FOR
ARGUMENT'S
SAKE

FOR ARGUMENT'S SAKE

A Guide to Writing Effective Arguments

THIRD EDITION

KATHERINE J. MAYBERRY

Rochester Institute of Technology

 LONGMAN

An Imprint of Addison Wesley Longman, Inc.

New York • Reading, Massachusetts • Menlo Park, California • Harlow, England
Don Mills, Ontario • Sydney • Mexico City • Madrid • Amsterdam

Editor in Chief: Patricia Rossi
Publishing Partner: Anne Elizabeth Smith
Associate Development Editor: Karen Helfrich
Senior Marketing Manager: Ann Stypuloski
Project Manager: Donna DeBenedictis
Design Manager/Cover Designer: Wendy Ann Fredericks
Cover Illustration: © Julia Talcott/Laughing Stock
Prepress Services Supervisor: Valerie Vargas
Electronic Production Specialist: Joanne Del Ben
Senior Print Buyer: Hugh Crawford
Electronic Page Makeup: Ruttle, Shaw & Wetherill, Inc.
Printer and Binder: The Maple-Vail Book Manufacturing Group
Cover Printer: Coral Graphic Services, Inc.

For permission to use copyrighted material, grateful acknowledgment is made to the copyright holders on p. 197, which is hereby made part of this copyright page.

Library of Congress Cataloging-in-Publication Data

Mayberry, Katherine J., 1950–
    For argument's sake: a guide to writing effective arguments/
Katherine J. Mayberry. —3rd ed.
      p.   cm.
    Includes index.
    ISBN 0-321-01467-7 (pbk.)
      1. English language—Rhetoric.   2. Persuasion (Rhetoric)
3. Report writing.   4. Logic.   I. Title.
PE1431.M39   1999
808′.042—dc21   98-21403
                                              CIP

ISBN 0-321-01467-7

Please visit our website at http://longman.awl.com

12345678910—MA—01009998

Contents

3

The Claim   18

4

An Argument's Support   36

5

Making Reasonable Arguments: Formal and Informal Logic   50

6

Arguing Facts   65

7

Arguing Cause   90

9

Arguing Recommendations 139

10

Writing and Image   160

11

Introductions and Conclusions   171

Preface

The focus of *For Argument's Sake* is the process of writing effective arguments. By dividing written argument into its four most common modes—factual arguments, causal arguments, evaluations, and recommendations—and outlining the steps of argument composition, from the earliest stage of invention through audience analysis to final revision, this text provides a comprehensive guide to the creation of responsible and effective written arguments.

For Argument's Sake came out of my own experience teaching a college course in "written argument" at the Rochester Institute of Technology. At the time, my textbook choices were limited to theoretical treatises on logic and reading-focused argument anthologies. But what my students needed was practical advice about how to write arguments. In the absence of such a text, a colleague (Robert Golden) and I decided to write our own. In the first edition of *For Argument's Sake,* we created a practical guide to writing effective argument that is helpful to students from a variety of disciplinary backgrounds, new in its approach to some fundamental issues, and detailed without being unnecessarily complex.

ORGANIZATION

The text is organized around the three major phases of argument writing: focusing, supporting, and reviewing. Chapters 1 through 5 discuss how to bring a developing argument into focus, including finding and focusing a claim, identifying and accommodating the audience, and understanding the relationship between claim and support. Chapters 6 through 9 show students how to support the four different classes of argument (arguments of fact, cause, evaluation, and recommendation). And Chapters 10 through 12 present the reviewing activities necessary to refine and polish an argument: considering image and style, composing openings and closings, and revising and editing the argument draft.

These three writing phases are presented in the order students typically follow when composing arguments, but there are of course perfectly acceptable and effective exceptions to the typical. The order presented is meant to guide, not prescribe. Further, the sequential presentation of phases is not meant to contradict the received wisdom about the recursive nature of good writing; in the real practice of writing, changes made in one phase lead to changes in the others.

SPECIAL FEATURES

The discussion of dissonance in Chapter 2 is unique to argument texts. The question of what moves people to write arguments is a critical one for students that can lead them to make a greater personal investment in their own writing.

The treatment of formal and informal logic is also unique to argument texts; in this book, they are introduced at the point in the argument process where they are most useful: the development and evaluation of support. Too often, argument texts include the theory of logic and examples of informal fallacies without addressing how they are useful in the actual writing process. Chapter 5 presents both formal and informal logic as practical tools for creating reasonable arguments.

The inclusion of an entire chapter on style and image (Chapter 10) enriches the traditional view of argument, which sometimes seems to suggest that effective arguments have more to do with formulas and principles than with using language fairly and effectively. Here, a writer's style—the image he or she projects through the writing—is a fundamental component of argument, not just a lucky accident of talent.

For Argument's Sake contains many examples that today's college students (both traditional and nontraditional) can relate to, as well as examples from a range of academic and career areas. The range of applications helps students see the importance of writing effective arguments not only in college courses, but also in their postcollege careers.

Because improvement in writing comes only with practice, the emphasis in all the activities in the text is on *writing*. Each chapter gives students many opportunities to practice what they are learning by writing (and rewriting) full and partial arguments.

NEW TO THIS EDITION

The third edition of *For Argument's Sake* retains the overall structure of the first two editions, as well as the emphasis on invention, composing, and overall practicality. My experience of teaching from the first two editions, as well as invaluable advice from many colleagues, has, inevitably, led to some changes in this third edition that make the text even stronger.

The most substantive changes appear in Chapters 4 and 5. In Chapter 4, the discussion of definition now includes a more extensive treatment of the stipulative definition. The discussion illustrates how stipulative definitions can constitute arguments in their own right, rather than support for another argument.

In Chapter 5, the presentation of Toulmin logic has been expanded and made even more accessible. Furthermore, in Chapters 6 through 9, the logical frameworks introduced in Chapter 5 are applied to the relevant classes of argument. For example, the discussion of evaluative arguments in Chapter 8 includes illustrations of the role that the formal syllogism can play in supporting and evaluating student arguments. The demonstration of the ties between theory and practice is a truly distinctive feature of the text.

Chapter 6, "Arguing Facts," now includes an entirely new section on "Evaluating Electronic Sources." This section includes both a brief "how-to" discussion on accessing electronic information and a list of evaluative criteria particular to electronic sources.

The overall tone of the third edition is relaxed and student-friendly, illustrating the importance of matching tone and style to audience. Many of the references and examples have been updated to reflect changes in the external environment. Further, more attention has been paid to selecting and creating examples that are accessible and familiar to students; this edition includes a good mix of familiar and unfamiliar ground for students, providing them opportunities to work from what they know *and* to stretch into new territory.

Finally, the activities throughout the text now give students greater opportunity to work in groups—both in evaluating and in composing arguments. These modifications, as well as a discussion of peer reviewing in Chapter 1, are intended to persuade students of the value of collaboration in their thinking and their writing.

I am pleased to offer this third edition of *For Argument's Sake* as an even more useful, accessible, and manageable guide for college students at all levels who must write arguments.

ACKNOWLEDGMENTS

While new professional obligations have prevented my colleague Robert E. Golden from participating further in the revisions of *For Argument's Sake,* this third edition would not be possible without the energy and intelligence that Bob devoted to the project at its outset. The third edition has specifically benefited from the expertise of John M. Ackerman, Northern Arizona University; Alice Adams, Glendale Community College; Virginia Anderson, Indiana University Southeast; Donna R. Cheney, Weber State University; Anthony C. Gargano, Long Beach City College; Margaret Baker Graham, Iowa State University; Patricia H. Graves, Georgia State University; Ruth M. Harrison, Arkansas Tech University; Lorraine Higgins, University of Pittsburgh; John Jablonski, Ferris State University; Ben E. Larson, York College; Kenneth Mendoza, California State University—San Marcos; Peter Mortensen, University of Kentucky; William Peirce, Prince George's Community College; Lynn Rudloff, University of Texas at Austin; and Ellen Strenski, University of California—Irvine. I am grateful to the Division of Academic Affairs of the Rochester Institute of Technology for absorbing the copying costs of preparing this edition, and to Karen Helfrich, Associate Development Editor, and Anne Smith, Publishing Partner, of Addision Wesley Longman for their tactful encouragement.

KATHERINE J. MAYBERRY

FOR
ARGUMENT'S
SAKE

1

An Introduction
to Argument

AN EXTENDED DEFINITION

If you grew up with siblings, or if you and your parents had a particularly stormy relationship during your adolescence, you may think you know all there is to know about argument. And you may be right, if you understand the word *argument* to mean a verbal battle where reason is absent and agreement rarely reached. A teenager engaged in this kind of argument with her mother might proceed as follows:

> Mom, I don't believe you! You are so unfair! Why can't I stay out 'til three? You never let me do anything fun. None of my friends have curfews. How do you think it feels to have to be the only one who has to leave a party early? Everybody thinks it's ridiculous, and I bet they're all really glad they don't have you for a mother.

The unpleasant and usually unproductive practice illustrated in this example is not the subject of this book. In fact, the kind of argument focused on in these pages is almost the exact opposite of the above illustration. Of concern here is the formal, traditional meaning of *argument:* the process of establishing, through the presentation of appropriate evidence, the certainty or likelihood of a particular point or position (what we call the *claim*).

Another daughter, using the principles of traditional argument, might make the following case about her curfew:

> Mom, I would really like to stay at this party tonight until it's over. I know you have a problem with my being out late, and I understand you're concerned about my welfare. But I'm eighteen now, I'll be leaving for college next month, and maybe it's time you let me start testing my own judgment. You and I both know I'm not going to do anything stupid, and I would really like to get some practice making my own decisions about my comings and goings.

While there is no guarantee that Daughter 2 would succeed with such an argument, it *is* a reasonable argument. Daughter 2 is acknowledging her mother's chief concerns and citing a sensible reason for lifting the curfew: she needs some practice at being grown up while still in the safety of her home environment. Daughter 1, on the other hand, has a lot to learn about making her point successfully; indeed, she commits about every foul imaginable in reasonable argument, including insulting her mother, irrelevantly and probably inaccurately appealing to crowd behavior ("None of my friends have curfews"), and failing to offer any sensible reason why her mother should change her mind.

Daughter 2's request is an oral argument, and the subject of this book is written argument; yet the principles and practices are essentially the same. The objective of each is to gain agreement about a point through the use of reasonable evidence. When you think about it, much of the writing you will do in college and in your careers following college falls under this definition. Research papers, lab reports, literary interpretations, case studies—all these forms of writing seek to convince an audience (your professor) of the reasonableness of certain conclusions. All these forms of writing, as well as application letters, instructional manuals, and corporate annual reports, are built around the simple objective of making a point.

An argument, whether written or oral, is different from an opinion. An *opinion* is based not so much on evidence as on belief, intuition, or emotion. Argument, on the other hand, is a position supported by clear thinking and reasonable evidence, with a secure connection to solid facts. While arguments rarely prove a conclusion to be absolutely true, they do demonstrate the probability of that conclusion. Opinions tend to be expressions of personal taste that have not been tested by the application of reasonable principles. Your opinion may be that history is a more interesting subject than literature, or that yellow is prettier than red, but these remain only opinions until they are thoughtfully and fully justified.

Effective arguments are ethical as well as reasonable. They make their points openly and honestly, avoiding underhanded methods and false promises, and seeking to remove ambiguity rather than exploit it. We make arguments in order to advance a reasonable position, not to trick a reader into serving our self-interest. As writers of ethical arguments, we recognize the influence that skilled writing can exert over credulous or ignorant readers, and we are committed to exercising that influence reasonably and responsibly.

Of course, what constitutes a reasonable and responsible argument is sometimes up for grabs. When they argue, people disagree about basic assumptions, beliefs, and values, and those disagreements affect their understanding of what is reasonable. Daughter 2 in the example above is working from the assumption that children should be encouraged to behave maturely. This seemingly inarguable assumption leads her to the conclusion that she should be allowed to exercise her own judgment about curfew. But perhaps her mother believes it is a parent's responsibility to protect her child from harm—another seemingly inarguable assumption. This reasonable assumption leads her to conclude that she cannot put her child at risk by lifting her curfew. Both daughter and mother are being reasonable, but their differing beliefs take them in two very different directions.

So this book will not be able to define what constitutes a reasonable argument for every writer, every audience, and every occasion. But it can introduce you to some concepts, processes, and tools that will help you make informed and effective decisions about how to construct your own arguments. And the many writing samples included at the end of most chapters will demonstrate how the principles and practices of formal argument carry over into a wide variety of writing contexts.

THE CLASSES OF ARGUMENT

Once you begin paying attention to the writing you do for school and work, you will notice how frequently your assignments fit within the definition of argument. You may also notice that the claims, or propositions, of these arguments tend to fall into certain patterns. Papers in economics or history courses may tend to concentrate on identifying the causes of certain events, while lab reports in biology or physics focus on describing a particular process and interpreting its results. In fact, argument can be divided into four classes: (1) factual arguments, (2) causal arguments, (3) evaluations, and (4) recommendations. These classes are distinguished both by the type of claim being argued and the degree of agreement expected from the reader.

Factual arguments try to convince an audience that a certain condition or event actually exists or has existed. Factual arguments, though they sound quite simple, are the most ambitious type of argument, for they try to convince readers of the truth or factuality of a claim. Those laboratory reports from biology or physics are examples of factual arguments, and their purpose is to convince their reader (usually a professor) that certain steps were taken and certain things actually happened.

Causal arguments—often found within those economics or history papers—try to convince readers that one event or condition caused another or is likely to cause another in the future. A paper identifying the complex economic reasons for the 1987 stock market crash would be a causal argument. Causal arguments can only rarely claim truth or certainty; most are judged successful if they establish a certain cause or future effect as *probable*.

Evaluations, or evaluative arguments, make value judgments. The film critics Gene Siskel and Roger Ebert are in the business of oral evaluations, as they share their judgments about the quality of recent films with their television audience. Because evaluations are often tied up in personal tastes and opinions, they are the hardest of all arguments to make successfully; nevertheless, they *can* be reasonable and effective.

Finally, **recommendations**, as their name suggests, try to get readers to *do* something, to follow a suggested course of action. While the other three classes of arguments aim for armchair agreement, most recommendations want the reader's agreement to be translated into action.

This book will take up the principles and practices of each argument class in isolation from the others, but you should realize from the outset that many of the writing assignments you will do for this course, for other courses, and on the job will *combine* these classes. In fact, the most common type of argument is the combined, or *hybrid,* argument.

ARGUMENT THROUGH IMAGE

An argument's success depends on many things: the clarity and exactness of its claim, the appropriateness and adequacy of its supporting evidence, and the particular *image* it projects. Image is the total impression a reader gets by reading your writing, and it is composed of a number of elements. Among these is the writing *style,* which consists of word choice, sentence length and structure, and the writer's tone of voice. Other elements of image include grammar, punctuation, neatness of the page, and quality of graphics. Together, these elements compose an overall impression of the writer and the work that will influence the reader's final acceptance or rejection of the argument. A positive image will help to secure the reader's confidence, respect, and attention; a negative image inevitably gets in the way of the agreement that all arguments seek from their readers.

Consider the example of an application letter for a job. Let's say that you are the head of the work-study program at your college, the person responsible for placing students in campus jobs. You have whittled the pool of applicants for the desirable job of dean's assistant down to two applicants: Jon Marshall and Becky Quinn. Both students have comparable academic qualifications, and both have been highly recommended by faculty and former employers. Becky's application letter is a well-organized, neatly typed business letter that carefully lists and develops Becky's qualifications for the job. Jon's letter also contains his qualifications, but it is filled with misspellings and faulty punctuation, it addresses you by your first name, and it has a grease spot on the upper-right-hand corner. All other things being equal, which candidate is likely to have the edge? Which image better argues the writer's suitability for the job?

THE ARGUMENT PROCESS

It is one thing to recognize the prevalence of argument in the writing you do but quite another actually to create effective written arguments. While this book contains no single blueprint or recipe for writing effective arguments, it will suggest a practical process, as well as theoretical principles, that will help you reach the desired product of an effective written argument. Unless you are extraordinarily gifted—one of those rare students who can produce a perfectly acceptable essay in a single sitting—your writing process will consist of at least three broad stages: forming the argument, supporting the argument, and reviewing the argument.

In order to explain and illustrate these stages, we have created the hypothetical case of Rob Wade, a journalism major with the ambition of becoming a radio sports announcer—the Vin Sculley of the twenty-first century. In this age of high-tech video, you may find Rob's ambition a bit old-fashioned, but it is based on his belief that television is ruining sports for the American public. After watching the television coverage of the 1998 Winter Olympics in Nagano, Japan, and the 1997 World Series between the Florida Marlins and the Cleveland Indians, Rob's convictions have grown so powerful that he feels compelled to communicate them to a large audience. He decides to kill two birds with one stone: his professor has assigned a "Letter to the Editor" as part of his journalism portfolio, and Rob plans to use this requirement to communicate his strong disapproval of television sports coverage. Let's watch how Rob moves through the three stages of argument composition as he creates his letter.

Forming the Argument

Forming your argument consists of discovering a motive for writing, identifying an audience to address, and discovering and sharpening the point or points to be argued.

Most successful arguments originate in the writer's strong personal interest, which often includes a desire to change the status quo. The origin of Rob's letter to the editor, his *motive* for writing it, is his long and growing discomfort with television sports coverage. He is disappointed in this coverage, angry at how it packages sports for the public; the desire to communicate these feelings and to remedy the harm he sees being done are powerful motives that will energize his writing.

Once Rob has decided to act on these motives, he needs to think seriously about where he would like his letter to be published—in the school newspaper, the city newspaper, the *New York Times,* or *Sports Illustrated?* This decision must be made before he begins writing; otherwise he will lack the necessary sense of audience. *Audience* is an inescapable consideration in writing, yet writers often underestimate its importance, forgetting that argument always consists of one person addressing another person, or a group of people. In Rob's case, a letter to the editor of the school newspaper, whose readers consist largely of young men and women in their late teens and early twenties, would be very different from a letter to the editor of *Sports Illustrated,* whose readers are typically educated males of all ages. Also, *Sports Illustrated* will be more selective in choosing which letters to publish than the school paper is likely to be. Regardless of where Rob decides to send his letter, his argument will gain focus and immediacy if he has a clear sense that he is writing to a particular audience, with particular backgrounds, expectations, values, and beliefs.

Rob also must be clear from the outset about the exact point or points he plans to argue. Sure, he knows he wants to attack television sports coverage, but he will soon find that such a goal is too vague and too emotional to inform what must be a clear and reasonable argument. Before he starts writing, he'll need to compose a clearly focused statement of the point or points he wants his readers to agree with. In most arguments, such a statement is a one- to three-sentence summary of the argument's conclusion called the *claim.* Some claims come to writers early and easily in the writing process, while others are the result of considerable reading, thinking, and narrowing. Though Rob knows generally what he wants to write about, it will take him some time to develop a claim that will interest his readers, that will be clear, and that he can reasonably support.

After more thinking than he had anticipated, Rob finally comes up with the following as his working claim: "While television coverage of sporting events allows us to be armchair spectators of exciting athletic contests that we would otherwise never see, we are paying a price for the convenience of this coverage. For what we are watching from our comfortable vantage point is glossy, high-tech artifice, not *real* sports."

Supporting the Claim

Having identified his claim and his audience, Rob now must decide how to support that claim. An argument's *support* is all the material that turns a tentative claim into a justified conclusion. Support is the most important component of argument. Without adequate and suitable support, a claim remains merely a hunch or an opinion; with appropriate support, it becomes a sound and credible conclusion.

At the very least, Rob can support his claim through his own viewing experience, which is, after all, what led him to the claim. But he's pretty sure that one person's experience is not enough to support an argument, so he knows he has some work to do. Identifying the class of his argument will help Rob select appropriate support, because certain kinds of support tend to apply to certain classes of argument. After careful consideration of his claim, and a thorough review of the four classes to which it might belong, he decides that his claim introduces an evaluative argument: it is making a negative judgment about the quality of television sports coverage.

This identification will help him, but there is more to selecting support than matching it to the class of the argument he is making. Rob will also need to ensure that the relationship between his claim and its support will be *reasonable,* that it will accord with the principles of formal and informal logic. So he will review carefully the material in Chapter 5 of this book, which presents these principles.

Reviewing the Argument

The product of these three steps—identifying an audience, composing a claim, and selecting appropriate support—will be a first version, or *draft,* of Rob's argument. As a journalism major, Rob has a fair amount of writing experience; he knows how difficult it is to evaluate your own writing, particularly when you have no distance from it. So, as he always tries to do, he puts his first draft away for a couple of days, so that when he returns to it, he has a fresh perspective that allows him to see problems in style and organization and reasoning that he hadn't noticed two days ago.

While getting distance from his argument will help to freshen his perspective, there is no fresher perspective than that of a second party who is unfamiliar with the work. In his writing classes, Rob has learned how well the process of "peer reviewing" works. As the name suggests, peer review is getting a friend or classmate or coworker to read your writing before you submit it to your professor, or, in Rob's case, for publication review. Peer review works best when you ask your reviewers to consider certain questions as they read. In the case of Rob's argument, these questions might be listed as follows: Does the argument effectively address its intended audience? Is its claim completely clear, and does it stick to that claim throughout? Is the supporting material reasonable and relevant to the claim? Does the argument project a positive image of its writer? Does the argument convince its audience? Friendly readers of your writing can identify problems and suggest solutions that you yourself are too close to the writing to see. Peer review is not cheating; it is not the same thing as getting someone else's answers to a calculus test. Peer review is a perfectly acceptable form of collaboration, providing an invaluable supplement to the writing process that the writer alone simply cannot supply: a *reader's* perspective. As a college student, Rob is lucky to have plenty of reader perspectives to call on. And his experience tells him that he would be foolish to ignore them, that without this collaboration, the revision process might become nothing more than superficial editing for spelling, punctuation, and grammatical errors. While editing is a necessary part of the review process, it is the final "spit-and-polish" step; revising often entails significant changes.

One addition that Rob will make to the first draft during the revision process is composing an introduction and conclusion. Like many writers, he finds it difficult to write interesting and representative introductions right out of the gate; the problem is partly psychological (first paragraphs are always the hardest) and partly practical (he won't know the exact content of the argument until he has finished a first draft). Likewise, it makes little sense to labor over a conclusion if the content of the first draft is going to be changed substantially during the revision process.

CONCLUSION

Having provided an extended definition of argument and a brief overview of the writing process, let's proceed to a detailed description of the steps involved in creating effective written argument, the reasoning principles that inform effective argument, and the special elements and requirements of each of the four classes of argument.

SUMMARY

An Introduction to Argument

- Written argument attempts to convince the reader of the writer's point of view, using reasonable and ethical methods. Most effective writing contains some form of argument.

- The *image* projected by the argument is the overall impression the writer makes on the reader. Image is created through writing style; correct spelling, punctuation, and grammar; and the physical appearance of the document.

- Argument can be divided into four classes: arguments of fact, cause, evaluation, and recommendation.
- While the process of argument composition varies from writer to writer, most writers follow these three stages: (1) forming an argument, which can consist of discovering a motive for writing and identifying an audience to address, discovering and sharpening a position, and developing an appropriate style; (2) supporting the argument; and (3) reviewing the argument, which can include considering the image projected by your argument, making substantial additions or deletions to a first draft, and adding an introduction and conclusion.

SUGGESTIONS FOR WRITING (1.1)

1. If you are planning on finding a summer job or a part-time job while in school, you will probably need to write a letter of application to your prospective employer. Give yourself some practice by writing a one-page letter of application for a real or made-up job. Try following a sequence like the following:

   Paragraph 1: State the position desired and your primary qualification for it.

   Paragraph 2: Expand on the primary qualification.

   Paragraph 3 and following: Develop other qualifications for the job.

   Concluding paragraph: State your willingness to answer questions and be available for an interview.

   Before writing, be sure to identify to yourself the needs and expectations of your reader, that is, your prospective employer. Then be sure your letter addresses these needs and expectations through such elements as the content of the letter, its level of formality, and the overall image projected by the letter.

2. Find an editorial in your local newspaper. With two or three classmates, analyze your responses to the editorial. Do all members of the group find the argument convincing? Why or why not? Do your disagreements reveal anything about your different concerns and values as readers? What image is projected by the editorial? Does the image appeal to all members of your group? Why or why not? Are there ways that the editorial could be changed to be effective for all members of your group?

3. With a small group of your classmates, review an essay examination that one of you has written recently. As a group, identify the expectations of the professor giving the exam. To what extent does the claim, the support, and the overall image of this one essay meet these expectations? As a group, rewrite the essay so that all of these considerations are met.

2

Where Writing Begins: Motives and Audience

Most of us write because we have to, not because we want to. As a college student, you write a research paper because your political science professor has assigned it; a sales rep writes a monthly report because her boss requires it; a mother writes a note explaining her son's absence from school because school policy insists on it. Yet the best writing, the kind we read voluntarily and the kind that endures over centuries, springs from some source other than mere necessity. And even when necessity drives great writing, other motives are also at work. Shakespeare wrote *Hamlet* to make a living, Dickens wrote *David Copperfield* to feed his many children, but these writers were surely inspired by some motive beyond making money.

MOTIVES FOR WRITING

What are these other motives for writing? They are powerful intellectual and emotional drives of enormous variety—from the desire to create a lasting record of some important experience (think of Anne Frank's *Diary of a Young Girl*), to the yearning to express love or joy (a common motive for music through the ages from Renaissance musicians to Tracy Chapman), to the need to disagree strongly or even complain (Harriet Beecher Stowe's *Uncle Tom's Cabin* was written from a deep disagreement with the institution of American slavery). One common motive for writing, especially for writing arguments, is our drive to resolve personal dissonance. *Dissonance* is actually a musical term meaning an inharmonious arrangement of tones that the listener wants resolved into harmony.

On a more general level, the term *dissonance* suggests tension or uneasiness. It is a good word for describing the mismatch between the way we want life to be and the way it is. Dissonance drove the angry voice of the prophets in the Old Testament, the determined defiance of the Declaration of Independence, and the heartfelt challenges in the *Communist Manifesto*. Driven by intense dissatisfac-

9

tion with the way things were, the writers sought a resolution of this tension by expressing it in writing.

The Value of Dissonance

The principle of dissonance is a useful starting point whenever you are at a loss to discover an argument worth making. If you find yourself doing nothing but staring at a blank page when you are supposed to be writing a ten-page paper for an English composition class, try asking yourself the following questions: "What really bothers me? What do I wish were different? What could be done to improve the situation?" The cause of the dissonance may be anything from parking problems on campus, to the status of women in large corporations, to the chemistry professor you don't understand.

If you begin the process of forming your argument by identifying a cause of dissonance, you will find both a subject to write about and a position to take on that subject (i.e., a claim). Because this position comes from your own interests and experience, developing it into an argument will be interesting to you, and if it's interesting to you, it's likely to be lively and interesting to your reader.

Let's assume that in an English composition class, you are asked to write about the impact of technology on education. An obvious position to take would be that the computer and associated technologies like educational CD-ROMs and the World Wide Web enhance the learning process for children and young adults. A solid position, certainly, but a bit predictable: probably 90 percent of your class will take this or a similar position. Plus, though you know it's a defensible position, it's not one that you find particularly exciting. So put that tentative claim on a back burner, and take some time to probe the general topic for personal dissonance. What discomforts, uneasiness, or inconveniences have you experienced from the new educational technology? Perhaps you were an avid reader as a child, someone who treasured the physical properties of books—the texture of the pages, the shape and heft of the volumes, the warm look of a filled book shelf. As you think about it, you realize that as amazing as educational technology is, it threatens the reader's important physical relationship to books, to tangible texts. Reading about the Byzantine Empire or cell mitosis from a computer screen just isn't the same as learning about them from a volume taken down from your living-room shelf. This could be the beginning of an interesting argument about the losses incurred when screens replace pages, when electronic texts make the comforting tangibility of books obsolete.

This approach has a number of advantages. First, it promises to be different, unusual. In writing, an unusual approach, as long as it is intelligent and not merely eccentric, is often effective: it gets people's attention. Second, working from dissonance lets you get to the core of your discomfort by discovering reasons for it. Turning an opinion into an argument is a great way to challenge and define your unexamined views. And finally, focusing on problems is more useful and productive than ignoring them; neither you nor your readers can improve a situation until you have identified and accounted for its problems.

Don't take this advice to mean that you should turn every writing assignment into an occasion for complaining. Searching for dissonance should help you learn to be a critical and discerning thinker, not a cynic or whiner. And one of the hallmarks of a discerning thinker is the ability to recognize value where it exists: a student writing on the disadvantages of educational technology should acknowledge its obvious positive impacts. To pretend that they don't exist will only make the argument seem nearsighted and unfair. Of course, sometimes balance and fairness are not appropriate; the Declaration of Independence would be much less effective if it presented a balanced view of the British government. But extreme situations calling for one-sided appeals are relatively rare.

Writing Arguments That Are Meaningful to You

Of course, not every writing assignment will allow you to call on your own feelings and opinions; sometimes you are required to write about topics that simply don't interest you. Yet there are ways to make even those assignments more relevant to your interests and experience. The next time you find yourself working with an uninspiring assignment, try these three suggestions for making that assignment more meaningful to you:

1. *Search for the most interesting facets of the assignment.* If you must write on the American Civil War—a topic that holds little interest for you—try to find one aspect of the war that is at least potentially more meaningful to you than any other. You may need to do some research, but your time is well spent if you get excited about the topic. If you are interested in medicine, for example, why not write about the medical treatment of the wounded during the war?

2. *Don't lie.* Express only those opinions you honestly believe in. If you are unsure of your claim despite your best efforts to become comfortable with it, don't hesitate to use qualifiers such as *perhaps, probably, usually,* or *likely.* Never be lukewarm when you can be hot or cold, but don't take a position simply for the sake of taking it. A qualified claim, such as "Athletes who train with professional coaches usually perform better than athletes who do not," is preferable to the unqualified statement "Athletes who train with professional coaches perform better than athletes who do not" because there are bound to be some exceptions to this rule.

3. *Don't be pompous.* You don't want your writing to be too informal and colloquial, but you also don't want to sound like someone you're not—like your professor or boss, for instance, or the Rhodes scholar teaching assistant. Good writing is always genuine writing.

These suggestions apply to any assigned writing, from a monthly sales report to a memo on improvements in office procedures, to a lab report, to an anthropology research paper. You may not have chosen to do the writing in the first place, but energy spent making the project your own will result in a more lively and credible argument.

ACTIVITIES (2.1)

1. Look at the last four things you have written: letters, reports, essays, memos, and so on. What were your reasons for writing them? How many of them were not written out of choice? Would these have been better if you had tried to write about what is important to you? Adjust the topic of one of these to make it more meaningful to you and then rewrite it following the suggestions presented in the preceding part of the chapter.
2. List four aspects of your life or of the world around you that you wish were different. From these four aspects, derive tentative topics for essays.

THE IMPORTANCE OF AUDIENCE

When you prepare writing assignments for a college professor, you are usually writing for an audience of one: a professor who is a specialist in the subject of the paper, who has certain expectations of the paper, and who is obliged to read it carefully. Having such a predictable audience is actually a luxury to students, freeing them from one of the most important steps in argument formation: identifying the audience. But in most of the writing you will do outside an academic setting, you won't be able to ignore this step. Written argument assumes a relationship between a writer and a reader: the writer speaks and the reader listens and reacts. As a writer, your first and most basic goal is simply to engage your audience—to get their attention. Taking the time before you write to consider your audience will help you avoid boring or offending or confusing them. Considering your audience will also add focus and purpose to your writing: you will write with an imaginary "reader over your shoulder," as poet Robert Graves put it, which is vastly preferable to writing into a void.

Audience consideration is important to all writing, but particularly to arguments. Since the purpose of all arguments is to convince someone of something, knowing who that "someone" is is crucial. An argument seeking to convince college students of the need for a tuition hike would proceed very differently from an argument seeking to convince the school's board of trustees of the same claim.

Developing an accurate sense of audience depends in part on experience, but you can sharpen this sensitivity by considering the following questions each time you prepare to write: *Who* is the audience? *Why* will the audience read your argument? *What* should the audience be able to do after reading your argument? You should try to keep the answers to these questions in mind not only as you form the argument, but also as you write it.

Who Is the Audience?

Sometimes this question will be answered in terms of specific individuals (my supervisor, my prospective employer). More frequently, it is answered in terms of categories or groups of readers (readers of a certain magazine, users of a certain product, students in a particular class).

Having identified your audience, you will want to consider how familiar they are with the subject matter. Readers usually know much less than writers about the topic at hand; even readers in the same organization with similar education and experience may be unfamiliar with the subject matter of your report. With this in mind, consider where you might provide background information, what terminology you might define, what difficult concepts you might explain or illustrate. No matter how convincing your argument is, if it baffles its readers it's not going to succeed. Most readers, if they have any choice in the matter, will stop reading a difficult argument before they will struggle through its unfamiliar language and concepts. If you don't know how much your audience is likely to know, or if they have different levels of knowledge, you are better off providing too much explanation than too little. Most people prefer feeling superior to feeling ignorant.

Finally, audience identification also includes considering your readers' probable disposition to your claim. Are they likely to be friendly or hostile to your position? The answer to this question will influence a number of your argument strategies. For example, if you expect your audience to be hostile to your claim, you might give them credit for their views at the outset. In recommending an expensive federal crime prevention program to an audience already frustrated by the cost of crime to taxpayers, acknowledging and legitimizing that frustration may help to neutralize their hostility: "There is something wildly unjust about living in fear of crime *and* having to pay for that crime as well." Once you have conceded that your audience probably won't want to pay more to prevent crime, you could proceed to argue for a new crime bill that, while temporarily costly, offers an excellent chance of reducing crime and its costs to the taxpayer. Telling the audience that they are selfish or pigheaded or shortsighted will not gain you much agreement, but expressing a genuine understanding of their frustration may convince them that your motives and theirs are essentially the same.

When you know that someone in your audience holds a view completely different from your claim, or even when you know that there is a good counterargument to your position, you may need to include a *refutation* of that opposing argument. (Refutations are discussed in Chapter 4, under "Addressing the Counterargument.") Even if you don't refute such a counterargument directly, acknowledging that you are aware of its existence can convince your audience that you have taken time to learn about the issue.

If you are confident that your audience shares your views, your work will be easier, but don't let yourself become sloppy, or you may lose the agreement you started with. To guard against triteness and predictability, try playing devil's advocate (appearing to support the opposing view), or expressing your central claim outrageously, or reminding your audience of the dangers of knee-jerk responses.

If you have no idea how your audience might respond to your claim, perhaps you can get some information about their general beliefs and values, which you can then appeal to in the course of your argument. Some arguments—particularly evaluations and recommendations—depend on successful appeals to readers' values and beliefs. An argument written for the *New Left Journal* recommending the recitation of the Pledge of Allegiance in public schools will succeed only if it appeals to a value held by the *Journal*'s politically liberal readers. These readers will not be moved by a "Your country: love it or leave it" approach. But if your claim rests on the principle of free choice, arguing that every student should

have the choice of saying the pledge, your argument may succeed with this difficult audience.

In considering these questions about your audience—who they are and what
they know, think, and believe—you are considering audience psychology. But it is
important that you understand your reasons for doing so. You are not going to the
trouble to understand your audience so that you can manipulate them through
underhanded, unreasonable, unethical methods. Rather, you are giving your good
argument the best chance at success by trying to ensure that the audience will approach it fairly and reasonably.

ACTIVITIES (2.2)

1. Examine a copy of *four* of the following and try to identify the probable audience for each. Estimate the level of education and the kinds of occupations
   each audience would probably have.

   Example: *Publications of the Modern Language Association* (PMLA). Level of
   education: usually at least some graduate education. Occupations: primarily
   graduate students in English or foreign language and literature and college-
   level instructors in these subjects.

   a. The *Wall Street Journal*
   b. *Time* magazine
   c. *Cosmopolitan*
   d. *People* magazine
   e. The *New England Journal of Medicine*
   f. *Popular Mechanics*
   g. *Soldier of Fortune* magazine
   h. Instructor's manual for the Apple Macintosh computer (or some other per-
      sonal computer)
   i. *Mad* magazine
   j. The *New York Times*

2. The following passage is from a brochure on how employees can use statistics to improve the quality of their organization's products. The intended audience for this brochure is company employees with a seventh-grade reading
   level and with no previous knowledge of statistics. How well does this passage communicate with its intended audience? If you believe the passage
   would be difficult for its intended audience, rewrite it so that it addresses its
   audience more appropriately.

   Quality can be best maintained by preventive action in advance of complete tool wear or predictable machine maintenance. If we check characteristics of parts on a sampling basis as they are produced, it is better
   than sorting through a bin of hundreds of parts looking for the defective
   parts and then trying to determine which parts can be salvaged.

   Collecting and analyzing data on current operations is essential in supplier and company plants. By studying the data, the causes of defects for
   each main quality characteristic can be investigated and determined. Appropriate solutions, including redesign or reprocessing, can be developed. Once problems are identified, a decision can be made whether to
   analyze past data, to collect new information, or a combination of both.

Why Will the Audience Read the Argument?

Readers can be divided into two broad groups: those who _have_ to read the argument (a professor, a supervisor, etc.) and those who are free to read or not read, depending on the argument's appeal (think of the fickle magazine browsing you do in waiting rooms). As part of your preliminary consideration of audience, it pays to determine why your audience will read your argument—because they have to, or because they want to.

If your readers are a captive audience—if they have no choice about reading your argument—you are not freed from making your writing interesting and engaging. In fact, the captive audience puts considerable pressure on the writer to be engaging. The professor with piles of student compositions to read, or admissions committee members with hundreds of application essays to evaluate, are likely to be bored and irritable by the time they come to your composition or essay. Knowing this, you should put more, not less, effort into getting and keeping their attention. In some cases, this may mean getting to the critical issues quickly and directly, or it may mean taking care to follow directions exactly, or putting a unique spin on your argument that will distinguish it from all the others your audience has to read.

When your audience is a purely voluntary one—readers of popular magazines, for example—they may not approach your work bored and irritable, but they are under no obligation to read further than your title if they don't find your argument interesting. Writers who write for daily or weekly periodicals are continually looking for "hooks" that will attract their readers to subjects that are already quite familiar. For example, in the Summer Olympics of 1996, Kerri Strugs's courageous vault landing received a landslide of positive attention from the international press. Patricia Dalton, a weekly columnist, wrote one of the hundreds of articles on the Kerri Strugs "moment." But she distinguished her article from the rest by opening with a very different take on Strugs's moment of valor: "I wanted to shout to the millions of kids watching [Kerri's heroics] on TV two weeks ago: This might not be good for Kerri—and it certainly isn't good for you." A position so different from the popular one was far more likely to get and keep the reader's attention than one that took the more predictable route of praise and applause.

ACTIVITIES (2.3)

The following audiences are likely either to be uninterested in or hostile to the following claims. Working with two or three students in your class, rewrite the claims, and add whatever additional sentences would help to engage audience attention. Be prepared to justify your changes to the rest of the class.

1. Parents of a college student: Tuition must be increased.
2. A social worker: Because of budget cuts, your caseload will increase.
3. An African-American woman: Affirmative action results in reverse discrimination.
4. An inner-city high school principal: Metal detectors are unconstitutional.
5. A software specialist: Our society looks at too many screens.

What Should the Audience Be Able to Do
After Reading the Argument?

All arguments want something from their readers. At the very least, they want to convince their readers that the claim and its supporting material constitute a reasonable position, even though readers may not agree with it completely. Many arguments are more ambitious, looking for their readers' full agreement, which may mean changing readers' minds. The most ambitious arguments want not only full agreement from their readers, but also action taken on the basis of this full agreement. What you expect from your audience will influence the nature and extent of your supporting material as well as the overall tone of your argument.

For example, if you were trying to convince an audience that fraternity term-paper files on your campus are a problem, you would argue why and to what extent they are a problem. But if you wanted your audience to take action to solve this problem, your argument would need to include specific steps to be taken, such as applying pressure on fraternity councils, setting up a more rigorous honor code for students, and encouraging faculty to change term paper assignments yearly. Including these steps means convincing your audience that they are likely to be effective: fraternity councils will monitor the problem more carefully if they are in danger of losing campus support; term paper files will be useless if assignments are not repeated from year to year; and so on. Arguments that seek to inspire the reader to action should be specific about the action proposed, show the connection between the claim and the proposed action, and convince the reader that the action will lead, or at least will probably lead, to the desired changes.

The expectations you have of your readers should also influence your argument's tone. If you want to convince gently, the tone can be mild: "Members of the International Students Club need to consider an alternative to their international banquet for raising money for travel." If you intend to exhort, the tone should be more forceful, as in Winston Churchill's famous address to the British people in their darkest days of World War II: "We shall fight on the beaches, we shall fight on the landing grounds, we shall fight in the fields and in the streets, we shall fight in the hills." If you want to command (in which case, you are no longer seeking reader agreement), you can afford to be very blunt: "No smoking is allowed in this computer room."

ACTIVITIES (2.4)

For which of the occasions below should the argument spell out the actions it wishes its readers to take? Why?

1. **Claim:** The flood of no-fat and low-fat packaged foods is turning a generation of kids into low-fat anorexics.
   Audience: High school dietitian.
2. **Claim:** My experience as a student senator, my active participation in four student clubs, and my 4.0 grade point average qualify me for the job of student government president.
   Audience: Student body of your college.

3. **Claim:** The new mandatory bicycle helmet law is an infringement of personal liberty, depriving the citizen of his or her right of self-determination.
   Audience: Listeners of a local call-in talk show.
4. **Claim:** Bicycle helmets should be made mandatory in this state, just like motorcycle helmets.
   Audience: Your state legislature representative.
5. **Claim:** While I have had some academic difficulties over the past year, my commitment to receiving a college degree and my newfound understanding of study strategies will contribute to my eventual academic success, if only you will agree to waive my suspension.
   Audience: Dean of your college.

SUMMARY

Where Writing Begins

- Dissonance—the mismatch between the way we want life to be and the way it is—is a motive for effective arguments.

- When you write, try to write about what is important to you, expressing only those opinions you honestly believe in and avoiding pomposity.

- Before you write, consider these three questions:

  - *Who* is the audience?

  - *Why* will the audience read the argument?

  - *What* should the audience be able to do after reading the argument?

SUGGESTIONS FOR WRITING (2.5)

1. From your list of topics from Number 2, Activity (2.1) at the end of the first section of this chapter, "Motives for Writing," select one of the topics and write a two- to three-page essay proposing a solution to the problem that bothers you.
2. Write a letter to your parents asking them for something you know they won't want to give you, for example, a raise in your allowance, a charge card, or a round-trip ticket to Europe. What steps can you take to neutralize the objections you know they are going to have?
3. Examine the last report or essay you wrote, and answer the following questions: Who was your audience? Why would they read what you wrote? What did you expect them to do after they finished reading? How well does that report or essay, when viewed in light of these questions, communicate with its intended audience? What changes would you make?
4. To recognize how audience affects the tone and content of an argument, write an informal evaluation of one of your current professors for your student E-mail conference system; then write a one-page evaluation of that instructor for the instructor himself or herself.
5. Attend a lecture or speech sponsored by your college or university. Then write a letter to the speaker evaluating her or his sensitivity to audience.

3

The Claim

You've discovered a subject and motive for your argument, and you've considered some key questions about your audience. Now you are ready to begin focusing your argument. Focusing—clearly defining the center and extent of your argument—occurs throughout the writing process, from discovering a motive to revising a final draft. This chapter concerns an early and critical stage in the focusing process: formulating, modifying, and positioning your argument's claim.

While some writers compose their claims before they begin writing, others let their claims evolve during an exploratory first draft, clarifying and modifying as they write. You can experiment with the sequence that works best for you, but regardless of how and when you reach your claim, your argument is not focused until you can summarize its principal point within a few sentences.

HOW CLAIMS WORK

An argument's claim is a short summary of its central point or points. All arguments have at least one claim; some longer arguments have more than one. Usually, the claim is stated directly, but sometimes, it is only implied by its supporting material. Regardless of where and whether it appears in an argument, the claim shapes and moves the argument, giving it structure and energy.

Claims can be short and tightly packed, as in the statement "America's youth are entirely apolitical," or they can be long and intricate, reflecting the argument's structure as well as its main points: "Because a capitalist system rewards aggressiveness, competitiveness, and intelligence, it is an almost perfect economic extension of Darwinism. In a capitalist society, the 'fittest' get rich; the unfit stay poor."

Crystal-clear claims are extremely useful to readers. All readers, whatever their levels of interest, knowledge, and intelligence, approach an unfamiliar manuscript clueless about its content and direction. An unequivocal, succinct statement of an argument's chief point or points alerts them to the argument's goal and prepares them to understand the relationship between the parts and the whole.

Good claims also help readers evaluate an argument. Knowing the proposition to be argued, they are equipped to judge how successfully it has been made. A claim such as "Television coverage of the O. J. Simpson criminal trial turned our already tarnished criminal justice system into no more than a serial plot for a tabloid news show" provides a benchmark against which readers can judge the supporting argument. On the other hand, a claim such as "The O. J. Simpson trial was a joke" is too vague, too unfocused, to serve as a useful benchmark.

While claims can be discovered or changed at virtually any point in the writing process, you will probably find that formulating a tentative working claim early in the process is quite helpful. Such a preliminary claim will help you determine the kinds of supporting evidence you will need, will guide your argument's organization and direction, and will keep you from darting off on tangents.

Finding a Claim

Many student writers are insecure about their ability to come up with a position worth arguing. But even experienced, mature writers with a wealth of experience and opinions often have to work to find a claim. For inexperienced and experienced writers alike, claims tend to evolve gradually from reading and thinking (at both the conscious and the unconscious levels) about the subject or from personal discomfort with a particular situation or issue.

On occasion, however, the process of developing a claim can be short-circuited. In many college classes, particularly introductory ones, claims are actually assigned. Students in English composition courses, for example, are often assigned a particular thesis (claim) to develop ("Write a two-page essay supporting your view of the effectiveness of student orientation at this college"). And essay exams offer students at least the foundation of a claim. For example, the question "Was dropping the atom bomb in 1945 on Hiroshima and Nagasaki necessary to achieve Japan's surrender? Support your answer with specific reasons" dictates the form, though not the content, of the claim that will begin the essay: "Dropping the bomb was/was not necessary, for the following reasons."

And some writers do come to their work with their main point firmly in mind. But what usually happens to these seemingly lucky folks is that this main point gets modified, changed, and sometimes even reversed as they go about the business of developing and supporting it. And this is as it should be; clinging to a claim that clearly needs modifying can doom an argument at the outset. So if you find yourself passionately attached to a particular position at the beginning of the writing process, try to treat that position as a starting point, a tentative claim that will guide your research and thinking, not a commandment set in stone.

Some assignment topics cause problems because they are too vague. A literature student assigned a fifteen-page analysis of the early poetry of William Wordsworth will set out with little focus or sense of direction. A new employee asked to evaluate the product quality and cost-effectiveness of a particular supplier would probably be equally adrift.

How do such writers move from vague assignments like these to working claims that will give the developing argument some direction and discipline? There are many answers to this question, because coming up with a claim—indeed, the entire writing process—is a highly idiosyncratic business. Some writers logically deduce claims from the evidence, in Sherlock Holmes fashion, while others discover them unexpectedly while daydreaming or jogging or listening to music. Claims can be slowly and painfully dredged from the earth, or they can come like lightning from the sky.

When you find yourself doing more dredging than you'd like, consider the following suggestions:

1. Don't press to arrive at a claim prematurely. More time is wasted following up a forced, dead-end claim that eventually has to be scrapped than there is in thinking, reading, and taking notes as preparation for deciding exactly what your position is going to be.

2. Instead of rushing the claim during the preliminary research phase (and research can mean nothing more than tapping the contents of your own brain without ever opening a book), concentrate instead on gradually narrowing your topic. For example, if you're preparing to write the paper on the poetry of Wordsworth, your reading and thinking might lead you originally (and accidentally) in the direction of thematic content, then to the narrower concern of images of nature, then still more narrowly to the recollection of nature as an inspiration to poetry. By the time you have gathered material on this focused subject, you will not be far from imposing a particular point of view on the subject. This point of view on a focused topic will be your claim, which might be something like "Wordsworth as a poet was inspired by nature, but nature sifted through memory, not nature as it is immediately perceived." While you may have accumulated a lot of seemingly useless notes along the way, you should be saved the agony of distorting your paper to fit an unworkable claim you have discovered with too little consideration. As you are closing in on a claim, keep in mind that good claims are rarely too narrow, and that poor ones are often too broad.

3. In the early stages of writing, don't spend too much time polishing and refining your claim. At this stage, a claim needs a narrow topic and the expression of a definite attitude toward that topic. A good working claim could be no more than "Smoking in public places is harmful to everyone." Later, after the first draft, you can refine and shine, adding a summary of supporting reasons if necessary.

4. Today's computer technology offers valuable tools for narrowing a broad topic to a focused position. Huge databases are available to you through your library computer system, including electronic catalogs and major bibliographic indexes stored on CD-ROMs. You will probably also have access to the Internet (a huge network of computers) through the World Wide Web, which contains not only databases, but huge volumes of information in various forms. (Chapter 6 will discuss the pros and cons of electronically retrieved information.) We get at the information we want through *keywords* or *descriptors*—words or brief phrases that describe our subject. Searching for information by keyword can give you good ideas for narrowing your topic.

Say you're planning to write an evaluative essay on the films of Stephen King, and you search several film indexes (e.g., *Film Research: A Critical Bibliography* or *Film Review Annual*), using *King, Stephen,* as your descriptor. You get close to a hundred "hits" through this search, and you notice that many of the sources have to do with King's novels as well as his films. You become interested in the whole question of adaptation, so you search other film indexes using narrower descriptors like *King, Stephen, and adaptations* or, even more narrowly, *The Shining.* Through this early search for sources, you have imposed considerably more focus on your initial, broad topic—a focus that would soon lead to a working claim like "The true genius of Stephen King is in his ability to adapt the printed page to the medium of film."

Keeping Your Working Claim Flexible

As you proceed with a rough draft that works from a tentative claim, you may discover that the preliminary claim needs modification. Perhaps the thinking and research you have done on the subject have made you realize that your claim does not apply as widely as you thought, that there are significant exceptions to your position. Be flexible enough to accept these discoveries and change your claim accordingly. Writing is not simply the recording of previously established thoughts but also a way of clarifying your thoughts, of discovering if what you meant to say can be said in a coherent and defensible way. If possible, take advantage of the guidance offered by a thoughtful claim, while remaining open to those discoveries to which writing and thinking can lead you.

Let's say you begin the composition process with a claim that arises fairly easily out of your own strong opinions about the issue of affirmative action. Your preliminary or working claim is "Jobs should be given to the most qualified applicant, not to the most qualified minority applicant. To reject the best candidate on the grounds of his or her majority status is unjust and inequitable." This claim statement not only summarizes your position toward affirmative action but also points to the main support for that position—that affirmative action is unjust and inequitable. In order to argue this evaluative claim convincingly, to convince your audience that one's minority or majority status is irrelevant to considerations of merit, you will need to demonstrate the injustices of affirmative action.

So far, so good. Even though you aren't personally aware of a wide range of cases, it should be easy to come up with examples of the basic unfairness of affirmative action. In the course of your reading, however, you keep coming up against the stubborn argument that majority candidates are often more qualified for jobs and educational opportunities because they are more educationally and economically privileged than members of minority groups. To reward the most qualified, this argument continues, is to perpetuate this tradition of unequal opportunity. You find this position persuasive and reasonable, though it doesn't change your central view that qualifications, not race, should determine one's success in the job market. Gradually, you realize that this is a more complicated issue than you had recognized; a hard-line position is not completely defensible.

You consider ignoring the counterargument and sticking to your original claim, but you conclude that your argument will actually be stronger if it reflects the ethical complexity of the issue and your awareness of the unfair advantage long given to the majority group. So you rewrite your working claim to read:

> In the United States, all men (and women) may be *created* equal, but for many, that birthright of equality is fleeting at best. Few would argue that, where women and minorities are concerned, inequality in economic and educational opportunity has been our national tradition. The affirmative action legislation of the 1960s was designed to redress the harms resulting from this indefensible tradition. Impeccable in its intent, affirmative action has been problematic in application: hiring on the basis of race and gender with secondary consideration to qualifications does not solve the problem of inequity; it merely changes the victims.

This new working claim is richer and more balanced than the first, reflecting your new understanding of the issue as well as your continuing disagreement with affirmative action laws.

The primary lesson to be learned from this example is that working claims should be seen as starting points, not as immutable conclusions; the thinking and writing processes will inevitably influence the starting point of an argument, shaping and modifying and in some cases even reversing the original position. Your final argument will benefit if you remain flexible about the original claim; always be prepared to alter it in the face of contrary evidence or new ideas.

ACTIVITIES (3.1)

1. With a small group of your classmates, select three of the following topics to work with. For each selected topic, work together to narrow the topic to one that could be written about in a seven- to ten-page essay. From this narrower topic, derive a working claim for this paper. Remember that the working claim is the claim with which you would begin to write the essay, though it might be refined or changed as you write.

   Example topic: The risks of cigarette smoking.
   Narrower topic: The health effects of cigarette smoking in public places.
   Working claim: Cigarette smoking in public places is harmful to everyone.

   a. Japanese automobiles
   b. Jogging
   c. Women's rights
   d. College education
   e. Television
   f. Unemployment
   g. Presidential elections
   h. New York City
   i. Careers
   j. Popular music

2. With one of your classmates, agree on a very broad topic of interest to you both, for example, professional basketball, computer games, a certain actor. Then conduct independent computer searches on the subject, progressively focusing it (and focusing your keywords) as you get a sense of the information available. When you have reached a focused topic that could be ar-

gued about in a five-page paper, compare that topic with your classmate's. How similar or different are the two? Retrace the evolution of your keywords for each other.

POSITIONING THE CLAIM

Another important decision you'll have to make about your claim is where to place it in your argument. You can make this decision before, during, or even after your first draft, but whenever you make it, it's one that requires careful thought. Different placements will have different effects on your audience, in some cases influencing their ultimate acceptance of your argument. As long as you base your decision on audience consideration and the intended function of the claim, you can put the claim almost anywhere. There are two main points to consider in positioning your claim: First, what is the function of your claim? Second, what is your audience's probable disposition toward your argument?

Claim Stated Up Front

Stating your claim within the first couple of paragraphs makes sense

- if your argument is complicated or the subject matter is unfamiliar to readers (an up-front claim will let your readers know what's coming);
- if your audience is likely to be comfortable with your argument (so that its claim will not alienate them at the outset);
- if your claim is particularly engaging, curious, or intriguing (an up-front claim will lure readers into your argument).

The following excerpt from an article on fund-raising in higher education, where the claim (in italics) appears after a brief introduction, illustrates the second and third of these conditions. Readers of the *New York Times* (where this article appeared) are not likely to object to the article's claim, though they may be intrigued by the argument's redefinition of the traditional practice of fund-raising:

> As the last mortarboards are flung like Frisbees into the air and the last speaker winds up a peroration on endings and beginnings, at least one campus office marches on into summer on an unending mission: raising money.
>
> The task is ancient but the tools get more modern all the time. Colleges and universities, long seen as aloof from the commercial crush of life, are increasingly willing to pull out all the stops in getting alumni to give.
>
> *It's still called fund-raising—or development or even institutional advancement. But it's getting to look a lot like marketing.* ("Some Schools Won't Take No for an Answer," Janny Scott, the *New York Times,* June 19, 1994, section E, p. 3; emphasis added)

Claim Stated at the End of the Argument

Delaying your claim until the end of the argument can be effective

- when your audience may find the claim objectionable (readers who accept a claim's support as reasonable before they know precisely what the claim is may be less hostile to that claim once it is stated);
- when your evidence builds directly and inevitably toward your claim, which can then serve as your argument's conclusion.

Let's say you write for your school newspaper. An example of the first instance would be your editorial recommending stricter enforcement of quiet hours in the dorm—a position that may not be welcome to all student readers. In this case, you can first present all the problems associated with the nightly bedlam in the dorms. Once you have established the seriousness of the problem, you can conclude the argument with your recommendation for stricter quiet hours. Having been convinced of the seriousness of the problems, your readers will be more likely to accept the final claim as necessary and logical.

Or to exemplify the second case, if you were reviewing a film for your newspaper, you might choose to describe various elements of the film first—acting, plot, cinematography—before summarizing these remarks with the inevitable statement of the central claim: "Find the time to see this film."

Unstated Claim in an Argument

You may choose to omit an explicit statement of your claim in situations like the following:

- When your readers will see red at your claim (because it is so bold or so objectionable), regardless of where you place it.
- When the claim is very, very obvious.
- When stating your claim will oversimplify your argument.
- When stating your claim will break the momentum or shape of your argument.

A wise mother might use this strategy in a letter counseling her college age son to hit the books. She knows that outright directions won't work, but she might tell a story that implicitly makes her point—a story about an uncle who frittered away his college opportunities and always regretted it. She does not end her letter with the obvious point "Don't be like Uncle Jake"; that would be too obvious, too heavy-handed. Instead, she lets her narrative speak for itself.

A word of caution, however, about omitting claims: Make sure that you have a very good reason for using this tactic, and that the point or points of your argument are absolutely clear without being stated.

ACTIVITIES (3.2)

1. Read the following essays included at the end of Chapters 6, 7, and 9: "Statistics Lie, or Do They?" (6); "I, Too, Am a Good Parent" (7); and "The Side

Effects of Affirmative Action" (9). In a discussion with three or four class-mates, identify the central claims and consider the reasons for their place-ment in each essay.

CLASSIFYING YOUR CLAIM

Once you have come up with a claim—even a tentative one—you'll need to iden-tify the class it belongs to. Knowing at the outset of a first draft that you are work-ing with a factual, causal, or evaluative claim or with a recommendation will sim-plify the gathering and presentation of support, since each class uses different kinds and arrangements of support. Recognizing your claim's class requires famil-iarity with the characteristics and functions of each class. The following section of-fers a full discussion of the different categories and examples of claims from each.

Factual Claims

The purpose of *factual claims* is to convince an audience that a certain statement is factual—that a given condition or phenomenon exists or has existed. The fact can be as basic as "Despite appearances, the sun is the center of our solar system, not the earth," or as unfamiliar as "In 1993, 65,091,168 people flew in and out of Chicago's O'Hare Airport." Writers of arguments introduced by factual claims at-tempt to convince their readers that their claims are true, although perhaps not true forever and under all circumstances (in the Middle Ages it was a "fact" that the earth was the center of the solar system).

Perhaps you find the idea of arguing facts a contradiction in terms; to you, facts are unchanging statements about reality, not provisional statements requir-ing support and verification. If it's a fact, why argue it? But a statement becomes factual only if it is accompanied by evidence that makes it extremely probable to its particular audience. Because facts become the cornerstones of so much of what we know and expect of the world, we cannot afford to accept them on faith. In short, factual claims must be supported carefully.

Facts are crucial to argument; indeed, it is hard to imagine an argument suc-ceeding if it doesn't include some facts. In the arguments you write in college and beyond, facts will play three roles:

1. They will sometimes appear as an argument's central claim, as in a labo-ratory report claiming that "The addition of sulfur to the compound cre-ated sulfuric acid."
2. They will function as support for other claims. A general claim such as "All the teachers in the Child's Play Day Care Center have experience working with preschool children" would be supported by facts about the specific experience of each teacher.
3. They will serve as examples or illustrations of difficult, unfamiliar, or ab-stract ideas. Suppose you're writing an essay on photosynthesis for an au-dience unfamiliar with the process. You might follow the scientific defin-ition of the term ("the formation of carbohydrates in living plants from

water and carbon dioxide, by the action of sunlight on the chlorophyll"—
Webster's New World Dictionary) by the more familiar description of the
yearly cycle of a cherry tree.

The four types of facts that will figure most commonly in your arguments are
(1) common knowledge facts, (2) personally experienced facts, (3) facts reported
by others, and (4) factual generalizations:

1. **Common knowledge facts** are so widely acknowledged as true that they
   require no support or proof beyond mere statement.

   Examples: Men cannot bear children.
   Opposite poles attract.

2. **Personally experienced facts** are the events, observations, and conditions
   that you have personally experienced.

   Example: I have taken countless history courses in my life, and I have
   never had a teacher who excited me about the subject.

3. **Facts reported by others** are those that you have learned from second- or
   third-party sources. A second-party source is the person who ascertained
   the fact. A third-party source is the person or document reporting facts
   ascertained by someone else:

   Examples: "The 'man shortage' and the 'infertility epidemic' are not the
   price of [women's] liberation; in fact, they do not even exist"
   (Susan Faludi, *Backlash,* xviii; second-party source).

   "The mental health data . . . are consistent and overwhelming: The suicide rate of single men is twice as high as that of
   married men" (Faludi, 17; third-party source).

4. **Factual generalizations** claim that an assertion is true for a large number
   of subjects or over a long period of time. Factual generalizations can be
   common knowledge facts, personally experienced facts, or facts reported
   by others.

   Examples: Most of my friends are interested in sports.

   "In 1995, 14.9% of American children lived in blended families" (*World Almanac, 1995,* 962).

All factual claims are stated as definite and unequivocal assertions, as in the
following examples:

- New York City is the banking center of the United States. (The claim makes
  a quantifiable assertion that can be verified by a survey of the number of
  banks and banking transactions in major American cities.)
- Our solar system is approximately five billion years old. (While no individual can verify this claim through firsthand experience or knowledge, it represents the consensus of experts on the subject and can be documented in
  this way.)
- Steel radial tires last longer than tires made with nylon. (Again, this claim
  can be verified, though the process may be tedious and time-consuming.)

- Most of my friends are involved in intramural sports. (A statement of fact that can be supported, if necessary, by a listing of the number of friends who are involved and not involved in intramural sports.)

ACTIVITIES (3.3)

1. For each of the factual propositions listed below, identify the category or categories of fact (common knowledge, personal experience, second- or third-party, generalization) in which the proposition belongs.

   Example: The Cuban Missile Crisis occurred in October of 1962. Second- or third-party for most students; personal experience for older people.

   a. The disappearance of former Teamsters Union leader Jimmy Hoffa is still unexplained.
   b. The risk of getting cancer is decreased by a high-fiber diet.
   c. My communications professor routinely missed her 8:00 class.
   d. Alaska is the largest state in the United States.
   e. An apple a day keeps the doctor away.
   f. I get better grades on the papers I take the time to revise.
   g. Severe air pollution is dangerous for people suffering from lung disease.
   h. Women under age thirty have better driving records than men under age thirty.
   i. In Italy, people take more time to enjoy life than we do in the United States.

Causal Claims

Causal claims propose a causal connection between two events or conditions. They can argue that A caused B or, more speculatively, that A may cause B at some future time. Statements such as "The violence represented in movies and television has numbed us to the horrors of violence in the real world" or "High consumer spending will lead to greater inflation" are examples of causal claims.

It is human nature to be curious about cause. We watch the careers of prominent public figures and wonder about the reasons for their spectacular successes and failures. We reflect on a tragedy like the Holocaust and demand to know how such a thing could happen. We look for the reasons behind events to assure ourselves that the world is governed by certain rules, not merely by random chance. We also learn by discovering cause. Knowing what caused the crash of TWA Flight 800 off the south shore of Long Island in the summer of 1996 gives us a reasonable chance of preventing a similar event in the future. And you can be sure that the next Democratic presidential candidate will do whatever he or she can to reproduce those factors that led to Bill Clinton's successive elections.

Just as we are given to discovering cause, we are also fascinated by predicting *effects*. Stockbrokers must be skilled in this form of causal argument, as they try to enhance the interests of their clients by predicting market activity. Doctors practicing *preventive* medicine are also in the business of predicting probable effects: they tell their patients to reduce dietary fat in order to prevent a future heart attack, or to exercise regularly to maintain bone density. And in business and industry, the long-term health of a corporation often depends on the accurate prediction of future trends. Eastman Kodak, for example, with its enormously successful business of traditional photographic products, must determine the probable future of those products in the face of electronic imaging.

Under carefully controlled scientific conditions, it is possible to identify cause and even to predict effect with so much certainty that the causality can be established as *factual*. Researchers have determined that smoking increases the risk of lung cancer and that lobar pneumonia is caused by pneumococcus bacteria. But in the causal arguments that most of us make, arguments concerning human behavior—our actions, our successes and failures, our relations with others—certainty is impossible to reach. In these more speculative arguments, the best we can hope for is to establish *probable* cause or effect convincingly.

But because a claim cannot be proven with certainty doesn't mean it isn't worth arguing; if we always waited for certainty before acting, our progress would be slow. An argument that establishes probable cause or effect *can* be a reasonable basis for decisions or actions. In fact, probability is the goal of most of the arguments we write. But even probability isn't easy to achieve; in many cases, it calls for more skill than establishing certainty in factual arguments.

Causal claims are easy to spot because they (1) often contain words indicating causality—*cause, produce, effect, consequence*—and/or (2) involve the relationship between two phenomena occurring at different points in time. The following are examples of causal claims:

- According to social critic Neil Postman, technology is causing the surrender of American culture. (The word *caused* is a dead giveaway of a causal argument.)
- If Sally had written a better résumé, she might have landed that job. (An early event—Sally's poor résumé—caused a later one, her failure to land the job.)
- A balanced budget promises a stable government. (The claim proposes a close causal relationship between a balanced budget and a stable government. The verb *promises* indicates cause.)
- Increasing numbers of two-career families have contributed to the rising divorce rate. (*Contributed to* suggests a causal relationship between the two facts.)

ACTIVITIES (3.4)

1. Look back at the distinction between factual and probable causes on this page. For which of the following causal claims could you establish a factual cause—one that few people would dispute? For which could you establish only a probable cause—one for which you would have to argue?

   a. If Abraham Lincoln had not been assassinated, he could have lessened the bitterness between the North and the South after the war.

   b. The widespread use of computers in business and industry will increase total employment, not decrease it.

    c. If it had not snowed, Ohio State could have defeated Michigan in that football game.

    d. In most automobiles, failure to change the oil at regular intervals will damage the engine.

    e. The decline in the percentage of the population attending organized religious activities has caused the rise in the crime rate in the past forty years.

    f. The use of seat belts decreases the number of fatalities in automobile accidents.

    g. If newlyweds had more realistic expectations about marriage, there would be a decline in the divorce rate.

    h. The children of the affluent would be happier if they had to do more for themselves.

    i. Some cold medicines cause drowsiness.

    j. The existence of nuclear weapons has prevented the outbreak of World War III.

2. Write a claim for a causal argument for one of the following; then make a list of all the reasons you can think of that would convince a reader of the cause or effect you identify. Describe these reasons in a paragraph.

    a. The cause of a particular war

    b. A team's victory or loss in a certain game

    c. A change in some aspect of the government's social or economic policy

    d. A change in exercise or dietary behavior

    e. The cause of a person's career success or failure

Example of (c): "There would be fewer homeless people if the federal government increased its aid to cities."

Reasons: Money could be used for low-income housing. Money could be used for training programs that would give the poor a means of self-support. Other countries that give substantial aid to cities do not have the problem with the homeless that we do.

Evaluations

When we argue an evaluation, we are proposing our personal judgment of the value of a work of art, a policy, a person, an action, even another evaluation. No doubt you often find yourself making informal pronouncements of personal taste: "Your tie is ugly," "That restaurant serves the best chicken wings in town," "I enjoy playing basketball more than playing tennis." These pronouncements are so purely subjective, so clearly a matter of personal preference, that there is little point in trying to argue them reasonably. We are all inclined to pass judgment on what we observe, and frequently we don't much care whether these judgments are taken seriously.

But sometimes we do care about the impact of these judgments; sometimes we want our opinions to influence others. In these cases, we must understand how to argue judgments of value. And many value judgments, even those originating as unconsidered personal opinion, *can* be convincingly argued. Claims such as "Pornography is an offense to all women" or "The government was mistaken in trading weapons for hostages," if they are serious, carefully considered judgments, can be developed into meaningful arguments.

Evaluations are probably the hardest of all arguments to argue successfully. Not only do they originate in the writer's personal value system, they also speak to his or her readers' equally personal, passionately held, and often unexamined values. Changing someone's mind about an opinion or judgment is an uphill struggle, so your goals in arguing evaluations should be rather modest: to gain your audience's sympathy toward a conclusion that you have reached through responsible and reasonable evidence, rather than to change the mind of everyone who reads your argument.

An important variant of the evaluative claim is the *interpretive* claim. Interpretations are *explanatory* evaluations of a person, event, or object: "Dreams of beautiful gardens often suggest a state of profound satisfaction in the dreamer" or "Will's domineering and self-centered style is an expression of his profound insecurity." Neither of these examples is simply factual or descriptive; each reveals something unexpected beneath the visible surface of behavior. Interpretive claims surpass mere opinion only when they are supported by facts and reasoned argument. Reasonable, intelligent people may differ in their interpretation of a person or a situation, but not all interpretations are equally plausible or illuminating. To argue, for example, that Hamlet's actions are the symptoms of gout, when there is no evidence to support that view, is an example of poor interpretation.

The following statements are examples of claims introducing evaluative arguments:

- Many people do not realize that Herman Melville, the author of *Moby Dick,* was also an accomplished poet. (Evaluative claims often contain descriptive modifiers, like *accomplished* in this example.)
- Former president Jimmy Carter may not have been a great president, but he was an honorable one.
- Mary's constant chatter is an attempt to keep people from abandoning her. (An interpretive claim, in that it offers a beneath-the-surface explanation of Mary's behavior. Like many interpretive claims, this one contains causal elements, but what distinguishes it as primarily interpretive is the identification of a *coincidence* between visible and hidden phenomena.)
- For my money, soccer players are the most gifted of all athletes. (*Gifted* is a subjective term: it not only means different things to different people, but it also cannot be conclusively verified. Claims including superlative or comparative adjectives are likely to be evaluative claims.)
- "Human memory is a marvelous but fallacious instrument." (Primo Levi, *The Drowned and the Saved.*) (This claim makes two judgments about memory.)

ACTIVITIES (3.5)

1. Write claims for evaluative arguments for the following subjects.
   Example subject: theft of library books

Example claim: Stealing library books is not only a criminal act; it is a serious trespass against the ideals of community.
a. Political campaign spending
b. Computer games
c. Pass-fail grading
d. A particular television show
e. Teenage pregnancy
f. Your composition instructor
g. Rap music
h. Television sports coverage
2. Give an example of an interpretive claim for the following topics.

Example of topic (a): The cinematic revival of Shakespeare is an expression of fin de siècle anxiety.
a. The significance of a play, movie, or short story
b. The importance of a contemporary political figure
c. The meaning of a current trend in fashion
d. The attitude of students at your college toward their future careers
e. The attitude of young Americans toward religion

Recommendations

A common goal of argument is to convince an audience that existing circumstances need to be changed. Some *recommendations* seek only to gain an audience's agreement with an idea or a decision, but others have a more practical (and ambitious) purpose: they try to convince their audience to take a particular action or, more modestly, to convince an audience that a particular action should be taken by others. As a student in English composition, you might write a paper for your instructor arguing that the legal drinking age should be lowered, or you might make that same argument in a letter to your congressional representative, with the hope of getting him or her to take action. A lab technician might write a memo to her supervisor suggesting the purchase of new equipment. Or the chairperson of the history department might write to the dean requesting an adjustment in faculty salaries. All of these arguments would be recommendations.

All recommendations are concerned with the future, with what should be done at a later time, but they also imply a judgment about present conditions. Writers propose change because of dissatisfaction with an existing situation. Early in arguing a recommendation, you'll need to determine whether you want to concentrate on the current problem, or on the improvements resulting from your recommendation; in some recommendations, you'll emphasize both.

- The main goal of recommendations emphasizing *present* conditions is to demonstrate the problems in the current situation. Because these recommendations argue *that* something needs to be done rather than *what* exactly that something is, they usually don't discuss a proposed change in any detail.
- The main goal of recommendations emphasizing the *future* is to present a plan for change and to demonstrate that it is feasible and likely to produce the desired effects.

- Recommendations with *equal* emphasis on present and future argue the problems of the current situation *and* the likely effects of the proposed change.

You may have noticed that recommendations are hybrid, or combination, claims with elements of both causal and evaluative arguments. That is exactly right. When proposing that an existing situation be changed, you are at least implying a negative judgment of that situation. And implied in the changes you recommend is a positive evaluation of those changes. Furthermore, you will support the recommendation itself through an argument of effect—demonstrating the positive future effects of the change.

Because arguments of recommendation argue for an action not currently in effect, words such as *should, would, must, ought, needs to be, will* or *might* typically introduce these arguments. The following are some sample claims for arguments of recommendation:

- We need more emphasis on science and math in our schools to prepare the next generation for a world of international economic competition. (The claim proposes a *change* in the current curriculum.)
- In order to attract more nontraditional students, this university must review and revise its course offerings. (Again, this claim calls for a change in an existing situation—a change that will have positive effects in the future.)
- If this company is to regain financial health, it must divest itself of all divisions not directly connected to its traditional core business. (The words *must divest* identify this claim as a recommendation—a suggestion for a particular action is being made.)
- Take back the night. (A trenchant recommendation expressed in the imperative mode. In the word *back,* the command implies making a change in an existing situation.)

ACTIVITIES (3.6)

1. For the following situations, write two claims of recommendation, one focusing on current conditions and one on the results of recommended improvements.
   Example: Taking a typing course
   Claim with a focus on current conditions: I need to take a typing course because I can't use the word processor required in my English composition course.
   Claim with a focus on future improvements: I need to take a typing course so that I will be ready for the day when every office has its own word processor.
   a. Replacing a television
   b. Requesting a new strict policy on noise in a dormitory
   c. Advocating a freeze on the research for and manufacturing of nuclear weapons
   d. Purchasing a new car to replace your or your family's current one
   e. Increasing the number of police in the most dangerous sections of a city
2. Read the two recommendations at the end of Chapter 9. As you read, consider whether these recommendations emphasize the present, the future, or

both. See how well your ideas match up with those of a group of your classmates.

Combination Claims

A brief look at any essay anthology may persuade you that "real" claims in "real" arguments don't always fit neatly into the four categories presented in this chapter. But your experience of writing *and* reading arguments will persuade you that all arguments contain claims that fulfill one or more of these four functions.

In some cases, you will need to mentally recast claims to decide what kinds of arguments they are. For example, the famous claim "The only thing we have to fear is fear itself," which is a forceful, lively claim needing no revision, can be translated to mean "We should beware of the dangers of fear"—a recommendation based on an argument of effect identifying the negative consequences of fear. The claim itself need not be rewritten; having identified the category of the recast version of the claim, you can proceed to support the original claim.

Often, as the above example demonstrates, the context of a claim will help you categorize it. This quotation about fear is taken from President Franklin Delano Roosevelt's first inaugural address in 1933, during the heart of the Great Depression, when fear about the future pervaded America. In this context, Roosevelt's remark is part of a broad recommendation to the American people to regain their confidence and to begin to plan for the future with new hope. In a less urgent context, "The only thing we have to fear is fear itself" might be a causal claim meaning "The experience of fear is dangerous because it builds on itself."

If you are arguing a claim that doesn't seem to fit into any of the categories discussed here, and you can't seem to recast it mentally, ask yourself some questions about the function of the argument that will support the claim. For example, is the claim verifiable? If not, it is not factual. Does it make an unverifiable judgment about something or someone? If so, it is probably evaluative. Does it propose a course of action? If so, it is a recommendation. Does it account for or predict a particular phenomenon? Then it is a causal argument.

Some claims actually contain two propositions to be argued, as in the sentence "Acts of terrorism are serious offenses against human freedom and should meet with deadly retaliation." The first claim is the *evaluation* that acts of terrorism are serious offenses, and the second is the *recommendation* that they should meet with deadly retaliation. In supporting this double claim, you would have to defend the value judgment about terrorism before moving on to the second assertion, the recommendation. Ideally, both claims should be defended, though writers frequently assume that their audience agrees with them on the most basic points—that terrorism is abhorrent, for example—and concentrate on one or two more arguable points, such as the need for deadly retaliation.

While space constraints may require this kind of corner cutting, be careful not to assume too much about your audience's position. A writer dealing with the controversial topic of terrorism should at least *consider* whether terrorism is always completely unjustified, even if she doesn't address this question in her essay.

Often, a factual claim is combined with one of the other three kinds of claims. When this is the case, as in the statement "The rise in the divorce rate in the last thirty years may increase the divorce rate in the next generation," you must establish the accuracy of your facts (the rise in the divorce rate) before you go on to speculate about the possible effects of this fact. So, too, with the statement "The flight of business and industry from the Northeast to the Sun Belt will eventually have a damaging effect on the quality of public education in the Northeast." First, the flight of business and industry must be established as a fact, probably through outside research; then the long-term causal argument can be made.

The following are examples of combination claims:

- The recent rise in interest rates may contribute to higher inflation. (This statement combines a factual assertion about rising interest rates, which can very quickly be supported, with a causal argument predicting the effect of the higher rates. This second claim would be the focus of your argument.)
- No nation is truly free that does not offer its citizens equal opportunity in education and employment. (This statement combines a causal argument—lack of equal opportunity results in an unfree nation—with an evaluation judging the degree of a nation's freedom.)
- If the candidate wants to win votes, he must convince constituents that his reputation for moral laxness is undeserved. (This statement combines a recommendation that the candidate make his case to his constituents and a causal argument that making this case will win him their votes.)
- While men seem to be driven to success by a fear of failure, women are made comfortable with failure by their fear of success. (This breathtaking generalization combines interpretation—identifying hidden motives for behavior—with elements of a factual argument. The writer will have to present *many* instances of these gender-linked phenomena in order to warrant the generality of the claim.)

ACTIVITIES (3.7)

Into which of the four main argument types or combination of types do the following belong? Be prepared to support your answer.

Example: Automobiles should be designed so that they get a minimum of thirty miles per gallon of gasoline.

Type of argument: Recommendation

1. Excessive consumption of alcohol can lead to many illnesses.
2. Honesty is the best policy.
3. Cutting defense spending will create a safer world.
4. Tariffs on imports merely raise prices for domestic consumers.
5. Alley cats are a public nuisance in this neighborhood.
6. Politics is the art of the possible.
7. An improved sewer system would solve these flood drainage problems.
8. America should protect its domestic industries with tariffs and quotas.
9. Without a belief in God, life has no meaning.
10. Obesity can help cause heart disease.

SUMMARY

The Claim

- Claims help readers to understand and evaluate arguments, and they help you, the writer, to generate the direction and content of your arguments.
- If you have difficulty coming up with a working claim, you probably need to do more thinking and reading about your topic. When you are knowledgeable enough, a claim should come to you.
- Always be prepared to modify a working claim to fit with new ideas and information.
- Claims can be placed virtually anywhere in an argument. The most effective placement depends on the nature of your argument and its probable reception by your readers.
- *Factual claims* seek to convince an audience that a given object or condition exists or has existed. The four kinds of facts are common knowledge facts, facts experienced by you, facts reported by others, and factual generalizations.
- *Causal claims* assert that one event or condition produces or helps to produce another event or condition. In claiming *cause,* we look for what produced a past or current event or condition. In claiming *effect,* we predict a future occurrence on the basis of certain current or intended circumstances.
- *Evaluations* make a value judgment of a person, activity, or object.
- *Recommendations* argue for a particular course of action in order to change existing circumstances. Recommendations can focus on present conditions, future effects, or a combination of both.
- Some arguments work from claims that combine elements of the four classes.

SUGGESTIONS FOR WRITING (3.8)

1. Read an argumentative essay in a magazine like the *Atlantic Monthly* or the *New York Times Magazine,* and write a one- to two-page essay on what kind of argument it is and why. Be sure to give your instructor a copy of the argumentative essay you are analyzing.
2. Select a familiar document such as Martin Luther King, Jr.'s "I Have a Dream" speech, Lincoln's Gettysburg Address, the Declaration of Independence, or a famous Shakespearean soliloquy, and identify the class or classes of argument it represents. In a one- to two-page letter to your instructor, support your identification. Be sure to give your instructor a copy of the document you are analyzing.

4

An Argument's Support

Now that you have a working claim and a good idea about the kind of argument it summarizes, you are ready to begin supporting that claim. The body of your argument, the material that will convert your claim into a conclusion, is your presentation of support. Broadly defined, an argument's support is all the material you insert into your argument to strengthen the probability (and in some cases, truth) of your claim. To argue your claim successfully, you must know how to select appropriate support for your particular claim, how to determine how much support is necessary, and how to arrange that support in the most convincing way.

Once you have a working claim, you will probably find that you have some ideas for supporting it. The more your claim emerges from your experience of dissonance and from your own interests, the more likely you are to have solid support ready at hand, though you will have to do *some* research on even the most familiar topics. On the other hand, regardless of how much research goes into them, claims having no connection with your own experiences, interest, or knowledge will be more difficult to support.

Let's say that you are worried about your grandmother, who, although healthy, is growing increasingly depressed and withdrawn. You know from talking with her that she feels useless, ignored, and aimless. Your concern makes you angry about the way our society treats its older citizens, and you decide to let this concern and anger fuel an argument about age discrimination. Your grandmother's experience has given you a number of specific examples of age discrimination and its effects. Some of these examples will help to support the claim "American society, for all its public attention to human rights, is guilty of systematically depriving its senior citizens of countless 'inalienable' rights." But you know that in order to argue such a far-reaching claim convincingly, you will need to find support beyond your personal observations.

Since different classes of arguments often require different kinds of support, knowing the class of argument that your claim belongs to will help you know what kinds of additional support to look for. Chapters 6 through 9 discuss these specific requirements. There are also more general types of support, not specifically associated with a particular class, that you will want to be familiar with. And you will need to determine how much support will be enough, and how to arrange that support strategically. These generic supporting tactics are treated in this chapter.

SOME VARIETIES OF SUPPORT

It is useful to think of supporting material as separate units or building blocks that strengthen a claim in different ways and to different degrees. What follows is a discussion of some of the generic varieties of support commonly used to strengthen arguments.

Secondary Claims

All claims, regardless of their class, are supported by further claims, which will require their own support. Sometimes these *secondary* claims will belong to the same class as the main claim, sometimes to a different class. If you were arguing the factual claim "Students in my major are more interested in learning marketable skills than in truly educating themselves," you would need to support your fairly general claim with individual examples of this phenomenon. You probably would cite conversations in which individual students had expressed this preference to you and/or perhaps a survey asking students in your major to rank their educational priorities. In both cases, you are supporting your main claim with a secondary factual claim, which will itself need to be verified.

A recommendation claiming "This university should offer a pass-fail grading option to its students" may include as support the secondary *causal* argument "Removing the traditional evaluative system of letter grades will facilitate learning by reducing pressure." While not the chief point of this argument, this secondary causal claim still needs to be supported. One way to support it is through a third, *factual* claim. Perhaps the writer has access to a survey taken at another university that offers the pass-fail option, and this survey demonstrates a positive student response to the option. Or maybe the writer has friends at other schools who have spoken favorably about their pass-fail grading policy. Whether these responses are gathered through a large survey or individual conversations, they are facts that will strengthen the secondary claim (provided they are responsibly obtained and accurately reported).

As these examples illustrate, eventually all main claims will come to rest on factual claims that are supported by observations, examples, statistics, studies, and so forth. While some arguments depend more heavily on facts than others, no argument is likely to be convincing if it doesn't at some point refer to verified factual claims. In the first example above, the factual generalization about learning goals is supported by secondary factual claims: the expressed preferences of other students in your major and/or a survey of student learning goals. In the second example, a recommendation ultimately comes to rest on a secondary factual claim:

positive student response to the pass-fail option. As you will see in Chapter 6, these fundamental factual claims would be supported by the writer's assurance that they have been gathered, interpreted, and reported responsibly.

ACTIVITIES (4.1)

Supply secondary claims that would support the following main claims of arguments. In each case, identify the class of the secondary and primary claims.

1. The *Boles GRE Study Guide* is an excellent tutorial for students preparing to take the GRE.
2. Television newscasting influences how Americans think about social and political issues.
3. In my high school, food abuse was a far bigger problem than alcohol or drug abuse.
4. Dostoyevsky's *Crime and Punishment* is a ponderous novel of sin and redemption.
5. If we really want to eradicate racism, we must institute within the primary grades curricula that honor diversity.

Comparisons

You can support some claims by citing a comparable claim that has already gained wide acceptance. Note, however, that this supporting strategy will work only if the two claims are truly comparable, not just vaguely similar. In an argument predicting financial difficulties for a new snowboard store in your town mall, you might cite the failure of the three other stores that have rented the same space. Or if you are arguing against proposed cuts in state money for scholarships, you may cite what another state has done to avoid reducing its education budget. This comparison will work only if the fiscal situation of the state you refer to is truly comparable to that of your state. In order to know this, you will have to get considerable information on each and probably present that information in the argument itself.

Appeals to Authority

You can support any claim by referring to a similar view held by a recognized authority in the field. You could support an evaluative argument claiming that Michael Jordan is the most talented professional basketball player in the game today by quoting Charles Barkley pronouncing the same judgment (of course, Barkley has to have made this pronouncement—you can't make it up). Just be sure that the person whose judgment you cite *is* an established expert in the subject of your argument. Even though Barkley is a sports celebrity, his fame does not make him an expert on investment strategies or health care.

Appeals to Audience Needs and Values

Remember the emphasis of Chapter 2 on audience consideration, including an identification of audience needs and values? You can convert this preliminary identification into explicit support for your argument. Obviously, audiences will be more accepting of arguments that they see as likely to satisfy their needs or affirm their values. Many arguments presume these needs and values without referring to them explicitly. But you can strengthen some arguments by directly addressing these considerations, particularly when the match between claim and audience needs or values is not obvious. For example, a recommendation addressed to the administration of your college proposing a change from a trimester to a semester calendar should identify precisely how the change would benefit the administration—perhaps in the form of increased enrollment, higher student satisfaction, or long-term savings.

ACTIVITIES (4.2)

Get together with a small group of your classmates and discuss which methods of support (comparison, appeal to authority, appeal to audience needs and values) could be effectively applied to the following claims:

1. The costs of statewide and national political campaigns will discourage all but the rich from running for office.
2. The study of homosexuality is (is not) appropriate in a college course.
3. Regardless of what your mother used to tell you, you cannot catch a cold by going outside with wet hair.
4. Parents should recognize how they risk their children's intellectual development by parking them in front of a television.
5. The widespread use of antidepressant drugs has revolutionized the psychotherapeutic community.

Addressing the Counterargument

A defining feature of argument is that its claim or claims are subject to disagreement: they are arguable. Thus, any claim you argue should be capable of evoking a *counterargument*—a position different from and often directly opposed to your claim. Just as you must carefully consider certain questions about your audience before you begin arguing, you must also identify the probable counterargument or arguments. Though this statement may seem counterintuitive, your arguments will be strengthened by your acknowledgment of their most powerful counterarguments. Why? For one thing, it is entirely possible that your readers are aware of the counterargument and even convinced by it. In stating and rebutting this position, you are dealing head on with the opposing view. Second, even if your readers aren't familiar with the alternative view, identifying it in your own argument will contribute to your image as a responsible and well-informed thinker.

The following are approaches to dealing with your argument's counterargument:

1. You can omit direct reference to the counterargument when it is a weak position or likely to be unfamiliar to your audience. But note that omission does not mean ignorance: you should keep even the weakest counterargument in mind while you are writing, if for no other reason than that a reader may raise it.

2. You can acknowledge or identify the counterargument without directly re-
futing it. This technique shows your readers that you are aware of the complexity
of the issue and the legitimacy of other positions; it gives the impression that you
are reasonable and broad-minded. In the following example, Margaret Whitney includes a brief acknowledgment of some predictable objections to her claim that
competitive athletics are good for girls:

> I am not suggesting that participation in sports is the answer for all
> young women. It is not easy—the losing, jealousy, raw competition and
> intense personal criticism of performance.
>
> And I don't wish to imply that the sports scene is a morality play ei-
> ther. Girls' sports can be funny. You can't forget that out on that field are
> a bunch of people who know the meaning of the word cute. During one
> game, I noticed that Ann had a blue ribbon tied on her ponytail, and it
> dawned on me that every girl on the team had an identical bow. Some-
> how I can't picture the Celtics gathered in the locker room of the Boston
> Garden agreeing to wear the same color sweatbands.

Whitney has chosen not to refute these objections, probably because of the
relative brevity of her argument, but her identification of the objections does suggest that she is reasonable and flexible.

3. You should identify and directly refute an opposing position in the following situations:

- When you know your audience holds that position.
- When you know a credible, often-cited countercase exists, regardless of
  whether your audience subscribes to that position.
- If it is vital to your argument to project a broad-minded, well-balanced
  image.

The following excerpt from Martin Luther King, Jr.'s 1963 "Letter from Birming-
ham Jail" is an example of direct refutation. Here, King is responding to criticism
by Alabama clergy of his program of nonviolent resistance to racial segregation.

> You may well ask, "Why direct action? Why sit-ins, marches, and so
> forth? Isn't negotiation a better path?" You are quite right in calling for
> negotiation. Indeed, this is the very purpose of direct action. Nonviolent
> direct action seeks to create such a crisis and foster such a tension that a
> community which has constantly refused to negotiate is forced to con-
> front the issue. It seeks so to dramatize the issue that it can no longer be
> ignored. My citing the creation of tension as part of the work of the non-
> violent resister may sound rather shocking. But I must confess I am not
> afraid of the word "tension." I have earnestly opposed violent tension,
> but there is a type of constructive, nonviolent tension which is necessary
> for growth. Just as Socrates felt that it was necessary to create a tension
> in the mind so that individuals could rise from the bondage of myths and
> half truths to the unfettered realm of creative analysis and objective ap-
> praisal, so must we see the need for nonviolent gadflies to create the

kind of tension in society that will help men rise from the dark depths of prejudice and racism to the majestic heights of understanding and brotherhood.

Notice how King identifies the opposition's position and even concedes them a point (they're correct in calling for negotiations) before he refutes their position and moves to an idealistic statement of his own. This pattern of statement-concession-refutation is typical of effective refutations, though you have to be careful not to give away too much in the concession.

Direct refutations should be thoughtfully placed in your argument. If your audience appears to be firmly committed to an opposing position, you're not likely to convince them of the error of their views at the outset. On the other hand, readers without strongly held views are less likely to be swayed by a counterargument if it follows an impressive array of support for your claim. But if you include your refutation as the final piece of support, remember that it may linger in your reader's mind for some time, so make it as strong and convincing as possible. And finally, some very powerful arguments are exclusively refutations of opposing positions; these arguments gain form, precision, and intensity from the position they are opposing.

ARRANGING YOUR ARGUMENT'S SUPPORT

Having accumulated support for your claim, you now have to consider the best way to arrange it in your argument. You can make strong support even stronger by arranging it to have the most powerful impact on your readers. Once again, audience consideration is key: your decisions about the organization of your argument's support should be based on your readers' familiarity with the subject, their ability to follow the path of your argument, and their probable disposition toward your claim.

It helps to think of your support as separate units that can be moved around within your argument. In an essay claiming that "The Student Activities Board should bring the Dave Matthews Band to campus," the units of support could be listed as follows:

1. A survey shows that the Dave Matthews Band is the most popular performing group with students at your college.
2. The college would increase student satisfaction by showing their willingness to please students.
3. Ticket sales would be brisk, and therefore would substantially offset the cost of bringing the band to campus.
4. In a letter to the *Chronicle of Higher Education,* the vice president of student affairs at a college in the adjoining state praised Dave Matthews for his intelligent and thought-provoking lyrics. "This is a band that any school should be proud to host," the letter concluded.
5. The band has a solid reputation for being professional and audience-appropriate.
6. Bringing such a popular band to campus would increase the college's community visibility.

7. Student enrollment would increase as a result of bringing Dave Matthews to campus.

A good general principle is that the *strongest* support should be presented first, so that you gain some early agreement from your readers. If possible, you should also save an effective supporting point for the end of your argument; it will leave your readers with a positive final impression. In the list above, the strongest argument may be Argument 2, particularly if the college in question is, like most schools in today's competitive higher-education environment, extremely concerned about student satisfaction. Argument 6, a secondary causal claim, is likely to be persuasive to the Student Activities Board as well, since community visibility is always a plus to college administrators.

What constitutes strong support? To some extent, this will depend on your audience. A credulous, inexperienced group and a cynical or expert audience will be convinced by different points. However, relevant factual support (figures, examples, and statistics, as in Argument 1 above) is usually very strong, while highly speculative arguments (predicted effects with a remote chance of being realized) are weaker; for example, Argument 7 would be extremely difficult to predict convincingly and probably should be omitted altogether. Citing expert opinion, as in Argument 4, is usually effective, provided your expert is credible and his or her support is documented. In Argument 4, does the opinion of a vice president for student affairs qualify as expert in this context? Does she have an obvious bias that might weaken her statement? How respectable a publication is the *Chronicle of Higher Education?* Are your school and hers comparable?

Sometimes you have little choice about the arrangement of your support. Scientific experiments dictate a certain organization, as do causal chains, where Cause A must be discussed before Cause B, Cause B before Cause C, and so on. In these cases, you'll need to make sure that all supporting arguments are strong and that they fit tightly together, because one weak link can destroy the entire argument.

ACTIVITIES (4.3)

1. The following argument, written by student Sharon Bidwell, contains a number of varieties of supporting material. Pretend that you are the editor of your school newspaper and have decided to print Sharon's letter. In a two-page letter to Sharon, comment on the effectiveness of her choice and arrangement of support.

> The administration's decision not to allow Dr. Fasciano and his white supremacist group to participate in a roundtable discussion with the students on our campus is clearly an act of censorship and should not be tolerated in a country that prides itself on free thought and expression. Censorship, as defined by the Encyclopaedia Britannica, is "the suppression or prohibition of speech or writing that is condemned as subversive to the common good." It is obvious that the administration is making a

selective decision of what the "common good" is for the students of this campus.

There is no doubt that the administration has legitimate concerns that need to be addressed. First of all, Mr. Fasciano's visit will raise some eyebrows among those who make regular contributions to the university. Second, Mr. Fasciano's visit is likely to set off active protests which have the capacity to seriously disrupt the campus and even threaten the safety and security of the students.

Despite these very real risks, the administration must make it known that this university supports the Constitution of the United States--namely, the First Amendment--and does not bow to pressure when it comes to suppressing free speech. To paraphrase John Milton in his Areopagitica of 1644, we must allow that free and open encounter in which truth may indeed prevail over error.

The argument against censorship has been made by many who fought hard against it--against anything, in fact, that interferes with self-development and self-fulfillment. For example, in his first inaugural address, Thomas Jefferson addressed the necessity of free dissent: "If there be any among us who would wish to dissolve this Union or to change its republican form, let them stand undisturbed as monuments of the safety with which error of opinion may be tolerated where reason is left free to combat it."

The administration must give the students the freedom to be the best guarantors of quality and fairness. We rely on these institutions of higher learning to teach future generations by allowing them to choose freely and make difficult decisions. For those who oppose Mr. Fasciano and his views, let there be an open forum with a free exchange of ideas. Our forefathers fought for this privilege. Let's not let them down.

DEFINITIONS

Obviously, readers can't agree (or reasonably disagree) with what they don't understand. Clarity is the result of many different elements in written argument: precision of ideas in the writer's mind, an understanding of the relationship among these ideas, careful organization of claim and supporting material, clear transitions among parts of the argument, reliance on the conventions of grammar and punctuation, and comprehensible, unambiguous language. It is this final element—the clarity of your language—that concerns us here. Ideally, writers of argument would use only those words that they knew their readers would understand. But arguments can't always rely on simple language, and even the simplest words mean different things to different people. This is where *definition* comes in: the careful delineation of the intended meaning of a potentially troublesome word or term.

Knowing when and how to define terms is critical to successful argument. Because effective and strategic definition strengthen any argument by making it more accessible to readers, it can be viewed as a form of support. In some cases, definition moves from its clarifying supporting function to that of a secondary claim, where the writer must convince the reader to understand a term in a particular way before the central claim can be argued. Sometimes definition of a key term is so crucial and controversial that it becomes a central claim in itself.

When to Define

You should plan on defining the following types of language in your arguments:

1. *Unfamiliar terminology.* Any specialized or unusual terms that may be unfamiliar to your readers must be explained. If, for example, you aren't sure whether your readers will have heard of "Maxwell's Demon," or a "net revenue model," or "dysthymic disorder," provide a clear definition.

Unfamiliar terminology includes *jargon* (specialized vocabulary and idioms). Generally speaking, jargon should be avoided, but there are times when it is the best language for the job. If you must use phrases like "the dialogic principle of feminist discourse," don't assume that everyone in your audience will know precisely what you mean; provide a definition.

2. *Nonspecific language.* In general, avoid vague, fuzzy terms, particularly in statements of evaluation and measurement. If you claim, "The Dave Matthews Band is the most popular band in contemporary music," consider how little this statement tells the reader about the nature and extent of that popularity. Popularity based on tape and CD sales? Popularity based on money earned? On concert attendance? And popularity with whom? Certainly they are not the most popular band with people over sixty-five. A more specific statement, such as "The Dave Matthews Band has sold more CDs in the last year than any other contemporary band" is far more useful to the reader.

And when you use nonspecific words like *poor, excellent, large, grand,* or *considerable,* make sure you explain the meaning of your modifier as precisely as possible.

3. *Abstract terms.* While you should try to make your writing as concrete as possible, sometimes you can't avoid using abstract terms in argument, especially in evaluations. The problem with abstractions is that they can be understood in different ways; that is, they can be *ambiguous.* If you must use a term like *popular,* or *talented,* or *conservative,* be sure to pin down explicitly your understand-

ing of the term. While your readers may not agree with your definition, at least they will understand how you intend to use the word and will judge the success of your argument within those parameters.

4. *Controversial terms.* Some terms have been at the center of heated public debate for so long that they are emotionally and politically loaded. Their meaning is ambiguous—that is, it can be interpreted in more than one way—and people tend to argue over which interpretation is correct. *Euthanasia* and *socialism* are examples of such controversial terms; how one defines them often determines one's position toward them. When you use such terms in your arguments, you will almost certainly need to clarify what you mean by them.

Sometimes such terms are so controversial that your definition, because it implies a position on the subject, becomes the point of the argument. Consider, for example, an essay on doctor-assisted suicide: a carefully delineated definition of what the practice *is* (or is not)—the prescription of lethal amounts of medication to a dying patient at the patient's request, for example—would take you a long way in an argument supporting the practice. This is precisely the strategy adopted by student Robert Conway in his essay "The Moral Justification for Euthanasia" (pp. 131–134 in Chapter 8).

Types of Definitions

Terms requiring clarification can be defined briefly or extensively, depending on the needs of your audience and the importance of the term to your argument. The four types of definition you will most commonly use as support for your argument are the shorthand definition, the sentence definition, the extended definition, and the stipulative definition.

Writers often resort to *shorthand* definitions when the term in question requires only a quick explanation. A shorthand definition substitutes a familiar term for an unfamiliar one, as in the following example: "Acetylsalicylic acid (aspirin) is an effective medicine for most headaches."

A *sentence* definition, similar to a dictionary definition but written as a grammatical sentence, consists of the term to be defined (the *species*), the general category to which it belongs (the *genus*), and those characteristics that distinguish it from all other members of that general category (the *differentiae*). A sentence definition has the following structure:

Species = Genus + Differentiae

An example of this form of definition is "A heifer [species] is a young cow [genus] that has not borne a calf [differentiae]."

An *extended* definition includes this basic sentence definition *and* any additional material that would help a reader understand the term being defined. The following are strategies for extending a sentence definition.

Evolution of Definition.   Sometimes an understanding of the historical development of a word's usage will illuminate its richness for readers. The word *queer,* for example, means strange or out of the ordinary. Thus it was eventually coined as a derogatory term for a male homosexual. Recently homosexuals have embraced the term, converting it from a slur to a compliment. There is now an academic field called Queer Studies.

Comparison.   Readers can gain a better understanding of a term if it is compared to something with which they are familiar. An argument that needs to define the term *docudrama* might explain that a docudrama is similar to a movie, except the events depicted are based in fact.

Example.   Offering specific examples of unfamiliar terms is an excellent way to explain them. To define what a *haiku* is, for example, you would almost certainly present an example or two.

Definition by Negation.   Sometimes you can explain a term by telling your reader what it is not, what it should not be confused with. For example, at the beginning of this textbook, we defined the term *argument* by distinguishing it from *opinion,* a term often mistaken as being synonymous with argument.

Etymological Definition.   Providing the etymology of a word—the meanings of its original roots—can also help to explain its meaning. The word *misogynist,* for example, derives from the Greek *miso,* meaning "hate," and *gyne,* meaning "woman."

Definition by Description.   Unfamiliar or abstract terms can often be explained or introduced by a physical or figurative description. If you were defining a Phillips screw, you might explain what the screw looks like. Or in defining contrapuntal music, you could describe the sound: the listener hears two distinct melodies going on at exactly the same time.

Functional Definition.   You can explain some unfamiliar terms by telling readers what the object or person does or how it operates. It would be helpful for a reader unfamiliar with the meaning of *provost* to learn what duties that academic officer performs. Functional definitions are particularly helpful in explaining unfamiliar *objects* such as tools. After describing the appearance of a particular drill bit, for example, you could explain what that particular bit is used for or how it is used.

The following extended definition of "poetry," from Laurence Perrine's *Sound and Sense,* contains many of these strategies of extended definition:

> Between poetry and other forms of imaginative literature there is no sharp distinction. You may have been taught to believe that poetry can be recognized by the arrangement of its lines on the page or by its use of rime [sic] and meter. Such superficial tests are almost worthless. The Book of Job in the Bible and Melville's *Moby Dick* are highly poetical, but the familiar verse that begins: "Thirty days hath September,/ April, June, and November . . ." is not. The difference between poetry and other literature is one only of degree. Poetry is the most condensed and concentrated form of literature, saying most in the fewest number of words. It is language whose individual lines, either because of their own brilliance or because they focus so powerfully on what has gone before, have a higher

voltage than most language has. It is language that grows frequently incandescent, giving off both light and heat.

This definition uses a sentence definition ("Poetry is the most condensed and concentrated form of literature"), a definition by negation (indicating what poetry is *not*: poetry has little to do with line arrangement or rhyme or meter), comparison ("Between poetry and other forms of imaginative literature there is no sharp distinction"), and figurative description ("It is language that grows frequently incandescent, giving off both light and heat").

Stipulative definitions *argue* that a particular definition should be assigned to a term. In other words, a stipulative definition argues a claim about meaning. While all definitions can be seen as claims, in that they propose meaning, and meaning is never fixed, the types of explanatory definitions discussed so far record meanings that most audiences would agree on. Stipulative definitions, on the other hand, argue for a particular meaning rather than record a consensual one. Sometimes stipulative definitions are made for convenience and clarity: "When we use the term *argument,* we are referring only to its primary meaning of demonstrating the reasonableness of a proposition." In this example, the writer is clarifying, not arguing.

But extended stipulative definitions are often fully developed arguments supporting an arguable, often controversial, claim about meaning. Think of the often-repeated argument "Abortion is murder." This short sentence definition opens a Pandora's box of controversies about meaning. First, there is likely to be disagreement over the meaning of the term *murder* in this context. The dictionary tells us that murder is the "unlawful and malicious or premeditated killing of one human being by another" *(Webster's New World Dictionary of the American Language).* But abortion is not illegal, so an antiabortion argument would have to reject this definition and stipulate its own. Or to open another controversy: Is the fetus a "human being?" Is there consensus about the meaning of this term? Clearly not: a prochoice advocate would want to restrict or stipulate the meaning of *human being.* Through your stipulated definitions of *abortion, murder,* and *human being,* you are actually arguing your position on the issue of abortion.

Extended stipulative definitions are essentially interpretive arguments: in proposing a restricted, possibly unusual, definition of a concept, you are arguing a particular interpretation or understanding that is suggested and supported by the context of the argument. Stipulative definitions can be supported through a variety of supporting methods. One of the most useful is an argument of effect, that is, demonstrating the positive effects of adopting your particular definition of the term. For example, if you were proposing a new definition of the word *minor* as a way of making a case for lowering the legal drinking age ("The traditional definition of *minor* as someone under the age of twenty-one leaves out those eighteen- to twenty-year-olds who are considered old enough to die for their country, to get married, and to terminate their education"), you might introduce a supporting argument of effect that money could be saved if police didn't have to enforce the current drinking age. Or if you were arguing that education is a lifelong process, you might base your argument on a stipulative definition of *education,* supporting that definition through the secondary causal argument of the positive consequences that education, so defined, can lead to.

Chapter 10 of this book, "Writing and Image," begins with a stipulative definition of the word *image* as applied to written argument. This definition serves more of a clarifying than an argumentative purpose, but it does make the claim that despite the largely negative popular understanding of the term, a writer's "image" is positive and important.

ACTIVITIES (4.4)

1. Examine an extended definition in an encyclopedia, reference guide, or textbook, and write a one- to two-page essay that describes what elements (sentence definition, examples, history of the object or concept being defined, comparison or contrast, and so on) have been included in the definition and speculate on why they have been included. Are there other elements you believe should have been included to help the definition? Are there any elements that could have been omitted?
2. Write your own stipulative definition of *beauty, murder,* or *friendship.* Compare your definition with those of your classmates who define the same term.

SUMMARY

An Argument's Support

- An argument's support is all the material that transforms your working claim into a reasonable conclusion. Knowing the class of the argument you are making will help you determine the appropriate support, but there are some generic varieties of support that can be used to strengthen any class of argument. These are

  - secondary claims

  - comparisons

  - appeals to authority

  - appeals to audience needs and values

  - addressing the counterargument

  - defining key terms

- When possible, arrange your support to have the greatest impact on your readers, with strong support placed at the beginning and end of your argument.

- Any terms in your claim or the body of your argument likely to be unfamiliar to your readers should be defined by a sentence definition, an extended definition, or a shorthand definition.

- Stipulative definitions, which restrict the meaning of a term to one of the term's possible meanings, can be used to clarify an argument or to make an interpretive argument.

SUGGESTIONS FOR WRITING (4.5)

1. Write a claim that comes out of a position or belief you hold strongly (about a political issue, a policy at your university, or your relationship to your family, for example). Identify the category of your claim, and make a list of all the points you can think of to support your claim. Give your list to a classmate and see if he or she can add any supporting reasons you haven't thought of.

2. Write a two- to three-page extended definition of some concept or object, making sure your definition includes a formal sentence definition. Your instructor may have suggestions for this assignment, but we also suggest the following: entropy, eugenics, amber, ecosystem.

5

Making Reasonable Arguments: Formal and Informal Logic

In Chapters 6 through 9, you will learn the most appropriate supporting methods for each class of claim. But before you begin working at the specific levels of claim and support, you should have some understanding of the principles of logic. The primary definition of the term *logic* is "the science of correct reasoning." The many and complicated rules of formal logic do, in fact, make up an intricate mathematical system that yields absolutely right and absolutely wrong answers. But this system does not dominate the fuzzier province of written argument, where variations in context, occasion, audience, and purpose make absolute conclusions exceedingly rare. Nevertheless the fundamental principles of formal logic and their less formal derivatives do have their use in written argument: they are excellent tools for testing the reasonableness of the relationship between claim and support, for measuring the probability of an argument's conclusion. Think of it this way: You can't write successful arguments without some familiarity with logic, but this familiarity will not ensure that your arguments will be successful.

FORMAL LOGIC

The principles of formal logic were identified by the Greek philosopher Aristotle (384–322 B.C.). Today, almost 2,500 year later, these principles continue to influence what we mean by *reasonable* thinking. Just as children learn to speak their native language unaware of its underlying linguistic and grammatical principles, so we learn to think reasonably with little understanding of those complex principles informing reasonable thought. At some point in their education, children must learn the rules of grammar in order to refine their language skills; similarly, as educated adults and certainly as writers of argument, we must become familiar with the principles of logic to refine our reasoning skills.

Formal logic comes in two broad varieties: induction and deduction. *Induction,* or inductive reasoning, involves reasoning from observed evidence (the support) to a general statement (the claim or conclusion). *Deduction,* or deductive reasoning, involves reasoning from premises (assertions accepted as true or probable) to a conclusion or claim.

Induction:

Observed evidence: In the twenty years I've lived in New York State, warm weather has begun every year between March and May.

General statement: In New York State, warm weather begins between March and May.

Deduction:

Premise: All human beings are mortal.

Premise: Jane is a human being.

Conclusion: Jane is mortal.

In the first example, notice the movement from specific examples (every spring for twenty years) to a very general assertion. But notice also that the specific examples suggest only that the general assertion is likely or probable, not necessarily true. The move from specific examples to a general conclusion is often referred to as the *inductive leap,* a term which underlines the large gap between the truth of the individual instances and the truth of the generalized conclusion.

In the deductive example, on the other hand, the statement that Jane is mortal is *necessarily true* if the premises preceding it are true. If certain conditions are met, deductive arguments *can* lead to necessary, or absolute, conclusions. But the "if" is a big one; in reality, the principles of deduction will enhance the reasonableness of your argument, but they will rarely ensure its absolute truth.

As you'll see in the next four chapters, some logical principles are more useful with one kind of argument than with another. The remainder of this chapter offers a general introduction to the principles themselves.

Induction

In inductive reasoning, we make generalizations on the basis of individual instances. For example, if you observed repeated instances of male students dominating class discussion, you might conclude that at your school, male students participate in class more than female students. Your conclusion is useful not because it represents the absolute truth, which of course it doesn't (there are exceptions to any generalization), but because it summarizes a set of similar events that you have observed. Inductive reasoning comes naturally to all of us, whether we're highly trained in Aristotelian logic or don't know the difference between a reasoned argument and a shouting match.

But the process does carry risks. For one thing, irresponsible induction can lead to harmful misconceptions. There is a world of difference between the conclusion "Male political science majors at Miller College tend to dominate class discussion" and one claiming "Men are more skillful speakers than women." You can avoid making irresponsible conclusions if you heed the following three cautions: (1) be sure you have *enough* individual examples to warrant the conclusion (your experience in one political science class is not enough to warrant even the first conclusion above); (2) provide the context of your examples and conclusion—in this case, your observations of students in a particular major at a particular college; and (3) always qualify your conclusion by using verbs or modifiers that limit the degree of certainty you're insisting on ("Male students often dominate class discussion").

A second risk of inductive reasoning concerns the use to which we put its conclusions. Inductive conclusions are safest if they are used *descriptively,* as a way of summarizing a set of observations or facts ("Male political science majors at Miller tend to dominate class discussion"). But induction is more commonly used to *predict* events or behavior. Many of the predictions we make on the basis of induction are perfectly harmless. If you know that the shopping mall is usually crowded on Saturday afternoons, your decision to shop Saturday morning is a harmless and quite useful prediction based on inductive reasoning. But predictive inductive reasoning can lead to harmful stereotypes. It may be true that women in your major do not participate in class discussion, but if you assume, on the basis of these limited observations, that all the women you associate with will be quiet and unassertive, your false conclusion may put you in personal and political hot water.

Responsible inductive reasoning depends in large measure on recognizing and arguing factual claims, since induction involves supporting a general claim by individual factual instances. For this reason, a full discussion of induction is reserved for Chapter 6, "Arguing Facts."

Deduction

The basic form of the deductive argument is the *syllogism:* a three-part argument consisting of a *major premise* (a premise is an assertion or proposition), a *minor premise,* and a *conclusion.* The earlier sample of deductive reasoning is a classic example of a syllogism:

> **Major premise:** All human beings are mortal.
> **Minor premise:** Jane is a human being.
> **Conclusion:** Jane is mortal.

This syllogism is an example of thinking in terms of classes. The major premise establishes two classes—a larger one of mortal beings and a smaller one of human beings—and it asserts that the smaller class belongs in the larger. The minor premise establishes that a still smaller class—in this case, one individual (Jane)—belongs in the smaller class of the major premise. From there it necessarily follows that Jane will also be a member of the largest class, mortal beings. The syllogism can also be displayed visually.

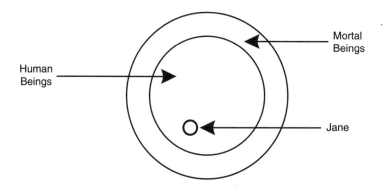

Thinking in terms of classes can be misleading if the process is done incorrectly. Examine the following syllogism:

> **Major premise:** All Catholics believe in the sanctity of human life.
> **Minor premise:** Jane believes in the sanctity of human life.
> **Conclusion:** Jane is a Catholic.

At first glance this argument may seem plausible, but as the following diagram shows, the argument is seriously flawed because the minor premise puts Jane in the larger group of those who believe in the sanctity of life but not in the smaller group of those who are Catholics. All the argument can really tell us is that Jane and Catholics share this one trait. They may differ in everything else.

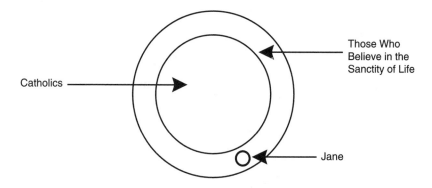

This sample syllogism leads us to an important distinction in deductive reasoning: the distinction between validity and truth. A syllogism is *valid* when it's set up correctly, according to the rules of formal logic. You can look these rules up in a logic textbook, but in many cases, you can tell when a syllogism doesn't follow them correctly because, as in the case of Jane's religious persuasion, you recognize instinctively that the conclusion doesn't make sense. On the other hand, a syllogism is *true* only if its premises are true. The syllogism about Jane's mortality is both valid and true. But consider the following syllogism:

> All women are feminists.
> Jane is a woman.
> Jane is a feminist.

Clearly, the generalization that *all* women are feminists is untrue; so, though the relationship between premises (support) and conclusion (claim) is valid, the conclusion is untrue because it works from a false premise. On the other hand, while the premises of the syllogism about Jane's religion are true, the syllogism is not valid because the relationship between premises and conclusion is incorrect.

Deductive arguments that are both true and valid are *sound.* Deductive arguments that are untrue, invalid, or both are *unsound.* Whether reading or writing arguments, you'll need to be on guard against the seductions of the valid argument built on false premises, and of the invalid argument luring you with the truth of its premises or conclusion.

Conditional Syllogism.   The conditional syllogism, sometimes referred to as the *if-then syllogism,* takes the following form:

> If John drops the glass on the sidewalk, then the glass breaks.
> John drops the glass on the sidewalk.
> The glass breaks.

This syllogism is valid, and if its premises are true, it is also sound.

With conditional syllogisms, however, you need to watch out for a very common error, usually called *affirming the consequent,* where the "then" clause of the major premise is turned into an affirmative statement in the minor premise:

> If John drops the glass on the sidewalk, then the glass breaks.
> The glass breaks.
> John drops the glass on the sidewalk.

The argument is invalid because the major premise merely claims that John's dropping the glass causes it to break; it does not exclude other ways of breaking the glass, such as hitting it with a hammer. Given this major premise, we cannot conclude that John has dropped the glass simply because the glass is broken.

Disjunctive Syllogism.   The disjunctive, or "either-or," syllogism takes the following form:

> Either the doctor gave the patient oxygen or the patient died.
> The patient did not die.
> The doctor gave the patient oxygen.

Note that this argument is invalid if the alternative is affirmed—that is, if it turns out to be true—rather than denied, or declared untrue, as above:

> Either the doctor gave the patient oxygen or the patient died.
> The patient died.
> The doctor did not give the patient oxygen.

The major premise merely asserts that we can assume that the first alternative occurred because the second one didn't. (In other words, if the doctor hadn't given the patient oxygen, the patient would surely have died.) But if the second one, the patient's dying, did occur, we can't turn around and assume that the doctor failed to give the patient oxygen. Again, the patient could have died from a number of other causes even if the doctor did his "duty."

Making Use of Deduction in Written Arguments. For writers of argument, classical logic offers a good way of "checking your work." Familiarity with the basic principles of deductive reasoning will probably not help you *create* arguments, but it will help you test the reasonableness of your claim and support once they are composed. Of course, the writing and thinking we do every day do not come packaged in classical syllogistic form, so that detecting sound and unsound reasoning is a little more difficult than in the examples above. But with a little practice, you can become adept at recasting your claim and support into the syllogistic model.

Let's say you are writing an argument claiming, "Pittsford State should create a substance-free dormitory." You plan to offer the following support for your claim: (1) considerable tension exists between drinkers and nondrinkers in the dorms at Pittsford State; (2) studies of similar schools with substance-free dorms show a dramatic increase in student satisfaction with dormitory life; and (3) student drinking is a fact of life that is not likely to be eliminated. To determine whether your claim and support are logical, you'll need to work with each supporting claim separately, finding the place it would occupy in a formal syllogism that concludes, "Pittsford State should create a substance-free dormitory."

So where would your first supporting claim be placed? Because it's fairly specific, it is likely to be a minor premise, since minor premises of syllogisms are almost always more specific than major premises. You now have an incomplete syllogism that looks like this:

> Major premise: ?
> Minor premise: Tensions exist in Pittsford State's dorms between drinking and nondrinking students.
> Conclusion: Therefore, Pittsford State should create a substance-free dormitory.

The syllogistic formula requires that the major premise establish a larger class of which the class in the minor premise is a subset. Here, the major premise would read something like "Where tensions arise between drinking and nondrinking students, substance-free dorms should be created." Now the syllogism looks like this:

> Major premise: Where tensions arise between drinking and nondrinking students, substance-free dorms should be created.
> Minor premise: Tensions exist in Pittsford State's dorms between drinking and nondrinking students.
> Conclusion: Therefore, Pittsford State should create a substance-free dormitory.

You don't have to state the major premise in your argument, but it is extremely helpful to know what it is so that you can determine whether that assumption—and its relationship to the rest of the argument—is reasonable.

To determine its reasonableness, you test the validity and soundness of the syllogism. The syllogism is valid: the internal relationship among premises and conclusion is deductively proper. But its soundness (the truth of the premises) is another question. Let's take the minor premise first. You would need considerable evidence of student tensions in order to justify this premise. One or two personal experiences with these tensions would not justify the premise. But if you have personally witnessed disagreements between drinking and nondrinking students and have heard similar reports from friends, and if, say, a group of nondrinking students has petitioned the residence government to address the problem, the premise could be accepted as true. (Chapter 6 will discuss the principles of support for factual claims like this one.)

The major premise is much more problematic. At the very least, it is debatable. Some might say that it is indefensible, since it asks readers to accept as universally applicable a single solution to a complex problem. Even if the premise is true, its truth is too controversial to be assumed; it must be justified through a careful secondary argument.

The incomplete syllogism discussed above (the one lacking a major premise) is an *enthymeme*—a form of syllogism common to spoken and written arguments, where presenting all components of the syllogism may be tedious for the audience. An enthymeme is a rhetorical syllogism that implicitly relies on an audience's existing beliefs to support the conclusion. Enthymemes are not inferior syllogisms; their very incompleteness helps to convince. An audience that helps to complete the argument will have a stake in it and thus will be more likely to accept it. But as in the case above, the writer must have good reason to believe that the audience will accept the premise provided. As you will see in Chapters 8 and 9, this process of uncovering the syllogism or enthymeme of an argument can be particularly useful when arguing evaluations and recommendations.

ACTIVITIES (5.1)

1. Identify the major premise of the following incomplete syllogisms, as in the following example.

   Conclusion: My physics professor is a skilled teacher.
   Minor premise: My physics professor knows her physics thoroughly, uses imaginative examples, is concerned that her students learn, and is an excellent speaker.
   Major premise: A skilled teacher knows his or her subject matter thoroughly and can present it imaginatively, is concerned that students learn, and speaks clearly and compellingly.

   a. **Minor premise:** Mack's résumé was poorly written.
      Conclusion: Mack did not get the job because his résumé was poorly written.
   b. **Minor premise:** Jessie made faces at the refs behind their backs, cursed members of the other team, and refused to congratulate them on their victory.
      Conclusion: Jessie is a poor sport.

  c. **Minor premise:** Professor Callahan constantly interrupts his students.
     Conclusion: Professor Callahan does not respect his students.
  d. **Minor premise:** Young people of today do not value family or community.
     Conclusion: Our young people will not grow up to be good citizens.
  e. **Minor premise:** Bill Clinton is a master of the art of compromise.
     Conclusion: Bill Clinton is a fine statesman.
  f. **Minor premise:** There is no way I can write my final research paper for this class.
     Conclusion: I will not pass this class.
2. With a small group of your classmates, discuss the extent to which the major and minor premises of three of the above syllogisms would need to be argued.
3. Examine an essay you wrote recently and present its major argument as a syllogism. What are the argument's major premise, minor premise, and conclusion? Are any of these components implicit rather than explicit in your essay? Is the syllogism sound and valid?

THE TOULMIN MODEL: A MODERN VARIANT OF FORMAL LOGIC

Formal deductive reasoning yields necessary or certain conclusions, yet written arguments about our complex, provisional, and messy world rarely presume to discover absolute truth. It is in this mismatch between the goals of formal reasoning and those of written argument that the limitations of deduction are exposed. The fact is that most of the arguments we judge to be worth making are worth making *because* they are arguable, because they admit the possibility of more than one reasonable position. Few people waste time, for example, arguing about whether the sun will come up tomorrow, but they do argue about whether the problem of ozone depletion in the atmosphere warrants strict regulation of pollutants.

Recognizing the limitations of Aristotelian logic for practical rhetoric, the twentieth-century philosopher Stephen Toulmin identified and formalized a slightly different relationship between an argument's claim and its support. Toulmin's model is a useful way to judge the reasonableness of many of the arguments you construct.

According to the Toulmin model, a claim is linked to its support through what is called a *warrant*. A claim's warrant indicates how one gets from factual support (which Toulmin calls *data*) to the claim. In many ways, the warrant resembles the supplied major premise of the substance-free dorm example above: it is the general belief, convention, or principle that permits the data to support the claim.

Suppose you were proposing that your college major institute a junior-year-abroad program. You have a number of supporting reasons for this claim: the program will attract students to the major; it will be an invaluable educational experience for students; it will allow the department to establish important international connections. The Toulmin model requires that each supporting reason be linked to the claim through some assumption or principle acceptable to the audience. Using the last support cited, a diagram of this argument would look like this:

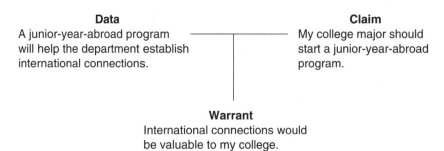

| **Data** | **Claim** |
| A junior-year-abroad program will help the department establish international connections. | My college major should start a junior-year-abroad program. |

Warrant
International connections would
be valuable to my college.

We can identify an argument's warrant (which is not always stated explicitly in the argument itself) by asking, "What is it about the data that allows me to reach the claim?" In this case, it is the *value* of international connections that makes the claim desirable. Just as major premises are sometimes left unstated in real arguments, warrants are sometimes only implied. If you have any reason to suspect that your audience will not accept the warrant as generally true or at least reasonable, you will have to support it with what Toulmin calls *backing*. In this case, one backing for the warrant might be identification of the benefits of international connections in a world where more and more college graduates will be working for international organizations.

A fifth element of the Toulmin model, which makes the concept particularly useful to written argument, is the *qualifier*. The qualifier is a word or words that modify or qualify the claim. In our example, that qualifier is the word *should,* a word that makes the recommendation less strong than *must,* but more strong than *might want to consider.* Unlike the syllogism, the Toulmin paradigm gives the writer room to entertain claims that are less than necessary or certain. Adding the backing and the qualifier to our example, we come up with the following diagram:

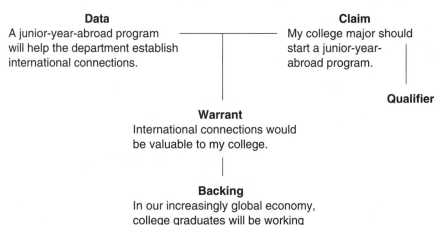

| **Data** | **Claim** |
| A junior-year-abroad program will help the department establish international connections. | My college major should start a junior-year-abroad program. |

Qualifier

Warrant
International connections would
be valuable to my college.

Backing
In our increasingly global economy,
college graduates will be working
for international organizations.

Applying Toulmin's model to your own arguments can help you to flush out the assumptions that generate your claim and to evaluate their reasonableness. You may find that this model is most useful in making recommendations (as in the example above) and causal arguments. The most useful point in the composition process at which to apply both the Toulmin and the Aristotelian models is after you have formulated a claim and collected some support. Fitting these elements into one or the other paradigm will help tell you what is missing, what needs further support, and what is patently unreasonable. Don't *begin* the argument process by trying to fit ideas into the models; this will only frustrate your thinking and limit your inventiveness.

ACTIVITIES (5.2)

1. Identify the unstated warrants for each of the following pairs of claim and support.
   a. **Claim:** Secondary smoke is harmful.
      Support (or data): The Surgeon General's report on smoking establishes this.
   b. **Claim:** Celebrities who stand trial for capital crimes are not likely to get fair trials.
      Support (or data): The media focus unrelentingly on celebrity suspects.
   c. **Claim:** If you have the flu, you should stay at home.
      Support (or data): This year's strain of the flu is highly contagious.
   d. **Claim:** Writing is a dying art.
      Support (or data): My freshman students don't know the difference between an independent clause and Santa Claus.
   e. **Claim:** Mick is an unorthodox runner.
      Support (or data): Mick holds his arms high when he runs, and his heels never touch the ground.
2. Which of the warrants supplied above would require some backing in order to be acceptable to readers? What kind of backing might you supply?

INFORMAL FALLACIES

Unfortunately, even when we pay careful attention to the logical principles discussed in this chapter, our reasoning can still go awry through any of a number of *informal* fallacies. Like the principles of formal logic, informal fallacies usually involve a faulty relationship between an argument's claim and its support. Familiarity with these flaws in reasoning is especially useful during the revision stage, when, with these fallacies in mind, you examine the relationship between your claim and its support. Since an inclusive list of these fallacies is a very long one— as inexhaustible as human inventiveness—included here are only those fallacies that frequently turn up in student writing. For each fallacy, the category or categories of argument in which it is most likely to occur are also indicated.

Ad Hominem Argument

An *ad hominem* argument is against the arguer (Latin *ad hominem* means "to the man") rather than against the argument: "Smith's argument against increasing taxes on the rich is worthless because he himself is rich." This fallacy, which substitutes irrelevant judgments of an individual for reasonable evaluations of an issue, is most likely to occur in evaluative arguments.

Ad Populum Argument

Ad populum is Latin for "to the people." One commits the *ad populum* fallacy when supporting a claim by referring to popular opinion or behavior to justify it. A teenager trying to convince her parents to remove her curfew because "everybody else's parents have done it" is attempting to convince her parents through an appeal to popular behavior rather than to reason. This fallacy is a corruption of the legitimate tactic of appealing to established authorities to strengthen a claim.

Circular Argument

A circular argument (also known as *begging the question*) is one in which the claim is already contained in the support: "John did not succeed on the track team [the claim] because he did not do well in track events [the support]." In this example, "did not do well in track events" really only restates "did not succeed on the track team"; it adds no new information about *why* John didn't succeed. Another common version of circular argument, or begging the question, assumes what has to be proven, as in the statement "This film should be banned because it contains immoral scenes." This claim requires a definition of *immoral* and evidence that the film meets this definition. Lacking such material, the claim begs the question of the immorality of the film. Evaluative, interpretive, and causal arguments seem to be particularly subject to this fallacy. One giveaway that your argument is circular is that your supporting statements repeat a key term from your claim.

Distraction

Distraction is bringing in irrelevant points to distract attention from the issue being argued: "Sure I cheated on my income taxes, but I've never broken any other laws." It is also known as the *red herring,* from the practice of dragging a dead herring across a trail to distract hunting dogs from the scent of their prey. Distraction is frequently used to deflect unfavorable evaluations.

Either-Or Argument

The either-or argument is setting up two extreme positions as the only alternatives and denying any possible middle ground: "The painting is either a masterpiece or trash." The painting could be something in between. Also known as *bifurcation* or the *fallacy of the excluded middle,* this fallacy can occur in any category of argument, though it is probably most frequent in evaluations (as in the claim about the painting) or in recommendations, where extreme solutions are sometimes seen as the only options: "Either we build a new computer facility or we give up on using computers at this school."

Emotive Language

The fallacy of emotive language involves making a case through slanted, value-laden language rather than through reasonable support, as in the statement "Smelling blood, the media will attack and destroy any candidate with a newsworthy weak spot." This claim, in its implicit identification of the media with carnivorous beasts, presumes a value judgment about the media that the claim does not justify. Writers of argument should try to refrain from using prejudicial language, at least until their claims have been made reasonably. Emotive or slanted language can be used in any kind of argument, but it is most common in evaluative arguments.

False Analogy

The false analogy supports a claim by comparing its subject to something not *essentially* similar: "Offering courses in gay and lesbian theory is no more defensible than teaching pedophilia or necrophilia." While both sides of the comparison refer to noncustomary sexual preference, there are more *differences* between gay theory and pedophilia than there are similarities, and comparing them attempts to prejudice the reader against gay and lesbian theory. As pointed out in Chapter 10, analogies can be useful in generating and illuminating arguments, but they can never prove a point. Just as legitimate comparison can be used to support any kind of argument (see Chapter 4), analogies can be misused in all of the four classes of argument. If you find that you have introduced an analogy to *support* rather than explain or illuminate a claim, you have probably committed this fallacy.

Hasty Generalization

Basically a misuse of the inductive method, hasty generalization consists of a general claim based on an insufficient sample: "Young professional people tend to be self-centered and materialistic. My friends Eric and Melanie certainly are." This fallacy typically occurs in factual arguments and in the supposedly factual support for evaluative statements about entire groups of people: "Women are sentimental"; "Asian-American students are good in mathematics."

Non Sequitur

A non sequitur claims a logical relationship between a conclusion and a premise where none exists: "Henry should make a good governor because he is tall and handsome." *Non sequitur* in Latin means "it does not follow"; non sequitur reasoning is behind almost all fallacies. The term is really a generic one that has been specifically applied to cases where the relationship between a premise and a conclusion is seriously askew. The term is also used to cover some fallacies in causal analysis: "I performed poorly on that speech because I wore my green tie rather than my red one." This is an example of our next fallacy—*post hoc, ergo propter hoc*. Non sequitur reasoning can occur in any category of argument.

Post Hoc, Ergo Propter Hoc

Post hoc, ergo proper hoc is Latin, meaning "after this, therefore because of this." It means claiming that because one event preceded another, it must have caused the subsequent event to occur: "I performed poorly on that speech because I wore my green tie rather than my red one." This fallacy is at the root of much superstition, as in the case of a pitcher who carries a red handkerchief with him whenever he pitches because he had one with him the day of his no-hitter. It is a serious risk in any causal analysis, and a writer can guard against it by following the principles of causal reasoning presented in Chapter 7.

Slippery Slope

Designating a first and a last step in a causal chain, when the intervening steps have not occurred, constitutes the slippery slope fallacy: "I didn't get the first job I interviewed for, so I guess I'd better forget about a career as an engineer." In this simple example, the speaker creates a worst-case scenario (forgetting about engineering) based on a series of events that has not yet occurred and will not necessarily occur, that is, repeated failure to be hired in engineering jobs. This fallacy appears most commonly in arguments of effect, usually when the writer wishes to prove that the consequences of a particular action are likely to be negative.

Strawperson Argument

A strawperson argument involves attacking a view similar to but not identical with that of an opponent: "How long will America tolerate softheaded opponents of gun control who want only criminals to have guns?" Advocates of gun control vary in their views, but they do not want only criminals to have guns. The adjective *softheaded* is an example of emotive language; in this sentence, it is designed to arouse a particular emotional response. Negative loaded terms are frequent in strawperson arguments. This fallacy is a common but misguided tactic of evaluative arguments.

You can improve your ability to analyze your own and others' arguments by familiarizing yourself with the kinds of fallacies previously defined, but you need to remember that what is considered "correct" thinking depends on your context. What may be incorrect in one context may be perfectly acceptable in another: *ad hominem* arguments are frowned on in academic writing (though they do occur), but they are perfectly acceptable in a court of law, where questioning and at least implicitly attacking witnesses' backgrounds and motives are frequently practiced. In addition, some of these fallacies are only a slight step off the path of correct reasoning. For example, there is nothing inherently fallacious about either-or reasoning, but this kind of reasoning goes wrong when either-or alternatives lead to excluding other, real possibilities.

ACTIVITIES (5.3)

Identify the informal fallacies committed in the sentences that follow. Select from the following list:

ad hominem argument	false analogy
ad populum argument	hasty generalization
circular argument	non sequitur
distraction	*post hoc, ergo propter hoc*
either-or argument	slippery slope
emotive language	strawperson argument

1. Legalized abortion puts us only a step away from legalizing murders of anyone we deem undesirable or inconvenient.
2. If you can't beat them, join them.
3. I strongly disagree with your proposal to allow women to join fraternities. Fraternities are men-only clubs.
4. Those traitorous, draft-dodging youths who preferred deserting their country to serving it should never have been granted amnesty.
5. Discrimination should be fought on every front—whether it's practiced against members of a certain race, a certain sex, or those who bear arms.
6. I spent two weeks at a military academy and realized that private school is just not for me.
7. It is unfair to penalize Eastman Kodak for harming the environment when it has been such a strong supporter of the local economy.
8. *Supercop* had the highest ratings of any television movie. Clearly it was a superior film.
9. Tom Hanks is a brilliant comedian; he should leave heavy drama alone.
10. Opponents of the Equal Rights Amendment believe that women should stay barefoot and pregnant.

SUMMARY

Making Reasonable Arguments: Formal and Informal Logic

- Understanding the principles of formal logic will help you link claim and support reasonably.
- The principles of inductive logic—moving from specific instances to general conclusions—are important to all writers of argument and are particularly applicable to factual arguments.
- The syllogistic formula, common to most deductive reasoning, can be applied to an argument's claim and support as a way of determining the reasonableness of their connection.

- The Toulmin model of claim-warrant-backing is particularly useful to writers of argument, as it does not make absolute certainty a requirement of the claim.
- Informal fallacies are any of those errors in reasoning that can undermine the credibility of a claim. The best time to consider the possibility of informal fallacies is during the revision process.

SUGGESTIONS FOR WRITING (5.4)

1. Pay attention to the informal conversations and discussions of your friends. Start a list of all the generalizations you hear them make. Then write a one- to two-page letter to your friends telling them what information and evidence they would need to support their generalizations reasonably.
2. Focus on three advertisements you see repeatedly on television or in print. Write a one-page essay on each advertisement, discussing your application of the syllogistic and Toulmin models. How would the advertisement look within the format of each model? What premises or warrants are only implied? Are those claims true? What would have to be argued in order to make the advertisement more reasonable? Finally, rewrite the ad so that it conforms to the principles of deduction and the Toulmin model.

6

Arguing Facts

An argument's claim can be supported in a number of ways—some common to all arguments, some particular to specific classes. As is mentioned in Chapter 4, one common form of support for a claim is another claim. For example, if you were arguing that students graduating from your major have had trouble finding jobs, you could support that claim with job placement figures for students in your major, and/or with anecdotes about the employment woes of your friends. In both cases, you would be supporting a central factual claim by further factual assertions.

But take a slightly more complicated example. Suppose that in arguing the claim "First-time DWI offenders should have their driver's licenses revoked" (a claim of recommendation), you cite as support the secondary claim "The threat of license revocation would deter many from driving while intoxicated." This secondary claim is causal (predicting the *effect* of the change) and would require support appropriate to causal arguments. Among others, one piece of support you might use for this secondary causal claim is a factual assertion about the effectiveness of similar laws in other states.

There are two points to be taken from these examples: First, arguments almost always consist of a central claim supported by secondary claims, which themselves must be argued appropriately. Second, sooner or later, all argumentative claims will come to rest on factual assertions. Because so many of the assertions we consider factual are themselves debatable, the facts holding up your arguments are not necessarily bedrock. Furthermore, even gathering the most reliable facts available seldom means that you will arrive at absolute truth. But some factual assertions are more solid than others, and it is the purpose of this chapter to show you what constitutes a reliable factual assertion or claim.

WHAT IS A FACT?

The New College Edition of *The American Heritage Dictionary* defines a fact as "Something known with certainty." According to this definition, a fact is a statement that is known to be true and about which there can be no debate or doubt.

Assertions like "My physics teacher is a woman," "George Washington was the first president of the United States," and "Human beings are mortal" would fall under this definition; they are inarguable, unambiguous, proven facts that in most arguments would require no support beyond their simple assertion. Facts like these often come from your own experience or have been confirmed by your experience; sometimes they fall under the heading of "common knowledge." In any event, they can be accepted as indisputable.

But what about statements like "Beta-carotene is a carcinogen," "Secondary smoke is not harmful," or "The FDA-established minimum daily nutritional requirements are inadequate"? While these claims are stated as if they are known with certainty, careful readers might hesitate to call them indisputable. For one thing, they come from fields in which most of us are comparatively ignorant; we lack the expertise to judge their accuracy. Second, anyone who reads the newspaper regularly knows that these are the kinds of "facts" that seem always to be retired or revised when new evidence or new research methods emerge. Indeed, each of these statements is a correction of an earlier assertion that claimed to prove the opposite: beta-carotene was for years thought to be cancer-inhibiting; the known dangers of secondary cigarette smoke have just recently been moderated; and millions of perfectly healthy people have based their diets on the minimum daily requirements suggested by the FDA.

Assertions like these fall more properly under the dictionary's secondary definition of *fact:* "Something asserted as certain." Such statements are made in good faith, based on the best available evidence, and stated with conviction, but they are the findings of incomplete and ongoing research in comparatively dynamic fields and thus are always subject to revision and correction as newer, more inclusive, more reliable evidence is gathered. In other words, such factual assertions are *believed* to be certain, but not *known* with certainty; they are more like state-of-the-art educated guesses.

Then there are the assertions that are true, but that are useless and sometimes downright misleading if their entire context is not known. You'll see an example in the second sample essay at the end of this chapter, where research findings about the correlation between obesity and morbidity are stated out of context by a journalist. The journalist has not lied: the research did demonstrate that the heaviest men in the study had higher death rates than the leanest men, but without all the research data, it is impossible to know whether this difference was significant or not.

Finally, there is the assertion that is stated with certainty, dressed up as factual, and credited to a seemingly impeccable source, but that is nonetheless utterly preposterous. Some of these impostor facts are easy to detect; we know never to trust anything we read in the *National Enquirer,* for instance. But in more cases than we'd like to admit—particularly with the proliferation of electronic information—these preposterous facts can sneak right by you without your even suspecting that they are unreliable. You may find yourself particularly vulnerable to accepting (and circulating) false facts if they will strengthen your own argument. If you are arguing for a pass-fail option at your college and come across figures linking this option to high student satisfaction, you may be tempted to make use of these figures, even if you are skeptical, simply because they support your position.

The more your argument relies on the first and second type of facts, the more solid it will be. Your job in presenting facts supporting your argument's claim will be to convince your readers of their truth or likelihood, to convince them, that is, that your supporting facts are "known with certainty" or "are based on the best available evidence." The principles that follow should help you with this crucial job.

SUPPORTING FACTS REPORTED BY PRIMARY AND SECONDARY SOURCES

Most of the arguments you will write will depend on facts you find in your reading and research. Sometimes these facts will be reported by what are called primary sources, sometimes by secondary sources. A primary source is the individual or group that determined the fact in the first place; for example, a manager reporting that sales declined 5 percent in the last quarter or a research oncologist summarizing the findings of her study on cancer remissions in a medical journal. A secondary source is the person or document reporting facts discovered by someone else, for example, a biology textbook describing some little-known facts about Darwin's work on the HMS *Beagle,* or a member of an electronic listserve summarizing information heard at a professional conference.

Because reliable facts are critical to successful arguments and because so many of the statements paraded as facts are unreliable, you'll want to be extremely discriminating about selecting facts from primary and secondary sources, recognizing that whenever you include a fact in your argument, you are tacitly saying to your audience, "I believe this to be a trustworthy statement." When your sources are printed texts (e.g., books, journals, newspapers), you have some assurance that the factual material has been reviewed by someone, though this assurance does not relieve you of responsibility for further evaluating the reliability of your source. But when your material comes from the Internet, that assurance may be completely missing. For both print and electronic sources, there *are* certain steps you can, and should, take to assure yourself—and thus your audience—that the facts you're presenting are relatively trustworthy.

Evaluating Print Sources

The first thing to look at when evaluating print sources is the identity of the author. Books and journal articles are almost always published under the author's name. If you are familiar with the author and know he or she is an acknowledged expert with a proven track record in the field, you have some assurance that the facts you wish to cite are reliable. You are probably safe trusting the facts given out by your college career counselor on postgraduate career opportunities, or facts about astronomy contained in an article by the noted astronomer Carl Sagan, because both have established professional reputations. But you should be wary of advice on the stock market obtained from a staff writer of your school paper. It's not that information obtained from nonexperts can't be reliable, but you should always be skeptical of these sources.

If you're not familiar with the author of the facts in question, it often pays to do a little digging. Your library has a number of professional biographical dictionaries either in its reference section or on-line. It pays to spend a little time looking up your the author's qualifications. One thing to consider is the objectivity of your author. If Tiger Woods writes that Nike makes the best running shoe in the world, accept that pronouncement with a good dose of suspicion.

If you can't discover anything about the reliability of the author, or if the author isn't identified (as often happens in reference books, magazines, and editorials), consider the reputation of the publisher. Most university presses, for example, are considered careful reviewers of the material they publish, and certain journals and periodicals have established a reputation for accuracy. The publisher's good reputation will not ensure that the material in question is accurate, but it does make the odds of accuracy relatively high. Certainly a report found in the *Wall Street Journal* is more credible than one found in *Star* magazine or the *National Enquirer*. If you don't know anything about the reliability of your source's publisher, ask a professor in the field.

You also want to be sure to check the date of your source's publication. While a book on Abraham Lincoln dated 1966 might not be considered outdated, a 1966 book on computer technology would be barely worth reading, unless you were doing a historical survey of the field.

Evaluating Electronic Sources

The huge growth in electronically accessible information is both a blessing and a curse to writers who must work with reliable facts. On the one hand, finding information has never been easier. Hundreds, even thousands, of sources on a given topic are available with a few keystrokes. But the sheer volume of information can make us lazier and less effective researchers. Furthermore, because anyone with the proper equipment can post information on the Internet, there is a lot more unreliable information on-line than between the pages of a book or journal that has gone through some kind of review process. (See the article "'Vonnegut Speech' Circulates on Net" at the end of this chapter for an example of how quickly misinformation can circulate on the Internet.)

For the most part, evaluating electronic sources isn't all that different from evaluating print sources. Begin by trying to determine the author's reliability—again, through biographical dictionaries or perhaps the *National Dictionary of Addresses and Telephone Numbers*. While you're on the Internet, try a search through the World Wide Web using the author's name as your keyword; you may find some useful information on his or her reputation.

Checking the electronic address of your source gives you some generic information about its origin and thus at least a hint of its reliability. *Edu* means it comes from an educational institution; *gov* is a governmental organization; *org* is a nonprofit organization; and *com* is a commercial organization.

Make sure to check the date of the material if it's available. Much of the material on the Internet has the virtue of being very current, but in quickly moving fields, information may become out-of-date in a matter of days.

If you read useful factual information on a listserve, try communicating with the author (whose name and E-mail address are included on the listserve posting) to get information about the sources of his or her information. Or if you find nonattributed information on a web site, try following up some of the related "links" on the site; these may lead you to the background you need on the sources of the web site material.

Citing the Source in Your Text

Another way to support the primary and secondary facts you present is to cite their source within your argument. Providing the source is a courtesy to readers, who may want to examine the subject in more depth. More important, including the source assures your readers that your argument is a responsible one—that your facts are not fabricated for the sake of argument but come from legitimate sources. Failure to cite the sources of the facts on which your claim rests will weaken your argument considerably.

In most cases, your citation of a source will take the form of a footnote, an endnote, or, increasingly, inclusion of the work in a "Works cited" list at the end of your argument. The subject matter of your argument will determine which citation form you should follow, and you can find models of these forms in most college writing handbooks. In addition to a footnote or bibliographic reference, you can also include a brief reference to your source within the text of your argument. For example, "According to the *Oxford English Dictionary,* the word *flick* at one time meant 'thief.'" In this case, the source would also appear in a works-cited or bibliography section at the end of the argument.

If your readers are not likely to be familiar with your source, you may want to provide credentials briefly within your text. For example, "In his book *The Mismeasure of Man,* Stephen Jay Gould, the noted Harvard paleontologist and popularizer of science, argues that the results of standardized intelligence tests can be misleading and also misused by those in power."

A note on citing electronic sources: most works on the Internet are copyrighted, so you must give full citations (including the FTP address and the path needed to obtain the file).

ACTIVITIES (6.1)

Write a one-page analysis of the credibility of two of the following passages. Consider the issues of expertise, bias, and currency of facts. You may need to do some research on the credentials of the author or of the publication in which the passage appeared.

1. Mailer had the most developed sense of image; if not, he would have been a figure of deficiency, for people had been regarding him by his public image since he was twenty-five years old. He had in fact learned to live in the

sarcophagus of his image—at night, in his sleep, he might dart out, and paint improvements on the sarcophagus. During the day, while he was help-less, newspapermen and other assorted bravos of the media and literary world would carve ugly pictures on the living tomb of his legend. Of neces-sity, part of Mailer's remaining funds of sensitivity went right into the war of supporting his image and working for it. (Norman Mailer. *The Armies of the Night.* New York: Signet Books, 1968. 15–16.)

2. **Chow chow,** powerful NONSPORTING DOG; shoulder height, 18–20 in. (45.7–50.8 cm); weight, 50–60 lb (22.7–27.2 kg). Its coat has a soft, wooly underlayer and a dense, straight topcoat that stands out from the body. It may be any solid color and is the only breed with a black tongue. A hunting dog in China 2,000 years ago, it was brought to England in the 18th cent. (*Concise Columbia Encyclopedia.* New York: Columbia University Press, 1983. 168.)

3. A SPECTER is haunting Europe—the specter of communism. All the powers of the old Europe have entered into a holy alliance to exorcise this specter: Pope and Czar, Metternich and Guizot, French Radicals and German police spies. (Karl Marx and Friedrich Engels. *The Communist Manifesto.* Ed. Samuel H. Beer. New York: Appleton-Century-Crofts, 1955. 8. Originally published in 1848.)

4. Many devices have been used in the attempted measurement of interests. The interest inventory is the most important of these both from the standpoint of the number of counselors using them and the number of investigators working with them. The inventory approach consists of the comparison of likes and dislikes of individuals through questionnaire items. Since the individual is asked to esti-mate his feeling, the method may be said to be subjective. A complete discus-sion of interest inventories is given by Fryer [Douglas Fryer. *The Measurement of Interests.* New York: Henry Holt, 1931]. (Harry J. Older. "An Objective Test of Vocational Interests." *Journal of Applied Psychology.* 28, 1944: 99.)

5. People who have a good sense of humor *suffer less constipation, acid stom-ach and sensitivity to cold* than those who don't get the joke, according to a study presented at the American Psychosomatic Society annual meeting. ("Medical Flash." *Self.* July 1994: 59.)

6. Sixty percent of schools in central cities . . . have insufficient phone lines, elec-trical wiring or electrical power to support communications technologies. (U.S. General Accounting Office. "Technology in Public Schools." 18 Dec. 1995. On-line. Internet. 22 Mar. 1997. Available http://www.gov/technology.html.)

SUPPORTING PERSONALLY EXPERIENCED FACTS

Sometimes you'll need to support a fact obtained through your own experience or observation rather than from a second- or third-party source. Personally experi-enced facts are supported by a credible and objective description of the experience or observation.

Describing the Experience

Let's say you are writing a report for a psychology class on phobias and you want to demonstrate how extreme and irrational phobic behavior can be. As evidence for this position, you cite your observations of a friend who is terrified to fly:

"Traveling with a friend on a short domestic flight, I observed firsthand what phobic panic looks like." Because this statement suggests extreme behavior, it requires a careful and accurate description of the panic as support: the pallor, the tremors, the hysteria you observed in your friend. (At this point, we are not talking about explaining or interpreting the fact, but about presenting it in such a way that your reader will accept that it happened.)

The principle holds in more complicated contexts. Take the scientific laboratory reports that are written in all lab courses from ninth grade through graduate school. The writer's basic purpose in these assignments—to report an experience in the lab—is achieved through a careful, detailed description of the steps followed and the results obtained. The student essay "The Properties of Enzymes" (at the end of this chapter) illustrates how the student's factual claim (i.e., that she obtained the results she reports) is supported by her careful description of her personal observations.

Establishing Your Own Credibility

Writers of argument must appear credible to their readers, projecting an image that inspires confidence and trust. This requirement applies to all components of your argument, but it is particularly relevant to the presentation of personally experienced facts. Since you, the writer, are usually the sole support of a personally experienced fact, you must give your readers no reason to mistrust your description of the experience.

If your readers have any reason to suspect that your description is dishonest or inaccurate, your argument is going to fail. For example, if you referred to your eighty-five-year-old grandmother as support for an argument against mandatory retirement, citing her daily five-mile runs, her ability to bench-press 300 pounds, and her current prize-winning research on recombinant DNA, your readers would be very suspicious of such obvious exaggeration, and your credibility as an observer would be seriously questioned.

In presenting facts derived from personal experience, you must also guard against the inevitability of your own bias. Without realizing it, we often see only what we want to see and ignore what is convenient to ignore. Ask two politicians on opposing sides of an issue their perceptions of a stormy meeting and you will almost certainly get two very different stories about what happened. They are not necessarily trying to falsify evidence, but their biases color their perceptions. In some contexts, such as sportswriting about the hometown team or essays on the opinion page of the newspaper, readers expect and even welcome a certain bias, but they tend to reject open manifestations of it in other contexts, such as front-page news, academic projects, or business reports. One way to avoid excessive personal bias when you report facts you have observed is to ask yourself whether a person making a different claim would have observed the same things; if the answer is no, you should aim for more neutrality in your description. Another way to guard against the possibility of bias in reporting fact is to consult other people who observed or experienced the same event to ensure that your view is essentially a shared one. If it is not, you must consider whether your own bias accounts for the difference.

SUPPORTING FACTUAL GENERALIZATIONS

Any claim, regardless of the class it falls into, can be stated as a *generalization*. For example, the factual claim *"People* magazine and *USA Today* use much the same format as television news shows" becomes a factual generalization when the communications scholar Neil Postman tells us that "the total information environment begins to mirror television." Similarly, the claim "Frank is a successful sales representative because his father was also a good sales representative" (introducing a limited causal argument with an element of evaluation) can be extended to the following generalization: "Successful salespeople tend to have other good salespeople in their families."

To support any generalization, you need to apply two sets of principles. First, you must convince your readers that your original claims about *People* and *USA Today* or about Frank and his father are plausible—that significant similarities do exist between the television news show *20/20* and *People* magazine, or that there is a demonstrable *causal* connection between a father and a son who are both sales reps. How you support your claim will depend on the category to which it belongs. The first example is a largely factual claim, and the second is a causal claim.

Second, you must show that your generalization is reasonable—that what you've observed about Frank and his father can be plausibly applied to salespeople and their children all over the world. We will use factual generalizations to illustrate this second principle, but it applies to all categories of argument.

Applying the Principles of Induction

All generalizations, even the most informal and sweeping, begin on a specific level. We see something a few times and assume that it happens frequently or even all the time. That is, we move from specific observations to general conclusions; from the particular, we infer the general. In traditional logic, this process by which we assume the widespread existence of particular instances is called *induction*. Conclusions drawn by inductive reasoning are always somewhat risky because they are based on incomplete evidence. You assume that because you have never seen or heard of a flying cat, no such creature exists, yet unless you have seen every cat that ever existed, your claim "There is no such thing as a flying cat" has made a rather staggering leap from the particular to the universal. Yet these leaps are the nature of induction.

Support for a generalization consists of identifying a number of specific, verified instances or examples. If you claim, for example, that American films increasingly show the dangers of casual sexual relationships, you will have to cite individual films to support your claim. Or if you write, "Many young American novelists find universities a supportive and economically secure place to work," you will need to point to specific examples. If the generalization is a factual generalization, the specific examples will be individual facts, which in some cases may need verification. What makes a factual generalization "factual" is not the absolute truth of the generalization, which can never be proven, but its foundation in singular factual instances.

The most credible generalizations are those supported by the most, and best, examples. You cannot reasonably conclude that all algebra teachers are women if your experience is limited to one or two teachers, but you can reasonably conclude that many teenagers like rap music if you have known hundreds of teenagers in many different settings who like rap. In supporting generalizations, you need to know how many examples are enough, whether they are representative of all the available evidence, and which examples to include. Unfortunately, no simple formula exists that answers these questions, but the following general rules of thumb are helpful.

How Many Examples Are Enough?   First, the more sweeping your claim, the more examples you will need. You can position a generalization at any point along a continuum of frequency: "*Some* business majors are good in math"; "*Many* business majors are good in math"; "*All* business majors are good in math." Although the word *some* does constitute a generalization, it is a very limited generalization, a safe one to make if you don't have abundant evidence. To support "some," you need only a handful of examples. "Many" requires more than a handful of examples, certainly, but is far easier to prove than "all." In fact, absolute statements using words like *all, everyone, never,* or *always* should be avoided in written argument unless every constituent in the group referred to can be accounted for. Otherwise, the claims these words make are too grandiose to be credible. The following passage supports its factual generalization with carefully chosen examples:

> A number of fraternity members on this campus contradict the broad and usually unflattering stereotypes circulated about "brothers." While I am not a fraternity member myself, I know a number of members well, and none of them fits the popular image of the beer-swilling, women-chasing party boy. For instance, my friend Judd, a dean's list electrical engineering major and obviously a dedicated student, says that fraternity living gives him the supportive environment he needs to excel in a difficult major. Two of my roommates from freshman year who have joined fraternities have become respected student leaders: Brad is vice president of Student Council, and Kelly is the student representative to Faculty Council. Both Brad and Kelly are well-rounded, academically successful students. Finally, I know that the entire pledge class of one campus chapter received the mayor's commendation for public service for their renovation of an inner-city recreation center. Of course, there will always be individuals who confirm the stereotype, but my observations question its widespread applicability.

In this passage, three examples, the last involving a large group of individuals, are presented to support the claim that few fraternity members fit the campus stereotype. In a more formal academic argument, we would probably insist on more rigorous, less personally observed evidence, but we would very likely accept these examples as adequate in a short, informal essay. As a general rule, three is a good number of examples for a short essay, since one or two examples may seem to be merely exceptions, while four or more would become tedious.

The less familiar your readers are with your subject matter, the more specific examples you should supply. If your readers are very comfortable and familiar with your topic, they will often accept sensible generalizations that are only minimally supported. If you refer in an internal business report to the "widespread problems with our new computer system," those familiar with the problem will accept the reference and not demand that it be supported. But a reader unfamiliar with this problem may demand evidence that the problem really exists. Of course, some readers unfamiliar with your subject area will accept dubious generalizations simply because they don't know any better. If these readers are misled, however, some of them will probably eventually learn that you were wrong in your generalizations, and they will then suspect your reliability in other situations, even when you are correct in your claims.

Do Your Examples Represent the Evidence Fairly?   In selecting which evidence for your generalization to include in your argument, you should make sure that the examples you choose represent fairly all the available examples, including the ones you omitted. Imagine, for example, that you support the statement "Fraternity hazing is obsolete on our campus" with examples of changes in the rules and practices of the three largest fraternities, but in the course of your research, you have discovered that there are significant exceptions to this generalization. You are misrepresenting the evidence if you fail to tell your readers about these exceptions. True, you may have provided enough examples to satisfy your readers, but you are misleading them by excluding the contradictory evidence. The best way around this problem is to qualify the claim in such a way that the evidence you omit is not contradictory. If you rewrite the claim as "Instances of fraternity hazing on our campus have decreased significantly in the last ten years," your three examples will perfectly support the claim, and the omitted evidence will no longer be contradictory.

Is Your Conclusion Too Broad for Your Examples?   Inductive reasoning always requires that the breadth of your conclusion match the breadth of your supporting evidence. If your generalized claim is very broad ("Art majors are the most politically liberal of all college students"), it must be based on proportionately broad examples—in this case, instances taken from a number of different colleges in different areas of the country that offer majors in art. If your claim is more limited ("Art majors at my college are the most politically liberal students"), you are justified in citing examples taken only from your college.

But even in this second, narrower case, you still must guard against generalizing on the basis of instances drawn from too narrow a context. If the art students at your school come from all over the country, yet you use as examples only those who come from the New York City area, your support is not broad enough to justify your conclusion. You will need either to limit your claim further ("Art majors from the New York City area are the most politically liberal students at my college") or to collect examples drawn from a broader geographic group.

ACTIVITIES (6.2)

1. The following conclusions are generalizations derived through inductive reasoning. What kinds of examples, and how many, would you need to make each one plausible?

   a. Most librarians are women.
   b. High school librarians tend to be women.
   c. In my experience, librarians have been pretty evenly divided between men and women.
   d. I have attended two major universities and have been struck by the number of librarians who are women.
   e. Library science departments tend to attract more women students than men.

2. Write a generalization that is adequately supported by the examples listed for each case below.

   a. John, Susan, and Jim prefer chocolate ice cream, while Jane prefers strawberry, and Henry prefers vanilla.
   b. Last Saturday night I sat alone at a showing of the new film *Anxious Hours,* and I saw no line for the film when I walked by the theater just before show time on Sunday.
   c. It is January 15 here in Minnesota, and so far this winter, we have had two snowfalls that just covered the ground and then disappeared.
   d. There were twenty-five Mercedes-Benz automobiles parked in the lot the night of my high school reunion, and as I recall, there were only about seventy students in my graduating class.
   e. When I returned from winter break to my classes here in Vermont, I noticed that Jack, Jeff, Mary, Matthew, Carrie, and Megan all had deep tans.

STATISTICS

Statistics are derived from the practice of drawing conclusions about a large number on the basis of a limited number of instances. Statistics are factual information compiled and reported numerically. The following are examples of statistical claims:

- Thirty percent of the American people believe a woman should never be president.
- The unemployment rate is 11 percent.
- One-quarter of all bridges in this state need repair.

In our world, statistics are an inevitable and integral part of our lives. We judge the quality of our manufactured products and of many of our services through statistics; we constantly encounter statistics on the health of our economy, our educational system, our sex lives, our souls. We tend to suspect claims that lack statistical support, and we use statistics in virtually every field in our society, from weather forecasting to managing baseball teams. But these general conclusions inferred from a limited number of instances are reliable only if the original process of information gathering was conducted according to certain principles. Whether you are conducting your own statistical studies as support for your argument or citing statistics obtained from other sources, you must be sure of the following:

1. The smaller group surveyed (or *sample,* as statisticians refer to it) must be *known.* If you read that eight out of ten women think they are overweight, but no reference is made to the source of the survey or who or how many were surveyed, you should not accept or use the figure. For all you know, only ten women were questioned, and they were picked from a list obtained from a weight reduction clinic. Every cited study should be identified and the sample group defined. Without such information, the figures are suspect.

2. The sample must be *sufficient,* or sufficiently large, in order for you to accept the conclusion drawn from that sample. That both of your roommates prefer classical music to rock does not justify the conclusion that classical music is more popular with college students; you need a much larger sample. Trained statisticians sometimes use small samples, but only under very specific conditions and with very specific mathematical models. Our inability to evaluate the use of these statistical formulas makes it hard for us to judge whether statistics are actually being used correctly. In such cases, it's important to learn as much as you can about the context of the studies and the methods by which the samples were gathered before relying on the figures completely. For example, researchers often critique each other's studies, and their analyses provide valuable information about the reliability of the results.

3. The sample must be *representative.* If a figure is given about the political inclinations of all Californians, the sample surveyed must represent a cross section of the population. If the 2,000 people questioned all have incomes of $40,000 and up, or if they're all over the age of forty-five, your sample is slanted, not representative of the variety of the population as a whole. Professional polling organizations like Gallup and Harris (groups hired to identify the preferences of large populations based on small samples) choose either a representative or a random sample. A *representative sample* is one that guarantees in advance that the sample will reflect the major characteristics of the population, for example, that the sample will have a percentage of Californians earning over $40,000 that is equal or nearly equal to the percentage of Californians earning over that figure in the total population. In a *random sample* on political attitudes in California, every adult Californian would stand an equal chance of being questioned. When chosen randomly, in 95 out of 100 cases a sample group of 1,500 people will be within 3 percentage points of duplicating the answers of the entire adult population. In evaluating the usefulness of any poll, you should know the method by which the sample was selected.

When you include in your argument statistics obtained from other sources, not only must you test them for the preceding three principles, you must also be certain they satisfy the requirements of second- or third-party facts. The source should have a reputation for expertise in the field and for objectivity, and the figures themselves should be recent. It is unwise to accept as support for your own argument any statistical data not credited to an authoritative source. If you cannot identify the instrument, individual, or organization through which these facts were obtained, chances are good that those facts are not reliable.

When using statistics in your argument, you also need to be aware of the variety of terms used to report large figures and of the way these terms influence the impact of the figures. A study on high school literacy could report its findings on extracurricular reading habits in a number of ways. It could say that out of 500 high school seniors surveyed, *100* had read at least one unassigned novel in the last year, or the same fact could be reported as *20 percent* of the students. Of those 100 readers, one could report the *average* number (or *mean*) of novels read (the total number of novels read divided by the 100 readers), the *mode* (the number of novels most frequently read by individual students), or the *median* (the midpoint of the range of frequency of novels read). The mean, mode, and median for this sample of students follow:

Students	Novels Read	Total Novels
25	4	100
10	3	30
45	2	90
20	1	20
Total 100		240

Average = 2.4 novels (total number of novels read divided by total number of students)

Mode = 2 novels (the most common number)

Median = 2 novels (the midpoint of the list of number of novels read according to the frequency of the number. Imagine the 100 students standing in a line, starting with all of those who read four novels, then those who read three, then two, and so on. The midpoint of this line of 100 would occur in the group of students who had read two novels.)

Statistics can be powerful tools in argument, but again, it is crucial to realize that they cannot *prove* claims; they can only *support* their likelihood. A recent poll indicating teenage hostility toward adult society is not proof that it was a teenager who attacked your English teacher or even that the students in a particular high school have hostile feelings toward their parents. It merely indicates that out of a sample of so many teenagers a certain percentage indicated feelings of hostility toward the adult generation. As the second student essay at the end of this chapter demonstrates, responsibly gathered statistics are not suspect, but the use to which we put these figures may be.

You should also be restrained in your use of statistics; if scattered profusely throughout a written text, they have a deadening effect on the audience. Often, a visual display of statistics in a chart or a table is more valuable to your audience than a verbal summary; graphic representations can clarify the meaning of the statistics and reinforce their significance. With statistics, it is easy to lose track not only of the "big picture" but also of any picture at all, and visual displays can give the reader the necessary perspective.

ACTIVITIES (6.3)

1. For two of the following statements based on statistics, discuss with a small group of your classmates the kind of information necessary to ensure the statement's reliability.
   a. Over 50 percent of the doctors surveyed in a nationwide study recommend Brand A medicine over any of the leading competitors.
   b. Brand C: The best built truck in America, according to a survey of truck owners.
   c. Over 60 percent of all Americans favor the president's plan for peace, while 85 percent oppose Senator Flag's call for more offensive weapons.
   d. Despite competition from television and VCRs, moviegoing is still popular in America. When asked how much they enjoyed going to the movies, 88 percent of moviegoers responded that they enjoyed moviegoing a great deal.
   e. A survey of leading economic forecasters indicates that a mild recession will occur in the next six months.

2. Conduct a survey of some of your classmates or of some friends. Ask them one or two questions that can be summarized in statistics, such as how many hours they studied last week. Compute the mean, mode, and median of these statistics. Write a one-page description of the results of your survey, and also present this information in visual form. Also state how representative you believe this group is of some larger, similar group, such as all students who studied last week.

SUMMARY

Arguing Facts

- All arguments rely on factual claims, either as their primary claim or as a form of support for the primary claim.

- To support facts reported by others, you must be satisfied of their accuracy and provide in your argument a brief reference to the source of the fact.

- To support facts founded on your own experience, you must describe the experience accurately and clearly and establish your own credibility through a responsible, objective, and accurate rendering of the experience.

- To support a factual generalization, you must cite a number of the verified facts that have led you to the general conclusion. The more sweeping the generalization, the more examples you will need to cite.

If your readers are likely to be unfamiliar with the subject matter, you should provide several examples as evidence. The examples cited must be typical of all the evidence discovered. The breadth of the examples cited must match the breadth of the generalization.

- Statistics can effectively support arguments, provided they are not overused and their significance is made clear.
- When including a statistical generalization, you must be satisfied of its reliability. It is reliable if the sample cited is known, sufficient, and representative.
- You must be aware of the exact meaning of the terms used to report statistical conclusions, particularly *average, median,* and *mode.*

THREE SAMPLE FACTUAL ARGUMENTS

The following laboratory report was written by a student in an introductory biology course. Like all lab reports, it is primarily a factual argument. The hypothesis in Paragraph 2 is the unsupported claim, which, by the final paragraph, has been converted into a supported conclusion. The writer supports her claim by reporting personally experienced facts: the procedure she followed and its observed results. Through her attention to detail and her adherence to the conventional lab report format, she implicitly demonstrates that she is a reliable reporter of personal experience.

THE PROPERTIES OF ENZYMES

Purpose: The purpose of this lab is to demonstrate (1) the enzyme activity of Catalase, (2) that enzyme concentration affects the rate of enzyme activity, and (3) that substrate concentration affects the rate of enzyme activity.

Hypotheses: (1) The higher the concentration of enzymes, the faster the reaction rate. (2) The higher the substrate concentration, the faster the reaction rate.

Procedure:

Part One:

Step 1: The lab group prepared a 40% enzyme concentration (4 ml of potato extract and 6 ml of buffer) and poured this solution into a watch glass.

Step 2: We then prepared a 1% hydrogen peroxide solution by measuring 30 ml of water and 15 ml of the H_2O_2 and mixing them together in a rinsed graduated cylinder. We labeled this solution 1% substrate.

Step 3: To observe the effects of enzyme concentration on enzyme activity, we poured 10 ml of the H_2O_2 and water solution into a clean beaker, making sure to fill the beaker exactly to the 10 ml mark. Then, using forceps, we dunked a small round piece of filter paper into the enzyme extract for five seconds. We then drained the paper by letting some of the solution fall onto a clean paper towel.

Step 4: To measure the reaction rate, we placed the moistened paper disk in the bottom of the beaker with the 1% hydrogen peroxide solution. When the disk reached bottom, the timer was started. The timer was stopped when the disk reached the top of the beaker. We repeated this procedure 3 times (each time with a new solution of hydrogen peroxide and a new piece of filter paper), recording the times and their average.

Step 5: Control: Following Steps 3 and 4, we placed a piece of filter paper in water and placed it in the beaker with the H_2O_2 solution. We timed the process of the paper from the bottom to the top of the beaker and recorded it.

Part Two:

After completing the first part of the lab, we were ready to observe the effects of varying substrate concentration on enzyme activity.

Step 1: We also prepared a 60% potato extract solution and poured it into a beaker and labeled it.

Step 2: We prepared another solution with a 1.5% substrate concentration in a graduated cylinder and poured it into a beaker that we labeled "1% H_2O_2."

Steps 3-4: We repeated Steps 3 and 4 from Part One of the lab to measure the new reaction rate, using a fresh hydrogen peroxide solution each time. Individual times and the average time were recorded.

Step 5: Control: The control for this part of the experiment was to dunk a paper disk in boiled potato extract, drain it, and place it on the bottom of the substrate beaker and record the time it took to reach the top of the beaker.

Materials: potato extract
100-ml graduated cylinder
10-ml graduated cylinder
buffer solution of water
goggles
3% hydrogen peroxide solution
uniform-sized filter paper disks hole-punched
from a larger piece
paper towels
small beakers
stirring rod
forceps
glass-marking pen or wax pencil

Data/Observations for Part One: While waiting for the disk to float to the top of the beaker with the substrate, we noticed that as the reaction occurred, bubbles of oxygen gas were released, causing the disk to lift off the bottom of the beaker and float to the top. The times and average time we recorded for this part of the experiment are as follows:

Data: Enzyme concentration = 40% Substrate concentration = 1%

	Trial One	Trial Two	Trial Three
Time (seconds)	6	6	7

Average of trials: 6.3 seconds
Time for Control 1: 0.0

Observation: The paper sits on the bottom, the solution gets fizzy, and then the paper rises.

After obtaining our own results, we compared them with those of our classmates. These results are recorded in the chart below.

Group	Enzyme Conc. (%)	Substrate Conc. (%)	Class Avg. (Seconds)	Total Avg. (Seconds)
1	20	1.0	10.4	12.5
2	40	1.0	6.9	7
3	50	1.0	5.9	4.58
4	60	1.0	5.3	5.6
5	75	1.0	4.4	4.86
6	100	1.0	3.9	3.2

The chart shows that as the enzyme concentration increases, the reaction time decreases.

Data/Observations for Part Two: In Part Two, we measured the effect of changing substrate concentration on the time of reaction. During this procedure, the filter paper also released a gas before rising. In timing the rising of three separate pieces of filter paper, we found the following information:

Data: Substrate concentration = 1.5% Enzyme concentration = 60%

	Trial One	Trial Two	Trial Three
Time (seconds)	5	4	4

Average of three trials: 4.3 seconds
Time for Control 2: 0.0 seconds

Observation: The paper released some gas before rising.
    After obtaining our own results, we compared them with those of our classmates and found the following:

Group	Enzyme Conc. (%)	Substrate Conc. (%)	Group Avg. (Seconds)	Total Avg. (Seconds)
1	60	2.0	4.63	4.5
2	60	1.5	4.6	4.0
3	60	1.0	4.35	1.5
4	60	0.8	6.11	5.3
5	65	0.6	6.2	7.3
6	60	0.3	8.1	7.8

This chart shows that the rate of enzyme activity is influenced by the amount of substrate. Up to a point, the more substrate present, the faster the reaction. However, when the substrate concentration is so high that an enzyme is working as fast as it can, further increases of substrate concentration will have no effect on the rate at which that product is formed.

Conclusion: The prelab material stated that four main factors influence the rate of enzyme reaction: temperature, pH, the concentration of substrate, and the concentration of enzymes. In this lab, we performed an experiment studying the last two of the factors. To ensure accurate results, we performed three trials and averaged the results.

There were many places where errors could have contaminated our results, such as the wrong amount of one of the liquids, a dirty beaker or graduated cylinder, and changes in temperature. The first two errors can be prevented by being careful and making sure everything is clean.

The first control showed that it was the enzyme that made the filter paper rise. In the control, the filter paper dunked in water and placed in the beaker with the substrate did not rise.

The second control was similar to the first in that it proved that what we were doing was caused by one thing and not something else. We could tell that the increase of time from high to low concentration of substrate was caused only by the changing of that concentration.

The chief determinations of this lab have been that variations in the amount of substrate and in the amount of enzyme concentration affect the rate of reaction.

The following argument exemplifies how a primary factual claim is supported through other facts and through appeals to authority. The argument, written by a student majoring in statistics, also indicates why it is so important to exercise caution and restraint when we rely on statistical support. This essay is based on the second "Suggestion for Writing" at the end of this chapter.

STATISTICS LIE, OR DO THEY?

Benjamin Disraeli, English statesman and writer of
the nineteenth century, once quipped, "There are three
kinds of lies: lies, damned lies, and statistics."
Disraeli was not a mathematician, but his judgment about
the reliability of statistics is one that many intelligent
people still hold today. Those not trained in the field
assume that Disraeli's stereotype is a just one.

The stereotype is not without foundation.
Advertisers, politicians, news reporters, and lawyers
misuse statistics so frequently that we, the public, have
come to have little faith in the numbers they quote to us
daily. But the fact is that it is rarely the statistics
themselves that are suspect, but the use that these people
make of them. Statistics don't lie; the people who use
them do.

Many of the statistics that we read in newspapers are
reported from retrospective, case-control studies,
particularly epidemiological studies. A retrospective
study is one in which a control group is selected that
does not currently possess the characteristic under
examination, and a study group is selected that does
exhibit the characteristic. In epidemiological studies,
the purpose is to find correlation between the presence of
some disease and a small group of factors that may
influence the course of the disease (Heafey 674). For
instance, Jane Brody reports in the New York Times that
Dr. I-Min Lee, epidemiologist at the Harvard School of
Public Health, has "found a direct relationship between
weight and mortality, with heavier men at all ages being
more likely to die." Here the living are the control
group, and weight is the discriminating factor. Dr. Lee
said that she found a correlation between men's weight and
their death rate. She was quoted, "So I believe the upward
trend in desirable weights is not justified" (emphasis
added). Dr. Lee did not say that excessive weight in men
was the cause of their higher death rate, merely that she

believed it to be so. But Brody's entire article, even the
headline, "In Midlife, the Leanest Men Survive," implies
that the cause of higher death rates is greater body
weight. Brody, the reporter, has interpreted for us as
cause what the epidemiologist (biomedical statistician)
had presented only as a strong correlation.

The fact that two events are correlated does not
necessarily imply that one causes the other. In the
courtroom, statistical correlations are not admissible as
proof that cause exists even for correlations as high as
98.95% (Heafey 685).

A classic example of the misinterpretation of cause
versus correlation is found in the relationship between
the number of stork citings and human population
statistics in Oldenburg, Holland. Seven years of
population statistics (beginning in 1936) imply a direct
relationship between the number of stork citings and the
total human population of the city. The population of
Oldenburg is plotted against the number of storks
observed each year. Few people would hypothesize that the
increased number of storks caused the increase in
population. Did it really require more storks to bring

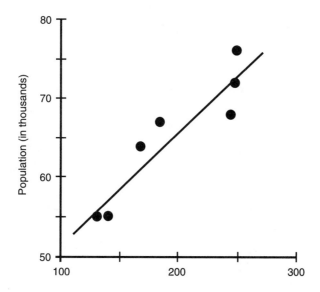

all those babies? Correlations between two variables Y and X often occur because they are both associated with a third factor W. In the stork example, since human population Y and the number of storks X both increased with time W over this 7-year period (each dot in the graph represents a year in the study), a correlation appears when they are plotted together as Y versus X. Maybe there is real cause and effect in the stork versus human population correlation. It is possible that more storks were cited just because there were more people around to see them. But these figures can't demonstrate cause, even if it should exist.

Statistics are also distorted by their method of presentation. For example, the American Cancer Society reported in 1991 that women have a 1-in-9 chance of contracting breast cancer (Blakeslee). But 1 in 9 is the cumulative probability that any woman will get breast cancer sometime between birth and age 110. Women at age 40 typically have a 1-in-1,000 risk of getting breast cancer, and that risk climbs to 1 in 500 by age 50 (Blakeslee). So even with the hard statistical evidence at hand, the American Cancer Society has chosen to report the numbers in such a way as to stretch the truth, to scare women about this terrible disease. The statistics are not disputed; it is the users of the statistics that are to be questioned.

The Brody article also shows how sound statistical findings can be manipulated to mislead the reader. Jane Brody failed to give us the actual numerical death rates that Dr. Lee had correlated. Dr. Lee found that men in the upper 20th percentile for body weight had death rates two and a half times greater than men in the lowest 20 percent. But what is the actual death rate? If the rate is 2 in 10,000 for lean men, then Dr. Lee's findings indicate that it would be 5 in 10,000 for the heaviest men. This is hardly a difference worth reporting (perhaps that's why it was omitted). However, if the death rate for thin men is 1 in 5, then the heavy men would presumably be dying at a rate of 1 in 2. Without this essential information, readers are led down the path again by sensationalism, perpetrated through underreported statistics.

Do statistics really lie? Can statistics be used to prove anything? A statistician will answer no to both of these questions. The trained statistician uses statistics to make informed decisions in the face of uncertainty. Statistics can be used only to show the likelihood of some event or process; by themselves statistics prove nothing. Properly used, statistics are a form of scientific evidence that helps us get closer to the true state of nature. When misused by partial omission (whether deliberate or not) or improper interpretation, statistics can be contorted to fit anyone's aim. Liars will use statistical half-truths to further their cause, and statistical novices will make interpretive mistakes. But the numbers themselves do not lie.

WORKS CITED

Blakeslee, Sandra (Fall 1993). Faulty Math Heightens Fears of Breast Cancer. The New York Times. Themes of the Times, Mathematics, p. 8. Englewood Cliffs: Prentice Hall.

Box, George, & Hunter, William, & Stuart, J. (1978). Statistics for Experimenters. New York: John Wiley & Sons.

Heafey, Richard J. (1989, v38, n5). Trial by Lottery: the Misuse of Epidemiology and Statistics to Prove Causation in Drug and Chemical Litigation. Defense Law Journal, pp. 673-692.

Huff, Darrell (1954). How to Lie with Statistics. New York: W. W. Norton & Company Inc.

Monypenny, W. F., & Buckle, G. E. (1968). Life of Benjamin Disraeli, Earl of Beaconsfield. New York: Macmillan.

The following article was posted on the World Wide Web site of *Wired* magazine on August 4, 1997. The posting, itself a factual argument, is an excellent cautionary tale about the pitfalls of trusting what we read on the Internet.

"VONNEGUT SPEECH" CIRCULATES ON NET

DAN MITCHELL

A copy of Kurt Vonnegut Jr.'s recent MIT commencement address made heavy email rotation on Friday. The characteristically pithy, funny, thoughtful speech was passed from friend to friend stamped with such comments as "worth a read" and "check this out—it's great."

And it *was* great. Trouble is, it wasn't Vonnegut's. "Kurt Vonnegut Jr. had never given a commencement address at MIT," said Robert Sales, associate director of the school's news office.

It turns out the "speech" was actually a column penned by the *Chicago Tribune*'s Mary Schmich. The column ran on 1 June—five days before UN Secretary General Kofi Annan delivered the actual commencement address at MIT. That speech "was a lot longer and maybe not as clever" as the purported Vonnegut address, Sales said.

Much of Schmich's column—which consists of advice for graduates—sounds like stuff Vonnegut might say: "Don't be reckless with other people's hearts. Don't put up with people who are reckless with yours. . . . Remember compliments you receive. Forget the insults. If you succeed in doing this, tell me how. . . . Keep your old love letters. Throw away your old bank statements. . . . Do one thing every day that scares you."

Nobody—least of all Schmich—can figure out why Vonnegut's name was slapped onto her column. "Some prankster apparently decided it would be funny. Why is it funny? If you can figure that out, you're a genius," she said Monday.

Perhaps the act itself wasn't funny, but some of the fallout has been. First of all, there's the fact that (ahem) Wired News ran part of the column as its Quote of the Day on Friday. Also, Schmich says she's gotten as much attention from the incident as just about anything she's written. "My email's just flooded with messages," she says. And she says she's actually been accused of plagiarizing Vonnegut—and vice versa. On Friday, she managed to reach Vonnegut, who, Schmich says, said the whole thing is "spooky."

In her column on Monday, Schmich writes that she wrote the piece "one Friday afternoon while high on coffee and M&M's." And, she insisted, "It was not art."

In part, Schmich blames the "cyber-swamp" of the Internet for all the trouble. "At newspapers, things like this have to go through a barrier before they go out to the world," she said. But on the Net "anybody can put anybody's name on anything."

Nonetheless, she added, "No one involved in this did anything bad, except the person who started it."

SUGGESTIONS FOR WRITING (6.4)

1. Write a two- to three-page essay supporting a fact that runs counter to popular opinion. This fact can come from your own experience, from your studies in college, or from your general knowledge. Examples of such surprising facts are "Despite predictions to the contrary, the increasing use of computers has created more new jobs than it has eliminated existing ones"; "Milk does not always do a body good." This surprising fact can be about yourself, your family, your friends, your hometown, your college, your job, your major, or whatever else comes to mind.

2. Stereotypes are misleading factual generalizations that make the false claim that all members of a group have a certain trait: "The English people have stiff upper lips in times of crisis"; "American men like to watch football." Take a prevalent stereotype and analyze to what degree the stereotype is true and how the stereotype is misleading. Make sure the stereotype is one you can deal with in a three- to four-page essay, such as "Engineering students of my college don't get involved in extracurricular activities." You don't have to do a statistical survey to gather data for this essay, but you should carefully examine and present samples to support your claim.

3. Analyze either a newspaper or a television news show for examples of bias or misleading generalizations (for the television news show, you may have to videotape the show so that you can view it two or three times). How objective is the reporting of the news? Are there any examples of misleading generalizations? What kind of news is *not* included? Write a two- to three-page essay addressing these questions. *good one*

7

Arguing Cause

The goal of causal argument is to establish a probable cause or effect for a given
condition. A claim arguing "Many teenagers abuse alcohol because they are desperately disappointed by their 'real lives'" will establish the *cause* of teen alcohol
abuse, while the claim "Today's generation of college students will be far more
successful in marriage than their parents have been" argues the *effect* of certain
conditions. In order to convince your readers that the cause or effect you argue is
reasonable, you must have a good understanding of the nature of causality and of
the processes used to determine and report causes and effects. Written causal arguments are essentially reports of the process the writer followed to determine
causes or effects.

The first part of this chapter concentrates on arguments of *cause:* arguments
that identify and support the cause or causes of an existing situation. As you'll see
in the last part of the chapter, the principles and processes involved in arguments
of cause are identical to those you'll rely on when you write arguments of *effect:*
arguments predicting the probable future effects of an existing situation.

DETERMINING CAUSE

Any single effect is the consequence of a number of causes—some powerful and
direct, others less influential but still contributing. For this reason, arguing cause
usually involves more than isolating *the* single cause of a given effect: most extended causal arguments discover and support those causes most useful to the
context, purpose, and audience of your argument. If your goal is to give as full a
causal explanation as possible for the effect in question, you will identify and support a number of causes, both direct and indirect. But if the point of your argument is to assign responsibility, you will address only the most immediate causes
(such as who did what, regardless of why). If the purpose of your argument is to
instruct, or if you want some future action taken or avoided on the basis of the

causality you demonstrate in a comparable situation, you are likely to emphasize both the immediate and the more remote causes of the current situation. For example, if you wish to improve your GPA, you might try to reproduce as many of the habits of a successful student friend as you can: careful budgeting of time, keeping up with assignments, regular class attendance, and so on.

Brainstorming for Possible Causes

Whether or not you begin with a particular causal claim in mind, it is a good idea to begin the argument process by listing all the facts and conditions you can think of that seem to be causally linked to the effect you are explaining. Depending on your subject, this list may come from your own thinking and brainstorming and/or from any reading and research you might do. The list should include as many facts or conditions you can think of that seem even remotely connected to the effect. The next step will be to apply your knowledge of causal principles to this working list in order to identify the most influential causes.

Let's assume you are arguing the reasons for the high student dropout rate at your college. Part of your argument will consist of a discussion of individual cases: why particular people you know decided to leave school. You know one student (we'll call her Emma) who explains her plans to drop out of school by saying, "I just don't like college." But you know this is not a satisfactory explanation. Why doesn't she like college? What events and conditions have made her unhappy enough to make this extreme decision? So, in a couple of long conversations, you press Emma further, and you talk with some of the people who know her well. The result of these discussions is a list of more specific possible reasons for her decision.

For one thing, Emma's grades have not been very good. Though her grades were good in high school, Emma can't seem to pull her GPA above a 2.0. It's clear to you from talking to her that she's the kind of person who expects a lot from herself, so her undistinguished grades have to be a blow to her self-esteem. It makes sense that she would want to leave a place where she doesn't feel good about herself. You also learn that Emma is the first person in her family to go to college, and her parents have made many sacrifices to give her every educational advantage. Their ambition for Emma puts a lot of pressure on her, which has probably made it even harder for her to relax and do her best. And Emma's family situation has worked against her in another way: it offers no close role models to emulate, no family tradition of academic success. Add to these factors Emma's crazy roommate and their closet-size room, and you begin to wonder how Emma lasted through the first semester.

Your examination of the situation has identified a number of possible causes for Emma's decisions—all much more specific and useful than her vague claim that she doesn't like college. Some of the possible causes on your list seem directly influential, like her mediocre grades, their blow to her self-esteem, and her crazy roommate; others are more remote, like her parents' lack of a college degree. But you conclude that, one way or another, each of these factors may have influenced Emma's decision.

Only a thorough investigation like the one you have conducted will yield a full explanation of the causes of a particular effect. The next step is to determine more precisely the relative influence of each point in this cluster of causes, and in order to take this step, you must know something about the causal properties of the different points on your list.

ACTIVITIES (7.1)

1. For the following effects, brainstorm a list of possible causes.
   a. The popularity of John Grisham's novels
   b. The success of Japanese products in the American market
   c. The popularity of disaster movies
   d. An increase (or decrease) in the size of the student body at your school
   e. The popularity of a particular major at your school

Necessary and Sufficient Causes

Understanding the concepts *necessary cause* and *sufficient cause* will help you identify which of the causes from your original list are likely to have been most influential in bringing about the effect you are explaining. To qualify as a cause for a given effect, a causal candidate *must* satisfy the conditions of a necessary or sufficient cause, or both. If it does not, it is not a direct cause of the effect, though it may well have contributed to the effect in some way.

A *necessary* cause is a cause without which the effect could not have taken place. One cannot get typhus without the introduction of a rickettsia, or gram-negative microorganism, into the bloodstream. This rickettsia is necessary to the contraction of the disease. Thus you can be certain that anyone who has contracted typhus has been infected by this particular microorganism. But while introduction of the rickettsia is necessary to the contraction of typhus, it doesn't guarantee that the disease will result. People with a vigorous immune system or those who have been inoculated against typhus will be safe from the disease.

Necessary causes are usually easy to identify: if we know the effect, we know that certain causes or conditions had to be operating. To use a nonscientific example, if you had not parked your car next to a construction site, it would not have been hit by falling debris. Parking your car in that spot was necessary to the effect. In the case of Emma, the cause necessary to her withdrawing from college is her unhappiness there. Presumably, if she were happy and liked college, she would stay.

Sometimes identifying the necessary cause will not be particularly helpful in your attempt to explain an effect. Necessary causes can seem like redundant restatements of the effect itself: the necessary cause of a company's filing for bankruptcy is that it ran out of money, but that doesn't tell us very much about the significant factors that led to the bankruptcy filing. In the case of Emma's planned withdrawal from college, the necessary cause—her unhappiness with college—does not shed much light on the question of the student dropout rate. In order to understand her decision, we have to work backward from the necessary cause, identifying those factors that set it up.

Sufficient causes, on the other hand, are always helpful in causal analyses. A sufficient cause is one that by itself is capable of producing a particular effect. A person's decision to join a health club can have a number of sufficient causes: for example, winning a year's membership in a raffle, wanting to meet new people, or wanting to become physically fit. Any one of these motives would be enough to prompt an individual to join a health club, but none of them *has* to exist for that decision to be made; that is, they are all sufficient to the effect, but not necessary. In Emma's case, a number of sufficient causes are operating: her poor self-esteem, her crazy roommate, and her distaste for dormitory life. Any one of these might have been enough to prompt her decision, but none of them was necessary to that decision.

Sometimes a single cause combines the properties of necessity and sufficiency. The example of the rickettsia demonstrates this combination. Not only *must* one be infected with that microorganism to contract typhus (the necessary cause), but this infection is by itself enough to cause the disease (the sufficient cause). For every effect, we can expect at least one necessary cause and any number of sufficient causes.

In determining which factors on your initial list have been most influential, you need to identify those that are necessary and those that are sufficient. Unless you are writing a full causal analysis, you will usually find yourself concentrating on the sufficient causes for the effect in question.

Identifying Sufficient Causes

The ability to identify a factor as causally sufficient depends on your good sense and your personal experience of causality. There is no rule or formula to follow in isolating sufficient causes, yet most of us have little difficulty answering the question "Is this factor by itself sufficient to have caused this effect?"

When your subject involves human behavior as either cause or effect, there is a useful test you should apply to those factors you think are sufficient. Actions performed by an individual or group are linked to their causes by some commonly accepted principle or motivator of human behavior. If you argue, for example, that a sluggish economy is a cause of the increased popularity of taped movie rentals, you are accounting for a particular human behavior: the rental of taped movies. Your claim is a simple claim of cause, with a fact at the causal end and an action (also a fact) at the effect end.

Sluggish economy	Increase in movie rentals
(cause)	(effect)

This causal proposition is plausible only if its two sides are linked by some acceptable motive. Why would people rent more movies for home viewing in a sluggish economy? What motive or need would urge them to react to a particular condition with a particular behavior? In this case, a linking motivation is easy to identify: in tight times, people need to economize, and it is considerably cheaper to watch rented movies at home than to pay high prices in a theater. The cause and the resulting behavior can be linked by a motivation that everyone can understand and identify with:

Sluggish economy . . . . Increase in movie rentals
{Desire to economize in tight times}

Identifying this motivation doesn't tell you whether this is the only sufficient cause, but it will reassure you that the link between this cause and the effect is plausible. If you can supply no such motivation between cause and effect, your theory is probably not plausible, and it's time to look for another cause.

Applying the Toulmin Model

The Toulmin model discussed in Chapter 5 is particularly useful when you are composing causal arguments. Indeed, the relationship just presented among possible cause, existing effect, and linking principle fits perfectly into Toulmin's data-claim-warrant formula. Here is the example about increased movie rentals translated into the Toulmin model:

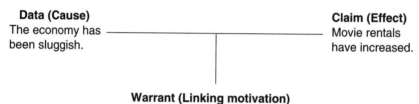

Data (Cause)
The economy has
been sluggish.

Claim (Effect)
Movie rentals
have increased.

Warrant (Linking motivation)
Most people find ways to economize
when the economy slows down.

In this case, the warrant is that general behavioral principle that connects the cause, which is placed in the data position, and the effect, which is placed under "Claim" (even though the actual claim of the argument is the causal relationship between data and claim). When you are trying to identify sufficient causes for a particular effect, you may find it useful to apply the Toulmin model to your cause and effect, making sure that you can provide a warrant that would be widely acceptable to your readers. Remember that in many cases, the warrant will not be acceptable without further support, or what Toulmin calls *backing*. In those cases, the warrant and its backing will need to be provided explicitly in the argument. If the warrant does seem immediately acceptable, it need not be stated outright.

ACTIVITIES (7.2)

1. With three or four other students, study the following effects and possible causes. For each effect, which of the possible causes, if any, do you think are necessary? Which would you class as sufficient? Make sure you can defend your choices.

   a. **Effect:** John's car accident.
      Possible causes: John was driving at night on a poorly lit road; the road was wet from rain; John had taken a very difficult exam that morning; John was driving ten miles per hour over the speed limit.

b. **Effect:** The dramatic increase in the use of VCRs in the last few years.
Possible causes: The cost of VCRs is now at an affordable level for most Americans; videotapes of films are increasingly available; viewers can choose what films they will watch with the VCR; many Americans have a large amount of leisure time available.

c. **Effect:** The decline in oil and gasoline prices in the middle 1980s.
Possible causes: On the average, cars were more fuel-efficient than they had been ten years before; there was a growing awareness that petroleum is a nonrenewable resource; the oil-exporting countries were producing more oil than the world consumed.

d. **Effect:** Louise's winning an award for the best violin recital at the music festival.
Possible causes: Louise practices the violin three hours each day; Louise's parents found the city's best violin teacher for her when she was five; from a very early age, it was obvious that Louise was talented musically; Louise prefers Mozart to any other composer.

e. **Effect:** Charles's favorite hobby is cross-country skiing.
Possible causes: Charles wants to stay in shape, and cross-country skiing is very good for the cardiovascular system; he likes winter and being out-of-doors; he is on a tight budget and cannot afford downhill skiing this year; he was once injured while downhill skiing; in high school, he won prizes in cross-country ski races.

2. For each pair below, place the cause and the effect within the Toulmin model and supply a warrant that links the data and the claim acceptably. For which warrants should you also supply backing? What would that backing be?

a. **Cause:** Increased leisure time
Effect: More participation in sports like skiing and windsurfing

b. **Cause:** Fifteen percent increase in tuition
Effect: Decrease in enrollment

c. **Cause:** Special incentives that reduce the price of automobiles
Effect: Higher automobile sales

d. **Cause:** More women receiving professional degrees
Effect: A rise in the average age of women having first children

e. **Cause:** The banning of a book
Effect: Increased demand for the book

DISTINGUISHING AMONG SUFFICIENT CAUSES

Sometimes, in analyzing causes, you will discover a number of possible sufficient causes for an effect and not know which were actually operating. In these cases you will need other methods for determining probable cause. The following strategies were formulated by the nineteenth-century philosopher John Stuart Mill to determine cause in such situations. While Mill was looking for ways to establish cause with scientific certainty, his methods are also very useful in situations where certainty is unreachable.

Method of Agreement

The method of agreement is useful when you are investigating the cause of *two or more* similar effects. In these instances, you determine what the sets of events preceding each effect have in common; you are looking for a single sufficient cause that operated in all these similar cases.

If you were investigating the reason or reasons for the success of the five best-selling hardbound books of the year, you would list all the factors that might have contributed to the success of each book, that is, the significant characteristics of each. If all the books center on the subject of personal relationships in the 1990s, you could safely identify subject matter as a leading cause of the books' success. Sometimes you will not discover a factor common to all your effects; perhaps the five best-sellers have no single common characteristic, so that a number of sufficient causes are operating in these instances.

Method of Difference

Mill's method of difference can be used to determine why two essentially similar situations turned out very differently. If you want to know why one self-help book succeeded while another failed, why one calculus class with Professor Jones was interesting while another was boring, or why the Confederate army lost the battle of Gettysburg but won the battles of Bull Run, you can apply the difference method by looking for the factor present in one case but absent in the other. If the only difference between your two calculus classes with Professor Jones was that the subject matter of the second class was more advanced, that could well be the reason for your unhappiness in the second class.

This method will work only when you are examining truly similar situations that share a number of common factors. If you were trying to account for the difference between your career choice and that of one of your grandparents, the situations would be too dissimilar for the method of difference to tell you anything; your grandparents faced an entirely different range of career choices than you did.

Method of Proportional Correlation

The method of proportional correlation is useful in determining the cause of an effect that is continuing and varied: the movement of the Dow-Jones industrial average, the increase and occasional decrease in the gross national product, the enrollment of college students in certain kinds of majors. In trying to identify possible causes of such measurable trends, you should look for conditions preceding the trends that vary and persist proportionally. In considering the reasons for the rise in the divorce rate since the 1960s, you might discover that there has been a congruent increase in the number of two-income families over the same time period, that is, that there has been an increase in the number of married women who are economically self-sustaining. This increasing economic independence of women is a plausible explanation of the increased divorce rate if it satisfies the following three conditions: (1) if it is truly independent of the effect (not a result of the same cause); (2) if the two trends, with all their fluctuations, are truly proportional; and (3) if the cause and effect are plausibly linked by an accepted behavioral principle—in this case, the principle or motive of independence or self-reliance. If these three conditions are satisfied, we would accept that the economic independence of wives is a sufficient cause of divorce.

ACTIVITIES (7.3)

1. Take a group of at least three of your classmates or friends who share a common trait, such as their academic major, a hobby, or some other favorite activity, and try to determine what sufficient cause made each member of the group have this trait. Try to find a common sufficient cause for the entire group, but be prepared to end up with different sufficient causes if a common cause does not reveal itself. Write a one- to two-page essay describing the results of your investigation.
2. Compare two classes you have taken sometime in your education, one that you liked and one that you disliked. The two classes should be as similar as possible in subject matter and level of difficulty. What made the one class likable, while the other was not? Write a one- to two-page essay addressing this question.
3. For the next week, compare fluctuations in two phenomena that you believe may be related, such as the weather and attendance at one of your classes. Make a chart comparing the movement of these two phenomena, and then see if any proportional correlation exists between the two. If there is such a correlation, ask yourself if the two are the result of the same cause and if some plausible behavioral principle links the two. Write a one- to two-page analysis of your study. Be sure to give your instructor the chart you have created.

CAUSAL CHAINS

Some effects are best understood in terms of a directly related series of causes, like links in a single chain, or a row of sequentially falling dominoes. In these cases, identifying the entire chain of causes is far more useful than isolating those causes that are closest to the effect, or isolating the more remote cause that originally set the chain in motion.

If someone told you that closed captioning of television shows (where subtitles can be seen on specially equipped televisions) is a result of the rubella epidemic in the United States during the 1960s, you might initially reject the connection as utterly implausible. What you have been given is the first cause and the final effect in a causal chain; if the links in the causal chain are filled in, the connection is reasonable. In the 1960s, there *was* a widespread outbreak of rubella, or German measles (at the time, there was no rubella inoculation). Rubella is a relatively harmless disease except to the fetuses of pregnant women; babies whose mothers contract rubella during pregnancy often suffer birth defects, one of which is deafness. Because of the epidemic, huge numbers of babies were born deaf. In the last thirty years, as these children have grown, we have seen increased sensitivity to the needs of the hearing-impaired, one of the most notable being the media's provision of closed captioning for television. With all the links in the chain identified, the causal connection between a common virus and closed captioning is no longer implausible, though there were other factors at work, including the increasing emphasis on the rights of the handicapped in the last thirty years.

The constellation leading to Emma's planned withdrawal from college contains a causal chain. Beginning with her decision to withdraw, we can move straight back as far as her parents' lack of a college education. The chain works as follows: Emma plans to withdraw from college because she doesn't like it. She doesn't like it because she feels low self-esteem in this setting. This low self-esteem is a result of poor grades, which at least in part have been caused by the enormous pressure she has been under to do well. This pressure comes from her parents, who, because they have never been to college, desperately want Emma to be the first in the family to get a college degree. Not all of the points in the constellation we identified earlier appear in this chain. So while the chain explains much about the evolution of Emma's decision, it does not explain everything, just as the chain linking the rubella epidemic with closed captioning is not the fullest possible explanation of the situation.

CONTRIBUTING FACTORS

In analyzing causes, we occasionally find a circumstance that is neither necessary nor sufficient yet is somehow relevant. This type of circumstance is labeled a *contributing factor*. If Kathy continues to jog even when she is run-down and then catches a virus, her jogging is not a sufficient cause of her illness; the presence of the virus without sufficient antibodies to combat it is the sufficient cause. Nor is the jogging a necessary cause, since she might have gotten the virus even without jogging. Yet her pushing herself while not feeling "100 percent" certainly didn't help and may have made her more susceptible to disease. In this case, we can label the jogging as a probable contributing factor.

Emma's situation contains at least one contributing factor: her lack of a close role model. Clearly, this factor is not necessary to the effect, nor is it sufficiently influential to have caused her decision to withdraw. Yet it has made a bad situation worse, depriving Emma of any positive example from which to take heart. Contributing factors are present in most complicated situations; if your goal is a thorough analysis of cause, you need to take contributing factors into account.

ACTIVITIES (7.4)

1. For two of the following causes and remote effects, find a plausible causal chain that links the cause with the remote effect.
   a. **Cause:** The rise of industrialization
      Effect: The growth of the conservation movement
   b. **Cause:** The invention of gunpowder
      Effect: The decline of knighthood
   c. **Cause:** Jane's high absenteeism in third grade
      Effect: Jane's difficulty with cursive writing
   d. **Cause:** The invention of printing
      Effect: The growth of democracy in Europe and America

e. **Cause:** Jack's love of parties
   Effect: Jack's becoming the mayor of his city

2. Review the clusters of causes presented in Number 1 in Activities (7.2), and identify possible contributing factors for each cluster.

SUMMARY

Determining Cause

- Because causality is always multifaceted, keep your mind open to all possibilities early in your causal investigations.

- The ultimate purpose of your argument (to explain, instruct, or designate responsibility) will determine which causes you will concentrate on in your argument.

- To determine the most influential causes for your effect, you need to be able to identify the necessary and sufficient causes. A *necessary cause* is a cause without which the effect could not have occurred; a *sufficient cause* is one that by itself is capable of producing the effect.

- Where human behavior is concerned, sufficient causes must be linked to their effect through an assumable motive.

- When you have a number of potential sufficient causes for an effect, use the following methods to determine the most probable cause or causes: the method of *agreement* will help you determine the cause of similar effects; the method of *difference* will help you determine why two similar situations turned out differently; the method of *proportional correlation* will help you determine the cause of an effect that varies over time.

- Some effects are best explained by a chain of causes, often originating at a time remote from the effect.

- Thorough causal arguments may also identify *contributing factors* to the effect—circumstances that are neither necessary nor sufficient causes but do play a role in creating an event or condition.

SUPPORTING CAUSAL CLAIMS

You support most causal claims by (1) establishing the factuality of the effect(s) and cause(s) you present; (2) identifying, sometimes only implicitly, an acceptable motive in arguments involving human action; (3) in some cases, describing the process that helped you validate a causal candidate (method of difference, agreement, or proportional correlation); and (4) qualifying the degree of certainty your argument claims.

Establishing Factuality

Facts are the foundations of causal argument. While in most causal arguments you will write, the causal relationship you propose between two events will rarely be certain and verifiable, there can be no room to doubt the certainty of the events you are linking; they *must* be true if your argument is to be meaningful and plausible. If you exaggerate, understate, or misstate the effect, your identification of cause is useless; you are explaining something that didn't actually occur.

If an article in a campus newspaper claims that the firing of a popular hockey coach has resulted in lower student attendance at home hockey games, the reporter needs to be absolutely sure that (1) the coach *was* fired (perhaps this is only a campus rumor and the coach got a job offer elsewhere) and (2) student attendance at home games really has declined since the coach's departure. Both cause and effect need to be presented and, if necessary, supported as individual factual claims before their causal relationship can be explored (see Chapter 6 for supporting factual claims).

Identifying an Acceptable Motivation

When you're dealing with human behavior as either cause or effect, your argument should suggest a common human motive. If a generally acceptable linking motive is obvious, you probably won't need to identify it explicitly. For example, if you are arguing that a decrease in DWI arrests is a consequence of tougher DWI laws, you don't have to point to people's unwillingness to risk the new penalites as the linking motivator between cause and effect; it is so obvious that it can merely be implied.

But let's take a more complicated example: an argument accounting for the increased divorce rate since the 1960s by a proportional rise in two-career families. Here, you would want to state the motive linking the proposed cause and effect, because it may not be immediately obvious to your readers: women who have some degree of financial independence and employment security are more likely to leave unhappy marriages than women who are financially dependent on their spouses. If the motive you identify may not be immediately acceptable to your audience, you will have to provide some backing for it.

There is a tendency among student writers to omit identifying the linking motivation when they should include it; that is, they find obvious what may not be so obvious to their readers. So if you have any doubt about whether or not to include this explanation in your argument, go ahead and provide it. It is usually better to err on the side of too much information than too little.

Describing the Process of Validation

In arguments where John Stuart Mill's processes of determination have been useful to you, you can support your claim by reporting in your argument how the method was applied. You don't need to use the formal terms *method of agree-*

ment and so on, but you should provide a summary, a kind of narrative of your investigation.

If you were to identify the reasons for the failure of four different food concession stands at your school, you would make use of the method of agreement, because you are looking for a single explanation common to the closing of all four operations. Your report of the process might read something like this:

> Between 1993 and 1997, four different concession stands have been opened in the foyer of the Student Union. Not one of these stands was able to draw enough customers to keep operating; each closed within five months of its opening.
>
> The stands had little in common. One was run by students from the hotel program and sold gourmet coffee and pastries; one was a national fast-food franchise; one was a "mom-and-pop" frozen-yogurt stand; and the fourth was a minideli operated by campus food services. Prices at the gourmet coffee stand were slightly on the high side, so when it failed, it was replaced by the inexpensive fast-food stand. Frozen yogurt from the yogurt stand was competitively priced, and it was the only frozen yogurt available on campus. Finally, the deli offered the most choice to customers, with food ranging from sandwiches to chips to pasta salads to drinks.
>
> The stands operated at different times of the day: the coffee stand in the mornings between 7 A.M. and 11 A.M.; the fast-food concession between 11 A.M. and 2 P.M.; the yogurt stand in the afternoons from 1 to 5; and the deli between 11 A.M. and 3 P.M.
>
> In short, campus food services tried very hard to learn from its mistakes, trying to eliminate every reason for failure. But the one factor common to all four concerns that they did not address was *location*. All were set up in exactly the same spot in the foyer of the Student Union. The thinking was that since this space saw more daytime student traffic than anywhere else on campus, food sales would be brisk. But the problem with this particular space in the union is that it is very close to the student-faculty cafeteria (on the same floor and open during lunchtime), and to the large student snack bar (in the basement of the union and open for lunch and dinner). It is reasonable to conclude that the food market in this heavily trafficked building was already saturated; if food services wants to make a success of the "portable food" idea, it will have to locate the next food stand in another area of campus.

As indicated in the preceding section on determining cause, some of Mill's methods of determination carry particular risks that you'll want to avoid. The difference method, for example, is reliable only if the effects you examine are truly comparable. And when using the method of proportional correlation, you'll need to be sure that the trends you identify are independent, that is, that they are neither effects of another cause nor mutually contributing (for example, bad tempers causing quarrels and quarrels exacerbating bad tempers).

It's a good idea when supporting your causal argument to point out that your use of a particular method of determination has avoided the associated pitfalls.

For example, if you use the difference method to determine why you like golf but your friend with similar athletic ability and experience in golf does not, you should demonstrate that the apparent differences between you and your friend—family background, interest in other sports—are not significant in terms of your argument.

Qualifying Your Argument

Since certainty is rare in causal arguments, you must not mislead your reader and thereby undermine your own credibility by claiming more certainty for your argument than is warranted by its support. You have a wide range of words indicating degrees of causality to choose from, so make sure you use language that accurately reflects your level of certainty. If you are very certain about your causal proposition, you can use such definite words as the following:

necessitated

caused

resulted in

attributable to

produced

created

brought about

was responsible for

But use these words with caution. Without qualifiers like "may have," "probably," "seems to have," and so on, they claim a certainty that may be difficult to document.

The words listed in the following group also indicate causality, but a causality that is clearly qualified:

contributed to

is associated with

is a function of

facilitated

enabled

influenced

increased

decreased

improved

You are better off using words such as these when the causality you propose is not certain. By using such terms, you are both indicating causality and admitting *some* degree of uncertainty.

ACTIVITIES (7.5)

For two of the examples below, write a paragraph on each indicating what would be needed to make the causal argument more convincing. This additional material may include establishing facts, reporting the process of determination, describing motives, demonstrating the independence of two elements in a proportional correlation, or adding qualifying language, though other steps may also be necessary to make the argument credible.

1. Bill's alleged cheating on the exam was certainly a result of his low grades early in the semester and his desire to be accepted into a reputable law school.
2. Police report the arrest of Hubert Midas, the oil and gas billionaire, for shoplifting a thirty-five-dollar shirt from a downtown department store. Midas must have forgotten to pay for the shirt.
3. As more women have entered the workforce, the number of families without children has risen proportionally. The increasing number of women in the workforce has caused this rise in childless families.
4. Without Martin Luther King, Jr.'s charismatic personality, the civil rights movement of the 1960s would not have had the impact it did.
5. The Roman Empire fell because of the moral decadence of many of its citizens.

SUMMARY

Supporting Causal Claims

- To support a cause, you must establish the factuality of cause and effect; identify an acceptable motivation in cases where human actions are at least part of the cause; usually report how you determined the causes; if necessary, qualify your assertions about the certainty of your argument.

ARGUING EFFECTS

Because arguments of effect are concerned with the future, with events that haven't yet occurred, their claim to certainty is even less absolute than arguments of cause. Even the most carefully constructed argument of effect, one firmly grounded in the principles of causality and in experience in the relevant field, can go awry. We have only to look at the accuracy rate of weather forecasters and political analysts to recognize how frequently the future refuses to cooperate with our plans for it. But if executed carefully and according to certain principles, arguments of effect *can* be reasonable and convincing, serving as useful guidelines for many courses of action.

Claims of arguments of effect can be stated in a number of ways, as in the following:

1. If John continues to drink heavily and drive, it's only a matter of time before he will have a serious accident.
2. The number of high school graduates will continue to decline for the next five years, then begin to stabilize.
3. I will not see a woman president in my lifetime.
4. Consumers are so comfortable with certain companies that they will buy almost anything carrying those companies' logos.

While they may seem quite different, these four claims share certain features common to all arguments of effect. Most obviously, all predict that something will happen in the future (or in the case of the third claim, that something will not happen). Claims 1 and 4—John's heavy drinking, and brand appeal—also identify a causal relationship between a current condition and a future event. Claims 2 and 3 don't identify a current condition that will lead to the effect the writer predicts. In order to make them qualify as arguments of effect rather than mere assertions, the writer will have to identify current conditions that might lead to these effects and claim that the conditions and effects are causally linked. For Claim 2, those conditions could be certain demographic trends that have persisted over time; for Claim 3, those conditions could be the conservative disposition of most voters, or perhaps a poll indicating strong opposition to a woman president among teenagers and young voters. These current conditions and trends set the ground for an argument of effect. An argument of effect demonstrates that the existence of these conditions and trends is enough to cause a particular future effect. Lacking identified causes, these kinds of claims are nothing more than random predictions, similar to the bizarre predictions on the covers of the sensational magazines found in supermarkets: "Psychic Foresees Economic Collapse Following Landing of Martians on White House Lawn!"

Determining and Supporting a Probable Effect

The processes of determining and supporting a probable effect overlap considerably. If you identify a future effect through sound methods, the best supporting strategy will be to report these methods, which we discuss in the following paragraphs.

Applying the Principles of Causality.   To argue an effect, you need to identify a sufficient cause for the effect and prove that this cause exists or could exist. Are the causes that are currently operating (or that might be set in place) enough to bring about the effect? If you can identify an existing sufficient cause or causes for the effect, your prediction is probably a good one.

Let's take the case of a publishing-house editor trying to decide whether to publish a book submitted to her on personal relationships. The editor will accept the book if she thinks it will sell well; her job is to decide whether current circumstances will make the book a best-seller. In other words, the projected effect is excellent sales. The circumstances operating are as follows: the market for books on this topic has been very strong; the writer has written popular books on this subject before; the book itself, in the view of this experienced editor, is interesting, original, and provocative. An analysis of these circumstances reveals that all are sufficient causes; in the absence of the other two, one cause alone would be sufficient to create the effect. The editor's experience with bookselling makes her a good judge of the sufficiency of these causes. Our editor knows how important these three circumstances are because she has seen them again and again. In projecting any effect, the arguer must understand the principles of the subject matter.

Missing from this list of current circumstances is a necessary cause, one that has to operate in order for the effect to occur. The absence of a necessary cause does not make the projected effect implausible; often it is the sufficient causes that create the necessary cause. In this example, the necessary cause of high sales would simply be that people buy the book, and they will buy the book in the presence of one or more of these sufficient causes.

Causal Chains.   In some situations, you can argue a future effect by revealing a chain of causes that plausibly connects Cause A with Future Effect D. To demonstrate the connection between a past or present cause and a future effect, you need to make a series of arguments of effect; if A is the remote cause and D the predicted effect, you will argue that A will cause B, which will cause C, which finally will cause D.

The field of economics often uses causal chains as a basis for future action. A classic example is the Federal Reserve Bank's setting of interest rates on money it lends to banks, which in turn affects the interest rates banks and other financial institutions charge customers on mortgages and other loans and the interest they pay to customers for savings and other deposits. One key step the Federal Reserve Bank can take to reduce consumer spending is to raise its interest rates, which means the banks will raise their rates, and customers will find that it costs more to get a mortgage on a house, to finance a car loan, or to buy other items on credit. Faced with these rising costs, consumers will decide to spend less. Also, because these same banks are now paying more interest for deposits, consumers have an incentive to save rather than spend—another reason why they will reduce spending. Visually, the causal chain looks like this:

(A) higher government interest rates → (B) higher bank interest rates → (C) lower consumer spending

This causal chain can be extended, since lower consumer spending may lead to a lower inflation rate or to less importing of consumer goods from other countries. With causal chains, however, the greater the length of the chain, the less predictable become the effects.

Sometimes causal chains simply don't work the way they are supposed to. When Prohibition became law in 1919, its proponents predicted that alcohol consumption would decrease and along with it a host of evils, including crime, broken homes, and absenteeism from work. They did not foresee a roaring fourteen years of speakeasies, bathtub gin, and bootleg whiskey before Prohibition was abolished in 1933. Especially when trying to predict human behavior through elaborate causal chains, you should always keep in mind the adage about the road to hell being paved with good intentions.

Comparable Situations.   You can also determine the probable future result of current conditions by examining comparable situations in which this cause and effect have already occurred. In trying to raise the educational standards of American primary and secondary schools, teachers, school administrators, and government policymakers look to the experience of other countries. The average scores of students from some other industrialized countries are higher than the average scores of American students on certain standardized achievement tests in areas such as math and science. In some of these countries, notably Japan, children spend much more of the year in school, and the schools introduce rigorous academic material earlier in the student's academic career. Some proponents of reform argue that the same methods used here will improve students' performance.

This comparison method will work only if the situations being compared are *significantly* similar. In arguing that the United States should follow Japan's example, advocates of these changes also need to look carefully at what each country expects from its schools and how these expectations relate to the general culture. What seems comparable at first may turn out to be more complicated on closer inspection, since the American and Japanese cultures have very different expectations about the role of the individual in society.

The more comparable the situations you find, the more convincing your argument of effect will be. If you can demonstrate that a certain cause has had the same result over and over again, and that the current conditions you are considering are truly similar to these other causes, your identification of effect will be well supported.

ACTIVITIES (7.6)

1. For two of the following actions, project two effects that might be caused by the action. State whether the action would be necessary or sufficient to the effect.

    Example action: Graduating summa cum laude.

    Possible effects: Being accepted into a prestigious graduate school (sufficient); receiving eight job offers (sufficient).

    a. Getting an A in a course
    b. Arranging a date with someone you don't know
    c. Reducing the danger of theft at your college or in your community
    d. Finding a good place to live
    e. Being stopped by the police for speeding

2. Write a two- to three-page essay describing a causal chain for some area or activity with which you are familiar (for example, gaining or losing weight, saving money, raising your grades).

3. For the five predictions listed below, cite a truly comparable activity or situation that can be used to support your prediction.

Example: Extending the academic year in primary and secondary education in the United States. A comparable situation could be the long academic year in Japan, to support the prediction of higher test scores for American students.

a. Being governor of a state
b. Student success in graduate school
c. Decreasing alcohol consumption at fraternity parties at your school
d. Being removed from academic probation
e. Making the varsity lacrosse team

SUMMARY

Determining and Arguing a Probable Effect

- To argue an effect, you need to identify a sufficient cause for the effect and prove that this cause exists or could exist.

- You can argue that a certain effect is likely if you can create a causal chain that demonstrates how you move from one cause to an effect that is the cause of the next effect, and so forth. The longer your chain, however, the less likely it is that the chain will perform as predicted.

- You can demonstrate that an effect is likely in a situation if you can prove that a similar situation produced a similar effect.

TWO SAMPLE CAUSAL ARGUMENTS

The following argument is a sample of causal analysis. Based on an essay written by college student Michele Statt, the essay considers possible causes of the recent growth of student interest in liberal arts majors. The essay is not an elaborate and definitive causal argument, but it is a good example of an exploration of the possible causes of an interesting phenomenon. (Note the qualification of Michele's causal claims.) As you study the essay, see if you can locate where Michele establishes the factuality of her cause and effect. Does she report on a process of determination used to test her main cause? What is it? Do you find any reference to a common human motivation?

THE NEW INTEREST IN THE LIBERAL ARTS

In 1978, only 443 students were enrolled in liberal arts majors at my college. Today, with the recent establishment of new liberal arts majors, 604 students are enrolled in these majors. (In the same period, the total enrollment at my college has decreased by 40 students.)

Many other schools have also reported that interest in liberal arts majors has been increasing. According to Michael Useem, Director of Boston University's Center for Applied Social Science, across the nation "the proportion of baccalaureate degrees in the liberal arts in 1986 was the largest in four years, and the proportion of first-year college students reporting an interest in a liberal arts major in 1987 was the highest in 10 years" (46).

Several causes may have influenced this increase in interest. Many students entering college are unsure of their career choice and gravitate to the liberal arts because such programs typically do not insist on early declaration of a major. Even if the undecided student then chooses to pursue a major outside the liberal arts, she will find that her liberal arts courses can be applied to her new major. However, having started in the liberal arts, she is likely to find a liberal arts major that appeals to her.

Another cause probably associated with this increase is the growing emphasis on career training within the liberal arts majors themselves. At my college the liberal arts majors include such programs as economics, school psychology, criminal justice, and communications—all of which include a significant element of career preparation that appeals to today's college students. Several of these programs at my college are relatively new. Their existence as additional options for students certainly helps to explain the growth in liberal arts enrollment here.

Liberal arts enrollment, however, has been increasing throughout the country, even at institutions that have not added many new liberal arts programs. The central cause of this growth is very likely the increasing demand for liberal arts majors in the job market. Michael Useem's article, based on research supported by the Corporate Council on the Liberal Arts and the President's Committee on the Arts and Humanities, states that since the early 1980s, many business leaders have stressed the importance of the liberal arts as preparation for a career in business (46). Useem received responses to his survey from 535 large and mid-sized American corporations. The results indicated that corporations do indeed hire liberal arts graduates, with 44 percent of the respondents recruiting liberal arts graduates on campus and 47 percent hiring such students for internships and cooperative education programs; 29 percent reported other efforts to recruit liberal arts graduates, and 61 percent have created programs to train liberal arts graduates for jobs in their corporations (47).

Students are becoming aware of this demand for liberal arts graduates. I chose my field of communication both because of my interest in it and because I was aware of job possibilities after graduation. Twelve students that I talked to said that career preparation was one of the two major causes of their choosing a liberal arts major, the other being their interest in the subject. These results are hardly scientific proof, but they are another piece of evidence demonstrating the importance of the job market in rising liberal arts enrollments.

Useem's study also notes that although many companies hire liberal arts graduates, they are often looking for accomplishments in addition to a liberal arts major, including campus or community involvement and a good grade point average. Another important requirement of most of these corporations was exposure to business courses or experience in business before graduation (47-48, 50-51). The increasing emphasis on career training in at least some liberal arts majors undoubtedly enhances the attractiveness of these majors to employers.

Ten or fifteen years ago, many college students felt that they were forced to make a choice between a liberal arts major or preparing themselves for a career. Because they wanted to find a good job, some of these students chose a program outside of the liberal arts even when they really preferred a liberal arts major. Today's students are more fortunate. They know that in choosing a liberal

arts major, they can also prepare themselves for their
future after college.

WORKS CITED

Useem, Michael. "The Corporate View of Liberal Arts."
    Journal of Career Planning and Employment. Summer
    1988: 46–51.

The following argument, "I, Too, Am a Good Parent," combines elements of a causal argument and a recommendation. The author, Dorsett Bennett, claims that the continuing custom of granting child custody to the mother is a result of the prejudice of older male judges who continue to dominate the courts. Is the cause Bennett identifies necessary or sufficient? Is it adequately supported by facts and examples? Do you find any further causal arguments embedded in the essay? What are they?

I, TOO, AM A GOOD PARENT
Dads Should Not Be Discriminated Against

DORSETT BENNETT

Divorce is a fact of modern life. A great number of people simply decide that they do not wish to stay married to their spouse. A divorce is not a tremendously difficult situation unless there are minor children born to the couple. If there are no minor children you simply divide the assets and debts. But you cannot divide a child. The child needs to be placed with the appropriate parent.

In my own case, my former wife chose not to remain married to me. That is her right and I do not fault her decision. My problem is that I do not believe it is her right to deny me the privilege of raising our children. Some fathers want to go to the parent/teacher conferences, school plays, carnivals and to help their kids with homework. I have always looked forward to participating on a daily basis in my children's lives. I can no longer enjoy that privilege—the children live with their mother, who has moved to a northern Midwest state.

I tried so hard to gain custody of my children. I believe the evidence is uncontradicted as to what an excellent father (and more important, parent) I am. My ex-wife is a fairly good mother, but unbiased opinions unanimously agreed I was the better parent. Testimonials were videotaped from witnesses who could not attend the out-of-state custody hearing. I choose to be a father. When I was 3 years old, my own father left my family. While I've loved my father for many years, I did and still do reject his parental pattern.

A couple of centuries ago, a father and mother might have shared equally in the care and raising of children above the age of infancy. But with the coming of the Industrial Revolution the father went to work during the day, leaving the full-time care of the young to the mother, who stayed at home. It was easier to decide who should get child custody under those circumstances. That would be true today even if the mother were put into the position of working outside the home after the divorce.

Now, a majority of married mothers are in the workplace—often because the family needs the second income to survive. With the advent of the working mother, we have also seen a change in child care. Not only have we seen an increase in third-party caregivers; there is a decided difference in how fathers interact with their children. Fathers are even starting to help raise their children. I admit that in a great many families there is an uneven distribution of child-care responsibilities. But there are fathers who do as much to raise the children as the mother, and there are many examples where men are full-time parents.

But, because we have this past history of the mother being the principal child caregiver, the mother has almost always been favored in any contested child-custody case. The law of every state is replete with decisions showing that the mother is the favored custodial parent. The changes in our lifestyles are now being reflected in our laws. In most, if not all, states, the legislature has recognized the change in childcare responsibilities and enacted legislation that is gender blind. The statutes that deal with child custody now say that the children should be placed with the parent whose care and control of the child will be in the child's best interest.

This legislation is enlightened and correct. Society has changed. We no longer bring up our children as we did years ago. But it is still necessary to have someone make the choice in the child's best interest if the parents are divorcing and cannot agree on who takes care of the kids. So we have judges to make that enormous decision.

The state legislature can pass laws that say neither parent is favored because of their gender. But it is judges who make the ultimate choice. And those judges are usually *older males* who practiced law during the time when mothers were the favored guardians under the law. These same judges mostly come from a background where mothers stayed home and were the primary caregivers. By training and by personal ex-

perience they have a strong natural bias in favor of the mother in a child-custody case. That belief is regressive and fails to acknowledge the changed realities of our present way of life. Someone must be appointed to render a decision when parents cannot agree. I would ask that those judges who make these critical decisions re-examine their attitudes and prejudices against placing children with fathers.

After the videotaped testimony was completed, one of my lawyers said he had "never seen a father put together a better custody case." "But," he asked me, "can you prove she is unfit?" A father should not be placed in the position of having to prove the mother is unfit in order to gain custody. He should not have to prove that she has two heads, participates in child sacrifice or eats live snakes. The father should only have to prove that he is the more suitable parent.

Fathers should not be discriminated against as I was. It took me three years to get a trial on the merits in the Minnesota court. And Minnesota has a law directing its courts to give a high priority to child-custody cases. What was even worse was that the judge seemed to ignore the overwhelming weight of the evidence and granted custody to my ex-wife. At the trial, her argument was, "I am their mother." Other than that statement she hardly put on a case. Being the mother of the children was apparently deemed enough to outweigh evidence that all the witnesses who knew us both felt I was the better parent; that those witnesses who knew only me said what an excellent parent I was; that our children's behavior always improved dramatically after spending time with me; that my daughter wished to live with me; and that I had a better child-custody evaluation than my wife.

So I say to the trial judges who decide these cases: "Become part of the solution to this dilemma of child custody. Don't remain part of the problem." It is too late for me. If this backward way of thinking is changed, then perhaps it won't be too late for other fathers who should have custody of their children.

Source: *Newsweek,* July 4, 1994.

SUGGESTIONS FOR WRITING (7.7)

1. Write an essay describing the necessary and sufficient causes for a major event in your life. Be sure to indicate to the reader how you determined that these causes were operating. Make the essay as long as necessary to describe fully the causes of this event.
2. Analyze at least three persons or organizations that share major common traits, and determine what similar causes, if any, made them the way they are. As examples, you could analyze successful or unsuccessful teams in some sport, or successful or unsuccessful television shows. Report your analysis in an essay of approximately four pages.
3. Analyze two persons or situations that share significant traits but that have ended up differing in some major way. What caused this major difference? For this essay, you might analyze why you and a close friend or a sibling chose different colleges or majors or why you performed differently in two similar classes. Report your analysis in an essay of approximately four pages.
4. Examine two trends that you believe may be causally related to see if there is any proportional correlation between them. An example might be the national crime rate and the national unemployment rate, or the national unemployment rate and the inflation rate. If you expect to find a correlation and you do not, speculate on why the correlation is not present. For this essay, you might start with a good almanac, since it will contain many trends with statistical data, but you will probably also need to consult a more detailed source such as the *Statistical Abstracts of the United States*. Report your analysis in an essay of approximately four pages.
5. Fewer and fewer college students are completing bachelor's degrees in the traditional four-year period. Do some research at your own institution, and find out the average time students are taking to graduate. Then write a four- to five-page essay that explores possible causes of this phenomenon. Make sure that the causes you suggest originate in the same time period as the effect.

8

Arguing Evaluations

EVALUATIVE SUBJECTS AND TERMS

All evaluations include a subject to be judged and an evaluative term that is applied to the subject. In the claim "John is a good writer," *John* is the subject, and *good writer* is the evaluative term; in "Tracy Chapman is a gifted musician," *Tracy Chapman* is the subject and *gifted musician* the evaluative term. Some evaluative claims include only partial evaluative terms, but their context should suggest the missing parts. In the claim "Capital punishment is immoral," the full evaluative term is *immoral act,* and in "Rembrandt was a master," the evaluative term is *master painter.*

To make a successful evaluative argument, you need to lay some careful groundwork. First, you must define the evaluative term. In the claim "John is a good writer," where *good writer* could mean different things to different people, you'll want to specify your understanding of the term. In many cases, you can do this by a shorthand definition: "John is a good writer; he communicates ideas clearly and gracefully." (see Chapter 4 for a discussion of shorthand definitions). This definition establishes clarity and grace in the communication as the criteria by which John's writing will be judged.

Sometimes evaluations are expressed negatively, as in "John is a poor writer," or "The instructions for this camera are useless." A negative evaluation can either imply its opposite as the standard of judgment or establish a definition of the negative term itself. The writer of the claim "William Faulkner's *Fable* is a failed novel" could work from a definition of *successful novel,* showing how this novel falls short of that definition, or could establish criteria for the term *failed novel* and apply those to the subject.

The second piece of groundwork necessary to most successful evaluations is gaining your readers' agreement about your definition of the evaluative term. If your readers' understanding of the criteria for good writing do not agree with yours, however clearly you have presented them, your argument won't get very far. Perhaps they agree that John's writing is clear and graceful, but because their understanding of good writing includes rich ideas and original expression, they will never be convinced by your argument that John is a good writer. In this situation, and in many evaluations, you will need to argue the definition of your evaluative term, convincing your readers that the criteria by which you define the term are reasonable and complete. Only then can you proceed to the heart of your evaluation: demonstrating the match between your subject and your evaluative term.

ACTIVITIES (8.1)

1. What is the evaluative term (implied or stated) in the following assertions?
   a. Mark Twain's *Adventures of Huckleberry Finn* is an American classic.
   b. When Roger Bannister broke the four-minute mile barrier in 1954, he accomplished one of the greatest athletic feats of this century.
   c. Calvin Coolidge was a mediocre president.
   d. Calculators are a real boon to mathematics students.
   e. The terrible losses in wars in the twentieth century show the bankruptcy of nations' using war as an extension of foreign policy.

2. Write a paragraph giving a brief definition of one of the evaluative terms you identified in Activity 1.

ESTABLISHING THE DEFINITION OF THE EVALUATIVE TERM

How much space and energy you devote to establishing your term's definition will depend on your audience and the nature of the term. There is so little dispute about some terms that an extensive definition is unnecessary—an honest bank teller, for example, or a reliable car. And in cases where you are very confident about your readers' values, about what is important to them and why, you may not need to argue or even propose a definition. A doctor writing to other doctors about the unprofessional behavior of a certain physician could probably assume agreement among her readers about the definition of unprofessional behavior. But when the following conditions apply, you should define your evaluative term and argue its definition:

- When your audience consists of people with expertise and/or values different from yours;
- When your definition of the evaluative term is unconventional or controversial;
- When there are different definitions of the term.

Whether or not you define the evaluative term explicitly, remember that very vague or inflated evaluations are usually harder to argue than those that are limited and precise. It would be far easier to convince an audience that "Indigo Girls are ingenious lyricists" than that "Indigo Girls are the best songwriters ever."

Presenting the Definition

In most cases, the actual definition of the term can be stated quite briefly, usually as part of or directly following the claim: "Alison is the ideal management trainee: she is intelligent, ambitious, congenial, and hardworking"; "In his highly original and influential reflections on the American spirit, reflections that affected common citizens as well as fellow philosophers, Ralph Waldo Emerson proved himself to be a great thinker."

When defining an evaluative term, you are proposing a *stipulative* definition—a definition that restricts the understanding of a term to a particular meaning appropriate to your context. (See Chapter 4 for a full discussion of definition.) In the argument about John's writing skills, the definition of good writing as the clear and graceful communication of ideas is stipulative: it asks readers to accept this particular and limited definition of the term for the context of this argument. In most cases, your definition will take the shorthand, sentence form identified in Chapter 4, although if the term is very difficult, you might want to provide an extended definition.

As in all definitions, the explanation you offer must be clear and precise. Your definition will be useless if it offers only broad or abstract generalizations. If you write, "The brilliance of the film *Citizen Kane* lies in its wonderful structure," but you fail to define *wonderful structure,* you will leave readers guessing. Try also to avoid definitions that include highly subjective terms. If you define a "talented soprano" as one whose voice is beautiful at all points in her vocal range, you have not done much to clarify the evaluative term. What is beautiful to one listener may be mediocre, or heavy, or thin to another; "beautiful" is a measurement that frequently provokes disagreement. So if you wish the term to be useful, define it by offering comparatively objective standards, like fullness, or clarity, or fluidity. While these, too, are subjective terms, they are more precise and are less a matter of personal taste than a term like *beautiful.*

Here are three examples of promising opening definitions; each is clear, precise, and informative.

1. A good argument is one that directly identifies its central proposition; supports that proposition with reasonable, relevant, and concrete evidence; and admits the possibility of alternative points of view.
2. A dedicated mother devotes herself to her children because she knows she should; a good mother devotes herself to her children because she can't imagine doing otherwise.
3. A good education will prepare a student not only for a career but for a fulfilling life outside a career. As important as careers are in our lives, they do not and should not occupy all of our time and energy. The well-educated person is the one who can view life outside work with zest, knowing that there are many other interests aside from a career.

While the qualities included in your proposed definition should be as clear and precise as possible, the very nature of evaluations will not always allow you to avoid subjective terms. In Example 3, the term *fulfilling life* is inherently subjective, yet it is not meaningless. There are certain qualities and activities we can identify that constitute a fulfilling life, including having friends, having hobbies or other recreational interests, and being curious about the past, the future, and the world. It may not be easy to measure each of these qualities or activities precisely, but they do exist, and they can be gauged on some comparative scale.

ACTIVITIES (8.2)

Using the preceding definitions as a model, give a brief but useful definition of the following. After you have written your definitions, compare them with the definitions written by two other students in your class. How much agreement is there among your definitions? How do you account for the differences that exist?

1. A safe automobile
2. An inspiring professor
3. An honest politician
4. A natural athlete
5. The perfect roommate

Arguing the Definition

Based on your assessment of their backgrounds, needs, and values, you may conclude that your readers will not automatically agree with your definition of the evaluative term. In such cases, you have one more job before you move to the evaluation per se: to *argue that your definition is just, that the criteria you have* assigned to a term such as *necessary war, master craftsman,* or *inspired teacher* are reasonable and complete. You can argue the justness of your definition using any of the methods for supporting definitions presented in Chapter 4, including appeal to assumed values, identification of effect, appeal to authority, and comparison.

To illustrate the application of these methods, we'll work with the following example: As a branch manager for a local bank, you are asked to write a formal evaluation of three new management trainees. Your reader will be the bank's vice president for personnel. There is no fixed evaluation form or criteria to work from; *you* must decide which qualities constitute promising performance in a new trainee. The qualities you settle on (in unranked order) are (1) honesty, (2) the ability to foresee the consequences of decisions, (3) attention to detail, and (4) courtesy to customers. Because you have created this list, you will need to justify it, however briefly, to the vice president. Your justification for each item on the list could use the following methods of argument:

1. *Honesty:* Appeal to assumed value. You wouldn't have to say much about this quality. For obvious reasons, bankers place a premium on honesty in their employees.
2. *Ability to foresee the consequences of decisions:* Identification of effect. This criterion may not be as obvious as the first, but bankers must base decisions about lending money, setting interest rates, and making investments on the probable consequences of these decisions. You could briefly point out the positive results of having this ability and the negative results of lacking it.

3. *Attention to detail:* Appeal to assumed value. Like honesty, the importance of this quality doesn't have to be argued to bankers.
4. *Courtesy to customers:* Identification of effect. You can easily demonstrate that good customer relations lead to good business. For many bankers, this criterion would be an assumed value.

You can buttress these criteria with other support. To bolster the third criterion, attention to detail, you might cite recognized authorities who stress this quality and the grave risks banks run when they hire employees who lack it. To support the fourth criterion, courtesy to customers, you might use the method of comparison, pointing to the success of a competing bank that stresses good customer relations.

If you can make a reasonable argument for your definition of the evaluative term, your readers are likely to accept the qualities you cite. But they may still object to your definition on the basis of omission: your definition is acceptable as far as it goes, but you have omitted one quality critical to them. Without the inclusion of that quality, they cannot accept your evaluation of the subjects. So, in formulating your definition, try to anticipate the reactions of your readers; if they are likely to be concerned about the omission of a certain quality, you must explain why you chose to omit it. Any of the methods previously identified will help you make this explanation. For example, you could justify your omission of a knowledge of computer programming as a criterion for judging trainees by using the identification of effect, pointing out that few bank employees do any programming anyway and that it is cheaper and more efficient to hire outside programming experts when they are needed. In this case, you are pointing out that no bad effects are caused by these trainees' inexperience with programming.

Ranking the Qualities in Your Definition

In some evaluative arguments, it is not enough to establish a list of qualities constituting your evaluative term; often you will need to indicate the relative importance of these qualities by ranking them. Ranking is almost always necessary in evaluations of multiple subjects. If you are evaluating four models of home coffee brewers, for example, you might establish the following qualities as essential: reasonable price, good-tasting coffee, a quick-brew cycle, and an automatic timer. A reader may agree with each of these qualities yet disagree with your final choice of brewer. The reason for the disagreement would be that you and your reader rank the four qualities differently. If a quick-brew cycle is most important to you but least important to your reader, he or she will not accept your final evaluation of the three machines.

In some evaluations, particularly those that are likely to directly affect your reader, you may have to justify the relative value you place on each quality. If you are evaluating dormitory life as a valuable freshman experience, you will let your readers (incoming freshmen) know which of the criteria you cite is most important and which is least important. Suppose you rank the qualities as follows: (1) quiet study atmosphere, (2) good social opportunities, (3) proximity to campus, and (4) comfortable surroundings. You could argue the importance of the first quality, a quiet study atmosphere, by a number of familiar methods: appeals to value or authority, comparison, or identification of effect. Regardless of the method you choose, you must be able to demonstrate that without a quiet study atmosphere, one that allows students to work hard and succeed academically, all of the other qualities are meaningless. If a student flunks out of school the first year, the other three qualities will have been useless. Thus the first quality is the most important because, in your view, it is the *essential* quality.

ACTIVITIES (8.3)

For one of the following subjects, list in order of importance the criteria you would include in its definition. Compare your definition with your classmates' criteria, and based on any disagreement you find, write a two-page essay justifying your selection and ranking of the criteria.

1. A college or university
2. A musical concert
3. A campus newspaper
4. A church or synagogue
5. A textbook for a college course

ARGUING THE EVALUATION

Having laid the necessary foundation for a successful evaluation, you're ready to make the evaluative argument.

The evaluation itself will be largely *factual.* By verifying data and presenting concrete examples, you will argue that your subject possesses the criteria you have cited. Establishing this match is especially important when your subject is a service—a travel agency, a long-distance phone service—or a functional object, such as a coffee brewer or a pickup truck. In these cases, where the evaluative term is defined by objectively measurable qualities (for example, speed, efficiency, accuracy, and price), your job is to verify the existence of those qualities in your subject.

Suppose you were evaluating portable FM radios in terms of affordable price, portability, and power of receiver. In your judgment, a good radio of this type is one that costs no more than forty dollars (your definition of affordable price), can be carried and listened to comfortably when you are walking or jogging, and holds the signals of local radio stations without interference. Using these standards, you evaluate the Euphony "Jogmate" as a *good portable radio.* Your evaluation will be convincing as long as you can establish the following three facts: the suggested retail price of the Jogmate is below forty dollars; it is easy to carry; it holds local stations firmly.

These facts can be convincingly established through reference to your own experience, provided you present yourself as reliable and objective. (Other supporting sources—the experience of friends or impartial analyses of the Jogmate found in consumer guides—could be referred to as well.) You could cite the actual price of the Jogmate at three local stores to verify the first fact. The second, which is the most subjective, can be verified by your physical description of the Jogmate—its weight, dimensions, earphone style—and a description of your experience running with it: "The small, cushioned earpieces fit comfortably into my ears; there is no connecting band to slip off the head or tighten uncomfortably; the small radio clips easily onto a waistband or can be held comfortably in one hand." The third fact can also be established by reference to your own experience: "I have run distances of four to five miles with the Jogmate at least twenty times. On those occasions, it has never lost the signal of the three stations I like to listen to." As with all factual arguments, the key to success in arguing evaluations is to cite reliable and authoritative experience and observations, and to include specific, concrete examples of general statements.

Not all evaluations are as neat and objective as the preceding example. Let's look at a very different example involving more subjective measurement and see how the principles of factual argument apply. This evaluation argues that your friend Ellen knows how to be a good friend: she respects her friends, accepting and loving them for who they are, and she expects the same treatment from them. Because the definition included in the claim is not a standard definition of friendship, it requires some preliminary support (see the preceding section on "Arguing the Definition").

Once supported, the definition must be applied to the subject, your friend Ellen. The quality of respecting others—a key criterion of your evaluative term—cannot be measured as objectively or established as definitively as the price of a radio or the fuel efficiency of an automobile. Yet general agreement exists about what constitutes respectful behavior: it is attentive, considerate, accepting behavior. The best way to demonstrate the applicability of the quality to your subject is through specific examples illustrating such behavior. As in any factual argument, you must *describe* the experience faithfully and objectively. Because you want to establish that Ellen's respectful treatment of her friends is habitual, not occasional, you should cite a number of examples.

Beyond citing the examples, you might also need to point out what is respectful in the examples cited, particularly if your readers might interpret the behavior differently. But in general, the more concrete and immediate your presentation of examples, the less explicit commentary you will need.

Testing Your Evaluation Through the Syllogism

A good evaluative claim falls very neatly into the basic syllogistic model presented in Chapter 5. Once you have come up with your claim, you can test its reasonableness and completeness by rewriting it in syllogistic terms. The definition of the evaluative term will be the major premise, the application of the defining criteria will be the minor premise, and the claim itself will be the conclusion. The preceding example regarding Ellen's friendship would compose the following syllogism:

> **Major premise:** A good friend respects her friends, accepts them and loves them for who they are, and expects the same treatment from them.
> **Minor premise:** Ellen respects me, accepts me and loves me for who I am, and expects the same from me.
> **Conclusion:** Ellen is a good friend.

The major premise establishes characteristics that constitute friendship; the minor premise applies those same characteristics to Ellen; and the conclusion makes a very specific claim derived from the relationship between the two premises. This syllogism tells us that the claim is valid, but we can accept it as true as well only if the two premises are also true. If the major premise (the definition of friendship) does not appear to be immediately acceptable, it will have to be argued in the ways we have suggested. Similarly the truth (or probability) of the minor premise may have to be established through a factual argument that provides examples of Ellen's behavior toward you. While you may not be able to *prove* the absolute truth of both premises, you can strengthen them by providing appropriate support, thus moving the entire argument much closer to a position of soundness.

ACTIVITIES (8.4)

Working from the definitions you created for Activity (8.2), compose a specific claim from each. Then turn the definition and the claim into a syllogism. To what extent would the major and minor premises of each syllogism need further support?

FURTHER METHODS OF SUPPORTING EVALUATIONS

Definition and factual argument are central to evaluations, but there are other ways to support these arguments. The tactics that follow can be used along with definition and factual arguments or by themselves.

Identification of Effect

Since an action, policy, or object is generally considered valuable if its effects are valuable, a good way to support evaluations is by identifying the positive effects of the subject. Freedom of speech is good because it encourages the widest exchange of ideas, which is more likely to lead to the truth or to solutions to problems. Child abuse is bad because it causes physical and mental anguish in children. Of course, such a causal support of evaluations will work only if it accords with the principles of causality discussed in Chapter 7, and if your audience agrees with your assessment of the effect. If you anticipate any disagreement from your audience, you'll need to argue, if only briefly, your evaluation of the effect.

Appeal to Authority

You can support any evaluation by appealing to the similar judgment of a recognized authority. If Chris Evert has publicly expressed her admiration for the tennis game of Martina Hingis, this statement would be effective support for your argument that Hingis is the finest tennis player on the women's tour. Just be sure, when you cite the judgment of an expert, that that person truly qualifies as an authority on this particular subject.

Comparison

You can often support your evaluation by showing similarities between your subject and one that your audience is likely to evaluate in the same way. For example, many feminists have supported their arguments against sexual discrimination by comparing it to racial discrimination. The two forms of discrimination are similar in many ways: both base inequitable treatment on irrelevant and immutable characteristics: race and gender. An audience that would object to racial discrimination would, when the similarities were pointed out, be likely to object to sexual discrimination as well. But as with any comparative argument, make sure the similarities between the two subjects are essential, not peripheral.

ACTIVITIES (8.5)

With a small group of your classmates, identify which kinds of support (factual argument, identification of effect, appeal to authority, comparison) would be most appropriate for two of the following evaluative claims. Discuss your reasons for choosing each form of support.

1. Shakespeare is one of the world's greatest writers.
2. Mercedes-Benz makes many of the world's best cars.
3. Failure to build a water treatment plant for the city would be a serious mistake.
4. Strato Airlines has the best customer service record of any airline in America.
5. Military involvements by major powers in small countries are usually unwise in terms of lives lost, money wasted, and the increased suspicion of other small countries.

THE VARIETIES OF EVALUATIONS

By now, you realize that different kinds of evaluations demand different kinds of support. While there are no hard-and-fast rules in this area, if you can identify the *kind* of evaluation you're arguing, you'll have a better sense of how to support it. Evaluations usually fall into one of three main categories: ethical, aesthetic, or functional. Included in this section is a fourth subclass as well: the interpretation. Strictly speaking, interpretations are not evaluative arguments, but since they are argued in much the same way as evaluations, they are addressed here.

Ethical Evaluations

The word *ethical* is one of those terms that we all understand in a vague way yet might be hard pressed to define precisely. To avoid confusion, consider the following definition: *ethical* describes behavior that conforms to an ideal code of moral principles—principles of right and wrong, good and evil. That code may be derived from any number of cultures: religious, professional, national, or political.

All of us operate within many cultures: we are members of families, communities, organizations, religions, professions, and nations. Each one of these cultures has its own set of ethical standards. For example, among the many ethical principles of Judaism and Christianity are the Ten Commandments. As United States citizens, we are subject to other standards of conduct, such as those recorded in the Constitution—including the Bill of Rights—and the Declaration of Independence. Your college also operates by certain standards that it expects its members to follow: respect for school property, respect for faculty, and academic honesty. In most cultures, these standards are formally recorded, but in some instances they remain implicit. There also exist certain ethical ideals common to virtually all cultures, ideals such as fair play, kindness, and respect for others.

Because individuals are tied to a number of different cultures, clashes between standards are inevitable. Some pacifist groups, for example, see a clash between the religious commandment "Thou shall not kill" and the government's standard that citizens must be prepared to defend their country in time of war. Sometimes conflicts occur between standards of the same culture. Such clashes are commonplace in law. What happens, for example, when the right of free speech collides with the right of a person to be free from libel? Free speech cannot mean that someone has a right to say anything about another person, regardless of how untrue or harmful it is. On the other hand, protection from libel cannot mean protection from the truth being told about mistakes or misdeeds, particularly when they have some impact on the public. Throughout our history, the courts have struggled to find a balance between these two competing claims, sometimes slightly favoring one value, sometimes the other, but always denying that either value can have absolute sway over the other.

Defining the Evaluative Term in Ethical Arguments.   Whenever you evaluate a subject in terms of right or wrong conduct, you'll be appealing to certain ethical values or standards that you believe your audience holds. When asserting that "Hitler was an evil man," or "Ms. Mead is an honorable lawyer," or "The coach used unfair tactics," you are assuming that your readers both *understand* what you mean by the evaluative term and *agree* with that meaning. As in all evaluations, if you have reason to doubt your readers' understanding of the term, you'll have to define it, and if you're uncertain about their agreement with the definition, you'll have to support it.

The Argument in Ethical Evaluations.   Most ethical arguments concentrate on demonstrating what is unethical or immoral about the subject being evaluated. At the center of these evaluations, then, is a factual argument. In arguing that Hitler was evil, your focus would be on documenting the behavior you identify as evil, and on demonstrating that your evaluative term fits the examples you are citing.

You can also strengthen your evaluation through other supporting methods, including comparison (Hitler was as bad as or worse than certain other dictators) or identification of effect (in addition to all of the bad he did in his life, the war Hitler started led to the division of Europe into two opposing camps, or to a pervasive sense of victimization among Jews of later generations).

ACTIVITIES (8.6)

Using one of the following evaluative assertions (from Activities 8.5) as your claim, write a two-page "Letter to the Editor" of your local city newspaper. Or create your own claim derived from a current local or national controversy.

1. Shakespeare is one of the world's greatest writers.
2. Mercedes-Benz makes many of the world's best cars.
3. Failure to build a water treatment plant for the city would be a serious mistake.
4. Strato Airlines has the best customer service record of any airline in America.

Aesthetic Evaluations

Writing a convincing evaluation of a work of art—a poem, an opera, a painting—is not as futile a task as many believe, provided you understand the goals of such an argument. Just as personal tastes in clothes or food are usually immune to reasonable argument, aesthetic preferences—liking Chopin's music and despising Mahler's—are often too much matters of personal taste to be arguable. There is much truth in the Latin saying *De gustibus non est disputandum:* There is no arguing about taste. Nevertheless, while changing aesthetic tastes or opinions is difficult, it is possible and often useful to convince an audience to *appreciate* the strengths or weaknesses of a work of art by giving them a greater understanding of it. A successful aesthetic evaluation may not convince a reader to like Rubens or to dislike Lichtenstein, but it will at least give a reader reasons for approving of or objecting to a work.

All artistic fields have their own sets of standards for excellence, standards about which there is surprising conformity among experts in the field. Most literary critics, for example, would agree on the standards for a successful short story: coherence of the story, careful selection of detail, avoidance of digression, an interesting style. When critics disagree, and of course they do so regularly, they usually disagree not about identified standards of excellence but about the application of those standards. Often such disagreements are matters of a personal preference for one kind of artist over another. Even professional critics are not immune to the influence of their personal tastes.

When you argue an aesthetic evaluation, you should work from standards currently accepted within the field, though you may not have to do more than briefly or implicitly refer to them. Your evaluation is likely to fail if you ignore these standards, or if you try to effect an overnight revolution in them. Like ethical standards, aesthetic standards usually change gradually, though there have been periods of revolutionary change, as occurred in artistic tastes in the early twentieth century.

Usually, then, your chief task is to demonstrate that these standards apply (or don't apply) to your subject. This demonstration consists of careful description and concrete examples, as in the following excerpt from an essay on the famous comedians the Marx Brothers ("From Sweet Anarchy to Stupid Pet Tricks"). In this excerpt, Mark Edmundson gives a description and examples from a particular scene in a Marx Brothers film and then presents his criteria for rich "antiestablishment comedy."

Groucho always rebels against his own success. When it seems that Trentino might treat him on equal terms, as a gentleman, Groucho stages an imagined encounter between himself and the Sylvanian ambassador that ends in disaster. "I'll be only too happy," Groucho pledges in most statesmanlike tones, "to meet Ambassador Trentino and offer him, on behalf of my country, the right hand of good fellowship." But then, Groucho worries, maybe the ambassador will snub him (stranger things have happened). "A fine thing that'll be! I hold out my hand and he refuses to accept it! That'll add a lot to my prestige, won't it? Me, the head of a country, snubbed by a foreign ambassador! Who does he think he is that he can come here and make a sap out of me in front of all my people?" Then, rising to a boil, "Think of it! I hold out my hand and that hyena refuses to accept it! . . . He'll never get away with it, I tell you! . . . He'll never get away with it."

Enter Trentino, looking haughty. Groucho, raging now, "So! You refuse to shake hands with me, eh?" Groucho slaps Trentino with his gloves. This means war!

It's Groucho's contempt for his own high-mindedness and posing— "I'll be happy to meet Ambassador Trentino and offer him the right hand," blah, blah, blah—that sends him into a spin. Groucho was about to act decorously, something for which he cannot forgive himself. As his predecessor Thoreau put it, "What demon possessed me that I behaved so well?"

Our current outsider comics—Roseanne, Eddie Murphy, Martin Lawrence—attack incessantly, and they sometimes score. But what they don't generally do is what Groucho does so superbly, turn the lens back, dramatize their own flaws. The richness of Groucho's antiestablishment comedy is that it compels us not only to challenge social hypocrisy but to consider our own. And it's that double vision, it seems to me, that helps make Groucho and the Marx Brothers as indispensable now as they were in the 1930s.

Edmundson's chief measure of the success of antiestablishment comedians is what he calls their "double vision," their ability to "turn the lens back, dramatize their own flaws." With the criterion clearly identified, the reader can discover it easily in the detailed description of the film scene.

As with all arguments, when composing an aesthetic evaluation, be sure to consider your readers' level of knowledge—both of the subject being evaluated and of the field in general (comedy, tragedy, jazz, autobiographies, etc.) Edmundson assumes that his readers are familiar with Marx Brothers' films, but he also reviews individual scenes in some detail to ensure that his points are made. In cases where your subject and your evaluative criteria may be less familiar to your audience, you may want to offer not only a careful description of the subject, but also a lucid explanation of the criteria. People often fail to appreciate what they don't understand, so if your evaluation can teach them about the standards of a particular field, it will have a better chance of convincing them that your subject meets (or fails to meet) those standards.

Another useful tactic when arguing a positive evaluation to an inexperienced audience is to relate your subject to one with which they are more familiar. If, for example, you want to convince an audience familiar with and appreciative of modern abstract art that the art of ancient Egypt is also interesting, you might point out the similarities between the two: "Although they are widely separated in time, modern abstract art and ancient Egyptian art both concentrate on the essence of a person or object, not the surface appearance." In taking this approach, you are borrowing from your readers' appreciation of modern abstract art, shining its positive light onto the subject of your evaluation.

ACTIVITIES (8.7)

For each of the following forms of art or entertainment, list at least three standards by which you would judge the quality of a specific work of this type. Then, for one of the categories, write a two- to three-page essay demonstrating how a specific work of that type does or does not fit your standards of excellence. (You should make these standards explicit in your essay.)

1. An action film
2. A mystery novel
3. A jazz recording
4. A portrait photograph
5. An abstract painting

Functional Evaluations

Functional evaluations stand a better chance of changing readers' minds than do ethical and aesthetic evaluations. It is easier to convince a reader that her views about turbo engine cars are inaccurate than that her views about abortion are wrong. While people do form sentimental attachments to objects and machines, they can usually be convinced that however powerful that attachment, it has nothing to do with the subject's actual performance; an audience's preconceptions about performance quality are less matters of cultural values and personal tastes than of practical experience, assumptions, or hearsay.

Functional evaluations always work from a definition of ideal standards: you can't demonstrate that Sony makes an excellent CD player without some criteria for measuring the player's performance. Some functional evaluations require an explicit presentation of evaluative criteria and some can safely assume reader familiarity with the relevant criteria. Certainly, if your criteria are unusual or innovative ("The most important feature of a car for me is that it *look* good"), you'll have to state them explicitly and argue their relevance and completeness (using any of the methods discussed earlier in this chapter).

Sometimes functional evaluations work best from a ranked list of criteria. For example, a lawnmower can be evaluated in terms of safety features, cost, and noise, but the three criteria may not be equally important. To justify your evaluation, you should explain and support the relative weights you've assigned to each criterion.

Any of the other supporting methods discussed earlier in this chapter (identi-fication of effect, appeal to authority, comparison) can also be used in a perfor-mance evaluation. Of these, the most valuable is identification of effect. "Virginia Wensel is a good violin teacher" because she has produced a number of fine play-ers; "My college provides an excellent education" because 85 percent of its gradu-ates go on to graduate school. In each case, the subject is judged in terms of its positive effects. Note that sometimes the effect you identify as an evaluative crite-rion must be argued. Why, for example, does acceptance into graduate school mean you have received an excellent undergraduate education?

If the effect you are citing has already occurred, your support will be a factual argument. In arguing that "Virginia Wensel is a good violin teacher," you would cite the number of fine players she has produced and briefly support your positive judgment of those players. In other cases, where the effect has not yet occurred, your argument is necessarily more speculative: "Based on the evidence we have, this car is likely to give you years of reliable service."

ACTIVITIES (8.8)

List in ranked order at least three standards by which you would judge the perfor-mance of the following. Then, for one of the categories, write a two- to three-page essay demonstrating how well one person or object in that category meets your standards of performance.

1. An automobile for a family with three small children
2. A president of a college or university
3. A personal computer
4. A United States senator
5. A college reference librarian

Interpretations

The purpose of an interpretation is to disclose the meaning of a particular sub-ject—often a meaning not immediately obvious to a casual observer or reader. At some time or other, all students must practice interpretive arguments in litera-ture classes. The following are examples of possible claims for literary interpreta-tions: "Beneath the apparently modest and conventional surface of Christina Ros-setti's lyrics lie fiery manifestoes of independence and rebellion"; "In placing the last scene of *Tess of the d'Urbervilles* at Stonehenge, Thomas Hardy reminds us that Tess is a pagan, not a Christian, heroine." But interpretations are not solely the province of literature; we make interpretive arguments all the time about the behavior of people we know ("Paul says he craves a close relationship with a woman, but it's easy to see he's terrified of intimacy") and about the productions of popular culture ("Television advertisements are selling one thing: sex").

Interpretations are often paired with explanatory causal arguments. In claim-ing that "Hamlet's indecisiveness is a symptom of his unresolved Oedipal com-plex," we are really making two claims, both of which propose an increased under-standing of the play *Hamlet*. First, we are identifying the *cause* of Hamlet's indecisive behavior (his unresolved Oedipal complex), and second, we are claiming that an unresolved Oedipal complex can be discovered within Hamlet's character. Now, if you've read the play, you know that Shakespeare is never explicit about the oddities of Hamlet's relationship with his mother. No character ever says to Hamlet, "Oh Hamlet, cast thy infantile and possessive love of thy mother off." But keen readers who recognize some of the telltale symptoms of the Oedipal complex detect one in Hamlet's words and actions. And that detection is the interpretive argument: the demonstration of meaning beneath the surface. You will remember that causal claims are always somewhat speculative; this brand of causal claim is even more so, because the cause it identifies is interpretive, not factual.

Interpretations can imply a positive or a negative evaluation, but they are not evaluations per se. Nevertheless, the processes for arguing the two are very similar. The subject of an interpretive argument is the visible surface we wish to understand or explore further; it is the behavior, data, or event that openly exists for all to observe. The interpretive term is the summarized explanation of the reality beneath the visible surface. In the interpretative claim "The current baseball cap craze among boys expresses their rejection of tradition and authority," the subject is *current baseball cap craze among boys* and the interpretive term is *rejection of tradition and authority.*

As in evaluations, your central task in interpretive arguments is to demonstrate a match between the subject and the interpretive term. But also as in evaluations, you will need to lay some groundwork. Most solid interpretations satisfy the following requirements: (1) the interpretive term is clearly defined; (2) the interpretive term and the subject are matched, that is, demonstrated to be equivalent or coincident; and (3) evidence is supplied to support the interpretation.

Defining the Interpretive Term. Like evaluative arguments, interpretations work from assumptions about definition—about what elements make up a certain condition or reality. In interpretations, we are stating that X (the subject) is Y (the interpretation). To prove or support this assertion, we must define Y in such a way that it restates X or restate X in such a way that it coincides with Y. In the interpretive claim "Television news broadcasting is no longer news; it is entertainment," we must demonstrate the coincidence of our definition of entertainment on the one hand with what we see of television news on the other.

In the following passage, we see a similar assertion of coincidence, where Sigmund Freud equates literature (the subject) with the play of children:

> Now the writer does the same as the child at play; he creates a world of phantasy which he takes very seriously; that is, he invests it with a great deal of affect, while separating it sharply from reality. Language has preserved this relationship between children's play and poetic creation. It designates certain kinds of imaginative creation, concerned with tangible objects and capable of representation, as "plays"; the people who present them are called "players."

The first step in assembling an interpretive argument is to consider whether to define the interpretive term and argue your definition. As with evaluative arguments, you should define the term if you are using it in an unusual or controversial way, and you should justify that definition if you think your audience is likely to object to it. In the first example, the term *entertainment* probably should be defined, as it is a very broad and even subjective term. You might define the term as "any brief, self-contained, sensually pleasing performance that amuses but does not challenge." If your audience is likely to disagree with this definition, you will have to support it with the methods discussed in the preceding section titled "Arguing the Definition" in this chapter.

Of course, you can work from an unstated definition, provided your argument clearly reveals the elements of that definition. The following example illustrates this tactic:

> Much of television news broadcasting is no longer news; it is entertainment. Most local and national news broadcasts, news shows like *60 Minutes* and *20/20,* and even public television news are putting out slick, superficial performances that are usually neither challenging nor controversial, but that capture huge audience shares.

Here the definition of entertainment is contained in the characterization of television news.

Extensive interpretations of a series of events or continuing behavior work somewhat differently, though the basic principles are the same. In these cases—for example, an interpretation of a character's actions in a novel or of quarterly stock market activity—the subjects are usually explained in terms of a coherent and preestablished theory, system of thought, or belief. Instead of demonstrating the coincidence or equivalence of the subject and a single concept (like children's play or entertainment), these more ambitious interpretations reveal the existence of a series of related concepts—an entire system—behind the visible activity of the subject. The system identified could be Christianity, Marxism, Jungian psychology, feminism, Freudian drive theory, capitalism, semiotics—virtually any set of facts or principles logically connected to form a coherent view of the world.

Examples of this kind of systematic interpretation are especially prevalent in artistic and literary interpretations, though they are not limited to these contexts. A feminist interpretation of a literary figure like Emily Dickinson would work from a thorough understanding of feminist theory. The interpretation might explain Dickinson's poems in terms of the tension between her vocation as a poet and the very different expectations that nineteenth-century society had for women.

However compelling such an interpretation, readers are not likely to be swayed if they strongly object to the interpretive system—to the Freudian, or Marxist, or feminist model of human behavior. Even if the construct used to explain the subject is not formally named, the principles contained in that construct must seem at least plausible to your readers. If you interpret modern American history on the basis of tensions and conflicts between different social and economic classes, your readers may not give your interpretation fair consideration if they are opposed to this set of principles. On the other hand, a good interpretation often helps readers gain sympathy for a philosophy or point of view they were previously hostile to or ignorant of. When you write interpretations, you should be sensitive to your audience's beliefs and prepared at least to acknowledge their probable objections as you proceed. In doing so, you may convince some hostile readers, bringing them to accept not only your interpretation but also at least some aspects of your underlying point of view.

Establishing Coincidence. All interpretations must demonstrate coincidence between the subject and the interpretive term. *Coincidence* in this context can mean equivalence (as in "Television news is the same as entertainment"), substitution ("Although marriage looks like a romantic partnership, it is often a formalization of female dependence"), or revelation ("Behind Jack's warmth and friendliness is a cold and impenetrable shield of defenses"). The challenge of interpretations is in demonstrating these coincidences.

When the interpretive term is concrete, this task is comparatively easy. We recognize such concepts as entertainment or economic dependence; they are verifiable. Once we agree on the meaning of the term, a simple factual argument will demonstrate the applicability of the term to the subject. If we know what economic dependence is, we can detect it in a relationship with little difficulty or little guesswork, provided we have the necessary facts.

But what about detecting a "cold and impenetrable shield of defenses" in an acquaintance? There is no sure way to verify the existence of such a "shield," so how do we argue its existence? Remember in Chapter 7 on causal arguments the principle of a generally accepted link between cause and effect? Just as a cause and its effect must be linked by some acceptable motivational principle that agrees with human experience and observation, so must the interpretation (the less visible reality) relate to the subject (the visible reality) according to an acknowledged principle of experience.

Let's take the case of Jack's misleading warmth and friendliness. Basically we want to demonstrate that his apparent friendliness is an expression of his need to protect himself. First, we'll have to recast the subject or the interpretive term so that the two are shown to be equivalent. We can do this by elaborating on the friendliness: "Jack is as friendly to a grocery clerk as he is to a lifelong friend. He is completely indiscriminate in how he relates to people. This may be good for the grocery clerk, who enjoys Jack's friendly manner, but not so good for the friend, who, in fact, has never gotten to know Jack any better than the grocery clerk has," and so forth. Having established the coincidence or equivalence of this brand of friendliness and defensiveness, you'll want to assure yourself (and your readers, if necessary) that the equivalence you cite agrees with the principles of human behavior that we generally accept: indiscriminate behavior (even friendliness) often expresses its opposite.

Documenting the Interpretation.   Interpretations need documentation, or evidence. As well as explaining your subject through an acceptable principle of experience, you'll have to document your claim through examples taken from your subject. Different arguments will provide different kinds of evidence, so it is difficult to generalize about the best kind of evidence. In literature papers, professors are looking for examples from the literary work that support the claim. For example, in a paper arguing, "Behind Othello's seeming self-confidence is a collection of debilitating insecurities," the student would need to cite a number of passages in the play that suggest these insecurities. In the student paper at the end of this chapter, an interpretation of popular media, the writer documents his interpretation of a magazine ad by carefully describing the visual details of the ad.

The Possibility of Multiple Interpretations.   Most subjects lend themselves to a number of different interpretations, and these interpretations are not necessarily mutually exclusive. Widely varied and equally convincing interpretations of Shakespeare's *Hamlet* have been written through the centuries; it is a testament to the brilliance of the play that it can accommodate so many different readings. Because of the likelihood of multiple interpretations of any subject, try to resist adopting a dogmatic and inflexible tone in your arguments. You don't need to constantly acknowledge the possibility of other interpretations, nor should you present your own interpretation too tentatively; on the other hand, don't lay out your argument as if it were immutable, inarguable dogma.

ACTIVITIES (8.9)

1. Write a brief interpretation (approximately one page) of a recent event. Your interpretation should include the interpretive term, the kind of coincidence, and the supporting evidence. Then write a second interpretation of the same event, again including all the necessary elements of an interpretation. Give both essays to a classmate to read, and then discuss with him or her which is the most plausible interpretation and why. Some possible events: a recent election, a political scandal, a friend's recent success or failure in some endeavor, an athletic contest.

2. Find in a magazine an interpretation of a film that you have seen recently. Write a one- to two-page letter to the magazine offering a different interpretation. Be sure to support your argument with concrete references to the film itself. (Give your instructor a copy of the magazine review.)

SUMMARY

Arguing Evaluations

- All evaluations include a subject to be judged and an evaluative term applied to the subject.

- Before you argue the evaluation, consider whether your readers will recognize and accept your definition of the evaluative term. When their acceptance seems questionable, you'll want to argue your particular definition. Definitions can be argued by appeals to assumed reader values, appeals to authority, identification of effect, and comparison. When evaluating more than one subject against a single set of criteria, you may have to rank the criteria and justify that ranking.

- Applying the syllogistic model to your evaluative claim can help you test its reasonableness.

- Evaluations are made in ethical, aesthetic, or functional terms. *Ethical* evaluations focus on applying the ethical standard (evaluative term) to the subject, or on arguing a stipulative definition of that standard. *Aesthetic* evaluations typically work from standards currently accepted within the field, demonstrating their applicability to your subject. *Functional* evaluations typically work from a number of ranked criteria in terms of which the subject is measured.

- *Interpretations* closely resemble evaluations in structure. They establish coincidence or equivalence between the subject and the interpretive term by linking them through an acknowledged principle of experience.

SAMPLE ETHICAL EVALUATION

The following essay on euthanasia, written by college student Robert Conway, is an example of an ethical evaluation. After carefully reading the argument, collaborate with a small group of your classmates in answering the questions following the essay.

THE MORAL JUSTIFICATION FOR EUTHANASIA

Euthanasia is usually defined as the act of allowing death to occur in someone who is terminally ill but whose life may be prolonged through continued medical treatment. Despite the frequent equation of the terms, euthanasia should not be confused with mercy killing. Mercy killing involves an action which <u>causes</u> death. It is the direct and intentional taking of a human life, and that is murder. Tacking the word <u>mercy</u> onto <u>killing</u> is really an inexcusable attempt to justify murder by stressing the motive rather than the act itself.

We should restrict the use of the term <u>euthanasia</u> to simply <u>allowing</u> death to occur through the withholding of life support systems. Free of life maintained by drugs and machines, the body simply dies in a natural, inevitable way. For those unfortunate people who suffer from terminal diseases or horrific accidents, and the loved ones of those people, this natural death comes as a great relief and a welcome end.

Often writers on this subject divide euthanasia into two categories: positive or active and negative or

passive, with active meaning mercy killing and passive
meaning euthanasia as I have defined it (Ladd 164). But
the meaning of the term should not be stretched so far,
because the positive and negative versions are so
different that it is necessary to have a clear and
unmistakable line drawn between them. Using the same term
for both acts makes it far too easy to confuse them.

That said, I wish to argue the moral rightness of
euthanasia. To my knowledge, none of the world's great
religions or ethical systems would dispute the
appropriateness of euthanasia for terminally ill patients.
According to my limited study, these creeds and systems
accept the inevitability of death, with caution to humanity
about the folly of trying to prolong life beyond its natural
limits. The Book of Ecclesiastes in the Bible tells us:

> To every thing there is a season, and a time to
> every purpose under heaven:
> A time to be born, and a time to die; a time to
> plant, and a time to pluck up that which is
> planted (3.1-2).

And classical Greek mythology warns us of the folly
of desiring immortality without also securing perpetual
youth in the story of Tithonus, who aged into a mere shell
of a human being, in one version of the myth finally being
turned into a grasshopper (Hamilton 289-90). Those who
make immortality possible are also punished in Greek
mythology, as we see in the story of Aesculapius, the
healer whom Zeus punishes by death for bringing a dead man
to life (Hamilton 280-81).

Closer to our own time, in a work of the eighteenth
century, the Struldbruggs in Swift's Gulliver's Travels
are still another caution against the folly of trying to
surpass human limits. The Struldbruggs are immortal but
continue to grow older and older, leading miserable lives,
a burden to themselves and to their society (Swift 167-73;
pt. 3, ch. 10).

We must also consider the incredible psychological
and financial stress on families of patients whose lives

are prolonged even though there is no hope of restoration to a reasonable life. Often these families must devote much or even all of their financial resources to this effort, while also undergoing the stress of watching the prolonged suffering of a loved one—with no real hope that this suffering might lead to a cure of the illness. Perhaps even worse than the strain on the families is the strain on the patients themselves, who, if aware of what is going on around them, are often experiencing great pain and are terribly frustrated by their own incapacity. For these patients, the natural outcome of their illness is far more humane than an artificial extension of a life that can no longer be satisfying.

Some opponents of euthanasia will counter that no illness is truly hopeless, since some day science may find a cure for all terminal illnesses, for death itself. Wouldn't it make sense to keep patients alive until that day? Perhaps it would, if society could bear the tremendous cost, and if we had the slightest shred of evidence that such a day is even possible. So far we do not: what science shows us is that individual organisms are mortal and that immortality, if it exists at all, belongs to the species. Those who look to scientific research as an argument against euthanasia seem to have a quarrel not so much with euthanasia as with death itself.

Of course, anyone who studies this issue soon discovers numerous questions with no simple answers, including, as the theologian Roger Shinn notes, questions about infants born with serious disabilities and about the definition of a meaningful life (23-30). Even the distinction between killing and allowing life to end must be examined in the context of specific decisions, as the philosopher John Ladd points out (164-86). Nevertheless, though we must be cautious, we can reach some conclusions. Euthanasia, as I have defined it and as I hope others will define it in the future, is consonant with traditional morality and with the acceptance of human mortality that traditional morality requires. Furthermore, it is the most

humane and realistic approach to the suffering of
terminally ill patients.

WORKS CITED

Hamilton, Edith. Mythology. New York: NAL, 1969.

The Holy Bible. Authorized King James Version. New York:
     Harper, n.d.

Ladd, John. "Positive and Negative Euthanasia." Ethical
     Issues Relating to Life and Death. Ed. John Ladd. New
     York: Oxford Press, 1979. 164-86.

Shinn, Roger L. "Ethical Issues." New Options, New
     Dilemmas: An Interprofessional Approach to Life or
     Death Decisions. Ed. Anne S. Allen. Lexington:
     Lexington-Heath, 1986. 23-30.

Swift, Jonathan. Gulliver's Travels. Ed. Louis A. Landa.
     Cambridge: Riverside-Houghton Mifflin, 1960.

Discussion Questions

1. What are the subject and evaluative term of Robert's argument?
2. Why do you think he provides a definition of the evaluative term?
3. Through what methods does Robert support his evaluation. Are these effective? Why or why not?
4. Identify and discuss the placement of the argument's claim.

SAMPLE INTERPRETATION

The following is an essay by first-year student Kevin Maloney on "Reading Popular Culture." Read it through carefully, then answer the questions that follow the essay. Compare your answers with those of your classmates.

READING POPULAR CULTURE

Hidden within the productions of popular culture are
quiet endorsements of specific values or attitudes. Such
attitudes are projected not only in print, but in music,
advertisements, and television programs. Just as it is
important to be able to read the written word, it is also
vital to know how to read these other forms of expression.
Being unable to recognize the sometimes hidden messages of
these forms of expression is like being in a foreign
country where you don't speak the language. In both cases,

you can easily fall prey to individuals eager to take advantage of your ignorance, to manipulate you into doing what they want you to do.

Often, the skill of discovering the values or attitudes promoted in popular culture involves nothing more than stepping back and seeing "the big picture," recognizing what is really pretty obvious. Take, for example, the popular sitcom Seinfeld. It is possible to watch and enjoy this show week after week without realizing how it is dominated by sexually promiscuous behavior. On a recent episode, Jerry Seinfeld pursued a female gymnast. His goal was to see if sex with a gymnast was more exciting and varied than with someone less physically flexible. Within a week's time, he was sleeping with the gymnast and joking about their sexual encounters. By the end of the show, he had broken up with her, merely because the sex wasn't really all that different.

Elaine, another character on the program, seems to have new sexual partners almost every episode. Since she can always find some very superficial reason to break up with them—she doesn't like one guy's name, another gets a haircut—none of these relationships lasts. But in show after show, she persists in her search for "the one."

None of the characters in the show disapprove of Jerry's and Elaine's promiscuity. In fact, their behavior is often the source of delight and envy for their friends, some of whom, like George, try to emulate it. I have watched the show regularly for at least three years, and I realize that I have never seen sex presented as anything other than a joke. The program never explicitly says that viewers should lead a promiscuous life, but that lifestyle is repeated again and again. And this is one way that cultural values are constructed and instilled—through repeated themes and behavior in television programming (George and Trimbur 228). Whenever a behavior—in the case of Seinfeld, sexual promiscuity—is repeated, the viewer is asked to accept it as a norm.

Television is not the only form of popular culture that promotes promiscuity as a norm. Magazine advertising does the same. As Jean Kilbourne says, these ads "sell a great deal more than products" (152).

Take the example of an ad from a recent computer magazine. A scantily clad woman stands in the middle of the page, her perfect body more prominent than anything else in the ad. She is wearing spotted, tight-fitting pants; her skin-tight T-shirt bares most of her abdomen; her shirt is covered by suggestive fishnet mesh; and a navel ring adorns her trim stomach. Apparently the waitress in this diner, she wears a pair of in-line skates and holds a tray. Everything about this woman suggests available sexuality.

And why is this ad set in a diner with a waitress as its focal point? The answers to these questions don't have much to do with computers, but they do have a lot to do with sex. As a waitress, the woman's job is to bring her customers what they want, and her dress suggests that this means anything. The table closest to the camera has partially empty cups sitting on it; clearly other customers have dined here before. And if they left something in their cups, they must have left satisfied— another instance of the advertisement's sexual insinuations. The text beneath the photograph tells us "Monday's Chef's Special" is "the obvious choice." What this woman can bring you is obviously what you want. And the sexual innuendoes go on and on.

Popular music also frequently contains implicit endorsements of sexual promiscuity. The words are often camouflaged by a good beat, a nice voice, and interesting harmonies, but their message is there.

Pop singer Bruce Springsteen has a song called "Secret Garden." The title suggests something pure and natural, but take a look at the lyrics: "She'll let you in her house if you come knocking late at night. She'll let you in her mouth if the words you say are right." Apparently these lyrics are about a woman who will engage in oral sex if the man sweet-talks her. The next line is "If you pay the price she'll let you deep inside." Again, sex is the reward for saying the right words to a woman. Later in the song, we hear "She'll let you into the parts of herself that'll bring you down." What is remarkable about these lyrics is how <u>clearly</u> they refer to promiscuous sex; you don't have to be a Houdini of interpretation to understand their meaning.

Some might say that such sexually promiscuous TV characters, sexually suggestive computer ads, and sexually symbolic song lyrics may <u>represent</u> promiscuous behavior, but they don't necessarily <u>promote</u> it. Yet the more behaviors and images are repeated in popular culture, the more "normal" they begin to seem. If we don't stop to recognize and evaluate these repeated behaviors and images, we will find ourselves influenced by their sheer volume. Without even realizing it, we may feel it's all right to repeat them in our own lives. So let's learn the language of cultural manipulation so we can avoid being its victim.

WORKS CITED

George, Dianna, and John Trimbur, eds. "Introduction to Television Culture." <u>Reading Culture: Contexts for Critical Reading and Writing</u>. New York: Harper, 1995. 228–29.

Kilbourne, Jean. "Beauty . . . and the Beast of Advertising." <u>Reading Culture: Contexts for Critical Reading and Writing</u>. Ed. Dianna George and John Trimbur. New York: Harper, 1995. 152–54.

Springsteen, Bruce. <u>Bruce Springsteen: Greatest Hits</u>. Columbia, 1995.

Discussion Questions

1. What is Kevin interpreting in this essay, and what is his interpretive term?
2. Do you agree with Kevin's decision about providing an explicit definition of the interpretive term?
3. Kevin does not address the possibility that the *Seinfeld* show is satirical, that it presents certain shallow and irresponsible behaviors to criticize or

poke fun at them. With a group of your classmates who know the show, consider this possibility and how it would affect Kevin's argument.

4. Discuss the evidence offered as support of the claim. Is it relevant and sufficient? Are you convinced by the argument?

SUGGESTIONS FOR WRITING (8.10)

1. Write a two- to three-page evaluation of a course you have taken or are taking in college. Your evaluation will be primarily a functional evaluation, one of the crucial questions being whether the course actually achieves its intended goals.
2. Write a three- to four-page argument for or against euthanasia based on your reading of the sample student paper at the end of the section on evaluation. Do you agree with the definition of euthanasia given there? What about the other supporting arguments? Are there other arguments for euthanasia, or do you have what you believe are more powerful arguments against it?
3. Write a combination interpretation and evaluation (three to four pages) of a recent artistic or entertainment event you enjoyed: a film, play, novel, concert, or something similar. Your evaluation will be primarily aesthetic, but it may be ethical as well.

9

Arguing
Recommendations

At one time or another, most of us—whether student, professional, or concerned citizen—will have to argue a *recommendation* (sometimes called a *proposal*). A recommendation is a written request for change of some sort: cable TV in the dorms, paternity leave in a company, or a new major in a university. Recommendations vary in format from a simple one-page letter to an elaborate minivolume with strictly prescribed components. But despite the many variations in format, all recommendations argue for change.

Recommendations are the hybrids of argument, drawing on the principles and practices of factual, causal, and evaluative arguments. So, for the most part, writing a successful recommendation is a question of applying what you have already learned about the different kinds of argument and their support.

All recommendations establish a current situation (how things are now) and a probable future situation (how they would be if the change were instituted). In other words, recommendations rely on arguments of fact and arguments of effect. How central either type of argument is to your recommendation will depend on the emphasis demanded by the particular situation.

If you focus on the current situation, which usually means showing that things have gotten so bad that change must be considered, much of your argument will be factual. Let's say you want to impress the authorities with the inadequacy of parking facilities at your commuter campus. You figure it's up to them to come up with the answer to the problem, but you know they won't do it without being convinced that a serious problem *does* exits. In this case, your recommendation would begin with a factual argument that establishes exactly what the current situation is.

But if you are the contractor asked to submit a proposal for new parking lots, your focus will be on the future effects of your particular plan and predicting its ability to solve the current problem. In this case, the recommendation will be largely causal, establishing the probable effects of the implemented recommendation.

Regardless of their emphases, all recommendations also make evaluative arguments; they include a judgment of the current situation (the parking situation is inadequate or unfair) and/or an evaluation of the proposed change (parking will be more available, more convenient, etc.).

AUDIENCE NEEDS AND VALUES

By now you've learned how important it is when making any kind of argument to know as much about your audience as possible. Nowhere is this knowledge more critical than in writing recommendations. Most recommendations asks readers to *do* something, not merely to give their armchair agreement to a claim. Human nature being what it is, people are more likely to take action if there is a possibility that the action will benefit them in some way. Thus a powerful way to support any recommendation is to appeal to the needs, values, and desires that you have identified in your readers. Making such an appeal means paying particular attention to the early stage of audience consideration: Who are your audience? What are their needs and values likely to be regarding your claim? Can you responsibly appeal to these in your recommendation? Luckily, it is usually fairly easy to answer these questions when you're preparing a recommendation because in most cases, you're addressing a very specific audience (often a single individual).

For example, suppose your favorite professor is denied tenure, and you and a number of other students write a letter to the dean arguing for a reconsideration of the decision. What kinds of appeals would most likely move the dean? To answer the question, you have to know what the dean's priorities and responsibilities are, which, in fact, you're never thought about. In speaking with faculty members, you learn that your dean is determined to enhance the academic reputation of the college as a way of attracting and retaining good students. Knowing this, you're not going to get far arguing that Professor Morris be granted tenure because he's a good shortstop on the faculty-student softball team or an easy grader. You'll need to find a way to demonstrate just how valuable Professor Morris is to students in the *classroom,* perhaps including testimonials from students.

Though you'll always need to be aware of the needs and values of your readers, you will rarely identify them explicitly in the recommendation. In the case of Professor Morris's tenure, you will identify the positive effects on students of granting him tenure, but you probably won't need to identify which of the dean's needs or priorities will be addressed by this action. Provided your assumption about these priorities is correct, you can trust her to recognize that the change you are proposing would satisfy them.

When Your Values Differ from Assumed Reader Values

Recommendations actually work with two sets of values: the reader's *and* the writer's. While a successful recommendation must appeal to the appropriate reader values, it will originate in values held by the writer. Indeed, most recommendations are born in the writer's experience of *dissonance,* that sense of mismatch between one's values and a current situation (see Chapter 2).

Often the values that move you to recommend a certain change will be the same as those that will move your reader to accept your recommendation. But sometimes writer and reader values do not coincide. Usually, as long as the two values or sets of values are somehow related and not directly opposed, their lack of coincidence will not weaken your recommendation. But you do need to be aware of the difference between them.

Suppose you are a commuter student who takes the city bus to get to campus each day. This term, you have an 8 A.M. class, the early bus from your stop has been overcrowded and unreliable, and you have been late to class a number of times. You decide to write a letter to the local transit authority recommending improvements in bus service. Your letter derives from your own experience of dissonance—your frustration at not making it to class on time—and it seeks to satisfy your rights to good service as a paying customer (your needs and values).

But you realize that these values are not necessarily going to move your audience—the transit authority—to make the necessary improvements to the service. The manager of customer service may not care much about your rights as a paying customer, but he does care about the value of *customer satisfaction.* No business, even one that holds a virtual monopoly, as most transit authorities do, can afford to ignore the importance of customer satisfaction.

In this example, the values of customer rights and customer satisfaction are not identical, but they can comfortably coexist in the recommendation because they are not in conflict, and they are *causally* connected: if your rights are being served, you will be satisfied.

Your letter to the transit authority might look like this:

Mr. Brian Rose
Manager, Customer Service
Metro Transit Authority
Collegetown, USA

Dear Mr. Rose:

   I am writing to complain about the quality of the morning bus service on Bus 15, which runs from Main and Winton to the community college. By the time the bus scheduled to stop at 7:21 A.M. gets to the stop at Main and Winton, it is usually late (in October, by an average of fifteen minutes) and always overcrowded, with standing room only. Two days in October (the ninth and the fifteenth) the bus was so crowded that some people could not get on at all. I have tried to take the 7:04 bus, but the situation is essentially the same, and I cannot take a later bus because I have an 8:00 class at the college.

   I and a number of others who rely on bus service are very unhappy. We are being cheated of the service we deserve, given the high fares we pay, and we would like some action taken to improve the situation. I am enclosing with this letter a petition signed by eight other students who depend on Bus 15 to get them to campus.

   Now that you are aware of this problem, I hope you will take action to correct it. I look forward to hearing from you about what that action might be.

                                        Very truly yours,

                                        Patrick Booth

This letter has a good chance of influencing its reader because the values from which it is written and the values to which it appeals are related and compatible. In cases where there is clear conflict between your values and your readers', you must search for other values to appeal to. You couldn't convince an audience of cigarette smokers that cigarette sales should be restricted because smoking is, as you believe, a stinking, filthy habit. But you might make some headway with an argument citing the risks of secondary smoke to loved ones—a risk that might concern even the most committed of smokers.

ACTIVITIES (9.1)

1. In each case below, the value cited to win the audience's acceptance of the recommendation is not appropriate. With a small group of your classmates, identify alternative values that are more appropriate. Then discuss your list with the entire class.

   Sample recommendation: A longer school year for elementary and secondary students
   Audience: Elementary and secondary teachers
   Inappropriate value: More work from teachers
   Alternative value: A greater opportunity to ensure students' mastery of skills

   a. **Recommendation:** Earlier closing of a college cafeteria
      Audience: College students
      Inappropriate value: Shorter hours and fewer headaches for cafeteria staff
   b. **Recommendation:** A new federal tax on gasoline
      Audience: Truck drivers
      Inappropriate value: Reduced reliance on trucks for transporting goods
   c. **Recommendation:** A curfew for everybody under the age of sixteen
      Audience: Those under sixteen
      Inappropriate value: Those under sixteen can't be trusted
   d. **Recommendation:** A law requiring motorcyclists to wear helmets
      Audience: Motorcyclists
      Inappropriate value: Reduced claims against insurance companies and therefore increased profits for insurance companies
   e. **Recommendation:** A shorter work week
      Audience: Employers
      Inappropriate value: More leisure time for employees

2. With the same small group of classmates, identify values that would be shared by the following pairs, or that would be compatible.

   Example: Republicans and Democrats
   Common value: Concern for the national interest—the country as a whole

   a. Planners of a new highway; homeowners whose property is in the path of the new highway
   b. Managers of a company; workers on strike against that company
   c. Parents planning to take away a child's allowance as punishment for bad behavior; the child in question
   d. Planners of a large rock concert; neighborhood groups opposed to the concert because of noise
   e. Proponents of legislation restricting the use of handguns; opponents of this legislation

RECOMMENDATIONS EMPHASIZING THE PRESENT

Some recommendations, like Patrick Booth's letter to the transit authority, concentrate on problems in a current situation, leaving a detailed proposal for change to another argument. The goal of such arguments is to demonstrate more *that* something needs to be done than *what* exactly that something is.)

To accept this kind of recommendation, your readers need an accurate and, usually, detailed picture of the current situation. They must grasp the situation as it is before they can agree or disagree with your evaluation of it. Recommendations emphasizing the present usually open with a factual argument.

Establishing the Current Situation

Patrick's letter to the transit authority does a good job establishing the current situation through facts and figures that Patrick collected: the average tardiness of the bus, the number of times the bus had to leave customers behind, and so on. Establishing these details is critical to the recommendation for a couple of reasons. First, readers are likely to take exact figures more seriously than irate vagueness. Exaggerations like "Huge numbers of people are regularly prevented from riding the 7:21 bus" are far less effective than exact figures.

Second, misrepresenting the facts, whether intentionally to strengthen your case or negligently through sloppy research, will be detected. The recipient of any recommendation is going to investigate the situation before taking action, and if the results of that investigation differ substantially from your figures, your recommendation will have reached a dead end.

Evaluating the Current Situation

All recommendations contain some evaluative elements. In recommendations emphasizing the present, the subject of the evaluation is the current situation. If you have a good understanding of your audience and their needs and values, you probably won't need to write a full-blown evaluation complete with a defined evaluative term. The transit authority letter, for example, doesn't require an explicit judgment of the situation presented. Any reader, whether an official of the transit authority or an occasional passenger, will recognize that the conditions described are undesirable. You could point to this fact for rhetorical emphasis, but the judgment is implicit within the factual presentation.

Sometimes your recommendation will be addressed to readers who may not immediately recognize the problems in the current situation. In these cases, you'd be wise to identify *what* is wrong by providing a clear and limited evaluative term. For example, a professor's schedule of assignments on a syllabus is unfair to students or hopelessly unrealistic. You can then proceed to match the subject (the syllabus) with the evaluative term according to the suggestions in Chapter 8, remembering the importance of considering audience needs and values.

Applying the Toulmin Model

The Toulmin logical model is especially useful when you're composing a recommendation. Placing your claim and support in the Toulmin paradigm (see Chapter 5) will help you detect any weaknesses of reasoning or wording in your argument and will suggest the secondary claims you'll need to support the central claim. Assume that an outside consultant, hired to analyze the employee benefits package of Quick-Stop Copy (the current situation), recommends that the company provide a benefits package more competitive with those of comparable companies (central claim). The consultant's recommendation would fit into the Toulmin model as following:

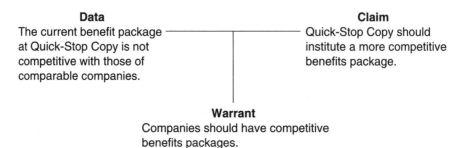

| **Data** | | **Claim** |
| The current benefit package at Quick-Stop Copy is not competitive with those of comparable companies. | | Quick-Stop Copy should institute a more competitive benefits package. |

Warrant
Companies should have competitive benefits packages.

Remember that in the Toulmin model, the warrant is equivalent to the major premise in a syllogism; it is the general statement about a class that enables the data (or the minor premise in a syllogism) to justify the claim (or conclusion in a syllogism). As noted in Chapter 5, sometimes both data and warrant need further support. Indeed, one of the virtues of the Toulmin system is that once you have stated your argument in its terms, you can recognize what further support (backing) your argument will need. In this example, you realize that the argument will need a breakdown of facts and figures to back the data (i.e., how the Quick-Stop package actually compares with those of other companies). And you should recognize as well that the warrant will need further backing if it is not self-evident to the reader that companies should have competitive benefits packages. Depending on the reader's point of view, the consultant may want to strengthen the warrant by supporting it with a secondary argument of effect, that is, demonstrating the negative results to employees and to the company of the inferior benefits package.

ACTIVITIES (9.2)

1. For two of the current situations below, what kind of facts would be necessary to convince readers that some change is necessary. Make a list of all the kinds of factual evidence you can think of.

   a. Traffic at an intersection
   b. Someone's physical appearance
   c. A friend's choice of a career
   d. A company's health care benefits
   e. The local court system

2. Using the material you developed for Number 1 above, create two claims of recommendation. Then state your argument in terms of the Toulmin model, indicating what additional support or backing is necessary.

RECOMMENDATIONS EMPHASIZING THE FUTURE

When your recommendation emphasizes the probable future effects of its proposed changes, you'll have to move beyond the current problems and the general claim that something must be done; you'll also have to identify, reasonably and convincingly, *what* that something is. A recommendation emphasizing the future will be effective if it can demonstrate (1) that your proposal is likely to produce desirable effects and (2) that the proposal is feasible.

Presenting the Recommendation

The recommendation itself—the proposed plan for change—must be crystal clear. Obviously readers can't agree with a plan they don't understand. Some situations will call for a rather general recommendation, leaving the details to others, while in other cases, particularly when you have some responsibility for implementing the plan, a detailed recommendation will be necessary.

Kate Quill is a second-year student at Carlson College, a small liberal arts college in Maine. Carlson has operated on a trimester calendar for years, with three ten-week terms per academic year. It is common knowledge at Carlson that many students are unhappy with the trimester system: they feel rushed and overworked by the short terms. Kate and a number of her friends think it's time to do something about this dissatisfaction, so they decide to write a letter to the college administration recommending that a committee of faculty and students look at alternatives to the trimester calendar. The letter they write, which follows, is an example of a *general* recommendation emphasizing the future.

Dr. Dale Hill
President, Carlson College
Carlson, Maine

Dear Dr. Hill:

It should be no surprise to you that students feel considerable dissatisfaction with the trimester calendar used at Carlson. Faculty report that students have complained about the excessively fast pace of courses for years. Given this long history of dissatisfaction, we feel it is time for a formal examination of alternative calendars. Such an analysis should determine once and for all whether our current trimester calendar is the best system for Carlson.

We recommend that you put together a calendar committee consisting of students, faculty, and administration to conduct such an examination. This group could research the calendars used by comparable institutions, determining the advantages and disadvantages of each case. If the committee concluded that our current system is the best, we believe that the current level of student dissatisfaction would be reduced. Similarly, if a different calendar more suitable to Carlson were discovered and implemented, students would be much happier.

Any of the students signing this letter would be eager to serve on such a committee. We appreciate your time in considering this proposal.

Very truly yours,

Kate Quill and
Carlson Students

Let's assume that President Hill has been hearing complaints about the trimesters for years and decides, on reading this letter, to take its recommendation seriously. After consulting with the deans and vice presidents, the president decides to constitute a "blue ribbon" committee to investigate the calendar issue. While Kate's recommendation was appropriately general (it's not a student's job to dictate details to a college president), the review process President Hill recommends to the chairperson of the Calendar Committee must be detailed and specific. This letter might read as follows:

Professor Rachel Eisenberg
Chair, Calendar Committee
Department of English
Carlson College

Dear Rachel:

Thank you for agreeing to serve as chair of the Calendar Committee. As you know, the calendar issue is extremely controversial; it is my hope that under your competent leadership the committee will put to rest once and for all the question of what calendar is the most appropriate for Carlson.

It is not my intention to direct the committee's work, but I hope you will allow a few suggestions about process and objectives:

- It will be critical to your deliberations to identify and verify the most common student complaints about our trimester system and the most common faculty complaints. This information can be obtained through survey instruments and through individual or group interviews.

- When exploring the alternative calendars currently used by other colleges, you should try to select schools whose size and mission are closely comparable to Carlson's.
- Please do not forget to factor in the budgetary implications of the various alternatives. While our primary concern should be with the quality of the education we deliver, an extremely costly calendar implementation could actually jeopardize our educational quality.
- While the final action taken on the basis of your report will be determined by the Carlson Board of Trustees, it would be helpful if the report included a ranking of the alternative calendars.
- The format and style of the final report I leave up to the committee, but bear in mind that it will be distributed to a number of different campus groups, so brevity and readability will be important.

Again, I thank you for agreeing to take on this challenging and important task. If there is any way that my office can help the work of the committee, don't hesitate to let me know.

Very truly yours,

Dale Hill
President

The preceding examples illustrate only two possibilities; recommendations can be more or less detailed than the second example. Generally, the more concrete your recommendation, the more effective it will be, provided your plan reflects a sound understanding of the operations of the group that will implement it. But there are times when a great deal of detail is inappropriate. Most editorials make recommendations without much detail; most politicians give few details in their speeches to general audiences. In deciding how much detail to include, be sure to consider your audience's capacity for and interest in the details, as well as their proposed role in carrying out the recommendation.

ACTIVITIES (9.3)

1. The sample recommendations below are extremely general. The writers have given no indication of how they expect their plans to be implemented. For each, provide at least three specific recommendations that will help an audience understand how the plans can be carried out. If you like, instead of working with the claims provided below, create your own general recommendations (the kind that might come out of a conversation with friends), and then provide more specific recommendations for each.

Example: We need a city with cleaner air.
Specific recommendations: (1) Encouragement of "park-and-ride" lots for commuters to decrease automobile traffic, (2) tighter inspection standards for automobiles' exhaust emission systems, and (3) restrictions on the burning of leaves and trash.

After you have made this list of recommendations, write a short essay (250–500 words) briefly explaining each of the recommendations and how they relate to the general recommendation.

a. Our college needs more school spirit.
b. Americans need to be more tolerant of racial and ethnic diversity.
c. Adolescents must be made more aware of the dangers of alcohol.
d. American industry needs to put more emphasis on the quality of its products.
e. Students and professors must learn to see each other as human beings.

2. In your student or local newspaper, find an example of a recommendation that you think is good, but that is too general to be implemented. Write a letter to the editor suggesting specific ways that the recommendation might be developed further.

Arguing the Effects of Your Recommendation

Recommendations with future emphasis always identify and evaluate the probable effects of the proposed plan. Identifying probable effects will take the form of an *argument of effect* and will follow the steps presented in Chapter 7. This part of your recommendation will be strong if you can show that the proposed changes (the causes) are related to the results you predict (the effects) through established causal principles.

In the example of the Carlson College calendar, the Calendar Committee might predict the following short causal chain: converting to a semester calendar (cause) will give students more classroom contact with their faculty (first effect), which in turn is likely to make students feel more satisfied with their college experience (second effect). Readers would be likely to accept the first causal link; a semester course meets something like forty-five hours per term, while a trimester course meets approximately thirty hours per term. Unless faculty use the additional time showing films and bringing in guest lecturers, the increase in hours will result in increased contact with faculty.

To support the second link in the chain, the committee needs to identify a linking behavioral principle. In this case, the principle linking increased student-faculty contact and student satisfaction has to be spelled out explicitly. That principle might be stated as follows: Young people go to college to receive an education and to become adults; faculty not only provide that education but offer a new brand of adult relationship based on mature, intellectual foundations. Thus substantial contact with faculty will meet a primary objective of many students. The committee report might also want to support this second effect in the chain by citing existing higher-education studies that have discovered this connection between student-faculty contact and student satisfaction.

ACTIVITIES (9.4)

With a small group of your classmates, discuss the likelihood of the projected results of the following three recommendations. Have one student write up the reasons for your judgment of each. Submit this write-up to your instructor.

1. **Recommendation:** Increase the price of tickets to films at the college theater from $2.00 to $2.50.
   Projected results: No significant decline in attendance; more revenue from tickets to allow the theater to rent better films, which will eventually lead to higher attendance.
2. **Recommendation:** Allow students to take one course pass-fail.
   Projected results: Students will feel under less pressure about grades and more willing to take tough courses; the students will work just as hard in the courses they take pass-fail as they would have if they had taken the course for a regular grade.
3. **Recommendation:** Increase school taxes to subsidize new athletic facilities at the high school.
   Projected results: Greater community involvement in and identification with high school athletic teams; improvement in high school image; increased student enrollment.

Judging Effects in Terms of Assumed Needs and Values

In developing your recommendation, you will probably identify several probable effects, only some of which will meet the needs and values of your readers. Suppose you support your recommendation to faculty of a pass-fail grading option by predicting the effect of students' doing less work in their courses. Such an effect isn't likely to appeal to faculty values. This does not mean that you should deny the effect if it seems probable, but at the same time, there is no reason to emphasize it.

You may not always have to evaluate the probable effects explicitly nor identify the needs and values that those effects will satisfy. But at a minimum, you must be aware of the values which the probable effects of your implemented recommendation will satisfy.

When Some Effects Are Undesirable. Few recommendations can promise exclusively positive results. But as long as the desirable effects outweigh the undesirable ones, your recommendation is worth making. When you know that along with the positive effects there may be some less desirable repercussions, you should acknowledge them in your argument. Provided you can demonstrate that the negative effects are less significant than the positive ones, you will not weaken your argument by mentioning them. In fact, an argument that acknowledges and measures its own weaknesses is usually more effective than one that fails to admit what any intelligent reader will recognize.

If you are on a committee recommending the building of a new expressway, you should admit that the building of the new expressway, whatever its ultimate advantages, will cause inconveniences. This is a more effective and responsible approach than ignoring altogether the obvious negative consequences of your recommendation. You will enhance your credibility by admitting what many people will know or suspect anyway.

Implementation.   To be successful, your recommendation must pass one further test: it must be feasible. Even the most brilliant recommendation will be rejected if its implementation is fraught with difficulties. While a detailed implementation plan is not required of all recommendations, some indication of the feasibility of your plan will strengthen your argument. At the least, you must provide a general indication that the recommendation *is* feasible. There is no point in advancing a recommendation that your audience will see as totally impractical, regardless of how desirable the results might be. Sometimes, your audience will expect a very detailed implementation plan, including a list of activities and the name of the person responsible for each activity, the dates for beginning and completing each activity, and the likely costs of each activity.

A crucial element of a general or detailed implementation plan is an analysis of costs. Many great ideas born in the heat of inspiration have failed to materialize because of a lack of cold cash; programs that many judge worthwhile (such as human exploration of Mars) have been delayed because of their expense. Whenever you present a proposal and outline its benefits, you also need to project its costs as accurately as you can. Remember that these costs often include not only the expense of constructing a new building or starting a new program but also the continuing costs once the proposal is a reality. Your community may need a new and larger airport, or a new bus service for the elderly, or new day care facilities, but once these are established, there may be additional costs of keeping the services going from day to day. The new and larger airport, for example, may need more employees to maintain it and may cost more to heat and cool than the old one did. These continuing expenses are easy to overlook or to minimize; the great temptation in making a recommendation that you believe in strongly is to overstate the benefits and understate the costs. You need to fight this temptation, remembering that some of your readers will be expecting just such a miscalculation.

People tend to accept recommendations that can be implemented within existing systems more readily than those requiring radical changes. Most of us are reluctant to make major changes on the strength of what *might* happen, however convincingly the probabilities are argued. Other things being equal, people usually prefer the least disruptive course of action.

On the other hand, sometimes existing structures need to be shaken up and disruptive measures taken. Much of our world, including the very existence of this country, is a result of radical changes. You should at least consider whether a drastic change will not be more effective ultimately and easier to implement than a piecemeal one. Sometimes piecemeal recommendations are like putting money into an old car that is going to break down anyway, or like eighteenth-century Americans hoping King George III and the British government would see the error of their ways. One test here, though a difficult one, is whether the piecemeal changes will improve the situation enough to justify the time and cost of the changes: the old car may not be worth keeping; on balance, it was easier to leave King George than to reform him.

Applying the Toulmin Model

The Toulmin model will help you evaluate the reasonableness and completeness of recommendations emphasizing the future. Applying the Toulmin format to the

Carlson College example, we get a look at what kinds of secondary arguments the recommendation calls for.

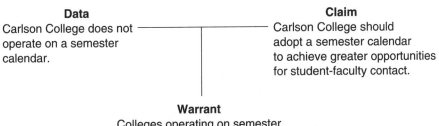

Data
Carlson College does not operate on a semester calendar.

Claim
Carlson College should adopt a semester calendar to achieve greater opportunities for student-faculty contact.

Warrant
Colleges operating on semester calendars provide the most opportunities for student-faculty contact.

Laying the recommendation out this way shows us what additional support the argument will need. The data in this case will need minimal backing (all the readers will accept it as true), but the warrant is clearly not self-evident and thus calls for backing. Depending on your assessment of the readers' needs, that backing may follow at least two directions. On the one hand, you'll probably want to support the generalization with a secondary factual argument that compares the number of student-faculty contact hours in semester and trimester systems: "Students at Rusk College, which operates on a semester system, meet in class with their course faculty four hours per week for fourteen weeks, as opposed to Carlson's three hours per week for ten weeks."

A second issue raised by the warrant is the unstated assumption that student-faculty contact is a good thing. If you think your readers need to be convinced of this assumption, then you'll want to provide a secondary evaluative and/or causal argument demonstrating the positive elements and results of student-faculty contact. Here, you can resort to anecdotal evidence, but your best bet is to cite some of those higher-education studies demonstrating the merits of this contact.

ACTIVITIES (9.5)

1. The following are recommendations that many believe are good ideas. For at least two of these claims, make a list of possible drawbacks to the recommendation that the writer would need to admit. Compare your list with those of some of your classmates. If you like, you may come up with your own recommendations—changes you would like to see occur—and consider the possible drawbacks.
   a. Sending astronauts to explore Mars
   b. Passing elementary and secondary students from one grade to another only after they have passed strict competency tests
   c. Prohibiting smoking in all public facilities
   d. Increasing the school year by an average of one month for all elementary and secondary schoolchildren
   e. Abolishing fraternities and sororities on your campus

2. Prepare an implementation plan for some change you would like to make in your own life, such as studying harder, learning a new sport or hobby, or exploring a possible career. Your implementation plan should include the sequence of activities you will undertake, the dates you plan to begin and end each activity, and the costs, if any, of the project. See the recommendation report "A Proposal for a Computer Facility in Marshall Dormitory" at the end of this chapter for a sample implementation plan.

3. Derive a claim of recommendation from three issues that you feel strongly about. Then place each claim within the Toulmin model, providing data and warrant. For each claim, where will you need additional backing? On the basis of your answer to this question, prepare an outline of a four- to five-page paper that would argue this recommendation.

Example: Our staggering divorce rate suggests that a course in marriage and relationships should be mandatory for all high school students.

RECOMMENDATIONS THAT CONSIDER PRESENT AND FUTURE

The two types of recommendations we have discussed rarely occur in pure form; many recommendations contain some discussion of both the current situation and the future possibilities. Obviously, such recommendations combine the strategies discussed in this chapter: they present and evaluate the current situation, lay out the recommendation, and finally identify and evaluate the probable results of the recommendation. Because these arguments consider what currently exists and what could exist, they provide the groundwork for a useful comparative evaluation. After you have examined both the present and future elements of your argument, you may wish to compare the two explicitly—to demonstrate that the probable effects will be preferable to the current situation. If you have an accurate grasp of your audience's needs and values, you should be able to make this comparison effectively.

SUMMARY

Arguing Recommendations

- Recommendations emphasizing present conditions include the following:
  - A presentation of the current situation, policy, and or practice (a factual argument).
  - An evaluation of this situation in terms of the values and needs important to your audience. The judgment expressed and the value appealed to may be stated or implied.
  - When applicable, a presentation of the existing effects (causal argument) and a judgment of these effects.

- When applicable, a presentation of the probable future effects (argument of effect) and a judgment of these effects.
- Applying the Toulmin model will help you identify the supporting secondary claims your argument will need to make.
- Recommendations emphasizing the future include the following:
  - Presentation of the recommendation. The degree of detail in this presentation is usually dictated by your degree of responsibility for implementing the recommendation.
  - Identification of probable effects of your recommendation if it is implemented.
  - Evaluation of these effects (both desirable and undesirable) in terms of audience needs and values.
  - In some cases, a suggested implementation plan and an analysis of costs.

  Whether or not you include such a plan, those recommendations requiring minor changes to existing structures are generally more acceptable, though not necessarily more valuable, than those requiring radical restructuring.
- Recommendations considering present and future include the following:
  - Presentation and evaluation of the current situation.
  - Presentation of the recommendation.
  - Identification and evaluation of the probable results of the recommendation.
  - In many cases, a demonstration that the probable effects of the implemented recommendation will be preferable to the current situation.

TWO SAMPLE RECOMMENDATIONS

The following sample recommendation report considers both the current situation and probable results of its implementation. The report is an example of what a student might include in a recommendation for a computer room in the dormitory. The format of the report, outlined here, is one of several possible formats for a recommendation report:

    I. Statement of problem
   II. Statement of recommendation
  III. Advantages of recommendation
  IV. Disadvantages of recommendation
   V. Costs and implementation plan

Many organizations and many professors have a preferred format for such reports; you would be wise to check whether there are such preferred formats before you begin to write this kind of report either at work or for a class.

This recommendation is briefer and more general than many. If a report with the same proposal were prepared by the university's office of computing, it would undoubtedly include more detail on the scheduling of the project, the nature of the renovations, and the kind of equipment that would be purchased. But a recommendation like this one—proposed by a student to an administrator—need not include an implementation plan (although some suggestions about implementation might impress the audience with how carefully the writer has thought about her recommendation).

A Proposal for a Computer Facility in Marshall Dormitory

Prepared for

Dr. Hector Martinez.

Assistant Vice President for Student Life

by Elaine Weston

Chair, Marshall Dormitory Student Committee

February 13, 1998

Statement of Problem

Currently many students living in Marshall Dormitory have difficulty getting access to a computer. The college's main computer facility is located over a mile away on the other end of campus, and that facility is often overcrowded; many students find that they can use a computer only after eleven at night or before ten in the morning. Some students bring their own computers with them to college, but not all students here can afford their own computers. I surveyed all students living on the third floor of Marshall and found that only 25 percent had their own computers, while another 50 percent said they use computers at least occasionally for course work. Of this 50 percent, 45 percent said that they have sometimes found it hard to get access to one of the college's computers, and 35 percent frequently had this problem. Clearly, this lack of access to needed computers is a serious problem for Marshall students. When I spoke with Helen Borshoff, the Vice President for Computing, she

confirmed the severity of the problem and said that her
organization is trying to deal with the problem within the
constraints of its limited resources.

RECOMMENDATION

We recommend that the Office of Student Life work with
the Office of Computing to convert the student lounge at the
west end of the second floor of Marshall into a computer
facility equipped with seven PCs connected to the central
campus computer system and three printers: Our discussions
with the Office of Computing indicate that the number of
computers and printers is the maximum that would fit into the
amount of space available and that this range of equipment
would be most appropriate for student needs. Since the need
for more computers and more access to computers is so
pressing, we recommend that the necessary renovations take
place this summer so that the facility will be ready by the
beginning of the next academic year on September 6, 1998.

ADVANTAGES OF RECOMMENDATION

If our recommendation is implemented, students who
live in Marshall will be able to use college-owned
computers without having to go all the way to the college
facility. There will also be more computers available than
there are now, and students without the means to buy their
own computers will be at less of a disadvantage than they
currently are. For students, then, there are significant
educational advantages if this proposal is implemented.

For the administration, there are several other
advantages as well. Construction of this facility will
alleviate at least some of the overwhelming pressure on
the main computer facility. Since the space for this new
facility already exists, renovating this space will be
less costly than adding new space somewhere on campus.
This new facility will also show the administration's
concern about increasing student access to computers, and
it will therefore help to reduce the growing tension
between students and administrators over this issue.

DISADVANTAGES OF RECOMMENDATION

Our recommendation does have some disadvantages. Probably the most significant is the security risk of having a small facility so far removed from the central computer facility, which means that it would not make financial sense to have someone on duty to guard the equipment. Another disadvantage is that some space devoted to student relaxation would be taken and used for another purpose. The placing of a computer facility in a dormitory also raises some new policy questions for the college, including whether only students in the dormitory can use the facility, or whether the facility would be open to all students of the college.

These disadvantages are real, but they can be dealt with. The Vice President for Computing assures us that new electronic security devices reduce the need for security personnel. In a poll taken two weeks ago, the Marshall students indicated that they preferred to see the current lounge converted into a computer facility, 68 percent expressing this preference, 18 percent opposing it, and 14 percent expressing no opinion. Finally, while this proposal does raise some new questions of policy, these questions must be addressed at some point in the near future anyway, as computers and computer facilities become more pervasive in the college.

COSTS AND IMPLEMENTATION PLAN

The following is a tentative and very general outline of the costs of the project as well as an implementation plan. These will have to be refined by the Offices of Student Life and Computing as they begin to work on the project. The Vice President for Computing has assured us, however, that the costs and implementation plan we have outlined here seem reasonable. On her advice, we have not included personnel costs for the time of administrators, since these costs are difficult to calculate and are not usually included in the budgets for small projects of this kind.

Activity	Dates	Costs
Initial planning with students, Student Life and Computing administrators	March	—
Work requests for construction; orders for equipment	April	—
Renovation of lounge	June–July	$15,000
Installation of security devices	Early August	$3,000
Purchase and installation of computer equipment	Late August	$30,000
Total initial costs		$48,000
Ongoing costs; maintenance of equipment		$3,000 per year

The following recommendation, is a more general argument than the preceding formal proposal, but like the preceding argument, its central claim calls for a new course of action.

THE SIDE EFFECTS OF AFFIRMATIVE ACTION

PAMELA J. HSU

In the 1960s, the civil rights movement said people could not be denied things like employment based on race. In the 1970s, affirmative action injected women and minorities into the workplace. In the 1980s, diversity programs stressed appreciating differences among all people. But are we starting to see some negative side effects in the 1990s?

During the past several decades, many programs have promoted the education and employment of women and minorities. Minority scholarships are readily available in just about every field. And most corporations track hiring, retention and promotion of women and minorities, and aim to improve performance in these areas.

As a 24-year-old Chinese woman, I benefit from these programs. I received a generous minority internship/scholarship package from a major corporation one summer during college. When I applied to graduate school, one university offered me a fellowship specifically for minorities entering that particular field of study.

I know that these opportunities have provided a boost in my career. I appreciate them. But there are times when I wish I could have competed against everyone else. I believe my ability would have made me at least a strong contender against all applicants.

I know we have not reached that ideal scenario. I realize that problems still exist and that economic and social conditions prevent some children from getting any chance at all. But we need to look at some of the actions taken in the name of fighting discrimination and promoting diversity to see if they are solving these problems—or just creating different ones.

I'm noticing a growing number of white males who say they are now being discriminated against. I'm talking about the professor who warns his white male students that a particular graduate program may be difficult to get into because they are favoring women and minority candidates. I'm talking about a former employer who ran a department one person short for months, even though many applied for the job, because the position had to be filled by a minority. There's a difference between fairness and force fitting.

Daniel J. Boorstin, the Pulitzer Prize-winning historian and best-selling author, said it best: "We must give everybody a fresh start and not try to compensate for past injustices by creating present injustices."

A growing number of groups are voluntarily segregating themselves from others to preserve ethnic identity. Just take a look at the average college campus, and you'll find Greek houses for minorities and organized student groups for just about every ethnic population. But some may be developing blanket beliefs about their own ethnic group. I've heard that you aren't being true to yourself if you "act" white or you aren't really happy if you've assimilated. The fact that I'm Chinese in blood and American in behavior rubs some people the wrong way. They dub me a Twinkie—yellow on the outside but white on the inside.

I was raised to assimilate, and I don't regret that. Just because I live an American lifestyle doesn't make me any less Chinese. It's ironic that groups which intend to promote an appreciation of their culture among others sometimes fail to reciprocate the respect among their own.

Competition between minority groups may be breeding another problem. One minority group complains that a university gave such-and-such group this much money, and how come they didn't get the same? Columnist William Raspberry pointed out that more students these days search for "discrimination nuggets" because if they find enough of them, they can trade in at the administration building for an ethnic sensitivity course or a minority student center.

It's time to step back and refocus on our ultimate goal. The idea that minority status equals money needs to change. Financial assistance should be available for those who need a chance. Ethnic groups should preserve traditions but not alienate those who do things differently. Sharing traditions with other people and encouraging those who are interested to get more involved—even if they do not belong to that ethnic group—would truly promote diversity.

Source: *Detroit News,* Sunday, 22 May 1994.

Discussion Questions

1. What is the claim of this recommendation? Is it stated explicitly or implied?
2. Does this recommendation emphasize the present, the future, or a combination?
3. How does Hsu support her presentation of the current situation?
4. Discuss with your classmates the overall effectiveness of this recommendation. Can you suggest any further forms of support?

SUGGESTIONS FOR WRITING (9.6)

1. Following the form of the first sample recommendation, write a recommendation report to improve some aspect of your college or university. Possible areas for improvement include dormitories or apartments, the library, the curriculum in your major, or the food service. Make your recommendation as realistic as possible by interviewing people with some responsibility for that area. From these people, you should try to learn why the situation exists in its current form and how feasible your recommendation is as well as to get some sense of the costs of the project. The length of this report will vary with the complexity of the problem and your recommendation, though it might be wise to limit yourself to a maximum of approximately ten pages.

2. Almost every community has its share of white elephants: elaborate projects or expensive buildings that ultimately had to be abandoned or converted to some alternative use because their cost greatly exceeded their benefit to the community. Look for a white elephant in your community and analyze why the project never met its original intentions. Your professor can help you get started. You will almost certainly have to consult the local newspapers and then perhaps the local archives. Since your time is limited and there may be a great deal of documentation, you might have to restrict your research to newspaper accounts of what happened and why. As with Number 1, the maximum length should be approximately ten pages.

3. Working from the outline you prepared for Activity (9.5.3), write a four- to five-page general recommendation emphasizing the future (along the lines of the Hsu sample above). Be sure to include and support all the secondary claims suggested by the Toulmin model.

10

Writing and Image

In our contemporary society of sound bites and spin doctors, the concept of *image* has developed something of a negative flavor, suggesting superficiality and deceit. Public personalities pay a great deal of money to have distinctive images packaged and popularized—images that may bring them enormous success but that bear little relationship to the real people behind them.

This book uses the term *image* differently and more positively, to suggest the ways in which writing honestly reflects to the reader the kind of person the writer is. In successful arguments, writers project an image of intelligence, probity, and trustworthiness. There is nothing false or superficial about this kind of image: these qualities cannot be created out of thin air; they must be true *reflections* of the writer and thus are developed over time and through experience. But whenever you write, you should strive to project such an image, while also being aware that this image will need to be slightly adjusted to fit the context of a given argument.

Image consists of many elements. Most obviously, the quality of the argument itself—its intelligence, honesty, and accuracy—will impress your readers. But image is projected on a smaller scale as well—by your argument's word choice, sentence construction, and figures of speech; by its spelling, punctuation, and physical format; even by its *sound*.

This chapter focuses on some of the conscious choices you'll be making about your image as a writer of argument, choices about voice, diction, metaphor and analogy, emotive language, and the sound of your prose. As you'll see in this chapter, the choices you make will vary from one argument to the next, depending on your subject, your purpose, and your audience.

THE ROLE OF VOICE

A writer's *voice* is the role that he or she takes for a particular occasion, almost like an actor taking a part in a new play. To many inexperienced writers, voice suggests insincerity or fakery, but all of us continually "play" different roles. We behave one way in a classroom, another way playing basketball; we talk to our parents in one way and to our friends in another. Voice is simply the written manifestation of this adaptability.

The following simple example demonstrates the variability of voice:

Dear Mr. Jones:

    At the suggestion of Ms. Hawkins, I am writing to inquire about an opening as an electrical engineer in your firm.

Dear Mom and Dad:

    Hi and help! You won't believe this but I'm broke again. Boy, were my textbooks expensive this quarter!

The same student wrote both of these openings and was completely sincere in both cases but the voices differ markedly. In the first case, the student was formal, polite, restrained. In the second, she was informal and very direct. In cases like these, the choice of a particular voice seems natural; the student did not spend much time or effort choosing these voices. But you can improve your writing by being conscious of the available choices and using them effectively. One crucial choice is between the formal and the informal voices—the voices of the first and second letters, respectively. Using an informal voice in a formal situation may have disastrous effects. What would happen to our student if she wrote to Mr. Jones (whom she presumably does not know) in the following manner?

Dear Mr. Jones:

    Hi and help! I ran into somebody Hawkins—I forget her first name—and she says you've got jobs. Boy, do I need one!

The Importance of Ethos

As the Greek philosopher Aristotle noted, a major element of a successful image is the *ethos* projected by the writer. The ethos is the impression of the writer's character that the reader gets; a positive ethos is one reflecting sincerity and trustworthiness. Readers are likely to accept arguments written by someone who comes across as honest, upright, and unselfish; they will distrust the claims of one known to be dishonest or selfish, or whose voice suggests these traits. So, in your own arguments, try to write from the most principled, unselfish part of yourself. And try not to emulate the ethos projected by the angry writer of the following letter to his campus newspaper:

> The grading policies of this college are rotten, just like everything else here at State. How can the administration put a student on probation for failing a course outside of his major? That's just outrageous. When I got an F in physics, they put me on probation even though I received at least a C in the courses in my major. I didn't want to take physics anyway, and the professor really stunk. Now I'm not eligible to play basketball! When are we students going to force the administration to get rid of this stupid policy?

The reasoning in this letter has many weaknesses, but the writer's failure to establish a respectable ethos also destroys its effectiveness. He presents himself as lacking balance (Is *everything* at State rotten?) and as concerned only about himself (What about the effect of the probation policy on others?). Almost all readers, including fellow students, would dismiss this letter as the howl of outrage that it is; certainly they would not be likely to join forces with the writer in an attempt to change school policy.

When Aristotle urged writers of argument to establish an effective ethos, he was not urging hypocrisy. In creating an ethos, you will present your best side, but this side is still part of you; it is not wholly fabricated. Our outraged student above is doubtless capable of balance and concern for others. Before writing that letter, he should have given himself the time to move from outrage to a broader perspective, using his anger to inspire dissonance but recognizing that hurt feelings and the impulse to dodge responsibility don't advance arguments.

A writer's ethos can be enhanced by the confidence with which his ideas are expressed. You should always appear confident about your claims, though not more confident than their support warrants. A credible ethos finds a balance between dogmatism and apology. Readers suspect writers, such as our angry student, who make sweeping claims (everything at State is rotten) and writers who make forceful statements that they can't possibly support ("the governor is the dumbest woman in the state"). On the other hand, readers will also suspect arguments that seem too wishy-washy: "I think it is probably true that this policy may lead us in the wrong direction."

Let's take a look at how the disgruntled student might create an ethos that works *for,* rather than *against,* him.

> After a painful experience with the academic probation policy here at State, I have concluded that the college should consider revising it. The policy states that any student whose grades fall below a C average will be placed on probation, so that that student will be ineligible for many extracurricular activities. The policy appears reasonable, but its effect is to place too much emphasis on courses outside a student's major. Many students, including three of my acquaintances, have found themselves ineligible to participate in extracurricular activities even though they were doing solid work in their majors. I now find myself in a similar situation, being ineligible to play basketball yet earning grades of C or higher in my major.

Here, the student comes across as someone who is honest about his own situation and also concerned for others, someone who allows for an apparently reasonable opposing view while remaining firm in his own.

ACTIVITIES (10.1)

1. Write a one-page letter to your parents or a friend asking for a loan to help with college expenses. Then write a letter to your college's financial aid office asking for the same loan. With two to three of your classmates, make a list of the differences in the two letters.

2. Go back to Chapter 8 and reread Kevin Maloney's essay "Reading Popular Culture." In a one- to two-page essay, characterize the argument's ethos. Your instructor may want to devote some class time to a discussion of the effectiveness of Maloney's ethos.

THE VIRTUES AND LIMITATIONS OF PLAIN WRITING

Most writing teachers and most writing textbooks encourage students to make their writing clear and straightforward, without distracting embellishments. Perhaps the most famous advocate of this plain style was British writer George Orwell, who formulated the following six stylistic rules in one of the most famous essays about writing style, "Politics and the English Language":

(i) Never use a metaphor, simile or other figure of speech which you are used to seeing in print.

(ii) Never use a long word where a short one will do.

(iii) If it is possible to cut a word out, always cut it out.

(iv) Never use the passive where you can use the active.

(v) Never use a foreign phrase, a scientific word or a jargon word if you can think of any everyday English equivalent.

(vi) Break any of these rules sooner than say anything outright barbarous.

The plain style Orwell urges arose as a reaction against the bloated and often dishonest prose of modern bureaucratic society, where military first strikes are called "anticipatory retaliations," visual materials in school curricula become "integrated systems learning designs," and simple sentences and direct expression disappear behind clouds of vague pomposity: "Please contact my secretary about an appointment regarding the project slippages in implementing the new on-line system." The writer could have said, "Please see me about the delays in starting the new on-line system," but to too many writers today, the first version seems more official, more important. A plain style of writing is an antidote to this swollen prose.

But plain writing carries its own risks, as Orwell notes in his sixth rule. Writers who use the plain style exclusively risk prose that is clear but undistinguished, serviceable but dull. To help you avoid this extreme, here are some friendly amendments to Orwell's rules:

(i) Don't be afraid to use metaphors, similes, or other figures of speech, provided they are not overworked.

(ii) When a long word is the best one, use it.

(iii) Use long sentences for variety and when they best suit your needs.

(iv) Dare to try something different.

(v) Break any of these rules rather than confuse your reader.

The following passage from Annie Dillard's book *The Writing Life* is a good sample of writing that succeeds by going beyond the plain style. The marginal annotations mark instances of enriched prose.

*Effective
exaggeration
-dare to be
different*

*Varied
sentence length*

*Inventive
language*

Ironic humor

It should surprise no one that the life of the writer—such as it is—is colorless to the point of sensory deprivation. Many writers do little else but sit in small rooms recalling the real world. This explains why so many books describe the author's childhood. A writer's childhood may well have been the occasion of his only firsthand experience. Writers read literary biography, and surround themselves with other writers, deliberately to enforce in themselves the ludicrous notion that a reasonable option for occupying yourself on the planet until your life span plays itself out is sitting in a small room for the duration, in the company of pieces of paper.

FIGURES OF SPEECH

A figure of speech involves a "turn" on the literal use of words, or using words to suggest something related to but different from their literal meaning. Two of the most common figures of speech are *metaphor* and *analogy*. A metaphor is an implicit comparison of two unlike subjects so that some aspects of one (usually concrete and familiar) illuminate aspects of the other (usually more abstract or unfamiliar). "The twilight of her career" is a metaphor comparing something concrete and familiar, the end of a day, to something more abstract, in this case the end of someone's career. "Global village" is another metaphor, where the abstract concept of the globe or world (the entire population of the earth) is compared to the more familiar and concrete idea of a village. A *simile,* a variant of a metaphor, is an explicit comparison, where the two subjects are linked by *like* or *as:* "Falling in love is like getting caught in a warm spring rain."

Analogy is like metaphor in that dissimilar subjects are compared, but in analogy, the comparison is usually extended through several points. The "global village" becomes an analogy when the world is compared to a village in several respects, for example, the need for certain agreed-upon laws and the importance of communication and cooperation among those in the community.

The following passage by historian Barbara Tuchman shows the value of metaphor in argument. In the first paragraph of "History as Mirror," Tuchman compares history to a mirror reflecting our own image:

At a time when everyone's mind is on the explosions of the moment, it might seem obtuse of me to discuss the fourteenth century. But I think a backward look at that disordered, violent, bewildered, disintegrating and calamity-prone age can be consoling and possibly instructive in a time of similar disarray. Reflected in a six-hundred-year-old mirror, a more revealing image of ourselves and our species might be seen than is visible in the clutter of circumstances under our noses.

Tuchman could not have made her point about history so succinctly without this metaphor. What aspects of history are clarified through its comparison to a mirror?

The following passage by psychoanalyst Carl Jung contains an effective use of analogy. Here Jung describes the collective mind of twentieth-century humanity through the analogy of a building:

> We have to describe and to explain a building the upper story of which was erected in the nineteenth century; the ground-floor dates from the sixteenth century, and a careful examination of the masonry discloses the fact that it was reconstructed from a dwelling-tower of the eleventh century. In the cellar we discover Roman foundation walls, and under the cellar a filled-in cave, in the floor of which stone tools are found and remnants of glacial fauna in the layers below. That would be a sort of picture of our mental structure.

Of course, Jung could have described the characteristics of the mind in more abstract language, but his description would have been less memorable than this picture of a house with a buried cave underneath. This example demonstrates how analogies crystallize abstract ideas into a sharp picture that both clarifies the ideas and makes them memorable.

Metaphors can also be valuable means of discovery—doors that lead you to important ideas and arguments. We are all naturally disposed to notice correspondences, to see the threads of similarity that unify experience. We have all had the experience of being spontaneously struck by similarities between two seemingly different subjects. Usually our minds hit on such a comparison because it is apt, because it contains a truth that we may not consciously recognize. On close examination, these correspondences or metaphors that come to us may reveal important truths about both subjects and may generate and even structure a theory or argument. When the noted computer scientist Edward Fredkin was struck by the correspondences between the operation of computers and the operation of the universe, he followed up that metaphor, creating a controversial but intriguing theory of digital physics from the implications of a seemingly simple metaphor. Like Fredkin and others, you should be alive to the generating power of your natural metaphor-making tendency, letting it work for you in the ideas you develop and the arguments you write.

Some Cautions About Figures of Speech

Metaphors, similes, and analogies can illuminate and generate ideas, but they can't prove a point; they offer clarification, not evidence. (See Chapter 5 for a discussion of false analogy as an informal fallacy.) Calling the world a village doesn't prove the need for world government. Ultimately all analogies break down if pursued too far; the two subjects of an analogy are, finally, *different* subjects. The world may be a village, but it is a village with more than five billion inhabitants, speaking thousands of different languages and following countless different customs and beliefs. Some village!

Analogies are risky if people take them too literally, as they did the "domino theory" analogy in the 1960s and 1970s. The domino analogy compared countries in Southeast Asia to a row of dominoes. When dominoes are placed on their ends in a row, they will fall down one by one if the first in the series is pushed. According to the domino theory, these countries would fall to communism in the same manner. The domino theory was a major reason for American involvement in Vietnam; American strategists believed that the fall of South Vietnam to the communists would lead to communist control of all of Southeast Asia and perhaps all of Asia. South Vietnam and some other parts of Southeast Asia are now communist, but other countries in Southeast Asia are not and do not seem to be in any danger of falling under such control. The domino theory may not always be this faulty, yet the theory cannot become an excuse for failing to analyze the particular complexities of a specific situation. Real countries are always more complicated than dominoes.

ACTIVITIES (10.2)

1. For one of the following analogies, write a one-page essay analyzing how the analogy illuminates aspects of the situation and how it does not. Our discussion of the "domino theory" above is one example of this kind of analysis.
   a. Sexual politics
   b. The family of humanity
   c. The game of life
   d. The war of ideas
   e. The corporate ladder
2. Write a paragraph that develops an analogy. You may use one of the analogies in Number 1, provided it is not the one you used in that exercise. The paragraph by Carl Jung previously cited is one model for this kind of development.
3. Read a classmate's paragraph from Number 2 above while he or she reads yours. Evaluate the effectiveness of the analogy, and discuss your evaluation with your partner.

CONNOTATIVE LANGUAGE AND SLANTING

Good writers must be aware not only of the *denotations* of words but of their *connotations* as well. The denotation of a word is its explicit meaning, its dictionary definition; the connotation of a word is the meaning or meanings suggested by the word, the word's emotional associations. The denotation of the words *apple pie* is a baked food made with apples. In our society, the connotations of "apple pie" are family life, patriotism, and innocence. Writers of arguments need to be sensitive to the connotations of words and to use these connotations appropriately. A writer urging the development of a suburban tract of land for offices and factories is more likely to succeed by describing it as a "high-tech park" than as an "industrial development area"; the term *high-tech* has a certain vogue, while *"industrial development"* smells of factory smokestacks. And have you noticed how frequently suburban office complexes are called something like Corporate Woods, even when there are few trees anywhere in sight? Beyond a certain point, words used for their connotative value cease to have any meaning at all; there are very few woods in Corporate Woods and nothing fresh in "lemony fresh" soap or in "fresh frozen" juice. And what is so natural about many of the products that advertise themselves as "naturally delicious"? Connotation is an inescapable element of argument, but it should not be used without regard to denotation. Some advertising disregards denotation and gets away with it, but most readers demand higher standards for other kinds of written arguments.

Writers are often tempted to use not only connotation but also blatantly emotional terms as illegitimate supports for their arguments. Suppose you were arguing for a new recreation center on your campus. You might refer to the necessity of having a place "where students can use their free time constructively, letting off the frustrations and pressures caused by rigorous scholastic demands." Here you are portraying students and their needs in a positive way: we tend to respect anyone subjected to "rigorous scholastic demands." But if you were arguing against the recreation center, you could completely alter this impression by using words with negative connotations: "Do our spoiled and spoon-fed students really need another service catering to their already well-satisfied needs?" The respectable students of the first argument have become the undeserving parasites of the second. Words like *spoiled, spoon-fed,* and *catering* are negative words, and their application to the students in question affects a reader's impression of the issue. The words used *slant* the argument, even in the absence of sound evidence. As a writer of responsible arguments, *you* must not fall into the trap of letting such language suggest conclusions your argument does not support.

The temptation to slant is probably strongest in arguments of ethical evaluation; of all the arguments you write, these are the most personal, the most self-revealing, and thus the most important to you. For these reasons, they may tempt you to resort to irrational means to convince your audience. You are not likely to invest high emotional stakes in arguing that four-wheel-drive cars are superior to other kinds of cars, but you can be passionately committed to an argument for or against capital punishment or abortion. Slanting, while almost unavoidable in such cases, must not become a substitute for sound support of your argument. (See Chapter 5 for a discussion of "Emotive Language" and "Circular Argument" as informal fallacies.)

ACTIVITIES (10.3)

With one other student in your class, select a subject to describe. Each of you should then write a description of that subject—one favorable, one unfavorable. Some possible topics are: city life, a particular television show, a book you both have read. Before you write your descriptions, agree on certain qualities to refer to in your descriptions.

THE MUSIC OF LANGUAGE

Any writer who ignores the importance of *sound* in argument is overlooking a valuable tool. We all know the power of advertising's jingles and catch phrases, which linger in our minds even when we wish they wouldn't. Less obvious but powerfully convincing is prose that holds our attention because of a fresh and pleasing combination of sounds. Such prose contains euphony and rhythm.

Euphony, a term which comes from Greek roots meaning "good sound," is a pleasing combination of sounds. We usually think of euphony as a characteristic of poetry or some kinds of prose fiction, but it can and should be present in written arguments as well. Euphony, of course, depends on the ear of the reader or listener, but ears can be trained to become sensitive to this quality of prose, just as we learn to be sensitive to different qualities of music.

Rhythm is a recognizable pattern of sounds through time. In prose, rhythmical units are often divided by grammatical pauses such as commas or periods, though a rhythmical break may also occur at some other place where we would pause to catch our breath if we were reading aloud. "I came, I saw, I conquered" is a simple example of prose rhythm, with three short, rhythmical units divided by commas. All of us have a rhythm to our prose just as we have a rhythm to our breathing or walking, and this rhythm varies with the situation, just as our walking rhythm does. Good prose writers learn to know their prose rhythms, to develop them as they gain experience in writing, and to recognize and use the appropriate rhythm for a specific purpose.

The following passage is from Jeff Greenfield's "The Black and White Truth About Basketball." Note Greenfield's sensitivity to euphony and rhythm:

> Basketball is a struggle for the edge: the half step with which to cut around the defender for a lay-up, the half second of freedom with which to release a jump shot, the instant a head turns allowing a pass to a teammate breaking for the basket. It is an arena for the subtlest of skills: the head fake, the shoulder fake, the shift of body weight to the right and the sudden cut to the left. Deception is crucial to success; and to young men who have learned early and painfully that life is a battle for survival, basketball is one of the few pursuits in which the weapon of deception is a legitimate tactic rather than a source of trouble.

For one thing, this passage makes effective use of the stylistic element of parallelism. Parallelism is the principle that equivalent thoughts demand equivalent expression. Notice how the actions described in the first and second sentences are presented in the same grammatical form: a noun modified by a verbal phrase ("the half step with which to cut around the defender for a layup, the half second of freedom with which to release a jump shot"). In addition to the grammatical parallelism within each of these sentences, Greenfield has made the two sentences parallel to each other: in each, two shorter phrases are followed by a third, longer phrase.

As well as parallelism, Greenfield also makes use of repetition ("half step" and "half second"; "the head fake" and "the shoulder fake") and opposition ("the shift of body weight to the *right* and the sudden cut to the *left*"). The overall effect of these strategies is one of balance—a rhetorical balance that nicely mirrors the physical balance of the intricate choreography of basketball.

The sound of your prose *will* affect how readers react to your argument, even if they are not conscious of the role sound plays in written prose and even if they have not developed the skill to create sound-pleasing prose themselves. As the rhetorician Kenneth Burke has noted, audiences tend to identify with skilled speakers and writers and are likely to be carried along simply by the very structure of the prose. A solid argument that is also aurally effective is hard to beat.

ACTIVITIES (10.4)

Read the following passages and choose the one whose prose style you find most memorable or striking. Write a one- to two-page evaluative argument demonstrating what is effective about the style and why.

1. You know how it is, you want to look and you don't want to look. I can remember the strange feelings I had when I was a kid looking at war photographs in *Life*, the ones that showed dead people or a lot of dead people lying close together in a field or a street, often touching, seeming to hold each other. Even when the picture was sharp and cleanly defined, something wasn't clear at all, something repressed that monitored the images and withheld their essential information. It may have legitimized my fascination, letting me look for as long as I wanted; I didn't have a language for it then, but I remember now the shame I felt, like looking at first porn, all the porn in the world. (Michael Herr. *Dispatches*. London: Picador, 1978. 23.)

2. Commercial exploitation and growing population demands will speed destruction of rain forests as well as oceans, grasslands, lakes, and wetlands. *Pleading ignorance of these vital and fragile ecosystems can only spell global disaster. What can you do?*

   You can accept this invitation to support World Wildlife Fund. *We have a plan for survival. We need your help to make it succeed.* (Letter from the World Wildlife Fund. World Wildlife Fund, 1987. 1.)

3. The stars awaken a certain reverence, because though always present, they are inaccessible; but all natural objects make a kindred impression, when the mind is open to their influence. Nature never wears a mean appearance. Neither does the wisest man extort her secret, and lose his curiosity by finding out all her perfection. Nature never became a toy to a wise spirit. The flowers, the animals, the mountains, reflected the wisdom of his best hour, as much as they had delighted the simplicity of his childhood. (Ralph Waldo Emerson. "Nature." *Essays and Lectures*. Ed. Joel Porte. New York: Library of America, 1983. 9.)

4. Many adults carry high school around with them always. It is a unique, eccentric, and insulated social system, a pressure cooker where teenagers rush from one class to another, shoved into close quarters with twenty-five or thirty others their age they may love, hate, care little about, or hardly know at all. It has its own norms, rituals, vocabulary, and even its own way to tell time— not by the minute and hour but, as sociologist Edgar Friedenberg has pointed out, by periods. As the setting for the adolescent search for identity, high school is, Kurt Vonnegut wrote, "closer to the core of the American experience than anything else I can think of." There is life after high school, but what we do as adults is powerfully shaped by those years. (Myra and David

Sadker. *Failing at Fairness: How America's Schools Cheat Girls.* New York: Scribner's, 1994. 99.)

5. Yes, Virginia, there is a Santa Claus. He exists as certainly as love and generosity and devotion exist, and you know that they abound and give your life its highest beauty and joy. Alas! how dreary would be the world if there were no Santa Claus. It would be as dreary as if there were no Virginias. There would be no child-like faith then, no poetry, no romance to make tolerable this existence. We should have no enjoyment, except in sense and sight. The eternal life with which childhood fills the world would be extinguished. (Francis Pharcellus Church. *New York Sun,* 1897.)

SUMMARY

Writing and Image

- The image you project through your writing is the result of a number of conscious choices you make about your style, your voice, and your use of language.

- You should write clearly, but you should also use various strategies to enrich your prose, including metaphors, similes, and other figures of speech, as well as long words and sentences when appropriate. In general, dare to try something different.

- Metaphor and analogy are valuable for illuminating and generating an argument, but they can never prove a point.

- You must be sensitive to the connotations of words, but you must defend your position with adequate support, not merely with connotation or open slanting.

- You should be sensitive to, and use, euphony and rhythm in your prose.

SUGGESTIONS FOR WRITING (10.5)

1. Write a one-page description of a friend for another friend. Then rewrite the description as a speech describing your friend at a ceremony where he or she will be receiving an award. Have a classmate read both versions and identify the stylistic details of each version.

2. Pick a famous brief essay or speech such as Kennedy's Inaugural Address, Lincoln's Gettysburg Address, or Martin Luther King, Jr.'s "I Have a Dream." Using this essay or speech as a model, try to capture some of the spirit of the original while using your own words and ideas on some topic of your choice in a two- to three-page essay. Pay particular attention to frequently recurring patterns of sentences, and try to use some similar patterns in your own essay.

11

Introductions
and Conclusions

Because your argument's introduction and conclusion are the first and last impression you will make on your readers, they require careful attention. Conclusions—whether a general closing or a specialized summary—are, of course, almost always composed late in the writing process, when you know exactly what it is your argument has concluded. Some writers compose introductions before they write the actual argument, but many delay until the last stage of the first draft, when they know more clearly what is to be introduced. This chapter discusses the importance of effective openings and closings and makes some suggestions for writing them.

INTRODUCTIONS

Because it is your readers' initial experience with your argument, your introduction must be particularly appealing to them. Regardless of what form your introduction takes, it is the hook that draws your readers into your argument.

The style and content of your introduction will be influenced by your argument's context (the occasion and audience for which it is written) and by its length, tone, and level of complexity. But no matter how you choose to open your argument, the basic purpose of any introduction is the same: to engage your readers. Usually an introduction succeeds in engaging readers if it is clear and inviting. Of these two features, clarity—the precise and accurate expression of carefully considered ideas—is probably the easiest to achieve, though for many writers it comes only with careful thought and considerable revision. To be inviting, your introduction must stimulate your readers' interest, as well as arouse their curiosity about the rest of the argument. Since being inviting is, for most of us, a learned skill, we offer some strategies for writing engaging introductions.

Strategies for General Introductions

Introduction by Narrative. Writers of "general interest" arguments (nontechnical arguments intended for a broad audience) often gain their readers' attention by opening their essay with a specific anecdote or short narrative. This kind of opening engages readers in two ways: first, in its narrative approach, it satisfies our delight in being told a story, and second, it gains our interest by its *particularity*—its details about people, places, and events that give readers a firm footing as they enter an unknown text. An essay entitled "Boring from Within," by English professor Wayne C. Booth, begins with the following paragraph:

> Last week I had for about the hundredth time an experience that always disturbs me. Riding on a train, I found myself talking with my seat-mate, who asked me what I did for a living. "I teach English." Do you have any trouble predicting his response? His face fell, and he groaned, "Oh, dear, I'll have to watch my language." In my experience there are only two other possible reactions. The first is even less inspiring: "I hated English in school; it was my worst subject." The second, so rare as to make an honest English teacher almost burst into tears of gratitude when it occurs, is an animated conversation about literature, or ideas, or the American language—the kind of conversation that shows a continuing respect for "English" as something more than being sure about *who* and *whom, lie* and *lay*.

Booth's essay, addressed to high school English teachers, goes on to identify the ways in which English is mis-taught and to suggest alternative teaching methods. As a renowned college professor addressing high school teachers about the problems of high school instruction, Booth must be careful not to alienate his audience by coming across as superior or critical. He does this in part by opening the essay (initially an oral address) with this personal anecdote, which immediately, but tacitly, says "I am one of you." As well as disarming his audience with the personal references, Booth captures their attention with the simultaneous specificity and universality of effective narrative.

Introduction by Generalization. Good introductions can also begin with a strong, unambiguous generalization related to the readers' experiences, as in the following opening paragraph of an article by David Brown published in a medical society journal:

> Few honorable professions have as much inherent hostility toward one another as medicine and journalism. Ask a doctor to describe journalists and you are likely to hear adjectives such as "negative," "sensationalistic," and "superficial." Ask a journalist about doctors, and you will probably hear about "arrogance," "paternalism," and "jargon."

Broad statements such as this should be limited and developed in succeeding sentences or a succeeding paragraph. In the second paragraph of this essay, the writer both justifies and develops the generalization made in the first paragraph.

> The descriptions are the common stereotypes and not wholly inaccurate, for the two professions occupy distant worlds. Physicians are schooled in confidence and collegiality; journalists seek to make knowledge public.

Physicians speak the language of science; journalists are largely ignorant of science. Physicians inhabit a world of contingencies and caveats; journalists inhabit a world where time and audience require simplification. Physicians are used to getting their way; journalists are used to getting their story.

This paragraph's development of the idea contained in the initial paragraph is echoed by the writer's syntax (the arrangement of his words): the last four sentences, neatly divided by semicolons into opposing clauses, emphasize the focus on this professional opposition.

Introduction by Quotation.   Some introductions begin with quotations that are eventually connected to the topic of the essay. While perhaps overused and over-taught, this technique *does* work if practiced thoughtfully. The writer using an opening quotation must be sure that it can be made to apply to the subject in an interesting way, and that the quotation is interesting, provocative, or well written (preferably all three). The following paragraph in an essay by Marilyn Yalom is a successful example of this technique:

> When Robert Browning wrote his famous lines "Grow old along with me!/The best is yet to be,/The last of life, for which the first was made," he was undoubtedly not thinking about women. The poet's Victorian optimism is difficult enough to reconcile with the realities of old age for men, and virtually impossible when we consider the condition of older women in the nineteenth century.

As in the article about the antagonism between the medical and journalistic professions, the initial statement here is immediately explained and developed in the succeeding sentence. Here, in fact, the explanatory sentence is also the claim of this essay on the older woman in Victorian England and America.

Other Types of Introductions.   There are a number of other strategies for making arguments inviting to your readers: startling statistics, a brief historical survey of the topic (which can have the same charm as the narrative introduction), a particularly startling or shocking statement (provided, of course, that it is relevant to the content of your argument), and even a direct announcement of the argument's subject (as in "This is an article about bad writing"). Any of these tactics will work as long as it connects in some way with the body of the argument.

Introductions in Professional Writing

Introductions written in a professional context according to established formats don't need to be as inviting as the previous examples, largely because readers of professional reports usually don't have much choice about whether or not to read a given report. Rather than trying to engage their readers, on-the-job writers are concerned about serving the needs of a known audience who will make some use of the report. In these cases, introductions are successful if they accurately represent the report's content. Company policy often dictates the form of a preliminary summary: some companies require an initial outline, others an abstract, still others a summary reflecting both organization and content. When the form is not dictated, the most useful is a simple summary of organization and content.

Take as an example an analysis of problems in customer relations assigned to a customer service representative of a local grocery chain. In her report, the representative first identifies, describes, and documents the different conditions she has found to be damaging to good customer relations: inadequate customer check-cashing privileges, a time-consuming refund policy, impolite carryout personnel, and inaccurate advertising of sale prices. She then estimates the loss of business resulting from each problem. Finally, she recommends possible solutions to the problems she has identified. Her report is clearly written and organized, but it is also lengthy and somewhat complex; it needs an introduction that will prepare its readers not only for the content of the report but also for the arrangement of its material. The preliminary summary will prepare readers for the sequence of the argument's main points, and it will serve as a useful reference should the readers become confused while reading the full report.

Our customer service representative introduces her report with the following preliminary summary:

> This report examines the recent quarterly decline in business at the seven Goodbelly stores. It attributes this loss of revenue to at least four remediable problems in the area of customer relations: (1) inadequate check-cashing privileges, (2) a time-consuming refund policy, (3) lack of concern for customers by carryout personnel, and (4) inaccurate advertising of sale prices. It is estimated that these difficulties may have cost Goodbelly's as much as $300,000 in revenue in the past three months. This report concludes by recommending specific personnel and policy measures to be taken to ease these difficulties and to regain the lost business.

Without being painstakingly mechanical, this brief paragraph identifies the central claim of the report (that the decline in revenue is due to poor customer relations) and prepares the reader for the organization and content of the argument. While an introduction such as this one may not engage a reader who has neither an interest in nor an obligation to the company, its concise and accurate representation of the report's content will be extremely useful to the obligated reader.

General Suggestions About Introductions

Finally, you may find these general suggestions about writing introductions useful:

1. Try writing your introduction *after* you've written your first draft. Often there's no point in agonizing over a preliminary summary for a professional report or a catchy introduction for a general interest argument before you know exactly how the argument is going to evolve. Even if you're working from a detailed outline, your organization and content will change as you compose.

2. On those rare occasions when a catchy opening sentence or paragraph comes to you early, giving you a hold on the overall structure, tone, and style of your argument, don't let this opening get away!

3. Don't make your introduction too long. Even the most interesting, captivating introduction is going to seem silly if it's twice as long as the argument itself. The turbot, a variety of anglerfish, has a head that takes up half of its total body length and is one of the silliest looking fish on the planet. Don't follow its example.

4. Make sure your introduction is truly representative of the entire argument. If you are writing a preliminary summary, be sure all the main points of the argument are covered in the introduction. In a less formal argument, don't let your desire to be engaging lure you into writing an introduction that is stylistically or tonally inconsistent with the rest of the argument. In short, the opening paragraph should never look as if it has been tacked on merely to attract reader interest, with no thought about its relationship to what follows. Rather, it should resemble an operatic overture, beautiful in its own right, but always preparing its audience for what is to follow.

ACTIVITIES (11.1)

1. For one of the following writing tasks, write two different introductory paragraphs using two of the tactics discussed in the preceding section: narrative, generalization, quotation, startling statistics, a brief historical survey, a startling statement, or an outright announcement of claim. Then write a two- to three-sentence description of the different effects of the two introductions.
   a. An essay on a relative whom you admire
   b. An essay on a law or policy of the federal government that you strongly support or oppose
   c. An essay on your favorite food
   d. An editorial in your local newspaper opposing teenage curfew
   e. A report to your supervisor (or a parent or a friend) explaining why you have failed to accomplish all the goals you set for yourself six months ago
2. For one of the arguments you have already written for this class, write (or rewrite) an introductory paragraph following the suggestions offered in the preceding discussion.
3. Working on a different argument written for this course, compose an opening paragraph that begins at a general level and ends with the argument's claim.

CONCLUSIONS

Once you have selected and presented the best possible support for your argument, you may feel that you have nothing more to say on the subject. But you're not finished yet. Until you have provided a final closing, a conclusion that rounds out your argument, your argument is incomplete. Most readers need to feel closure in all kinds of writing: letters, imaginative literature, and arguments.

Conclusions are not always easy to write, particularly because by the time we get around to thinking about writing an ending, we're often tired of the whole project. But you don't need to be a master rhetorician to write an effective ending. A conclusion that is direct, precise, and appropriate to the occasion will do the job just fine. Depending on the context, it can be as short as a paragraph or as long as a chapter.

Types of Conclusions

Arguments can have three basic types of conclusions: the findings or results of an investigation, a recommendation or set of recommendations, or a more general closing reflecting on the argument or raising other considerations related to the central claim.

Findings.   The findings or results conclusion usually ends an argument of fact, such as the reporting of a scientific experiment or a case study. Some causal arguments, such as certain historical studies, may also end with findings or results. Actually these findings are the argument's claim, which may be given in general form early in the argument and then with more detail at the end, or they may be given only at the end. The following paragraph (the second-to-last paragraph of an essay titled "Particle Accelerators Test Cosmological Theory") exemplifies the findings type of conclusion:

> Preliminary results from the machines indicate that there are at most five families of elementary particles. David B. Cline of the University of California at Los Angeles and the University of Wisconsin at Madison . . . has shown that the lifetime of the $Z°$ boson [a subatomic particle] is approximately what one would expect with just three families. Experimental uncertainties, however, allow for two additional kinds of neutrinos [another subatomic particle] and hence two additional families. . . . For the first time accelerators are counting neutrino types and getting a small number, one that was predicted by cosmological theory.

Recommendation.   Not surprisingly, recommendations typically conclude arguments of recommendation. Their purpose is to tell readers exactly what the argument expects of them. If the findings conclusion tells readers what they should *know,* the recommendation conclusion tells them what they should *do.* An example of this type of conclusion is found at the end of "A Proposal for a Computer Facility in Marshall Dormitory" in Chapter 9 of this book. The proposal ends with a "Costs and Implementation Plan" section that spells out in some detail the actions that need to be taken. In this proposal, the more general recommendations came earlier, so ending with more specific steps is a suitable way to conclude. In many other cases, the most appropriate conclusion is a general recommendation, as in this last paragraph from an essay titled "U.S. Economic Growth":

> Only if we increase investment in both capital and technology in all sectors of the U.S. economy (particularly manufacturing) and improve the quality of labor at all levels can the American standard of living rise at an acceptable rate. In the present highly competitive world market the U.S. has some historically demonstrated advantages, but it must take the longer view and pursue those seemingly trivial increases of a few tenths of a percentage point in growth rate each year.

General Closing.   The general closing is what we usually think of when we think of conclusions. This type of conclusion can work in several ways: it can move from the specific argument to a statement of the argument's broader significance, it can suggest future directions for research, or it can raise related issues. The general closing suggests a movement *onward* (where we go from here) or a movement *outward* (how this specific argument relates to other arguments), though the emphasis in any case will vary between these two elements.

The following paragraph (the closing of Mike Messner's "Sports and the Politics of Inequality") exemplifies a conclusion that moves to a consideration of an argument's broader significance:

> If this discussion of sports and inequality seems to make contradictory points, it is because sports plays a contradictory role in the larger politics of inequality. On an ideological level, sports strengthens and legitimates class and ethnic inequalities in society while simultaneously providing cultural space where ideologies supporting inequalities can be challenged and debunked. And for participants, sports offers a place where class and ethnic antagonisms and prejudices can be destructively played out *and* it can offer a space where participants can experience transcendent moments of play which are relatively free from the larger social inequities. In this space, it is possible to discover ourselves and each other as human beings. What all this means is that the role sports will play in the politics of inequality will be determined by "how we play the game," both individually and collectively.

The final paragraph of "Particle Accelerators Test Cosmological Theory" (cited previously) demonstrates the concluding strategy of pointing to new directions and future possibilities:

> The next step promises to be even more exciting. As new accelerators are completed and begin producing more data with fewer uncertainties the cosmological limit of three or at most four families will be checked with extreme accuracy. . . . The machines will probe the early universe with an effectiveness that no telescope will ever match.

A conclusion that raises related issues is found in the last two paragraphs of George Orwell's famous essay "Politics and the English Language." Throughout most of the essay, Orwell gives examples of bad English. But toward the end of the essay, he suggests connections between corrupt language and corrupt political systems. The final paragraph addresses this connection directly:

> One ought to recognize that the present political chaos is connected with the decay of language, and that one can probably bring about some improvement by starting at the verbal end. If you simplify your English, you are freed from the worst follies of orthodoxy. You cannot speak any of the necessary dialects, and when you make a stupid remark its stupidity will be obvious, even to yourself. Political language—and with variations this is true of all political parties, from Conservatives to Anarchists—is designed to make lies sound truthful and murder respectable, and to give

an appearance of solidity to pure wind. One cannot change this all in a moment, but one can at least change one's own habits, and from time to time one can even, if one jeers loudly enough, send some *melting pot, acid test, veritable inferno,* or other lump of verbal refuse—into the dustbin where it belongs.

A conclusion can contain more than one of the three basic types described above. The second-to-last paragraph of "Particle Accelerators Test Cosmological Theory" presents the results of the research, while the very last paragraph presents a statement on the future directions of this research. A results or recommendation conclusion may be supplemented with a more general conclusion that opens the argument outward.

A word of caution about all conclusions: The conclusion must not lie outside the boundaries of what you can legitimately claim in your argument. You should not, for example, turn an argument about the weakness of a certain school's curriculum into a conclusion uniformly condemning all schools, though your conclusion may suggest that the case you have examined is not an isolated one. In other words don't overgeneralize from the evidence you used to support your argument. Nor should you use your conclusion as the place to launch a whole new argument or to make claims that do not have some basis in what has preceded.

SUMMARIES

A conclusion is different from a *summary,* which is a restatement of the main points of your argument. Most short or medium-length arguments (five hundred to five thousand words) do not require a summary; final summaries are typically found in very long essays, in essays with difficult subject matter, or in books. This book, for example, uses sentence summaries at the end of each chapter to stress certain key points to an audience new to much of this material.

Writers of arguments sometimes provide a summary of the basic points *preceding* the argument. Such summaries are usually either separate from or at the very beginning of the argument. Typically they take one of two forms: the *abstract,* often used in academic or technical research, and the *executive summary,* often used in business reports and proposals.

An abstract is a summary, typically in paragraph form, that states the essential points of the essay so that readers can grasp these points without having to read the essay; in other words, the good abstract can stand alone, being meaningful by itself. If the readers read only the abstract, they will of course miss much of the argument, especially its support, but they will at least know what the argument's main claims are. With the flood of information confronting us all, abstracts have the obvious value of helping us decide what research needs further investigation and what can be left alone.

The following summary by King-Kok Cheung of her essay on Alice Walker's *Color Purple* and Maxine Hong Kingston's *Woman Warrior* is a good example of an abstract for academic writing:

The Color Purple and *The Woman Warrior* exhibit parallel narrative strategies. The respectively black and Chinese American protagonists work their way from speechlessness to eloquence by breaking through the constraints of sex, race, and language. The heroines turn to masculine figures for guidance, to female models for inspiration, and to native idioms for stylistic innovation. Initially unable to speak, they develop distinctive voices by registering their own unspoken grief on paper and, more important, by recording and emulating the voices of women from their respective ethnic communities. Through these testimonies, each written in a bicultural language, Walker and Kingston reveal the obstacles and resources peculiar to minority women. Subverting patriarchal literary traditions by reclaiming a mother tongue that carries a rich oral tradition (of which women are guardians) the authors artfully coordinate the tasks of breaking silence, acknowledging female influence, and redefining while preserving ethnic characteristics.

Here is an example of an abstract introducing a technical argument, "Cutting into Cholesterol," written by Bruce P. Kinosian and John M. Eisenberg:

We performed an analysis of the cost-effectiveness of treating individuals with significantly elevated levels of total serum cholesterol (>6.85 mmol/L [>265 mg/dL]), comparing treatment with three alternative agents: cholestyramine resin, colestipol, and oat bran (a soluble fiber). We simulated a program for lowering cholesterol levels that was similar to that of the Coronary Primary Prevention Trial, and then used the outcomes of the trial to calculate the incremental cost per year of life saved (YOLS) from the perspective of society. Our findings suggest that the cost per YOLS ranges from $117 400 (cholestyramine resin packets) to $70 900 (colestipol packets) and $17 800 (oat bran). Using bulk drug reduces the cost per YOLS to $65 100 (cholestyramine resin) and $63 900 (colestipol). Targeting bulk colestipol treatment only to smokers has a cost per YOLS of $47 010; the incremental cost of treating nonsmokers would be $89 600 per additional YOLS. Although pharmacologic therapy has substantial costs, it may be more cost-effective when low-cost forms are applied to particular high-risk groups, such as smokers. However, a broad public health approach to lowered cholesterol levels by additional dietary modification, such as with soluble fiber, may be preferred to a medically oriented campaign that focuses on drug therapy.

Executive summaries are often longer than abstracts, though they should not usually be longer than a page. Like abstracts, they give the main points of an argument, but they may also contain some background on why the report was written and on the scope of the original study. If the executive summary is of a recommendation report, the major recommendation should be included in it. Like abstracts, executive summaries should be written to stand alone; readers should be able to get the major points of the report without referring to the report itself.

The following is a sample executive summary with a format that might be used by a group auditing the overall effectiveness of a university computer center:

The audit completed a review of the Johnston Computer Center in February 1994. The Johnston Computer Center is one of three academic computing centers at the university and contains terminals and microcomputers for up to 200 on-site users, with access also available for up to 50 off-site users, so that it the second largest of such centers at the university.

The objectives of our review were to determine whether present and planned center operations are fulfilling user needs and are in compliance with university policies and procedures for computer security.

In our opinion, the center's operation is satisfactory in meeting the needs of its users and in using its internal resources to meet these needs, but unsatisfactory in meeting security policies and procedures.

Our survey of Johnston Computer Center users indicated that user satisfaction is high and that center personnel are responsive to user needs. While system response time has deteriorated in the last six months because of an unexpected increase in user demand, center management has addressed this problem by encouraging users to use the system during nonpeak hours and by recommending a hardware upgrade to the Vice President for Systems and Computing.

Our review of security showed that unauthorized users could gain access to and change another user's files. Since the center's computers are not directly connected to the university's administrative computers, which do contain other security safeguards, the university does not face a risk to its financial and personnel records because of these deficiencies. The student and faculty academic files contained in the center's computers are at risk, however. The center has reported three instances of tampering in the last six months. Center management is eager to address this problem but will need additional resources to purchase software and to obtain the necessary technical assistance.

Executive summaries have become increasingly common as business executives and other managers find themselves confronted with an overwhelming number of reports to read. The executive summary allows readers to decide if they want to read further, or if the summary alone provides enough information. Unlike abstracts, which are often intended for a specialist audience, executive summaries usually have a nonspecialist audience of higher managers who may be very far removed from the technical details of the report. The executive summary should allow for the audience's lack of familiarity with these details by avoiding specialized vocabulary whenever possible and by defining any specialized terms that are used. In other words, executive summaries demand great attention to the readers' needs and great precision in wording. Typically they are written after the report is finished, when the writer knows all its twists and turns.

ACTIVITIES (11.2)

1. Return to an argument you have written for this course, and write two different conclusions for it: first, a general closing, and second, a conclusion re-

stating the argument's findings or results. Give your argument and these two conclusions to a classmate to read; discuss with him or her which of the two conclusions seems more appropriate to its context.

2. Find a different argument from the one you used above and write a 250-word abstract (one double-spaced page) of the argument.

SUMMARY

Introductions and Conclusions

- The context of your argument will influence the style, content, and length of your introduction, but all introductions should be clear, engaging, and appropriate to the occasion.

- Some useful tactics for general introductions are:
  - Introduction by narrative
  - Introduction by generalization
  - Introduction by quotation

- Introductions of arguments in formal, professional writing should be precisely representative of the content of the report.

- Conclusions are usually one of three basic types: findings or results, a recommendation or set of recommendations, or a general closing. Which type of conclusion you use depends on the type of argument. Findings or results typically conclude reports of scientific experiments or case studies. Recommendations conclude recommendation reports. General closings are used for other types of arguments, especially interpretations and evaluations. The general closing has three subtypes: a statement of significance, suggested directions for research, and a raising of related issues.

- Do not confuse a conclusion with a summary. A summary is a restatement of the main points of your argument. There are three types of summaries: the ending summary, the abstract, and the executive summary. *Ending summaries* are typically found in books and in very complex or very long essays or reports. *Abstracts* and *executive summaries* are typically found at the beginning of or separate from the arguments on which they are based. Readers should be able to understand an abstract or an executive summary without referring to the report or essay on which it is based.

SUGGESTIONS FOR WRITING (11.3)

1. Locate a section of a newspaper or magazine that presents several editorial or opinion essays (the Sunday *New York Times* op-ed page is an excellent source; your local Sunday paper may have its own version). Examine the types

of conclusions used for three pieces, and write an essay of two to three pages describing the type of each conclusion, its effect on readers, and its overall effectiveness. Which of the three do you find the most effective? Why? Be sure to give your instructor a copy of the op-ed page you use for this assignment.

2. Write a one-paragraph executive summary one of your last papers, making sure that your readers will be able to understand the summary without reading the paper. When you hand in this assignment, give your instructor both the summary and the paper on which it is based.

12

Revising

Finally, you've finished your argument. It has an introduction and a conclusion, a claim and appropriate support, and you're ready to hand it over to your instructor with a sigh of relief.

But not so fast. You've certainly earned a break—writing is hard work—but if you want your paper to be as good as it can be, you've got to find the time and the energy for another crucial step in the writing process: revising.

Revising your argument means stepping back from it and seeing it whole. As the word's Latin roots (*re*—"again," and *visere*—"to look at") indicate, to revise is to see again, to have a new vision of the entire work. Sometimes this new vision leads to dramatic changes in any part of the argument, though the more attention you pay to the content and organization of your argument as you're writing the first draft, the fewer the major changes you will need to make (yes, that paper you've just finished is a only a first draft, not a finished argument). But even the most carefully composed first draft will require some changes. So, if you're not in the habit, it's time to make a practice of allowing plenty of time and attention for revision. It will pay off. Some people revise *as* they write, adjusting earlier parts of the argument to fit better with what they've just written or are about to write. This is a perfectly good practice that can save you time later on, but it shouldn't take the place of the revising process outlined below.

WRITING A FIRST DRAFT, REVISING, AND EDITING

Don't confuse revising with editing. Editing is a careful check of the spelling, grammar, punctuation, and overall consistency of a manuscript. Revising, as noted, is a more profound look at the argument's entire content, shape, and style. Revising involves considerable judgment on your part, because questions about claim, support, and style rarely have simple right or wrong answers. On the other hand, most questions about editing do have right or wrong answers; there are only so many ways to spell a word or to punctuate a sentence correctly.

Writing your first draft, revising, and editing require different attitudes and use somewhat different skills. Writing the first draft requires energy and egoism to keep you going through the bumpy parts; revising calls for detachment and reflection; and editing demands close attention to detail. Attempting a "perfect" first draft is actually one of the most dangerous and laborious ways to write. It is dangerous because you will lack the necessary distance to judge the quality of your argument, and laborious because you are trying to combine these three separate tasks. To some extent, of course, revising and editing occur during the writing of any draft; we all make minor changes in wording, organization, and mechanics even in the early stage of writing, and sometimes we decide on major changes as we write. Inserting these changes then makes sense, but you still need to set aside time for revising and editing, making each your major preoccupation in a separate review of the manuscript.

Many college students feel that they don't have time for anything but a first draft; in fact, they usually do. Students of roughly equal ability and with roughly the same amount of time available work in amazingly different ways, some finishing their work with plenty of time to spare, others doing everything at the last minute. Most students who claim that they were forced to write their papers just before the due date mean that writing the paper was not their highest priority and they could get motivated to write it only by the pressure of a deadline. Especially with word processing, writers who write a first draft, leave it for a while, and then revise it do not spend any more time writing than those who try to write just one polished draft.

SOME SUGGESTIONS FOR SUCCESSFUL REVISING

Offered here are some suggestions aimed at making your revising stage as effective as possible. These suggestions are based on years of writing experience, but they are only suggestions, not ironclad rules.

Suggestion 1: Give Yourself Some Breathing Space

After you've finished your first draft, give yourself some time—at least twenty-four hours—before you begin the revising process. This "breathing space" gives you some distance from your work, which you will need in order to review it objectively. And it gives your unconscious an opportunity to mull over the material, so that when you return to the argument, you'll find you have fresh ideas about how to make it more effective. You've probably had the experience of rereading a graded paper and wondering how you could have missed the problems that seem so obvious to you now (and that were far too obvious to your instructor). Putting some distance between first draft and the revision gives you an opportunity to gain this fresh perspective, and to put it to use *before* your paper is graded.

Suggestion 2: Avoid the Red Pen

As you're reviewing your first draft, avoid the lure of the red pen—the temptation to make small editorial changes before you have reread and assimilated the argument as a whole. Reread with your hands tied behind your back (figuratively, that is), and you'll get a much better sense of how the draft works as a whole.

Suggestion 3: Review Your Original Purpose and Audience

In writing your first draft, you've been intent on coming up with the right word and composing individual sentences. It's easy at this level to lose touch with your original purpose and intended audience. So an important question to ask yourself as you're rereading and revising is whether you've fulfilled your original purpose for your intended audience (of course, your original purpose and audience may have changed during the first draft, but that should be your conscious choice, not an accident).

It can be helpful to review your argument pretending that you're one of its intended readers. From this perspective, you can ask yourself: Do I understand the purpose and claim of this argument? Are the vocabulary and specialized terms clear to me? Is the argument meaningful to me? Am I convinced by the argument?

Suggestion 4: Review Your Organization

In reviewing the effectiveness of your argument, you'll need to consider not only your purpose and audience, but also the overall organization of what you've written, making sure that the parts fit together well and are logically sequenced, that nothing crucial is omitted, and that the structure is lean, with a minimum of repetition. If it's hard to keep the organization in mind, try reproducing it in outline form, as in the model below. Remember, you're outlining what you actually wrote, not what you intended to write. If you actually wrote your draft from an outline, don't look at it until you have completed this new one.

   I. Introduction (if appropriate)
  II. Claim (if appropriate)
 III. Supporting arguments:
     A.
     B.
     C.
     D.
 IV. Conclusion or summary (if appropriate)

If you have trouble constructing this new outline, your argument probably has organizational problems that need attention.

This is also a good time to review the effectiveness of your claim and your introduction. Ask yourself these questions: If I have an explicit claim, is it clearly stated? If it is implied, will my readers recognize it? Does my introduction prepare my readers for what follows? Should it be more interesting?

Suggestion 5: Review Your Argument's Coherence

Even the most carefully organized argument will puzzle readers if the relationship between its parts is not indicated in some way. In certain professions and businesses, standard formats include headings like "Introduction," "The Problem," "History," and so on. But such headings are inappropriate in many settings. You can make the elements of your argument *coherent*—establish their relationship to one another and to the whole—by using simple transitional words and expressions that indicate the nature of the relationship.

Words like *therefore, thus, so,* and *consequently* identify a conclusion and its evidence. Words like *but, however,* and *on the other hand* indicate exceptions to a stated point. You can alert your reader to the introduction of each new piece of support by using indicators such as *first . . . , second . . . , and furthermore,* and *finally.* Transitional words and expressions such as these are enormously useful to readers of arguments, particularly when the argument is long or elaborate. They help readers understand how one statement or section that may otherwise seem a digression or an irrelevancy relates to what has gone before or what might come later.

As well as using such brief signposts, you can also be quite direct about the role of different parts of your argument. Public speakers are often very explicit about the function of crucial parts of their speeches: "Let me give you two reasons why this land should be developed," or "To conclude, I'd like to remind you of a few lines by Walt Whitman." Such obvious signs are crucial when there is no written text for an audience to follow and ponder. But indicators such as these can be used in written argument as well, especially when the parts are many and complex.

Suggestion 6: Review Your Style

The revising stage is the time to consider the effectiveness of your argument's style: its tone, word choice, and general treatment of the reader. As discussed in Chapter 10, style is a crucial component of argument, often playing a major role in convincing or alienating readers. Poor style is just as damaging to an argument as a vague or unsupported claim; an effective style is just as convincing as compelling evidence. And while you're considering your style, think about the ethos projected by your argument: Does the argument reflect a writer who is fair, openminded, and appropriately confident?

This is also a good time to ask yourself if you have followed Orwell's rules for clarity, along with the friendly amendments offered in Chapter 10. Finally, check your draft to see if you have (1) used connotation effectively, (2) avoided slanting, (3) used metaphor and analogy effectively, and (4) paid attention to the sounds of words. Some of these questions will naturally occur during your consideration of claim (if you have one) and the organization of its support, as well as during your review of audience and purpose.

Suggestion 7: Review Your Argument for Faulty Reasoning

Chapter 5 introduced some basic principles of logic that will help you set up a reasonable argument. The "informal fallacies" presented there are most easily detected during the revision stage. As a final step in reviewing your argument, read it through to detect any unwitting fallacies, paying special attention to those that are particularly common in the kind of argument you've written.

Suggestion 8: Use a Word Processor

Fortunately (some students would say unfortunately), revising may lead to a drastic overhaul of your argument. But if you want your argument to be as good as it can be, you won't ignore the opportunity to make these major changes. Most students now write their papers on computers, which make large- and small-scale revising much easier than any other method. If you're one of those people who have resisted the move to computers, we strongly urge you to make the change. With a computer and a good word-processing program, you can switch entire sections of a draft around with ease; change words swiftly and even "globally," so that one word replaces another throughout an entire essay; and make corrections with no trace of erasures or correction fluid. Virtually all campuses have computer labs for their students, which save the expense of purchasing your own computer. And while a computer will not make you a better writer, it will give you the chance to make yourself a better writer. So get wired!

ACTIVITIES (12.1)

1. Write an outline of a paper or a draft of a paper that you have written for this class, using the format given in Suggestion 4. Then exchange this paper or draft with one of your classmates, while keeping your outline. Now prepare an outline of your classmate's paper, again using the same format, and then exchange outlines with your classmate. Compare your classmate's outline with your own. Do the two outlines agree on what the claim is and what the supporting arguments are? If there are disagreements, discuss these with your classmate. Find out why he or she saw your argument working in a different way than you did. Remember that if there is disagreement, you cannot simply assume that your classmate is wrong and you are correct: the purpose of your argument is to convince the reader, not yourself. After this discussion, make a list of the changes or possible changes you would make in your paper in the next draft.
2. Have a classmate read a clean copy of one of the papers you have written for this course. Ask him or her to write a one-page description of the overall image reflected in that paper and a one-page evaluation of that image. Do the same for a paper written by your classmate.

SUMMARY

Revising

- You should plan to spend separate portions of time writing a draft, revising, and editing.
- Allow breathing space between writing a draft and revising it. In your first review of the draft, concentrate on how the draft works as a whole.
- In revising, review your original purpose and audience, your organization, the adequacy and logic of your support, and your style.
- Knowing the principles of logic is a significant help in reviewing your draft.
- Using a word processor makes revising much easier.

AN EXAMPLE OF REVISION

Having read your manuscript all the way through at least once, and preferably twice, you are now ready to make major changes if they are needed. By avoiding the red pen until you have reviewed the entire manuscript, you are more likely to recognize the need for such major changes, and less likely to get lost in grieving over minor errors.

The following sample student essay is a good example of how to correct major problems in an argument. What follows is the first draft of the essay, along with the student's notes for revision, which he wrote in the margins during a second and third reading of the draft.

Drop- this idea not followed up ‖

When we think about computers, we usually think about how helpful they are to us: they enable us to process huge amounts of data, prepare large written documents with an ease undreamt of even twenty years ago, and by acting as the "brains" of robots, help us perform dangerous or monotonous tasks. But we often fail to think of the negative side of computers, including the threat they pose to our privacy. Also, in many cases, computers are replacing human labor in factories and offices.

One thing computers are used for is to store information about people. These computers contain databases, which are collections of discrete data that are divided into fields, such as age, sex, income, and place of residence. A user of a database can pull information out of the database on everyone who fits a category made up of some or all of these fields, such as every male between thirty and forty who earns between thirty and fifty thousand dollars a year and lives in Florida. An example of a database is the Internal Revenue Service's database, which contains basic information on tax returns along with demographic information on those who pay taxes. Other databases contain credit histories. If you have someone's Social Security number, you can find out just about anything you want about that person. Not just anybody can do this, but there are already too many people who can.

overstated →

A separate point, not related to ¶. Also, I have no proof. →

wordy, vague

As if it isn't bad enough to have someone go through all the information about you in one database, databases can even be linked to other databases because of the increased networking power of computers today. Having this ability leads to the potential problem of wrong information being kept on a person (especially if no written records are kept). Computers do fail, but the most important reason why a database would contain wrong information about someone would be because someone typed in incorrect information. If the police used computer databases to keep track of criminal records

Too many separate ideas in this ¶: Networking, human error, lack of paper copies. These need separate treatment.

without having another record of them on
paper somewhere, anyone could input harmful
data on innocent people that could cause
them a great deal of misery.

If the major problem with the accuracy
of information in databases is human error,
then perhaps new forms of electronic entry
of data will eliminate some of these
errors. Our phone bills are one example of
a completely electronic system. But these
phone bills can tell someone who wants to

No evidence.
statement un-
dermines my
credibility.

know all the people we called and when we
called them. Our phone companies could be
recording everything we say as well.

In our society, privacy is regarded as a
right--a right that is being threatened by
the increasing use of databases to maintain
large amounts of information on all of us.
A number of privacy bills have been passed

Ideas need de-
velopment. Is
situation hope-
less?

but are almost useless because they are so
hard to enforce. Violating someone's
privacy is hard to detect, and successfully
prosecuting someone for this offense is
harder still.

Not relevant
to what
I've written.

Computers are enormously valuable tools,
but they can be misused to violate privacy
and to manipulate people. We have a
population explosion today, and yet we
replace people with computers. We must

Is this conclusion
justified by what
I've written?

carefully examine the role of computers in
our society and learn to control them
before they control us.

First drafts (and final drafts, for that matter) are never perfect, as our student
has recognized on rereading his. Here is a list of the problems that his review has
discovered:

1. *Claim.* I have a combination claim focusing on the privacy issue and the
   issue of computers replacing human labor, but I do nothing with the

second issue. I should drop the second issue and concentrate on the first.

2. *Organization.* My ideas aren't clearly presented and organized, especially in the third paragraph, which talks about the three separate ideas of networking, human data-entry errors, and lack of paper or "hard-copy" backups. All of my paragraphs must be clearly tied to the privacy threat.

3. *Support.* I don't really support my argument because I talk a lot about the threat of invasion of privacy but give no actual cases. I need to distinguish clearly between the potential for abuse and actual cases. Is there a real possibility of abuse? Also, my conclusion about humans controlling computers before they control us isn't warranted by what I've written, since I've offered no suggestions for controlling computers.

4. *Style.* I undermine my credibility with sweeping statements like "If you have someone's Social Security number, you can find out just about anything you want about that person." Some of my writing could be much tighter, including wordy expressions like "As if it isn't bad enough to have someone go through all the information about you in one database . . ."

In his second draft, the student carefully attended to this list, ending up with a much stronger version of the paper. (Note that he has waited until his second draft to supply source references.)

> When we think about computers, we usually think about how helpful they are to us: they enable us to process huge amounts of data, prepare large written documents with an ease undreamt of even twenty years ago, and by acting as the "brains" of robots, help us perform dangerous or monotonous tasks. But we often fail to think of the negative side of computers, including the threat they pose to our own privacy. This threat may not seem immediate, but it is growing with the increasing power of computers, and so far society has done little to deal with it (Roszak 181).
>
> One thing computers are used for is to store information about people. Computers often use databases, which are collections of discrete data that are divided into fields, such as age, sex, income, and place of residence. A user of a database can pull information out of the database on everyone who fits a category made up of some or all of these fields, such as every male between thirty and forty who earns between thirty and fifty thousand dollars a year and lives in Florida. An example of a database is the Internal Revenue Service's database,

which contains basic information on tax returns along with
demographic information on those who pay taxes. Other
databases contain our credit histories, our history of
contributions to a specific organization, our personnel
records with our employers, and a variety of other
information. Businesses and other organizations already
use this information to bombard us with targeted
advertising through the mail; the information could be used
to monitor our opinions and activities (Roszak 182-87).

Databases can be made even more powerful by being
linked to other databases through networking. The
increasing capabilities of network systems raise the
possibility of a wide variety of information on us being
shared by numerous databases. Such information on specific
individuals would be a boon to marketers trying to find
target audiences, but individuals could end up with their
records of contributions to an organization in the hands
of the IRS, or their IRS files in their employers'
personnel records, without their even knowing it.

So far at least, cases of deliberate abuse or
manipulation of databases to violate an individual's
privacy have been relatively rare. Far greater problems
have arisen because of errors in the entry of data in
databases, with such undesirable results as individuals'
receiving bad credit ratings because of erroneous reports
of unpaid bills or even some cases of innocent
individuals' being denied government jobs because their
names appeared on computer lists of people belonging to
subversive organizations (Sherman 344). The risk of these
kinds of errors may increase with increasing use of the
"on-line" entry of data into computers, where a paper copy
(called a hard copy in computerese) of the transaction is
not necessary, so that no trace is left outside the
computer system of the source of the error. These errors
threaten our privacy, because this supposedly "private"
information may mislead others, damage our reputation, and
enormously complicate our lives. Common sense suggests
that with the increasing amount of "private" data being

kept on all of us, the likelihood of harmful errors also increases.

Most such errors are caused by human mistakes, but even computers can develop "glitches." Furthermore, even errorless electronically entered data can pose threats to our privacy. Our phone bills are one example of a completely electronic system which is almost always error-free. Yet these phone bills can tell someone who wants to know all the people we called and when we called them. The information may be accurate, but in the wrong hands, it can be seriously misused.

In our society, privacy is regarded as a right--a right that is being threatened by the increasing use of databases to maintain large amounts of information on all of us. A number of computer privacy laws have been enacted in the last twenty years, including the Medical Computer Crimes Act of 1984, the Cable Communications Policy Act of 1984, the Financial Privacy Act of 1978, the Fair Credit Reporting Act of 1974, and the Family Educational Rights and Privacy Act of 1974 (Organization for Economic Co-operation and Development 22). One aspect of all these laws is the protection of individuals from unwarranted use of data about them. But violating someone's privacy is hard to detect, and successfully prosecuting someone for this offense is harder still.

Nevertheless, protecting individual privacy against the threat posed by large databases is not a hopeless cause. The growing list of computer privacy laws indicates that the public is not blind to the threats posed by computers, though much needs to be done to make these laws meaningful. Even consumers can help, by insisting that their names not be sent to others when they subscribe to a magazine or join an organization. Faced with such insistence and the possibility of losing customers or members, many groups will stop sharing these lists.

Computers are enormously valuable tools, but they can be misused to violate our privacy. While the threat to our privacy is real, the situation is not yet severe. We still

have the time to control this threat before the threat
begins to control us.

WORKS CITED

Organization for Economic Co-operation and Development
(OECD). *Computer-Related Crime: Analysis of Legal
Policy.* Information on Computer Communications Policy
10. Paris: OECD, 1986.

Roszak, Theodore. *The Cult of Information: The Folklore of
Computers and the True Art of Thinking.* New York:
Pantheon, 1986.

Sherman, Barrie. *The New Revolution: The Impact of
Computers on Society.* Chichester, UK: Wiley, 1985.

Having read this second version carefully, do you think the student has solved
the problems he noted in his list? Do you see further changes that he might wish
to make before handing the paper in to his instructor?

ACTIVITIES (12.2)

Read the following draft of a student's essay (actually a composite of several essays), and make a list of what you feel the major revisions need to be. Compare
your list with those of your classmates; then revise the essay in accordance with
your list. Compare your revision with some of those done by your classmates.

Student Government: Why No One Cares

Being an engineering student here at High Tech, I
have very little free time. My time is entirely devoted to
academics. Occasionally I will have a few hours free on
the weekend, but then I work part time at odd jobs.
Tuition here is very high.

I am one of many busy students here who simply
doesn't have the time to take an interest in student
government. This same fact is true for most of us. Most
of us don't even know one person who is in student
government and could not tell you what student government
actually does.

We are very ignorant about student government and
what role we can play in it. Speaking for myself, even if I
saw posters announcing a meeting about student government,

I would not attend. Most of my fellow students would not either. What can just one student do? None of us has much of a voice in how things are run. The administration really runs the show here at High Tech, not the students. I believe that if the student government started putting up more posters and getting out more publicity about its activities, students would be more interested in its activities even if they did not attend them.

It is a whole lot simpler to just ignore what's going on and to assume that the student government is looking out for our interests than to take the trouble to get involved. Besides, life isn't all that bad around here, so why should we spend a lot of time and effort trying to improve a situation most of us already find satisfactory? By the time we solved some problem, we would be ready to graduate anyway.

SUGGESTIONS FOR WRITING (12.3)

1. Revise a paper you wrote earlier in this course, following the advice outlined in this chapter. Make a list of the major differences between the original paper and your new version, and indicate very briefly why you made these changes.
2. For this assignment, the class should be divided into groups of three or four. Each group will collectively write a three- to four-page paper (750 to 1,000 words) on the general question "What are the three things that infuriate me most about this campus?" Each group will brainstorm ideas that lead it to a working claim for an evaluative paper concerning student life at your school. From this working claim, the group will compose an outline; then each student will write a particular section of the paper. When the first draft is written, the group will discuss it and each student will revise his or her own section. Finally, the group will discuss this second draft and choose one student to prepare and edit a final version consistent in style and tone.
3. Write a description of the steps you typically follow when writing arguments. Start with the step of coming up with ideas and move through writing the first draft to whatever steps you take before you arrive at a final edited version. How efficient is this typical process in terms of time spent? How effective is it in helping you compose a convincing argument? Do you think the process can be improved so that you can write better arguments in a reasonable amount of time? Give the description to your instructor for comments and suggestions.

Credits

Index

A CUPCAKE CLUB ROMANCE, BOOK 2

SWEET STUFF

DONNA KAUFFMAN

KENNEBEC LARGE PRINT
A part of Gale, Cengage Learning

 GALE
CENGAGE Learning·

Detroit • New York • San Francisco • New Haven, Conn • Waterville, Maine • London

GALE
CENGAGE Learning·

Copyright © 2012 by Donna Kauffman.
A Cupcake Club Romance Series #2.
Kennebec Large Print, a part of Gale, Cengage Learning.

LIBRARY OF CONGRESS CATALOGING-IN-PUBLICATION DATA

Kauffman, Donna.
    Sweet stuff / by Donna Kauffman. — Large print ed.
      p. cm. — (A Cupcake Club romance series; #2) (Kennebec
  large print superior collection)
    ISBN 978-1-4104-4612-1 (pbk.) — ISBN 1-4104-4612-3 (pbk.) 1. Large
  type books. 2. Cupcakes—Fiction. I. Title.
  PS3561.A816S93 2012
  813'.54—dc23   2012001844

Published in 2012 by arrangement with Brava Books, an imprint of
Kensington Publishing Corp.

Printed in the United States of America
1 2 3 4 5   16 15 14 13 12
FD124

For the friends and family
who provide the roots
that bind us together,
and the foundation upon which is built
a happy and contented life . . .
no matter where we each
lay our heads at night.

CHAPTER 1

Later, she would blame the whole thing on the cupcakes.

Riley glanced through the sparkling window panes of the hand-stained, sliding French panel doors to the extended, multi-level tigerwood deck — complete with stargazer pergola and red cedar soaking tub — straight into a pair of familiar, sober brown eyes. "I know that look," she called out, loud enough so he could hear her through the thermal, double-paned glass. "Don't mock. I can too do this."

She turned her attention forward again and stared at the electronic panel of the Jog Master 3000. "I mean, how hard could it be?" A rhetorical question of course. Anyone, probably even the sunbathing mastiff, could figure out how to push a few buttons and —

"Ooof!" The belt started moving under her feet. Really fast. Really, really fast.

"Oh crap!" She grabbed the padded side bars, an instinctive move purely intended to keep from face-planting on high-speed rubber, with little actual athleticism involved. Okay, not a drop of it, but if she could keep pace long enough to get her balance, she could relax the death grip of just one of her hands and smack — press, she meant press — the electronic panel of buttons on this very — very — expensive piece of leased equipment. At which point her ill-advised, unfortunate little adventure would end well.

Or at least without the local EMTs being called. Or a lengthy hospital stay. She was way too busy for stitches.

"Yeah," she gasped. "Piece of cake." She managed a smirk at the irony of that particular phrase, but quickly turned to full panic mode as she realized she wasn't exactly gaining ground. Rapidly losing it, in fact, along with what little breath she had. "Crap, crap, crap," she panted in rhythm with her running steps. It had only been a few minutes — three minutes and forty-four seconds, according to the oh-so-helpful digital display — and she was already perspiring. Okay, okay, sweating. She just wasn't sure if it was from the actual exertion, or the abject anxiety that she wasn't going to get out of this latest catastrophe in one piece.

Where were those big, strong Steinway deliverymen when you needed them, anyway? Surely they could race right in and save her, in blazingly heroic, stud-monkey fashion. And she'd let them, too. Just because she prided herself on her total I-Am-Woman independence thing A.J. (After-Jeremy), didn't mean she wasn't above a little Rapunzel fantasy now and again.

She'd been awaiting delivery of the elegant baby grand for over an hour. So, technically, it was all their fault. The baby grand in question was the final component, and the *pièce de résistance,* of this particular staging event. With every other remaining detail attended to, she'd foolishly given in to the urge to run a test check — all right, play — with some of the toys she'd had installed. Once again, she had managed to get herself into a bit of a pickle.

Enough with the food analogies, Riles. Eight minutes, twenty-three seconds. At a dead run. The only way she could have ever pulled that off was if she were being chased by zombies. With machetes. And the world as she knew it would end if she didn't get to the edge of the dark, scary forest in time.

Instead, all she had was her mastiff and

his baleful stare. Not exactly adrenaline inducing.

Ten minutes, thirteen seconds. She was well past sweating and deep into red-faced overexertion. She glared back at Brutus, who kept faithful watch, but otherwise appeared unconcerned with his mistress's current distress. "No gravy on your kibble tonight," she called out. Well, in her mind, she called out. She was so winded it was all she could do to think the words. But her expression hopefully conveyed the message to her mutant, one-hundred-fifty-pound dog . . .

Who looked completely unmoved by her menacing glare. He knew she was a pushover. She'd taken him in as a rescue, hadn't she?

The sweet sound of the cascading entrance chimes echoed through the room, indicating the deliverymen had, indeed, finally arrived.

"Thank God," she wheezed. She didn't even care what they thought of the situation, or how horrible she must look. She'd bribe them with a few of Leilani's decadently delicious Black Forest cupcakes, featuring raspberry truffle filling, and topped with fresh, plump, perfectly rosy raspberries. There were two dozen of them, carefully arranged on the three-tier crystal display dish in the beautifully appointed breakfast nook. That, and maybe throw in a few bottles of imported lager presently chilling in the newly installed, stainless-steel Viking fridge with handy bottom freezer, and surely they wouldn't say anything to Scary Lois about Riley's less-than-professional activities.

Lois Grinkmeyer-Hington-Smythe was easily the most intimidating person Riley had staged showcase houses for thus far, or worked for in any capacity, for that matter. Given her former career as head food stylist for *Foodie,* the number one selling food magazine in the country, that was saying something. Even the most intimidating chef had nothing on Scary Lois, highest performing realtor for Gold Coast Properties, and Riley couldn't afford to annoy the source of her best bookings.

The chimes cascaded again. *Oh, for God's sake, come in, already!* She tried to shout, but all she could muster was a strangled, guttural grunt. Why weren't they just coming in? Open house meant the house was open!

She could see the headlines now.

Riley Brown Found Dead!

11

SUGARBERRY ISLAND'S PREMIER HOUSE STAGER IN HIGH-SPEED TREADMILL INCIDENT!

BARRIER ISLANDS, GEORGIA — Piano deliverymen and part-time models Sven and Magnus claimed they had no knowledge that the front door to the island's newly redesigned, prime lease property was unlocked, and that they could have entered the home and rescued the lovely and talented house stager from escalating terror and certain death. They did, however, make sure the reporter got their names right and photographed them from their good side.

Meanwhile, poor, dead Riley Brown probably wouldn't even warrant a hunky CSI investigator, who — clearly moved by her still glowing, cherubic face and bountiful blond curls — would posthumously vow to go to the ends of the earth to find out who was responsible for this terrible, terrible tragedy.

Of course, you couldn't exactly arrest a Jog Master 3000.

Right at the point where she knew her sweaty palms couldn't grip the rubber padding one second longer and her gaze had shifted to Brutus out on the deck for what could likely be the very last time, someone with a very deep voice that carried the warm caress of a slight Southern accent said, "Beg your pardon. I thought this was the house being leased. My apologies, I —"

Riley jerked her head around to look at the intruder. That was no Sven. Or even a Magnus. He was way — way — better than any Nordic fantasy. Framed by what she knew was a nine-foot archway, he was a rugged six-foot-four at least, with shoulders and jaw to match. Even in his white cotton button-down shirt, faded jeans, and dark brown sport coat, he looked like he could have delivered a baby grand with his left hand, while simultaneously saving the world with his right. Thick, dark hair framed a tanned face with crinkles at the corners of the most amazing bright blue eyes . . . Wait — she knew that face! How did she know that face?

Her jaw went slack the instant she realized who was standing, live and in the amazingly more-gorgeous-in-person flesh, right there in her Florida room. Well, not *her* Florida room, but . . . that didn't matter, because unfortunately the moment her jaw had gone slack, so had her hands.

She let out a strangled shriek as the

rapidly spinning rubber track ejected her from the back end of the machine as if she were a clown shot out of a circus cannon. Sans the acrobatic skills. Or clean landing.

The good news? The tastefully arranged indoor/outdoor cluster of salt-air tolerant baby cabbage and saw palmettos, cockspur prickly pear and Adam's Needle yucca kept her from being ejected straight through the sparkling clean, thermal double panes she'd spent a full hour on that morning. The bad news? Well, other than the part about saw palmettos and prickly pear not exactly being soft and cushy kinds of foliage? Yeah, that would be lying in a sweaty, red-faced, scratched-up heap . . . all while looking up into the breathtaking, turquoise blue eyes of the one-and-only Quinn Brannigan.

Dazed in more ways than one, Riley found herself thinking that if her life were ever made into a movie of the week, she sure hoped the screenwriter would give her some clever, witty line to say at that exact moment. One that would show her to be adorably spunky and utterly charming . . . despite her bedraggled, pathetic, utterly disastrous appearance.

Alas, she was more a visual person — which was why she was a stylist and a photographer, not a writer. Quinn Brannigan, on the other hand, was a writer. Of the number one with a bullet, *New York Times* best-selling variety. So, of course, he knew exactly what to say.

"I am sorry." That hint of drawl in his voice made him sound inherently sincere, while the concern etched in every crease of his perfectly gorgeous face only underscored the tone. "I don't know how I made such a mistake. I never meant to alarm you like that. Let me help you up, make sure you're all right." He extended a hand.

See? Perfect white knight, perfect amount of sincere contrition, perfect . . . well, everything. She'd always thought him handsome, staring back at her from the glossy book jackets of his many best sellers. What the photo didn't convey was the magnetism and charisma that packed an even bigger wallop in person. Not to mention his voice. Deep and smooth, with a cadence hinting at warm honey drizzled all over a hot, buttery biscuit. If they could package that voice along with his books, he'd double his already enormous sales.

"You know" — her words came out in more of a post-marathon croak — "you really should read your own books."

She closed her eyes when his expression shifted to one of confusion. *I said that, right out loud, didn't I?* Another rhetorical question, of course. "On tape," she added lamely, as if that was going to clear matters right up. "You know, audiobooks." Riley let her head drop farther back into the sharp fronds. "Never mind. I'm shutting up now."

"Give me your hand." When he crouched down, his handsome face and hot-sex-in-a-summer-hammock voice were even closer to her. "Are you hurt? Did you hit your head on the glass?"

Given her random commentary, his concern wasn't the least bit surprising. It was an easy out that a lesser woman might have taken. No one had ever accused her, however, of being lesser. Too much, maybe. All right, definitely.

"No," she managed. "Just a few scratches. I'm fine, I just —" She broke off, and, with a little sigh and a not-so-little huff of breath, tried to struggle her way out of the forest of serrated-edge foliage by herself. Then just as quickly gave up as the plants seemed to want to suck her in more deeply. She'd lost enough skin already.

She couldn't lose any more of her pride, however. That was all gone. She rubbed her dirty, still-sweaty palm on her pant leg, then took the offered hand, steeling her already fluttering hormones against the feel of his skin on hers. Not that she was normally so overwrought about such things, but, at the moment, her defenses were abnormally low. As in, completely missing.

And . . . yep. *Pow.* Right in the libido. Wide palm, warm skin, strong grip.

He lifted her overly tall, less-than-lithe form out of the tangle of deadly blades as if she were nothing more cumbersome than a downy little feather. She'd never once been accused of being a feather. Of any kind. She had to admit, it felt rather . . . blissful. So much so, that, if he'd asked her, she'd have happily agreed to strip naked, have his babies, or anything else he wanted, right there. On the evil Jog Master, even.

Because, oh yeah, that's what he's dying to do, Riles. Take you, take you hard.

Not that it mattered. Even if she had somehow managed to look adorably spunky and utterly charming despite the scratched-up flesh and blotchy red face, she'd sworn off men. Nineteen months, ten days, and dozens of cupcakes ago.

Not that all men were stupid, lying, cheating, ex-fiancé bastards like Jeremy. She knew that. And she hadn't held his actions against the rest of the male members of the human race. Most of the time. But given how thoroughly and completely duped and humiliated she'd been by the one person from that part of the population she'd most trusted with her deepest, truest self, not to mention all of her carefully guarded heart . . . yeah, she wasn't in a mad rush to find out if her judgment in that arena had improved. Hence the switch to baked goods for personal comfort.

Men were complicated. Cupcakes, on the other hand? Not so much.

"You've got a few scrapes," Quinn-the-hot-celebrity-savior was saying as he steadied her with a wide palm on her shoulder. *Rapunzel, eat your heart out.* Still working to get her heart rate back to some semblance of normal, she acknowledged that her studly savior was probably more to blame than the Jog Master.

After another moment passed, he carefully disengaged his hand from hers, which took a bit of doing as she'd apparently switched her Jog Master death grip to a Good Studly Samaritan one, but he kept the steadying hand on her shoulder for an additional moment before letting go completely. "Let me help you get cleaned up."

Riley belatedly realized she was staring at Quinn with God only knew what kind of glazed, starry-eyed expression plastered all over her blotchy and battered face. She might have sworn off men and wrapped herself in fiercely guarded independence, but that didn't mean she was quite up for inviting them to stare at her in abject horror. Or worse, pity. "I — uh, no, that's okay," she managed, finally pulling herself together. "That won't be necessary. Just a few scratches. Really. I can — I can take care of it. I'm . . . really sorry."

"*You're* sorry?" His eyes truly were the definition of piercing.

"To give you a scare like that, I mean. I was just . . ." She looked behind her at the Jog Master, which was still churning away. "Never mind. Not important." She turned and casually bent down, trying not to overtly wince at the parts of her that rebelled at being bent at that moment . . . and jerked the cord from the wall socket, using a wee bit more force than was actually required. Or perhaps a lot more force, as the plug snapped back and stung her ankle. Right in that tender, vulnerable spot that brought instant tears to the eyes. She dropped the cord like a live snake as she somehow managed to suck in every single one of the very unladylike, but totally appropriate-to-the-moment swear words, then forced herself to straighten, slowly, while giving herself a quick, silent talking-to. She could fall apart later, and swear to the heavens if she wanted to.

Right now, she had to salvage the few remaining bits of professionalism that hadn't been shredded along with the foliage. Only then did she turn back to face him, trying for a sunny smile, though that was likely ruined by the way the stretching of her lacerated skin made her flinch. "So, you're here for the open house?"

He was still frowning. The concerned, Good Studly Samaritan. It made her feel ridiculous and pathetic, though she was certain that wasn't his intent. Not that he needed to try. She could feel ridiculous and pathetic with no help at all.

"I really think we should give those scratches some attention, and you might want to sit down. At least for a few minutes. Get your balance. Again, my apologies for startling you like that." His frown eased into an abashed half smile that kept her pulse humming right along. "What in the world you must have thought, a strange man walking right into your home. I guess it's good you recognized me. I can't believe I got the number wrong. The island's not that big — wait." He paused, the half-smile turning back to a look of confusion. "Did you mean to say that this . . . *is* the house that's up for lease?"

For the briefest moment, Riley entertained the wild thought of pretending she was also there for the open house and had just made the unfortunate decision to give the Jog Master a try. But she ditched the plan almost as fast as she thought of it. Even if he bought the story, at some point, if he ended up leasing the place — which would be just her luck — he'd no doubt run into her around the island. Sugarberry was the smallest of the inhabited barrier islands and the only town on it was hardly big enough to be called a town. They couldn't help running into each other.

He'd quickly find out she was hardly in any position to lease the newly renovated and exceedingly high-end beach bungalow. The houseboat she lived on might give the impression of a decent annual income, but it was a loaner, and while nice, not exactly yacht club material. Not that Sugarberry had a yacht club. The *Seaduced* was presently tied up on the south end of the island alongside a bunch of commercial fishing trawlers, as it was the only pier that could take her.

For that matter, Sugarberry didn't have any other high-end beach bungalows. The old Turner place — bought at a bank auction by a pair of Atlanta investors looking to mine new Gold Coast development opportunities — was the first of its kind. And, if Sugarberry residents had anything to say about it — and they had plenty to say — the last.

Unlike Quinn Brannigan, who was exactly high-end, upscale bungalow, yacht club material.

"Yes, this is the one," Riley answered him, making a grand gesture to the room around them. Anything to take his concerned gaze from her face. "It's truly a gem. I'm so very sorry your first impression of the property was well . . . you know. Hugely unprofessional of me. Not the hoped-for introduction, I'm afraid." She deliberated a brief moment on asking him not to mention her little adventure to Scary Lois, but ditched that idea, too. Not a good idea to beg favors from the guy who'd just saved her life. Inadvertently, maybe, but still.

"You're not Lois of the multi-hyphenated last names, are you?"

That earned a real smile and a wince before she could control it. "No. No, I'm not."

Quinn gave her that ridiculously charming half smile again. "I didn't think so."

"You mean I don't look like the Gold Coast's most successful A-List Realtor?" she said dryly. "I'm stunned."

His half smile grew to a full smile and if she'd had any doubt her heart had fully survived her Jog Master marathon, that fear proved unwarranted. It was pumping just fine, thank you very much.

"I've not had the privilege of meeting her as yet," he said, a bit more of that honey-coated-biscuits-and-melted-butter tone flavoring his words. "But what communication we've had, well, let's just say you seem far more . . . approachable."

"You mean less scary?" Riley looked down at herself and sighed. "I don't know about that. I don't want to see myself in a mirror anytime soon."

"Come on. Let's find the kitchen and get you cleaned up a little."

A gentleman's way of saying, yep, super-scary looking. Not that it would have made a difference either way.

"That's okay, really. I'll go take care of it. Why don't you have a look around? Lois has all the literature with her, but once I'm cleaned up, I can give you a tour. I'm familiar with all the upgrades and should be able to answer most of your questions, at least as they pertain to the house itself."

In actuality, Riley knew every last inch of the place, before renovations and after. She knew every gizmo and upgrade that had been installed, as well as what parts of the property had been preserved, and why. Not because she had personal knowledge of Sugarberry history — she'd only been living on the island for a little over a year. This was actually the first project she'd done on the island itself. She normally worked farther down the barrier island chain, where the money was. She'd simply made it her business to know everything there was to know about the Turner place, just as she did with all the projects she was hired for.

In many ways, staging an entire home or condo wasn't any different than styling food for an elaborate magazine layout. She used to learn as much as she could about the cuisine being presented, including the history, the traditions, and, in many cases, preparing the dishes herself, or as close an approximation as she could, in order to come up with the most unique, authentically detailed settings possible. Knowing the history and setting of the property she was staging was as important as all the more glamorous, flashy details.

Not that every client, or even most clients, were interested in half of what she took the time to find out. They might not care, specifically, about the fact that the refinished, hand-carved sliding panel doors were original to the house, or that she'd purposely matched the colors of the pottery and doorstops throughout the house to the terra-cotta shingling on the roof, but she knew it was that attention to detail that ended up selling them on the place. It didn't matter that they didn't appreciate why they loved it, just that they loved it enough to write Lois a big fat check. And, in turn, Scary Lois kept signing hers.

"Why don't you start with the . . ." She'd been about to say the deck, pool, and gardens, but remembered the sunbathing Brutus. *Crap.* Normally she and her faithful companion were no longer on the premises when the actual event began. That she occasionally brought Brutus with her while staging various properties was also a teeny-tiny detail she'd neglected to tell Lois. This project had been so close to home, and she'd known he'd love lolling out on the deck. And, frankly, she enjoyed the company. Obviously not for protection purposes.

"Uh, bedrooms," she improvised, careful to keep her gaze averted from the sliding French doors. "Just up the stairs from the foyer entry. You'll love the master suite."

Too late, she remembered it had a second-story deck that looked right down on the first-story deck. "Though you might want to begin with the guest bedrooms along the front of the house. The, uh, lighting, right now . . . they have the morning sun. Truly spectacular."

If he sensed the slightly panicked edge in her tone, his affable expression didn't show it. "And risk my dearly departed Grams coming back to chase after me with her wooden rolling pin for being anything less than the gentleman she raised my pa and me to be?" The easy grin returned. "No, ma'am. Especially considering I caused the calamity in the first place." He gestured for her to lead the way to the kitchen. "Pretty sure she's capable of it, too," he added with a touch of dry reverence, as he followed her from the room.

Riley smiled, and didn't mind the wincing so much. It was impossible not to be charmed by him. But she needed to get him poking around upstairs as swiftly as possible. Not that she had any place in particular she could quickly stash a dog the size of a subcompact car, but she was due for a little luck.

She entered the kitchen, and if Quinn was impressed by the newly installed, state-of-the-art appliances, the marble-topped center island, or the array of terra-cotta-toned Calphalon pots and pans hanging from the hand-hammered silver overhead rack, he didn't mention it. Nor did he seem to even notice them. Of course, things like that were probably par for the course for his lifestyle.

He was opening cupboards and pulling out drawers, but she doubted he was taking inventory. "Not much to work with here," he murmured.

"I've got it." Riley stepped around the center island and walked over to the small breakfast nook table and the three-tier crystal cupcake display. She grabbed a few of the color-coordinated napkins that were artfully arranged next to the themed paper plates and plastic forks, then edged back around the center island to the twin stainless-steel sinks. "Really, you should take a look —"

"Here." He came right up behind her just as she'd turned on the water and shoved a wadded-up napkin underneath the steady stream.

As in, *right* behind her. Deep in her personal space. Like she hadn't just recently recovered her ability to breathe normally.

"Let me." Quinn put one broad palm on her shoulder and turned her to face him, relieving her of the soggy party napkins with his other hand, which he used to carefully dab at the scratches on her cheek and her forehead. And her chin. And her neck.

How lovely that must look.

She couldn't think about that. Unless she closed her eyes, there was nowhere else to look but directly into his, and though he was busy attending to her wounds and not really looking at her . . . she couldn't resist taking the opportunity to look at him. Really look at him.

And, up close? He looked even better. Every laugh line, every crinkle, even with a tiny scar just above one temple . . . he was truly and spectacularly gorgeous. So unfair. Even scratch-free, she wouldn't hold up to the same up-close-and-personal perusal. For one, she had freckles. And not that faint little scatter you got from being out in the sun. No, she had real freckles. Thirty-one years old. With freckles. Not adorable at that age. Then there was the whole mouth situation. Hers was wide and full, just not in that sexy and mysterious Angelina Jolie kind of way. Instead of a vampy pout that did wonders for selling lipstick and lingerie, Riley's was sort of perpetually curved in a big, goofy smile. At best, good for selling bubble gum.

She always looked like she was smiling, which shouldn't be a bad thing. But just try being taken seriously in an editorial meeting full of men when no matter how much you tried on your stern, I-mean-business face, you always looked like a brainless bimbo. Dolly Parton looked fiercer than she did.

And don't even get her started on being a natural blonde. With curls. Lots of them. Long or short didn't matter. Her hair fell in big, happy, springy sproings no matter what. No one took that seriously, either. No matter how sleek a bun she'd torture her hair into, curls sprang out to frame her apple-cheeked, freckled face. Throw in the bombshell-sized boobs, with a back porch to match and . . . yeah. Maybe slim, perfectly coiffed ice princess blondes got respect, but she couldn't pull off even a hint of that kind of frost. Smiley, sproingy, and stacked never added up to frost. No matter how you did the math. And that had been before factoring in a year's worth of Cupcake Club get-togethers.

"There," he said, with a final dab.

"Thanks." She felt herself flush as his eyes finally met hers.

The corners of his eyes crinkled ever-so-fabulously as he smiled. "Least I could do."

"Right." She heard the breathy note in her voice. She needed to get out of his personal space, pronto, or get him out of hers, before she made an even bigger fool of herself. If that were possible. "I mean, no worries. It was just one of those things. Could have happened to anyone." She took a step back, banged her hip into the counter, then turned with the intent of putting herself anywhere but in proximity to him and caught the edge of the refrigerator handle where it jutted out just a bit farther than the cabinets and counters. "Oooh, ouch!"

And just like that, his hands were on her again. On both shoulders, as he guided her back to safety. Dear God, didn't he know he was the more dangerous thing? She was a natural klutz on her best days — yet another minus from the ice princess equation — and what he did to her equilibrium was downright hazardous to her health and well-being.

"I'm fine, really, I just —" She turned around, attempting again to put space between them, but somehow only managed to wedge herself, front-to-front, between him and the counter behind her.

His gaze caught hers and held for that moment. You know, that *moment.* Like the one that happened in the movies, where a hundred things are said, but not a single word is spoken. And the tension is so tightly wound it all but makes its own soundtrack with its taut silence, fraught with so much promise, so many possibilities, if only one of the couple would just . . . do something. One little move was all it would take, and you watch, and wait, dying inch by inch, waiting for one of them to make that oh-so-crucial, heart-pounding *move.* The moment stretches, and expands, until you think you'll scream from the sweet, knot-tightening tension of it all.

A small furrow creased the center of his forehead. "I do think maybe you should sit for a bit. You're still a little flushed."

She slowly closed her eyes, and felt her cheeks flame hotter. *So not what the movie guy would say.* "Thank you," she murmured, making a point to be looking anywhere but at him when she opened her eyes. She edged herself to one side, away from the Viking monster, and Quinn mercifully stepped back.

"Why don't you sit at the table and I'll fix you some water. Unless there's something stronger —"

"No, really. You've been more than kind. You really should take advantage and go look at the place before the event starts.

Scary Lois will be here shortly and I —"
She broke off when he stifled a laugh with a
fist to his mouth, followed by a clearly faked
coughing attack.

"What did I — ?" Then she realized
exactly what she'd said. *Wow, just . . . wow.*
Apparently she really didn't want to work
again. Ever. Except she did. She loved her
job. Maybe not as much as the one she'd
left behind in Chicago, but as close —
closer, really — than she'd expected to find
again. Groaning in ever-deepening embarrassment, she turned toward the pantry
door and leaned her forehead on it. Any
other time she'd have given her noggin a
good rap, but she wasn't too sure, given how
the day had gone so far, that she wouldn't
end up in the ER with a concussion. Or in
a coma.

"Are there any beds? In the bedrooms?
Upstairs?"

"What?" She lifted her head and turned
to look at him. Had she rapped her head
anyway and hit it so hard she'd just forgotten? Clearly she did not just hear him say
— "Beds? Wh-why?"

"I think maybe a little lie-down would be
even better."

He didn't even give her the chance to
respond. He gently, but firmly, took her

elbow and guided her to the front hall and the staircase landing. Unfortunately not in that "Hurry! I must ravish you now!" kind of way. More in the way a person would when helping the frail and feeble-minded.

"And don't worry," he added dryly "I'll keep an eye out for Scary Lois."

Riley groaned again, her mortification complete. At least if she got him upstairs, she could redirect his attention to looking at the rooms, then slide back down, round up Brutus, and make her escape.

They were at the halfway landing when the entry chimes reverberated through the foyer, finally announcing the arrival of the piano delivery guys. How had she forgotten she still had a baby grand to stage? Not to mention there was foliage carnage to clean up.

It turned out the delivery guys weren't exactly Sven and Magnus.

More like Jeffy and T-Bone. Those were the names someone had actually stitched on their navy blue uniform shirts. She also doubted that either had enjoyed a modeling career. At any point in their lives. Though, with neither one of them clocking in at a day under sixty, who was to say that with less around the middle, and more on top of the head . . . and, well, teeth in the mouth, they might have, at one time, turned a lady's head.

Then Jeffy wedged a fingerload of Skoal inside his mouth and Riley thought . . . *then again, possibly not.*

"I'm — I need to go direct them to —" She didn't keep explaining. She just turned to make her escape. "Go on up and look around."

Quinn shifted so she could pass by him to head back down the stairs. He put a guiding hand on the small of her back as she took the first step, which sent a delicious shiver over her skin she had no business feeling. *He is just being kind to the feeble,* she reminded herself. She put her hand on the railing, just to be safe. As she started down the stairs, she felt a tickling little tug at the back of her head and almost lost her balance all over again when she instinctively swatted at it . . . only to freeze momentarily when her hand come into contact with Quinn's. She glanced back to find him holding a small palm frond that he'd apparently plucked from her hair. He gave her the briefest of smiles as he tucked it discreetly behind his back.

Apparently her cheeks were never going to be any shade but flushed as long as she was around him. She managed to nod a quick thank-you before turning back to oversee the matter at hand.

Mercifully, the task quickly enabled her to get her footing back — and hopefully her equilibrium — as she directed the two men to put the piano in the space she'd saved in the Florida room at the rear of the home.

"What the heck happened to you, missy?" Jeffy asked, nodding toward her face.

"Slight mishap with the foliage," she said, which reminded her she still needed to clean up that mess. "Nothing to worry about. Here, this way," she directed, not even so much as glancing back at the staircase. She could all but feel that half-amused smile heating up the back of her neck. "Right through there."

The two men put down protective runners on the hardwood flooring and rolled the piano — frame-packed on its side — into the house and carefully angled it through the arched doorway.

Naturally, that was when Brutus's up-to-then nonexistent protective instincts kicked in. He didn't so much bark as emit a very loud *woofing* noise that came from somewhere deep inside his mutant-sized canine frame.

"Good gravy. What on God's green earth is that?" T-Bone paused in removing the packing from the piano legs to stare through the French doors at Brutus, who was staring directly back at T-Bone from his position on the other side of the dog-slobbered glass.

The same glass she'd spent half the morning cleaning. Lovely. "That's just . . . my dog. Don't worry. He's fine."

"I don't rightly know that it was his health that concerned me," T-Bone replied. With one eye carefully still aimed in the general direction of the deck, he went back to work.

"Must be like feeding a horse," Jeffy commented around the lump in his cheek, less worried than his partner. Actually, he looked like he was trying to gauge how many of his family members he might be able to feed hunting with Brutus.

"If you could just position it here, so it's out of the direct sun, but facing the windows and the ocean view, that would be perfect," Riley directed, trying to keep them — and herself — focused on the task at hand. She worked at setting the potted plants back to rights and sweeping up the dirt and plant detritus while they finished up.

"You know it ain't tuned or nothing," T-Bone said. "We just deliver. You want to play it, you'll have to get in touch with Marty and set up an appointment."

"Yes, thank you." She didn't need it to be in tune. It was just for show. She had specifically chosen some sheet music — Debussy's First Arabesque, perfect for sunsets — to place on the rack above the keys, but intended to keep the key cover down, so hopefully no one would actually touch it. Marty was one of her better contacts, and she didn't plan to do anything to change that.

By the time it was all said and done and she'd signed the paperwork stating she'd personally be responsible for any damage done to the piece before its return, Quinn was no longer in the immediate area. Assuming he'd gone off to look at the rest of the place, Riley took a moment, after ushering the men out the front door, to duck into the bathroom off the foyer.

"Yet another bad idea." She sighed as she catalogued the damages in the beveled vanity mirror positioned over the transparent glass pedestal sink. She hadn't thought it possible to look worse than she'd imagined, but she'd managed to pull that off. Making a stab at cooling off her face with cold water, she cleaned up the worst of the scrapes on her arms and hands. The dirt smears on her plaid camp shirt were beyond repair, but since it was still damp and rumpled from her sweaty Jog Master marathon, there was no point in trying to salvage it.

She smoothed her hair and rewound it back into the knobby bun she'd previously been sporting — before the palmetto fronds had yanked it down and to the side, like a drunken harlot's. She addressed her reflection as she snapped the puffy, sky blue braided elastic back into place. "This is your life, Riley Brown." Smirking at herself, she squared her shoulders and took one last inventory of the cuts and scrapes. It was either laugh, or cry. And she'd learned one thing for certain in her year on Sugarberry Island. "Laughing is a hell of a lot more fun."

CHAPTER 2

Quinn was standing on the back deck, with snapped-in-half pieces of a pretty decent size tree limb in either hand, when the curly-headed blonde found him. Well, them, really. "I didn't get your name, before."

"Riley," she responded as she crossed the deck. "Riley Brown."

"Quinn Brannigan," he offered in return, well aware she already knew his name, but being polite nonetheless.

That dry smile tugged at the corners of her outrageously compelling mouth. "A pleasure to make your acquaintance, though perhaps I'd have chosen a different way to greet you, had I to do it again."

"You do know how to make a lasting first impression," he said, hopefully appealing to her dry sense of humor.

The wry hint of a smile remained as she inclined her head and performed a quick curtsy, but it was the rather lovely shade of pink that suffused her freckled cheeks that ended up captivating him. "I'm quite the master of all-eyes-on-me entrances," she replied gamely, "just not always executed in the most preferable manner."

He chuckled at that, but not wanting to cause her further embarrassment, he shifted his gaze back to the beast. "He's not much for fetch, is he?"

"Search and destroy is more his idea of a rousing sport."

Quinn hefted the weight of the longer chunk of tree limb in his palm and looked to the far end of the property, past the small pool, toward the gardens and the dunes that lined up beyond it. "Yep. I'd say he's got scholarship potential in that department. What's his name?"

"Brutus." She held up a hand when he choked out a laugh. "I didn't name him. It really doesn't suit him at all."

"If you say so. Here you go, big fella." Quinn gripped the limb, pulled it back, then launched it like a javelin, in a high arc, over the pergola and the organic sea gardens, to the more sparsely designed pine-needle-carpeted rear of the property. Scrub-covered dunes formed the rear fence line, some-where behind which, from what he could hear, was the ocean.

"Impressive." She followed the trajectory of the lofted limb with one hand framing her forehead to block out the sunlight. "High school quarterback, right? College, too, probably?"

"Nope. Too scrawny. Track and field. Decathalon." He smiled as he watched the limb sail. "Didn't know I still had it."

Quinn thought she might have muttered something under her breath after that last comment, but he didn't quite catch it. His attention was still on the beast.

Brutus remained seated next to him and calmly tracked the branch's entire trajectory along with them, not overly excited about the pitch or the game as far as Quinn could tell. Only after it hit the ground, stirring up a little cloud of pine needles and dried palm fronds, did the monster-truck-sized dog set off in a deliberate but unhurried trot down the tiled walkway.

"I guess I can see why he doesn't really feel the pressure to exert himself," Quinn commented. "Even if he's not first to the prize, who's going to keep it from him, right?"

"He's really a big, gooey sweetheart." Riley walked over to stand beside Quinn. "Wouldn't hurt a flea."

"Not unless the flea was trying to take

41

away his big stick." Quinn waggled the shorter end of the limb he still held in one hand, before tossing it in the hedgerow that edged the deck.

"He only cracked the stick because he thought you were playing tug-of-war. He loves tug-of-war."

"I'll bet. It's always fun to play games you never lose."

She laughed. "I wouldn't know much about that." She turned to watch her pet beast trotting back, tree limb clenched in his mighty jaws, but Quinn hadn't missed the brief wince when she'd laughed, or the way she'd reached up to put her hand over the worst of the scratches on her face.

She'd gamely applied her sense of humor to the whole ordeal, taking her bad spill with a great deal of grace. It was pretty much the only thing graceful about her, at least that he'd witnessed thus far. Perhaps his reaction simply came from long-evolved instinct. Having spent most of his formative years as a fast-growing young man with an awkward command of his gangly body, he understood what it was like to wish gawky long limbs would behave in a more coordinated fashion. Though she was obviously well past her formative years — as was he — just because he'd outgrown gawky didn't mean he wasn't empathetic to those who never did.

While she'd appeared to be a bit of an uncoordinated klutz, ditzy she definitely was not. Despite the bountiful blond curls and farm girl freckles framing that intriguingly deluxe set of lips, those big brown eyes of hers didn't miss much, he guessed.

Brutus trotted up and plopped himself on his butt right in front of Riley, dropping the branch on her toes, then looking up at her with what could only be termed pride and a great deal of self-satisfaction. "You're such a good boy." She rubbed his massive head, which leveled out above her hips, as if he were nothing more than a wriggling pup, needing approval. "Scoot," she told the dog, then bent down and picked up the stick.

Brutus instantly shifted his stance and faced Quinn, eyes alert, jaw tense.

"What?" Quinn said, holding up his empty hands, palms out. "I don't have the stick, she does."

Riley laughed. "Yes, but he knows I can't throw. He also knows, now, that you can."

"Ah."

She shadowed her eyes again when she turned and looked up at him. She didn't have to look up as far as most people, and he discovered he rather liked that about her. Perhaps still a bit gawky as a woman grown, her body was anything but. Lush was the word he'd use to describe the abundant curves that wrapped around her sturdy frame. Combine all that with the greater than average height, the equally lush mouth, and all those blond curls, and, klutzy or not, she was a definite attention getter. Actually, it was the klutzy part, and those farm girl freckles, that made the otherwise bombshell body all the more interesting. She'd gotten his attention anyway.

"Not much of a dog person, huh?" she said.

"I love dogs. Had them all growing up. It's just . . . been a while. Also, the dogs I had as a boy were a mite smaller than a half-ton pickup truck."

She smile-winced again, then looked away. "It's okay. Most folks don't look past the size to the heart."

She was talking about the dog, but something in her tone made him believe she meant something else entirely. Herself maybe? He felt like he'd been judged, and found lacking. Or, worse, predictable. He wasn't sure why that stung — but it did — or why he cared what she thought, but apparently, he did.

Before he could decide how he wanted to respond, she dug into the side pocket of her bleached white khaki trousers and came out with the world's largest dog biscuit, then slapped her leg.

"Come on, Brutus, let's get you out in the Jeep." She started off toward a gate in the fence that framed the sides of the backyard. "I'll be back in. I've got to finish setting up the breakfast nook area with the food. Lois should be here momentarily, and he needs to not be here when that happens." She glanced over her shoulder as she opened the gate for Brutus. "I know it's asking a lot, but I'd really appreciate it if we could keep my catastrophe in there our little secret."

"Given it was my fault, I don't see how that's a favor."

Her lips curved briefly. "You're being very kind. It was going to have a bad end, no matter what. I just — well, thanks. I owe you one." She let herself out the gate and trotted after Brutus, who was already out of sight before Quinn could reply.

She really was the damndest thing. And despite her attention-getting frame, not at all his type. That thought annoyed him. He liked to think he didn't have a type, that he took everyone he met as he found them. Maybe it was just that he'd never met anyone quite like her. He didn't know what to think about that.

Not that it mattered. He wasn't there to socialize. He was there to focus, to get a firm handle on his next book. The last thing he needed was Claire making her politely professional but pointed phone calls as the publisher started pressuring her for a due date, or worse, for his agent, Lenore, to start in. *If they only knew the depth of the concern they should already be having.*

The real reason he'd come back to Sugarberry Island was in hopes it would remind him of the handful of summers he'd spent there as a teenager with his grandfather, and, more important, the wisdom his grandfather had passed down to him. Quinn had to figure out what direction to take, not only with the manuscript in question, but with his career. He wished his grandfather were still alive, but hoped just being back would give him the balance and perspective he needed to think things through and make the best decision possible.

And to get on with the damn book. One way or the other.

Did he take the path he always took, the one he knew his readers wanted him to take? Or did he risk everything, and continue down the new, tantalizing trail that was calling to him, the one he had no idea if anyone would take along with him? He smiled at that and shook his head. "Being predictable. Good or bad? Right or wrong?"

He went inside and found Riley in the breakfast nook, putting the final touches on the crystal display stand filled with amazing looking, heavily topped cupcakes. He didn't have a huge sweet tooth, but looking at them made his mouth water and his stomach grumble a little with the reminder that he'd only fed it toast and coffee thus far that day. "Those look incredible."

She squealed and dropped the cupcake she'd been carefully sliding onto the top tier, which in turn, hit the cupcake on the tier just below it . . . and, of course, both plopped down to wipe out the entire side of the bottom tier.

"Oh, no. I'm so —"

"Sorry," she finished for him, sighing as she stared at the cupcake catastrophe. "Now I know why you write mystery novels. You're naturally stealthy."

"I like to think it's more about being observant, but I suppose if I truly was, I'd have noted your focused concentration and done something to announce myself before I spoke. The cupcakes just got my attention." He entered the nook area and stepped over to the display. "I am sorry, though."

Reaching out, he scraped a dollop of frosting from where it had been clinging to the side of the middle tier and licked it off his finger. "Wow" — he groaned a little as he swallowed — "if the cake part tastes half as good, you can leave them all right there in a pile. I'll just get a fork."

"Unfortunately, I can't leave them looking like that. The open house officially opens in" — she glanced at the clock and blanched — "fifteen minutes. I've got more of these stashed in the fridge, but I'll have to clean off —" She stopped talking and started moving.

He was savoring another scraped-off dollop of the rich, creamy frosting, so he stopped her the only way he knew how. He reached for her arm, turning her back to face him, belatedly realizing as she looked in surprise to where he held her, that he'd reached for her with his frosting-fingered hand. "Oops," he said, when she lifted her disbelieving gaze to his. He tried out his best disarming grin. "I don't suppose you have any ice-cold milk to go with these?"

Her mouth dropped open, and suddenly he forgot all about the cupcakes, distracted once again by her mouth. It matched her body, but was so incongruous with the splashy freckles and big, brown doe eyes.

At the moment, all he could think was how incredibly decadent those lips would be with frosting tipping the bowed curves in the middle and . . .

Still holding on to her arm, he impulsively reached out and snagged another cupcake — a perfectly intact one — and held it up to her mouth. "Have you tried one?"

"Mr. Brannigan —"

"Quinn. Please. And I'm not kidding. Try this." He nudged the cupcake closer to her mouth. "I'll replace the shirt. And the ruined cupcakes. Did you make these?"

"No, my friend Leilani Dunne made them. She owns the Cakes by the Cup bakery, in town. Now I really" — she tugged at her arm, gently but firmly — "need to get this display finished before —"

"What you really need is to try this." He drew her and the cupcake he'd proffered closer. He had no idea, less than zero, actually, why he was doing it, but couldn't seem to stop. The more annoyed she became, the more determined he grew. "After the day you've had, you've earned it." He nudged the frosting to her lips, leaving a chocolate smudge.

He'd been teasing, telling himself he'd wanted to make her smile again. He hadn't meant to smear frosting on her lips, but tell that to his body, which jerked instantly to attention. When his gaze shifted to that sweet little dab of chocolate fascination clinging to her lips, he was gripped by an almost overwhelming urge to take another little lick of frosting. A very specific little lick.

Her tongue darted out to remove the temptation, increasing his discomfort . . . and his impulsive urges.

"Why are you —"

"I honestly don't know. But you've got frosting on you now." He nudged the cupcake toward her again, careful not to leave any traces. He smiled as she narrowed her gaze. "Might as well, right? It's incredible, I promise."

"Mr. — Quinn — I really have to —" She broke off, and looked back at the wrecked display. "Lois is due any second, and I don't want her to find me standing here in the midst of cupcake carnage, sampling the wares, so to speak."

His body jerked to renewed attention, needlessly reminding him of just whose wares he'd really rather she sample. "She won't. I mean Scary Lois won't. Be coming. Not today."

"But, how is that possible? I can't run the open house, it's not my function. Besides, she has all the — is she okay? Has something happened?"

"She's fine, and yes, something has happened. While you were setting up the piano, I called my manager and had him make an offer on the place. A very nice offer."

"You — did what?"

"Leased the place. I believe there is a flurry of faxes going on between Scary Lois and even scarier David as I speak. I'm sure I'll have to sign something at some point, but the deal is done."

"So . . . no open house."

"No open house."

"But . . . it's been advertised. People will show up."

"Then they'll be disappointed to find a sign on the front door telling them the property is no longer available. I suppose I should go take care of that."

"Right, but —"

"But first . . . honestly, try this."

She stared at him over the top of the cupcake. "Are you always like this?"

"Like what?" He grinned. "Unpredictable?"

He watched as her gaze darted from his eyes, to his mouth, and back to his eyes again. Her pupils expanded, her brown eyes growing darker and deeper as her throat worked and the muscles in her arms tensed — quivered, actually. He wrote, in great detail, about all those little, telltale signs that took place when someone was aroused. Though, admittedly, it had been a while, a good long while, since he'd had an opportunity to personally observe them.

"That's not entirely a bad thing, is it?" he asked.

"Uh, no," she managed, still all hung up in his very direct gaze. "No, I guess it's not."

"Good. Now . . . lick."

She did — which surprised him, though he wasn't sure why. He'd expected an eye roll. Or a cupcake shoved into his face. Either of which he'd have deserved. Having brought her up earlier, he absently wondered what Grams would say about his rather . . . assertive behavior. But those fleeting thoughts vanished when Riley immediately closed her eyes and made a sound in the back of her throat as the rich chocolate coated her tongue, in that instinctive way a person did who was naturally, even viscerally connected to the sensuality of experience. Smell . . . taste . . . touch . . . Watching her, he felt a very distinct, deep-in-the-gut quiver of his own.

"Lani," she murmured. "Once again, you rule."

"Possibly the patron saint of baking," Quinn agreed, almost reverently, as he continued to watch, fixated, as she finished enjoying every last creamy bite.

She opened her eyes, and caught him watching — staring, really — and her cheeks bloomed once again. "I —" She tugged her arm free and took a short step back. "You — just, uh, let me know when you'll be moving your stuff in and I'll make sure to have all the staging furnishings and decor out of here. I, uh, it will take at least two days, but I could easily have everything ready for move-in by the weekend."

She jerked her gaze to his hand, which still held the cupcake, then back to his face again. He couldn't tell what was behind the hunger clearly written on her face, but it didn't seem to matter to every inch of his anatomy. Some inches more newly invigorated than others.

"I just have to make a few calls."

"I offered for it as is," he said, not any more in control than she appeared to be. Perhaps for entirely different reasons, but still proving that while unpredictability might be exciting, it wasn't exactly without risks. A point to remember.

"Oh. Oh! Well . . ." She gazed around a bit wildly.

Maybe it was just his interpretation. His own pulse was like a jungle beat at the moment.

"I guess I should just . . . uh, go then. I'll go." She looked back at him, and smiled brightly, though it didn't reach her eyes, which were still kind of half-glazed. "If you have any questions, Lois can just — or you could call me. Or — David, was that his name? He could. Actually, you should. Call me, I mean. I'm the one with the contacts for the furnishings and I'm here on Sugarberry, too. Full time. So, anything you don't want, I can just — do you want me to clean this up?" She gestured haphazardly toward the mangled display. "No," she answered herself when his gaze dipped to her mouth again. "Okay, I'll just — I'll go. Now."

He was still standing by the ruined cupcake display, cupcake in hand, as he heard the door shut and the crank of her Jeep engine a moment later. He rather thought the sound of sprayed gravel, indicating she'd torn out of his driveway like the proverbial bat out of hell, was perhaps a bit of an extreme reaction to the situation. Until he tried to take a step and realized he was so hard and his jeans so accordingly tight that he could barely move without risking damaging something . . . and decided maybe she'd had the right idea all along.

"Focus," he said. "You came here to focus." He promised himself he'd get on with it . . . just as soon as he finished every last bit of the cupcake in his hand. The one with the dollop of frosting missing. And that's exactly what he did, without questioning why, right down to the last swirl, fleck, and crumb. Savoring each bite, he stared at the ruined cake display, imagining how differently the afternoon might have gone if he'd simply pushed her back onto the breakfast nook table, peeled open her blouse, and drawn one of those frosted cups of heaven over the rosy tips of what he knew would be lovely, lush breasts . . . then followed up with his tongue. He wondered if her senses were engaged so rapturously when involved with pleasures of the flesh, rather than the decadent results of cleverly combined amounts of flour, butter, and sugar . . . and already believed he knew the answer to that question. A sensualist was a sensualist.

He groaned at the new round of images that idea brought to mind, tossed the crumpled paper on the table, and went off to find out how well the advertised drenching showerheads worked when they were set on ice cold.

Ten minutes later, when that hadn't worked, he switched to steam heat. At least, for the following ten minutes or so, he remained focused on something.

CHAPTER 3

"Land sakes! What on earth did you get tangled up with?" Alva Liles, the most senior member of the Cupcake Club, didn't add *this time,* but it was implied.

"Whatever it was, I think you lost." Young Dre, whose hairnet-draped purple Mohawk never failed to make Riley smile, immediately hunched back over a white fondant draped layer of cake, intently focused on squeezing out perfect rose petal after perfect rose petal along the curved edge. Four more individual tiers were on the stainless-steel table behind her, each covered with hundreds, if not thousands, of roses in all shapes and sizes. Dre took the practice-makes-perfect mantra to new and dedicated heights.

Riley hung her purse up on one of the apron hooks, and slid her HELLO KITTY apron off another, quickly looping the neck strap over her head and tying the dangling waist straps behind her hips. She liked the whimsical aprons that every Cupcake Club member adopted, inspired by Leilani's lifelong collection. It was certainly more fun and more comfortable than the chef's jackets she'd often worn in her previous life.

"What are you working on tonight, Miss Alva?" Riley knew full well the entire story of her lacerated self would come out, but she wasn't quite ready to entertain the troops with her latest misadventure. Actually, she didn't want to talk about Quinn Brannigan at all. He might not be able to read her thoughts — or maybe he had — but she knew her fellow baking buddies never missed a thing.

"Hey, you're here," Leilani said, as she bumped open the swinging door leading from the shop front of the bakery to the decently sized kitchen area, where they all gathered every Monday night after the shop closed early. She was around the same age as Riley, much shorter but sturdy, with light brown hair, usually pulled back in a haphazard ponytail, and a calm, competent demeanor that somehow managed to keep everything controlled and sane, even in the midst of chaos. "I have a new cake flavor I want you to try," she told them. "It's my take on a Dreamsicle."

Everyone let out a collective "yum."

"They just need to rest another five minutes, then I'll frost and we're all doing a taste test."

"Once again it does not suck to be us." Riley hauled her toolbox and quilted supply tote over to an empty space on the far stainless-steel worktable to set up shop. The bakery was situated on the main floor of an old rowhouse style shop, with the retail area out front taking up only slightly more than a front room or parlor's worth of space. The lion's share of the first floor was dedicated to the kitchen. Riley had initially questioned the inequitable division of space, thinking it made more sense to put on a splashier display up front, but, of course, that was her styling background speaking. For her, it was all about the presentation.

For Lani, it was all about the preparation. As Riley's friendship with Lani had developed, she'd quickly come to learn, the former Leilani Trusdale had been a James Beard–nominated executive pastry chef at New York City's famous Gateau patisserie. The pastry shop was still owned by her now-husband, Baxter Dunne, the famous British pastry chef seen weekly by millions of adoring fans — Riley included — on his network television cooking show, *Hot Cakes*.

Lani and Baxter, who'd gotten married just before Riley had moved to Georgia, were quite happily ensconced islanders now — Baxter taping his show in a gorgeous plantation house just over the causeway on the outskirts of Savannah, and Lani running her own little cupcake bakery on Sugarberry. When the big-city girl had initially designed her new little rural island shop space, she'd given in to her penchant to retain the one thing from her former life that she truly hadn't wanted to give up — the fully locked and loaded, professionally appointed kitchen her former profession demanded.

"Where's Franco?" Riley asked, referring to Leilani's swarthy, Bronx-born Italian pal, whom Lani had known and worked with, back in New York. He and their mutual friend, Charlotte, had also migrated south and set up a catering business in Savannah. Charlotte was involved with Carlo, one of Baxter's prep chefs from his television show. Franco was big, gorgeous, gay, and spoke with an affected French accent that made absolutely no sense, but was utterly and exactly Franco.

"He's in Savannah for the next few days, helping Baxter finish up the last part of this season's shoot. They're trying to piggyback the final three episodes and get them done in the time it normally takes to do one, so Bax can have a little extra time to finish up his next cookbook. With the first one out for over a month now, he was supposed to already have this one in to the publisher. But with the show moving to a major network after last season, and all the press he was asked to do for that and the cookbook release, well . . . you've heard me bitch about it all before. I swear, the man is superhuman. But now, added to that, one of Baxter's chefs is out with the flu. So Franco is stepping in to help."

Riley looked concerned at the news, and Dre noticed. She looked up long enough to say, "Don't worry. The son-of-a-bitch traitor is gone."

Riley's brows climbed halfway up her forehead, which made her flinch. Resisting the urge to press a cool palm to her scratched-up face, she said, "Brenton's gone?" referring to Franco's soulmate life partner. His *former* soulmate life partner. The son-of-a-bitch traitor. "As in *gone-gone?*"

Dre nodded, making her newly installed eyebrow ring — a bit bigger than her other two — jiggle with the motion. The weight of what looked like a tiny dragon charm hanging from a tiny loop on the ring added to the sway.

"Got an offer two days ago from a new place out in San Francisco," Dre explained. "Took it."

"Baxter was relieved when he turned in his notice," Lani added. "Told him he didn't need the two weeks, to just head on out. Brenton was gone that day. If Baxter could have fired him for what he did to Franco, he would have, but it wasn't business related and —"

"We know. No one blames Baxter." Riley said. "I don't know how Franco managed to help out on the show as much as he did."

"Baxter tried to mitigate that," Lani said. "It wasn't fair to not give Franco the work, especially since Carlo has partnered in with them to launch Sweet and Savory. We all know Franco's still doing a lot of work with the catering business, but I think, with Brenton out of the picture, he was feeling kind of homeless. I was honestly worried he might go back to New York.

"Baxter offered him a full-time gig with the show almost before Brenton had left the building, but Franco hasn't agreed to take it yet. I think for the time being he's planning to bounce back and forth from his continuing work with Char and Carlo to helping Bax out when he can."

"As long as Brenton is gone and Franco is still here, I'm happy," Riley said.

"Damn straight," Dre muttered, then groaned. "God, no pun, no pun."

Everyone groaned with her, then Lani added, "Franco will be here later, though. He's coming back with Baxter this evening. And guess what?" Lani wiggled her eyebrows. "I think he had company night before last."

"He did," Alva confirmed. "The kind you cook breakfast for," she added, in case anyone hadn't picked up on the inference.

Everyone turned to look at Alva, eyebrows lifted in question, but she merely lifted a shoulder. "We talk." She beamed at the assembled group. "I told Franco to bring his friend along so we could meet him."

"When did you talk to Franco?" Lani asked.

"Never you mind, missy. Franco and me, we're snug."

Riley and Lani laughed at that. Even Dre's lips threatened a smile.

"Tight," Dre finally offered when Alva looked surprised by the laughter.

"What's tight?" Alva patted her perfectly teased and lacquered bouffant of white hair, while looking down at her expertly pressed and color-coordinated hot pink tracksuit. Riley was pretty sure the feisty octogenarian was the only woman who could wear pearls with a tracksuit and make it work.

"You and Franco." When Alva merely looked confused, Dre sighed. "Never mind."

"I don't see what's so funny," Alva said, clearly a bit miffed.

"Franco is family and we look out for family. We don't know anything about this new young man. Who his people are, where he's from, what his designs are on our boy."

"If anyone is doing the designing, I'm pretty sure it's Franco," Dre offered in the kind of laconic drawl only a twenty-one-year-old, disaffected art school student could pull off with any real authenticity. Dre nailed it regularly.

"Be that as it may, I still say we should meet this young man sooner rather than later."

"I'm sure if shared breakfasts become a regular part of Franco's routine, we will," Lani said.

Riley began unpacking her supplies for her evening's baking endeavor, happy not to be the focus of the conversation. She'd gotten a workstation that would keep her back conveniently aimed at the kitchen's occupants, as opposed to her scratched-up face.

"Well," Alva said, "if he doesn't, I'll just drop by unannounced with a pan of my blueberry crumble." She smiled the innocent, twinkly smile of the elderly that everyone in the room knew to be a blatant and utterly false cover for her devious and perfectly sharp eighty-three-year-old mind, and went right back to work, humming as she triple sifted another two cups of cake flour.

Riley smiled to herself, privately hoping she'd be half the woman Alva Liles was by the time she reached the woman's advanced age. Half her age, even. Heck, given Riley's propensity for causing herself personal harm, she'd be thrilled to reach Alva's age at all.

Just then Franco swung through the back door, with all of his typical "making an entrance" insouciance. "*Bonsoir,* mes amies!" he announced cheerfully. "How are all the lovely bakers of *les petites cakes* this fine, fine hot August night? Speaking of hot August nights, Lani, do you have any old Neil Diamond on hand? I think we need a little 'Cracklin' Rosie' or 'Sweet Caroline.' " He grinned and made a show of primping his hair. "You can skip 'Solitary Man,' though."

"Wahoo!" Lani hooted. "You know, I think I might be able to accommodate you." It was well-known, at least among the group, that when alone in her kitchen, Lani often baked while shaking her groove thing to old movie soundtracks, hard-driving rock and roll, and dance music. On many occasions, they "pumped up the jam," as Charlotte put it, her proper Indian dialect making the eighties song phrase particularly amusing, at least to Riley, who laughed every time Char said it.

As yet, no one had turned on the stereo that particular evening. Last time they had was two weeks prior when Alva had brought in her latest contribution, a CD from that "very nice looking boy" Justin Bieber.

Riley tried not to smile and make her scratches sting again, but remembering Alva waltzing about the kitchen while lip synching "Baby, baby, oh," made it pretty much impossible. Of course, considering Alva's previous offering had been the *Best of John Denver,* she'd be happy to keep the Bieber on permanent rotation if it meant they never had to listen to Alva actually sing along to "Thank God I'm a Country Boy." Ever again.

"Let me see what I've got." Lani tipped

up on her toes to buss him loudly on the cheek as she passed by on her way to the stereo cabinet. "Where's Baxter?"

Even though she'd been married for over a year now, Lani's eyes still sparkled like a newlywed's whenever she so much as said her husband's name. If possible, Baxter was even worse. Or better, depending on how you looked at it. Riley looked at it happily, for the fairy-tale-come-to-life that it was. So what if she suffered a few incredibly selfish pangs of envy? That was her problem, not Lani and Baxter's.

"He told me to tell you he was going by the house first, *toute suite,* then will be by with some leftovers from today's shoot." Franco folded his arms and smiled a very smug smile. "And it won't be Baxter's baking, either. Guess who dropped by today?"

Lani turned around. "Who?"

"Let's just say somebody wanted a little throwdown with Chef Hot Cakes."

Lani's mouth dropped open. "No way! My TV chef boyfriend, Bobby Flay? Right in our Savannah house kitchen? And no one called me?" She made a little squeaking sound of outrage.

"Calm down, sister," Franco said, the accent disappearing, as it often did when he was giving Lani a hard time. "It wasn't a real throwdown. He was in town to see Miss Paula and came by to check out the setup, have a little chat. And, you know how it is . . . cooking happens." He went over to Lani and put a consoling arm around her shoulders, though his shameless grin was anything but. "You get to eat your TV chef boyfriend's amazing barbeque, so all is not lost."

Lani groaned. "He made barbeque." She dragged out the last word on a deep sigh of abject appreciation mixed with a healthy bit of envy.

"It was the end of the day. That's why we're late. He wasn't there long enough for you to get across the causeway."

"Fine, fine. But I'm like an elephant," she said, tapping her forehead. "I don't forget these things." She poked Franco in the chest. "You get to be the one to tell Char what she missed when she gets back." Lani took smug pleasure from Franco's blanched expression. "And no Neil for you. Tonight, we bake along with . . ." She whirled around and punched the play button, then spun back as the opening strains of "Ice Ice Baby" smoothed into the room, making Franco groan, as she'd known it would. As they'd all known it would. "Oh yes, my smug, Bobby Flay barbeque eating friend, it's harem pants on the dance floor night!"

Riley barely swallowed her smile as Franco spun away in aggrieved disgust.

"Does that mean it's going to be Hammer Time?" Alva asked. "Oh, goodie." She wiggled her hips as she spun the sifter handle, spraying a fine mist of white flour all over her workstation.

It was at that point Riley lost the battle entirely. Scratched face be damned. She loved these people. She laughed and boogied herself as she continued to unpack her supplies, humming with the bass line as she unrolled her knives.

"I hope he's bringing enough for everyone," Alva said.

"Oui, oui, mes amies," Franco said, his joie de vivre making a swift return. "Have no fear. And it is, I must say, *que magnifique.*" Franco kissed his fingertips.

Lani rubbed her hands together in anticipation as she boogied her way back to where she'd prepped to frost her Dreamsicle cakes. "MC Hammer, eat your heart out. Are you baking tonight," she asked Franco, "or just playing taste tester after being in the studio kitchens all day? Eating barbeque, and making goo-goo eyes at my TV boyfriend."

"May I respectfully remind you that both you and your TV boyfriend are happily married? To other people. As for me" — Franco's accent thickened — "tonight I will be baking zee perfect petite red velvet cakes, as I am in need of sweets for serving." He turned and shot a wink at Riley, who, still in her happy Hammer Time place, winked right back.

"Sounds like we all have a plan then. Oh, Dreamsicle taste test in five minutes," Lani told him. "New flavor I'm thinking of adding to the shop menu."

"I vote it's dreamy," Franco sang, giving in and moving to the beat as he shook out and put on the required crazy apron. Tonight he was sporting one of his standards, the always amusing Charlie's Angels apron that Dre and some of her graphic artist cohorts had made for his last birthday. "But then" — he assumed, as he did each and every time he donned the apron, all three Angel poses, with amazingly accurate precision — "everything in my world is dreamy." As soon as he finished the Farrah pose — always the last one — Franco twirled around and placed his tool tote perfectly at the empty space right next to Riley.

Riley marveled, as she always did, how a man his size could be so utterly graceful. If she'd tried even a fraction of that move, she'd have taken out half the kitchen and sent at least three of them to the ER. On a good night.

She wrapped an arm around his waist and leaned in to give him a quick squeeze. "It's so good to see you like this."

"It's good to be like this, *mon cher.*" His deep, basso voice, was sweet and ardently sincere.

So many times, especially right after it had happened, when Franco had been at his lowest, Riley had wanted to meet with him privately, to commiserate. But nothing was private on Sugarberry, and though she knew Franco had a great big wonderful heart, she also knew he couldn't keep a secret to save his own life. So, she'd done her best to be there for him in every way she could, but had always felt a bit guilty for not being more open with him. God knows they'd all been open about all sorts of things. She was so thankful, so incredibly thankful, for their friendship and the sisterhood that had evolved — Franco included — during the time they'd spent together.

She'd come to Sugarberry essentially to hide out and lick her wounds, with no real idea of where she'd head from there. She'd only known the one place she didn't want to be. What she'd found instead, without even looking, was so much greater than anything she could have ever hoped for. Almost thirteen months later, it was no longer a temporary port of call. The island had become home.

"What on earth?"

Riley jumped as she suddenly found her chin gently but firmly cupped in Franco's very broad palm as he turned her face to his.

"Who did this to you, mon cher?"

"Who do you think?" she said, through distorted lips.

He turned her head to one side, then the other, before letting his hand drop away.

"You know me." Using her fingers, she made a quick *L* on her forehead. "I . . . kind of fell off a treadmill into a bunch of plants, okay?" She spoke quietly, so as not to alert the rest of the gang.

So much for that. Eagle ears Alva turned right around. "What's going on? What were you doing on a treadmill?"

Dre and Lani looked up then, as well.

Riley sighed. "You know the Turner house —"

"Don't get me started on the Turner house," Alva said. "Monstrosity. I can't believe what they did to that place."

"Looks pretty awesome if you ask me," Dre said.

Everyone looked at her in surprise.

"What? Just because I dress like a street orphan doesn't mean I don't appreciate the finer things of life. I happen to appreciate comfort, that's all. I went by the place back when they completed the exterior. They expanded the rooflines, added the sunroom, but maintained the traditional style . . . and the landscaping is stellar. Shows what you can do with a little ingenuity in this scrubby, sea-salted wilderness. Even though it's upscale, it's really modestly done, not so gaudy and obvious like the ones in the lower islands. I thought the concept was respectful of the traditional, yet celebrated a unique vision." She shrugged. "Just my take."

Alva harrumphed. "We'll see how unique you think it is when the other developers start crawling all over the island, trying to get us to sell our properties so they can flop them to some of those country club snoots."

"Flip," Lani said. "Flip the houses."

"Flip houses, flop houses, I don't care what you call it. I think it'll be the ruination of our little island, and our quiet way of life. We like things peaceful and slow. We don't need fancy-shmancy. And I'm not afraid to say that I was a bit surprised you took the job." Alva looked right at Riley.

"She has to work." Lani tossed an apologetic look Riley's way.

"She's got a whole slew of islands south of here that love nothing more than to play Out-Jones-the-Joneses. We don't need to encourage it here."

"The house had already been renovated when I was offered the job to stage it," Riley reminded her mildly. "All I did was help get it back off the market and into the private sector as fast as possible."

"And did you?" Lani asked. "Was there a taker today?"

"Um, yeah, as a matter of fact, there was." To Alva, Riley added, "You'll be happy to know they didn't even end up holding the open house. It was snapped up beforehand." She made herself busy taking out the ingredients she'd brought along. "No one else traipsed through it, no investors pretending to be buyers. Hopefully this will be a one and done."

"Really?" This from Lani. "Wow, that's kind of unexpected. Who would take a place sight unseen?"

"I'll tell you who," Alva said. "The Jones-busters, that's who."

Dre snickered, but swiftly returned to her so-bored-too-cool expression when Alva spun her sifter in Dre's direction. Lani and Franco snickered at that. A little. Alva just gave them the eye.

Lani looked at Riley then. "Do you know who rented it?"

But it was Franco, standing right next to her, who spoke first. "Ooh, la la, *ma chère,* is that a blush *la rouge* I see blooming on those lovely luscious cheeks?"

Riley smacked away Franco's hands, but he was still beaming. "Do tell, my sweet. We'll find out soon enough anyway." He rested his hips on the edge of the worktable and folded his arms across his expansive chest. When she didn't immediately comply, he scooted a bit closer, then a bit closer still, until he could bump hips with her — which he did. Repeatedly.

"Franco." Riley knew she was doomed. So, after a brief sigh, she turned to face the room, reminding herself again how great it was to have such close friends.

"Oh, good." Franco clapped his hands together. "Leave out nothing juicy. And it's juicy, am I right?" He looked at the assembled group, each one of them having completely abandoned their baking projects. "It's juicy," he assured them. "Spill it."

"You're the one with the secret boy toy news," Riley retorted. "You spill it."

"The difference, *ma fleur hauteur,* is that *I* want to share my news. Fair to bursting with

75

it I am. But I promised myself I'd go slower next time, moderate my enthusiasm. You, on the other hand, don't want to tell us a peep — which automatically makes yours far more delicious." He crossed his ankles and batted his insanely luxurious and enviably naturally thick black eyelashes. "You know me, dog with a bone. I could put Brutus to shame. We're going to find out anyway." He warbled the last word.

"Okay, okay." Riley nudged him back a little. But she still took another moment to figure out how best to share only the parts she really wanted to share. She wasn't going to humiliate herself all over again by explaining the whole Jog Master thing. She was taking the rest of the day off from abject mortification. And she certainly wasn't going to talk about what she'd come to think of as the Cupcake Moment. She still had no idea what to think about all that. But Franco was right about the rest not staying a secret. "It's Quinn Brannigan."

Alva and Dre frowned, but Lani and Franco's mouths dropped open.

"Seriously?" This from Lani.

"As a heart attack," Riley said. "Which is what I almost had when he came into the house early and startled the daylights out of me."

Franco laughed, but then reached out to gently touch her cheek. "Ah, now I understand." His eyes twinkled affectionately, even as he tsk-tsked.

She swatted his hand away anyway. "Quinn took one look at the place and called his manager. Done deal." She shrugged. "End of story." She turned back to her bag and began unpacking her supplies.

" 'Quinn,' is it? End of story, my saggy senior patootie," Alva said.

Everyone spluttered a laugh at that, even Dre.

"Honey, you have a very fine senior patootie," Franco said, slipping into the Bronx borough dialect of his birth, except he sounded like gay Rocky. "Ain't nuthin' saggy 'bout that, sister."

It made everyone laugh even harder, except for Alva, who preened a little bit.

"Why, thank you, Franco, dear." She gave him her sweetest smile. "What can I say?" She turned to the rest of them, patting her coiffed curls once again. "The French know how to appreciate a real woman."

Not a single one of them attempted to correct her. About most things, Alva was one of the sharpest tacks on the board, but there were rare occasions when she was delightfully clueless in the way most would associate with someone her age. Or at least she did a damn good job of pretending to be. Riley was never quite certain.

"Now, Miss Riley May," Alva said, "are you going to tell us the rest of the story?"

Alva added "May" to everyone's name, except Franco and Baxter, especially when she wanted something from them. Riley had learned it was sort of a Southern endearment, and had never minded it much. In fact, it was rather sweet. If you overlooked the whole underlying manipulation part.

"There is no rest, Miss Alva. It's a six-month lease. He's here, I assume, to get some peace and quiet to work on his next book. There's really nothing more to add. He's taking the house as is, so I don't even have to ship back the staged furnishings. Win-win."

Alva merely folded her arms over her My Little Pony apron — the very same one Lani had saved since childhood, and which also happened to be the only one that would fit Alva's tiny-as-a-bird frame.

Riley sighed again. "I don't think he's going to be throwing any swanky parties with snotty guests, if that's what you're worried about. In fact, it's my guess he'd like nothing more than to be left alone while he's here."

"So, you talked to him." Lani inched closer. "Tell us, is he as dreamy as he looks on the jackets of his books?"

Riley gave up. "Dreamier," she admitted. Every last person in the room sighed.

"Do tell," Franco said. "Details. The eyes?"

"Yes, they are that blue. Bluer, if possible."

"I bet he's shorter in person. Those movie stars always are," Alva said.

"He's a writer, not a movie star, but no," Riley assured her, "he's not at all short. Quite the opposite. Quite," she added, before she could stop herself.

"And?" Lani begged her to continue.

"And, that's pretty much it. He's tall, tanned, gorgeous, with just a flavoring hint of a Southern accent. And a really deep voice."

"My, my." Alva fanned herself with her recipe card, sending a coating of finely sifted flour all down the front of her apron.

"Do you read his books?" Lani asked Alva. "I didn't think you recognized the name when Riley said it. I'm not surprised, though. He writes some pretty gritty stuff."

"Some pretty sexy stuff, too," Dre murmured.

Lani turned back around, and Riley looked at Dre, as well. But Dre was busily making more roses. A lot more roses. Like it was her damn job.

"So, you know who he is, too." Lani said to her.

"Duh," Dre said, not looking up. "He's a household name. Like Grisham, Patterson, and King. Who hasn't? I was just surprised he'd come to Sugarberry."

"How do you know about the sexy stuff?" Lani asked her.

Dre looked up, and blinked through the hot-pink-and-black leopard-print cat-eye cheaters she'd put on, the girlishness of which was in complete contrast to the overall goth-darkness of the rest of her ensemble. Riley was fairly certain that was exactly why Dre had chosen them. She was nothing if not a fan of incongruity, two thousand identical paste roses notwithstanding. Perched on the end of her nose, they only partially hid the four rings now piercing her left eyebrow, but left entirely visible the diagonal lines she'd shaved across the other.

With great patience, Dre tipped her head back so she could look down her nose through her crazy eyeglasses, which, Riley had to admit, did go with her much-favored

Johnny Depp Mad Hatter apron. "I realize I have the body of a twelve-year-old boy, and the relative height of said twelve-year-old boy's ten-year-old brother. But I assure you, at the age of twenty-one, I do know about the sexy stuff. In fact, I know where babies come from and everything."

"Come on, we know you date and all," Riley said, not wanting her to feel awkward. "I simply meant —"

"No, I do not date," Dre corrected her, clearly not needing the save. "I'm focused on my studies, and learning all things pastry from the master chefs Dunne and Dunne." She turned and performed a from-the-waist-up abbreviated version of the "I'm not worthy" bow in Lani's direction.

"What about Andrew, from your graphic illustrations class?" Lani said, giving her a quick salute back. "You've been to a couple things with him recently, right? Lectures and stuff?"

"Right. As friends. Colleagues. We share similar interests. We do not share a bed. Much less the clichéd backseat of a car."

Lani and Riley might have swallowed a little hard at that.

Dre rolled her eyes. "What? You can't have it both ways. You say you're cool that I'm dating, which implies I'm having sex, but then you seem all weirded out by the idea that I might actually be — never mind. I'm not having this conversation. Or sex. There. Happy now?"

Lani was too busy coughing — it had been that or choke — so Alva said, "You're a good girl, Missy Dre. I'm proud of you. Stand up for what you want, and don't lie down for anybody you don't."

It was Riley's turn to choke a little, though on laughter. To hide it, she ducked her chin so she could twist her hair up into a knot before she started working.

"As long as you're happy, you go girl," Franco told Dre. Then he turned right back to Riley. "What else?"

"Nothing else," she said, exasperated, as she snapped the hot-pink scrunchie into place.

"Well, I love his books," Lani said, turning back to her rack of tester cupcakes and picking up the pastry bag she'd filled with a creamy sherbety orange frosting earlier. "How he writes such gritty, horrible crime dramas, but wraps them up in such powerful love stories" — she sighed and fanned herself with the flap end of the pastry bag — "gets me every time."

"I bet he's good in the sack," Alva said, then turned back to her sifting. "I just read them for the sex. You can skip right past the gory parts if you don't like them. The sex parts alone are worth the price. I buy them in hardcover."

It was pretty much a group choke that time. Riley recovered first and grinned broadly, not caring that it pulled at the tender skin around her scratches. "Power to you, Miss Alva."

Franco started humming "Sisters Are Doin' It for Themselves," making Riley nudge him in the ribs.

But she was grinning. She did love this group, nosy busybodies, fake accents, mandatory crazy aprons, and all. They had no idea how much they'd done for her.

"Okay, everyone, taste test time!" Lani lofted the tray of freshly topped cakes. "I give you Leilani's Dreamsicle cakes, featuring mandarin orange soaked butter cake with cheesecake filling and sherbet whip frosting."

Everyone *ooh*ed together, sounding exactly like the little green men in the *Toy Story* movies.

As they shuffled over, still replicating the LGMs in the movies, Riley quickly took the butter out of the cold pack she'd stored it in before heading to Lani's table.

Franco swung back and cut her off, then

leaned down close. "We're not done talking, you and me, *mon amie.*"

She looked up at him. "Franco, I swear, there's nothing more."

Instead of a teasing or pleading look — he could teach master classes in both — his expression was uncharacteristically quite serious. "You've been there for me, Riley." When she started to brush that off, he placed his big hand gently on her arm. "You've been there. You don't have to confirm it, okay? I know. Those of us who've been there . . . we know. It's time for me to return the favor and be there for you. So . . . we're going to talk, *Mademoiselle* Brown."

Riley was surprised into momentary silence. She appreciated that he'd understood her desire to be there for him, and perhaps she really had been more of a help than she'd realized, just by providing a shoulder and words of comfort. It was a little disconcerting, though, that he'd ferreted out just how much she had understood about his pain. "I don't need a return favor, Franco. Not in this instance. I was glad I could be there for you. That's what friends are for."

"I know. And friends return favors." He bent down and looked into her eyes, then smiled broadly. "I saw the stardust in your eyes, *cherie.* And that's something I know a little about." He looped an errant curl behind her ear. "Just know, I'm here."

CHAPTER 4

Quinn stepped from the fixed pier onto the floating dock situated at the very back of the commercial moorings. It was where fisherman, commercial and local — he knew from past experience — could tie up temporarily without having to navigate through the maze of permanent slips, so they could run into Biggers' Bait and Tackle for supplies or a bag of ice. Old Haney Biggers had run the place back when Quinn's grandfather had run his trawler out from those very commercial piers. Other than a few fresh coats of paint, and an ATM parked out front, it looked much the same as it had fifteen or sixteen years ago. Quinn doubted Haney, who'd been older than his grandfather, still ran the place. Probably a son, or grandson by now.

Quinn wobbled a step or two as the dock dipped and swayed in the wake of an incoming slow-chugging trawler. It had been a very long time since he'd needed his sea legs, but he was happy to discover, as he gained more consistent balance, that it was apparently much like riding a bike. Something else he hadn't done in ages, he thought absently, as he made his way down the lightly swaying row of weathered planks. Maybe he'd pick up a bike while he was here and tool around the island. He knew many of the residents did, or had when he was younger.

He shifted his gaze past the bait shop to the boats tied up to the bigger, sturdier piers. Gavin Brannigan had kept his trawler there. He'd also harbored a little center-board, single-keel sailboat back on a tiny pier behind the house on the sound that he and Quinn's grandmother had lived in, on the west side of the island. Not too far from his beach bungalow in actual distance, but a lifetime away now. The house was no longer there; it had surrendered its weathered clapboard planks to a hurricane — what had it been, at least seven, eight years ago? Fortunately it had stood empty, both Gavin and his grandmother long deceased by then. The owner had been using it only as a summer cottage.

Quinn had gone by there yesterday, out of curiosity and sentimentality. A relatively new, modest lodge stood there now.

He'd thought about knocking on the door and introducing himself, asking if he could walk the grounds around the sound for old times' sake. There was no little pier behind the house, and the rest was so different, it hadn't seemed worth the intrusion. He had his memories, and looking across the calm, smooth waters of the inlet brought them back as clearly as if he and his grandfather had set out on a sunset sail the evening before.

Gavin had been a fisherman by trade, operating a commercial vessel for work purposes, along with many other merchant vessels. Those days were long, hot, sweaty and reeking of fish stink, filled with some of the most demanding physical labor and extreme tests of Quinn's patience the then fifteen-year-old boy had thought he could possibly endure. The former had taught him a lot about what kind of man he could be. The latter was the skill that would come in most handy for the man he had become.

Gavin Brannigan had lived to see his only grandson graduate from college, only the second, after Quinn's father, in their branch of the family to do so. By the time Quinn had published his first book a few short years later, Gavin had already joined his beloved wife, Annie, in the "great and grand beyond," as he'd called it, his rolling brogue always making it sound like the best adventure destination in the world. And perhaps it was.

Quinn thought about the summers he'd spent here, from the age of fifteen until just past his twentieth birthday. He'd worked the trawlers for the income, lending a hand where it was needed . . . and because Quinn had come to understand that what his father had wanted most was more time alone. Even from him. Maybe especially from him. Quinn had never been entirely certain. Still wasn't. As if the long, eighty-hour workweeks his father put in hadn't isolated him enough. Quinn's mother had died in a car accident just after his thirteenth birthday. His father had never been particularly geared to parenting, though he wasn't openly averse to it. But Mary Elizabeth had been born to the role, and he'd gladly left her to it, taking on the traditional patriarchal role, which was providing for his family. A role Michael Brannigan had taken seriously. They didn't live in the lap of luxury, but they'd never gone wanting.

His father had loved his wife, that much Quinn knew, if by nothing other than the depth of his father's grief. He wasn't a demonstrative man, even with her. Not that Quinn had seen, anyway. And Mary Elizabeth's death had pushed him to some place he'd never quite come back from, even now. So that had to speak of a deep bond.

Quinn didn't know for certain. It remained a subject that, to this day, he and his father didn't speak of.

He shifted his thoughts purposefully back to the handful of summers he'd spent on Sugarberry. When he'd been younger, his grandparents had lived farther south, and he'd rarely spent time with them. It hadn't been until their move to Georgia, and his mother's death, that he'd been shuttled off to their care, at least for the summer breaks. He smiled, remembering coming in from the backbreakingly long days, thinking there was no way in hell he'd be able to rise again the next morning and do it all over again. That if he never touched or smelled, much less ate, another fish for the rest of his life, he'd die a happy man.

Only to sit down to a solid hot meal, lovingly and always deliciously prepared by his Grams, and discover, to his absolute and continued amazement, that by the time the relaxed meal had been concluded, when his grandfather asked if he'd like to head out on a little sunset sail around the sound in the single keel, man against the sea and wind — rather than against what swam beneath it — Quinn had actually thought it sounded like a good idea. And it had been, every time. The leisurely loops around the inlet had provided opportunity for the two of them to talk, shooting the breeze and the bull. Workdays didn't allow for conversation of any kind, and the young man Quinn had been looked forward to those long, rambling conversations as the favorite part of his day.

Quinn could hear his grandfather's hearty chuckle as clearly as if he stood before him. He knew the pride that would have shone in his bright blue eyes upon hearing the news of his grandson's accomplishments. Quinn's smile spread to a grin. Along with it, the old man would have delivered a healthy dose of ribbing that his only grand-child had chosen to earn his keep making up stories rather than using his hands and back for what Granda Gav would deem an honest day's work.

There weren't too many Irishmen plying the southern shores back then, or likely now, for that matter. His grandparents and their families had come over from Doolin, a small fishing village on the west coast of Ireland, to build a fresh life in New England, where the hardier Brannigan souls continued to eke out a living fishing. It was only after he'd met and married his wife, the former Annie O'Sullivan, and they'd begun their small family that Gavin had pulled up stakes and moved south. The warmer climate was beneficial to Annie's poor health. First to the shores of the Gulf, and only much, much later, after Quinn's own father had grown up and gone on his own way, had they come to Sugarberry.

Quinn had never known, exactly, what had ailed her. He knew it to be something with her breathing, but Annie Brannigan was a proud woman and the very last to allow anyone to see that she might be running on less than full steam. It simply wasn't discussed outside what was held private between her and her husband.

Quinn's smile turned wistful as he thought about the two of them, how they'd been with one another. For all that his mother had been loving and warm, making him feel very loved, his parents' relationship had always been somewhat austere and reserved. Given his mother's predilection for hugs and kisses, Quinn had assumed she'd taken those cues from his father. Actually, he hadn't thought much about it one way or the other — his parents were his parents — until his mom had passed and he'd come to stay with his Granda Gav and Grams. Theirs had been an entirely different sort of relationship, the likes of which he'd never known could exist.

They were always as happy to see each other as if they'd been apart ages rather than hours. They were truly the light in each other's eyes, even when they were squabbling, which was done with more affection than anger. He'd come to know theirs had been a love story of epic proportions, one Quinn had never been able to come close to writing about. No one would quite buy just how inordinately and blissfully happy the two of them made each other.

It had been the best thing Quinn had ever learned about the capacity of the human heart, and one of the hardest, as well. Finding a partner who could be to him all that he'd witnessed them to be to each other had proven elusive. Quinn often wondered if he'd have been happy settling for less if he'd never known what could be. If he'd only observed his parents' kind of love.

Of course, he liked to think if he hadn't, he wouldn't be the writer he was, either. Although he couldn't completely capture the depth and breadth of his grandparents' love for one another on the pages of a book, the absolute knowledge that love like that existed was a large part of why Quinn wrote the kinds of stories he did. Not the murder, the grit, and the horror . . . that was the grip, the grab, the thing that pulled his readers in. But what kept them in, what made them invest more than their curiosity, wondering how he was going to solve the crime, was his ability to make them care — and care deeply — about the people he put at risk. Would they triumph?

Of course. They *had* to triumph. And the why of that was always — always — love. Love was the foundation that motivated his protagonists to fight off the evil that other men do. It gave them the will and strength to do whatever it took to win out, and why, in the end, they always — always — did. To that end, the love affairs he wrote about were epic as well. Perhaps not in as grounded and real a way as his grandparents' love — fiction demanded something of the tempestuous and fantastical — but his characters experienced love as deeply and fully as Quinn was capable of writing it.

Love was also the very reason he found himself at a crossroads. "What should I do, Granda Gav?" he murmured, looking out over the waters to the hazy blue horizon beyond, though his thoughts were much,

much further away. "What would you do?"

On the surface, it seemed easy. Go with his heart. His grandfather would tell him that much, Quinn knew. On a certain level, he knew that was the right decision. Maybe even the only one he could make. But there were other considerations. Not the monetary ones. In fact, money was the least of it. It was more that he felt an obligation to his readers, to the ones who had made possible the life he was so fortunate to have, the career he so loved and enjoyed. He didn't take lightly the idea that he would be potentially snubbing all that goodwill and trust. And for what? A self-indulgent choice that would possibly make only him happy?

His grandfather might not understand that specific commitment, the pact Quinn felt he'd made with each and every one of those readers who'd chosen to give him their loyalty and their hard-earned dollars. But he would have understood the emotion behind it. Commitment to the well-being and happiness of others, even at the detriment of your own success or happiness, was why Gavin relocated himself many hundreds of miles away from his own family and all they'd built on these shores. For the love of his wife, and her welfare, he'd started all over again. More than once. He'd never achieved a fraction of what he would have had he stayed north, where the strength and bond of their numbers alone had built a much sturdier trade.

His grandparents' lifestyle could be described as simple, basic, but Quinn had absolutely not a single doubt that his grandfather would have done any differently, given another chance. Granda Gav would have made any sacrifice if it meant keeping his beloved wife happy and healthy. He would have even said it was a selfish choice, not a noble one. Because he'd been rewarded with her companionship and love for all the additional years the move south had awarded her. Them.

Quinn sighed and rubbed a hand over the back of his neck as he felt the tension begin to creep in again. It seemed so ridiculous on some levels. Just write whatever damn book he wanted. It wasn't life or death. Not like with his grandparents' choice. But this was *his* life. In the absence of what his grandparents had, at the age of thirty-four, this was what fulfilled him and made him happy. This was what he invested his passion and energy in. This was what he stood for, what mattered. So, in that regard, it was a very big deal. To him.

He rubbed the same hand over his face,

then raked his fingers through his hair . . . and laughed. "Damn, Brannigan. Maybe you just need to think about getting a life."

No sooner had the words left his mouth than the entire dock shook and rumbled under his feet, followed by what could only be described as an inhuman-sounding bellow.

He actually knew that bellow. One glance over his shoulder proved that he'd guessed right.

Barreling toward him, jowls flapping, was all one-hundred-and-God-knew-how-many pounds of Brutus.

Quinn stood frozen for a moment, stunned that the behemoth was capable of such speed. He had just enough time to glance skyward and murmur, "Sometimes you have a really twisted sense of humor," before sidestepping out of the way, up onto the tips of his toes like a matador, so Brutus could skate right past him without taking them both into the water.

Unfortunately, with his intended quarry suddenly no longer in front of him, Brutus tried to scramble his huge, hulking frame back around with a skidding, surprisingly agile slide. But he didn't quite make it, and off the end of the pier he sailed, making a huge splash in the water. The cascading fountain naturally sheeted back over the dock . . . doing a decent job of soaking a good part of the front of Quinn's polo shirt and khaki shorts.

"Brutus!"

Quinn felt more dock vibrations and turned to see the star of his cupcake fantasies running down the pier, blond curls bouncing. Well, more than just the blond curls, if he were honest. And it might have been the other bouncing things that distracted him momentarily from responding.

Yeah. Definitely need to get a life.

Of course, if he knew how, wouldn't he already have one? Perhaps he should tell Finch to put it on the schedule. If anyone could figure it out, it would be his PA — Who was, for all practical purposes, more like his manager David's PA — since Quinn didn't work well with people actually underfoot. All he knew was, between the two of them, they expertly handled all the career and business stuff that didn't involve actually writing the books. Maybe they could arrange a social life for him while they were at it.

"I'm so sorry!" Riley called out, huffing a little as she also skidded to a stop a few feet from his damp form. "I was putting my bags on the pier back there, only took my eyes off him for one second. He usually doesn't go after anyone like that. I'm not even sure how he knew it was you, all the way down here." She framed her forehead to shield her eyes from the sun, so she could smile up at him. "He likes you."

She had dimples. How had he missed that the other day? Of course she had dimples. They suited her completely. They also made his body stir, which was nuts. Sunny freckles, apple cheeks, ringlets and now, dimples. Not remotely his speed. At the very least, she was definitely not the type of woman who might actually follow through on that fantasy he'd had in the shower. Much less the one he'd had later that night. Or the following morning in the shower. Again. Not because he wanted to have them, they just kept . . . appearing. It was the other part of having a very vivid imagination. Sometimes it handed him things he didn't ask for.

With this added detail, he had a strong suspicion his vivid imagination wasn't done toying with his subconscious quite yet.

Yeah. Really bad idea, remembering the cupcake fantasies. The way that delectable dab of chocolate had clung to those ridiculously earthy lips she had, smack in the middle of that girl-next-door face. And there was the matter of that body. That body could fulfill dreams he hadn't even thought up yet. As long as they didn't try anything particularly acrobatic, he amended, recalling her less than graceful treadmill dismount and general banging about in the kitchen.

He shifted his stance and looked out across the water, to where Brutus was presently paddling around. "Is he going to be okay out there? Do we need some kind of doggie life preserver?"

"He'll be fine. He'll come back over and I'll haul him up. The floating docks are good that way."

Quinn slanted her a look. "You *pull* him up? How many times do you end up in the water with him?"

The dimples deepened when she laughed. "Pretty much as often as you think I do. But he doesn't dive in often." She glanced up at him. "What brings you down here? Did you get the notes I sent to your personal assistant? Mr. Fincher? He's very nice, by the way. Super . . . efficient."

Quinn smiled. "Yes, Finch is definitely that." He might have phrased it as anal-retentive perfectionist, but, as he directly benefited from Finch's retentiveness, it didn't much matter how it was described. "And yes, everything came through fine. I appreciate your getting the necessary approvals and whatnot, so that I could keep the contents of the house for the duration of my stay. And so quickly. I was able to move in day before yesterday, ahead of the weekend schedule."

"Good. I'm glad it all went smoothly."

"I also made sure Finch and my manager David mentioned to Lois how pleased I was with your work and your help. I didn't realize you'd staged the house."

She tilted her head slightly to one side, clearly bemused. "What did you think I did?"

He smiled. "You mean after I realized you were work-jogging?"

He watched her cheeks bloom, and thought she might be the first woman he'd met who couldn't hide a single thing she was feeling. Her fair skin acted as a veritable bulletin board for her thoughts. She probably hated it. He found it rather tantalizing. And maybe a little adorable. She'd probably hate that last thought, too. Something about how she carried herself, the alertness that was always there in her eyes, and the bit of a shield she kept up, despite her sunny and outgoing nature, told him her waters ran a lot deeper than the dimples and freckles, curls and cleavage combination that what likely led most people to believe.

She cleared her throat. "Um, yes, after that part."

"Well — and don't take this as an insult — but initially I thought maybe the super-efficient Finch had set up a maid service for me."

She frowned. "Really. Before you even got there?"

Quinn flashed a grin. "He is amazingly efficient." She wasn't smiling. "Not that you looked like a maid! Anything but," he hurried to say.

"I've got nothing against maids," she said.

"It's just, Finch is also something of a . . . uh . . . caretaker, constantly nagging me to get more life in my life, if you know what I mean. So . . . at the time, it didn't entirely surprise me that perhaps he'd set up something like that because you're . . . uh —" He stopped, somewhat mortified to realize the hole he'd somehow dug for himself. He was usually the observer, watching other people chatter on. He was never the guy talking. Always the guy watching. The guy watching never got in trouble for opening his big, fat mouth, and inserting his foot.

"I think I get where you're going." Her tone was more acerbic than insulted. "And, clearly, I wasn't that."

"Right." He was relieved that she seemed to be taking his unintended slight with grace. "No, that I knew, obviously. Don't worry. I just wasn't sure what it was you did do."

That made her cheeks darken further, only he wasn't sure it was due to embarrassment. Not if the quick flash he'd seen in her eyes was any indication.

"So, after you safely determined that your PA couldn't have possibly hired me to see to your . . . personal needs — and by the way, is that a service he performs often for you? Because I have a really hard time believing, even if you were stranded in the remotest part of the desert or at the ends of an arctic tundra, that somehow, someway, you wouldn't find a willing partner, all on your own."

"First, no, he never has. He's just been more than typically concerned about me lately, and . . . well, his skill set runs more to the logical, linear solution than to the more socially acceptable ones. And, secondly, thank you. I think." Quinn had no idea how he'd arrived at this particular conversational juncture, but knew he had only himself to blame for the understandably wary concern still on her face. So maybe Finch wasn't the appropriate go-to guy for Quinn's Getting a Life campaign after all.

"So, when you ruled out the Julia Roberts *Pretty Woman* gig, and the J.Lo maid gig, what did you think I was doing there?"

"Working for Lois, I guess, in some capacity. Assistant? I wasn't certain. But I wish I hadn't brought any of this up, because clearly I've offended you and I sincerely didn't mean to. All I wanted to tell you was how impressed I was with everything you've done. I hadn't looked at the entire house while I was there —"

"Wait, back up." She frowned as if something had just occurred to her. "You sort of fudged over it, but how could Finch have already reserved some kind of 'maid service,' " — she used air quotes around that last part, and for the first time in pretty much as long as he could remember, his cheeks were the ones growing warm — "and had me already there before you'd even decided to lease the place? Didn't you put that into motion while I was getting Jeffy and T-Bone to set up the baby grand?"

"Right. That. Well, actually, I'd already put David in touch with Scary Lois. He handles all the personal contracts, my regular agent only handles dealings that directly relate to the work itself."

"You know, you really have to stop calling her that or somehow, someway, it will come back to bite me. I can't believe I ever said that out loud. Only, of course I did."

He smiled at that. She was such an unusual woman, this odd mix of someone with easily tweaked red cheeks but otherwise outspoken and pretty direct about most everything else.

"I'll do my best. And if I screw up, I'll take the blame. Just tell her I'm developing this amazing real estate character or something."

"I don't know that she'd be flattered to think you'd be making her some kind of intimidating villain — wait a minute, what am I saying? She'd be all over that."

Quinn laughed. "Then we're covered."

"So, then, you'd just leased the place sight unseen?"

"Well, I'd seen the brochure photos and write up, but, to be honest, I would have taken any place available on Sugarberry where I'd have unlimited privacy. You can't get that at a bed and breakfast, which was all that was available."

"It's true. Once folks come here, they tend to stick around. I can speak to that personally."

"I was excited when I found out there was

a place available. When you were with the movers, I confirmed with David and Finch that after seeing it, I hadn't changed my mind. I told them to finish up the paperwork."

"And to politely decline the maid service." She didn't use air quotes that time, and her self-deprecating smile had returned in full. "Thank you. For the good review to Lois. Your endorsement means a lot. Especially considering the . . . uh, work-jogging."

He grinned and her cheeks warmed a bit again. She felt it and purposefully turned around, ostensibly to keep track of Brutus, who had paddled around to the other side of the dock, but Quinn was pretty sure it was to hide her face from him.

Given his cloddish, ungentlemanly commentary, he could hardly blame her, but he wished she wasn't self-conscious about the blushing. It wasn't like she could help it. It was the contrast between the old-fashioned courtesan curves and straight-shooter personality that made her all the more interesting to him.

"The good review was sincere," he said, shifting so he stood beside her. He noted she kept her face framed from the sun as she looked over the water, but switched to using her left hand, to block her face from him as well. It shouldn't have bugged him. He shouldn't have cared if she wanted to hide. From him, or anything else. But it did bug him — which meant he did care.

He should probably cut that out. Any time now.

"The thing I made sure David mentioned to Lois specifically was how much the house felt like a home, like someone had already been living in it. You did a wonderful job keeping it sophisticated enough to match all the over-the-top upgrades, but you did an even better job of keeping it comfortable. I've rented other places that looked great in a magazine layout, but I couldn't sit anywhere, or touch anything for fear of leaving footprints or fingerprints. Those places leave me feeling like an intruder. But the bungalow . . . I really like it."

He hadn't mentioned to Finch or David that perhaps he really liked it because he knew she'd had a hand in designing the décor. Or because his recollections of her being in the house made him smile. Mostly because he hadn't been aware that was true until this very moment.

"Why do you lease places that leave you cold?" she asked, still without turning to him. "At the very least, why not refurnish it to your own taste?"

He laughed at that.

"What's funny? I mean, I don't want to be rude or indelicate, but I'm guessing it's not a financial worry for you. Is it that you don't stick around long enough, so it's not worth the effort?"

"Sometimes, but it wouldn't matter. Because I haven't the first clue what my style is. Other than I know it —"

"When I see it," she finished, nodding. "It always amazes me how many people are like that. I mean, I guess I understand it doesn't matter to everyone, but, speaking for me personally, I can't imagine not being influenced by my surroundings. As a writer, I'd think it would be imperative to be comfortable, or to set a certain tone or vibe. Or whatever it is you need to get your head in the space it has to be in."

"I don't know if that's so much a thing for me. All I really need is quiet. When I sink into the work, the world around me goes away. All I see is whatever I'm writing. The rest of the time . . . yes, I guess I do notice. And I want to be relaxed, comfortable. But I don't know that I've put any real energy into figuring out what works best or why. All I can say is, I knew I liked the cottage the moment I saw it."

She glanced up at him, then back at the

water again. "Even the baby grand?" she asked. "You don't strike me as a baby grand guy."

"Why not?"

"No particular reason. I guess it's that comfortable, lived-in vibe you spoke of. If that draws you, then I'd think the baby grand would be a little over the top. I worried about putting it in there, but Lois was adamant about having a few big statement showpieces. I was going for something more like a pool table or even foosball, but she —"

"Foosball," he repeated, with fond reminiscence. "Haven't seen one of those, or played on one since college. That would have been classic."

"I could have the piano removed. Put the foosball in, or the pool table, or maybe some more workout equipment. It shouldn't take more than a day or two, to —"

"No, no, I'm good. Actually, I like the piano. Statement piece and all." He grinned and looked more directly at her. "Does that change your opinion of me?"

She looked right at him then. "No."

He laughed outright.

"What?" she said. "I said it didn't change my opinion. My opinion wasn't a bad one."

"You just said it straight out, like having

an opinion of me doesn't come into play because that's not part of the job."

She eyed him. "You got all that out of a simple no?"

He studied her face for a long moment. "I'm pretty good at reading people."

She started to turn away from him again just as the pink rose to her neck, but he found he really didn't want her to escape. So, without thinking, he reached out and touched the side of her cheek, turning her face back to his.

"Mr. Brannigan —"

He rolled his eyes, but didn't take his hand away. "We're not business associates. Quinn. Please."

"As long as you have leased furniture in your bungalow, you're a client."

"I signed waivers on all of that. If anything happens to any of it —"

"That's not what I meant. I just meant . . . you're a client. You leased a home I staged, with pieces I'll still be responsible for again at some point, and that's business, so —"

"So, you can still call me Quinn. Unless you really want me to call you Miss Brown." He tilted her cheek a little. "The scratches have healed up fast. Doesn't look like they'll leave any permanent marks."

She shifted away from his touch. "They

have, thanks, and yes, it's all going to be fine." She turned again, watching Brutus as he came toward the dock.

"So, it's just the business thing, then?" he asked.

She looked back at him. "Is what just the business thing, then?"

"You retreat if I get close."

"You're right, I do. Partly because it's a business thing, but mostly because . . . well, I'm otherwise not —"

"You're not available," he finished for her. Of course she wasn't. He thought about his behavior with that cupcake. He was lucky she hadn't pushed it in his face and kneed him in the groin. Wow, he normally wasn't so slow on the uptake.

It shouldn't matter. This was the wrong time to play anyway, and she was the wrong woman to play with. He should be relieved. Game over. Back to work. "I'm sorry, I shouldn't have assumed otherwise. You're clearly — I mean, any man would be lucky to —"

He broke off as her cheeks bloomed anew. Her pupils slowly dilated — like they had over the cupcake in his dining room. Yeah, he definitely didn't need that to be happening, especially knowing she wasn't available. To him, that put her off limits even for fantasizing — which he really had to knock off. If he was going to fantasize about anyone getting any, it should be his characters. His needs could wait. As usual.

"I'm shutting up now," he said with a small grin, wondering if she remembered saying those same words to him, post treadmill launch.

She smiled briefly, letting him know she did. They didn't need things like in-jokes and meaningful looks between them. Not when he had a book to write and an entire career path to figure out.

And she had some other man to go home to.

They fell silent, and then Brutus hit the dock, making them wobble on their feet. Riley was still wobbling when she awkwardly knelt to heave the beast's hulking wet frame onto the dock, prompting Quinn to kneel beside her. "I can get him. Will he let me?"

"If he wants to get out, he will. You take that side, I'll take this side."

Quinn grabbed the side of the dog's collar with one hand and braced the other behind his front haunch and pulled as Riley did the same on the other side.

Brutus grunted, then scrabbled once his front paws hit the dock, half climbing, half leaping out of the water. It sent Quinn and

Riley sprawling onto their backsides, where they got to suffer the further indignity of Brutus extensively and quite enthusiastically indulging himself in a rather long, full-body shake, sending a cascade of seawater all over them.

"Brutus!" Riley spluttered, blocking her face from the spray. "Seriously?" She spit out the briny seawater and clambered to her feet, slipping a bit as she did. Quinn, having just made his feet, grabbed her elbow to steady her.

They stood like that for several moments longer than either of them needed to. *Drop your hand, Brannigan,* he thought, while simultaneously very aware she hadn't shrugged him off as she had before. *Spoken for,* his little voice reminded him, and he let his hand fall to his side, dismayed at how reluctant he was to do so. *Relief, Brannigan. That's what this is supposed to feel like. Relief.*

She stepped back, but not before he noticed the flash of color on the back of her hand. He reached for it without thinking, lifting it between them, holding on when she would have pulled it back as he saw it was an oversized Band-Aid. "What happened?" he asked, smiling briefly when he noticed the bandage sported Minnie Mouse faces all over it. "Are you okay?"

113

She slid her hand from his, but her smile was a rueful one. "Kitchen burn. Hit the back of my hand on an oven rack. It's fine. Happens. More often to some of us than others," she added dryly. She took the dog by the collar, turned to go, then glanced back at Quinn. "You really are soaked. And I know he got you when he first went in, too. Do you want to come aboard? I have dry towels, at least. Wash seadog off your hands? I'll be happy to have the shirt cleaned. The, uh, shorts, too, if you want." She looked him up and down, as if noticing the rest of him for the first time. "He really did get you. I am very sorry —"

"Aboard?" Quinn asked, as her words sank in. It had taken a moment because he'd been distracted by the fact that her shirt was soaking wet, too. If he'd thought her body distracting when it was clothed in dry, dirt-smeared cotton, well . . . he'd yet to understand the true meaning of the word distraction. Other than the fact that he was a guy, and therefore appreciated the female form, he otherwise wasn't typically a fan of women who were . . . generously endowed. Mostly because he wasn't a fan of plastics mixing with God-given body parts. But there was nothing plastic about Riley Brown. In fact, every last thing about her was about as non-plastic and God-given as possible. In fact, the big man upstairs had been most generous.

All that, Quinn thought . . . plus a gaze he recognized. Maybe he had from the first moment. He understood exactly what it was he saw there now — aware, attentive . . . observant — because he'd been recognizing the very same things for the better part of the past thirty-four years. Every time he looked in the mirror.

"My boat." Her gaze grew quizzical the longer he looked at her. Then, just like that, she shifted it away, but not before he saw the guards go up again. "Oh." She sounded . . . disappointed? Or maybe embarrassed again, though he couldn't, for the life of him, imagine why. "You didn't know I live here. I thought when I saw you on the dock, you'd come down here looking for me because there was a problem — or because, ah —" She abruptly waved that away with her free hand. "Never mind. None of my business. I do have towels though, if it would help. Again, Brutus and I are sorry." She tugged on the collar and gave the beast a pointed look. "Aren't we, big guy?"

Brutus actually looked slightly abashed. He hung his head a bit lower.

"Apology accepted," Quinn said. "And don't worry. About the rest. It's hot, so it felt good. I was heading back to the house anyway." Because the very — very — last thing he needed to do was climb on a boat with her, into a small confined space, with them both wearing wet clothes clinging to every inch of her body. Er, their bodies. But mostly her body. Yep. Definitely a bad idea.

Quinn reached out, started to give Brutus a pat on the head, then decided not to risk getting the dog wound up again, and sketched a quick salute to them. "Thanks, though."

"Okay, then," she said, as he moved around them so he could head back down the dock. "Dunking notwithstanding, it was nice to see you again. I mean, it's good to know that everything worked out okay with the house, not because it was nice to see you because I thought —" She stopped and he glanced back to see the blush — hot this time — creep up her neck. She made a self-deprecating face and ducked her chin. "Yeah," she said quietly, then lifted her head with what he knew was her fake sunny smile. He'd seen the real one. That one came with dimples. "Drive carefully," she said.

"I will," he replied, wishing she didn't feel

so flustered around him. Not that he supposed it mattered. He wouldn't be seeing any more of her. The thought drew his gaze down, whereupon he jerked it right back up again. Nope, definitely didn't need to be seeing any more of her. He'd seen more than enough. He nodded again and started off down the dock. With every step, his shoes made a rather comical squishing-squirting-squeaky sound, like something out of a cartoon. He grinned, which changed to a laugh when he heard her snicker behind him.

"You sure you don't want a towel or something to at least put on your car seat?" she asked. "You're pretty wet." She smiled when he looked back, a truer one this time, though dry rather than dimpled. "I saw your ride when I left the bungalow the other day. Nice rental when you can get it. I know it's just a short hop back home, but I'm pretty sure those were hand-tooled leather seats."

"You made a pretty quick exit." If she'd been in even half the state he'd been in, the last thing she should have noticed was what kind of seats he had in his old Carerra. "How did you notice that?"

"I'm a stylist. I pay attention to details. The smaller, the better."

"That's a skill set I can appreciate."

"Yes, I guess you would, given what you do. It's an entirely foreign concept for most people. I will say, I didn't realize they rented out vintage sports cars."

"They don't."

Her eyes widened slightly at that. "It's yours? You drove all the way here from — well, again, I speak without thinking. I don't even know where you drove from because I don't know where you call home, if that's even where you were. With your accent, it might only be Atlanta for all I know."

He tried not to grin, but she was babbling a little, as if she was nervous. The kind of nervous he was beginning to understand — intimately — when he was around her. Not that he had any business understanding it. Or enjoying it. "I guess maybe my accent has peeked out a bit since I've been back. Normally, I never notice it. My dad and his parents are from down this way, but I spent most of my life up north. My father has been up there for eons, since before I was born anyway. I have a place just outside D.C., in Old Town. Alexandria. That's in Virginia."

"Yes, I'm familiar with the name. That's where Lani's from originally. She owns the cupcake shop. And I meant D.C. Her dad was a police detective there, but her mom was from Georgia. They moved down here after he retired. He's our sheriff now. Leyland Trusdale."

"Doesn't sound all that retired," Quinn said.

"You probably don't really want to know all the details. Anyway, very nice ride. That's all."

"Actually, I love hearing about the people here. I have sentimental ties to this place, but people always interest me. And the car was the first one I ever bought and paid for, which I did right after I signed my first big book deal."

"That wasn't all that long ago, was it? I mean, I've read all your books. You were young to publish your first. That was what, ten years ago at the most?"

"Close, nine. But you're right, the car is a model from the mid-eighties. Neighbor of ours had one when I was growing up, and I've always liked the body style. Plus, to me, it symbolized success. Our neighbor was an attorney, middle-upper class, and well . . . we weren't."

She nodded, then smiled. "So, how did it feel, when they handed over the keys? Did it feel like you thought it would?"

He grinned. "Better. Way better. But that was pretty much all I wanted, or at least the only statement I felt personally compelled to make."

"But you kept it. That statement."

"I did. Mostly because I really ended up loving that car."

She grinned. "You're such a guy."

He lifted one hand. "Guilty as charged."

They stood there another drawn-out moment, grinning at each other, then she cleared her throat and said, "Sure I can't get you that towel? Protect those beloved, statement-making leather seats?"

He opened his mouth to say no, thank you. Because, pleasant conversation aside, that was the only real option. At least that was the one easy decision he could make. So, no one was more surprised than he when what came out was, "To be honest, I'd really appreciate it, if you don't mind. I'll make sure you get it back."

It was at that exact same moment he realized just how much trouble he'd already gotten himself into.

She nodded, then moved past him and motioned him to follow her. He did, fully and utterly mesmerized by every voluptuous inch of her as she strolled ahead of him in what looked like soaking wet men's long, black basketball shorts. They should have been the definition of anti-sexy, but they so incredibly weren't. They rode low on her naturally swinging hips, and it was her beautiful heart-shaped backside they were clinging to. If he dragged his gaze off that view, it was only to collide with the equally sodden, mango-colored tee that clung to her waist and rolling hips, which brought him to the mass of wet and wild blond curls tumbling down the center of her back that would easily be the envy of mermaids the world over.

He found himself clenching his fingers into his palms, but that didn't keep him from wondering what it would be like to sink his hands into those curls, to wrap them around his fingers and gently tug her head back so he could reach the creamy skin of her neck. That couldn't happen. She was not his to touch. Or taste. Not now. Not ever. *Taken, Brannigan.* Why was that so hard to imprint on his suddenly hormone-jacked brain? He'd never, ever, not once, pursued anyone who was otherwise in-volved. Beauty, body, brains, or any combi-nation thereof, no matter how alluring, didn't matter. The instant he discovered a woman was otherwise involved, it was like an instant off switch for him.

The woman he'd been looking for, wait-ing for, would only have one man on her mind. Him.

He watched as Riley's mutant pet trundled easily along beside her, though she kept her hand on his collar anyway.

Quinn thought he might as well have been the one with the collar around his neck. But she wouldn't have to tug him along beside her. The way he was feeling right at that moment, he'd have trotted along, panting, right behind her.

Yep. He was in deep, deep trouble.

CHAPTER 5

"It's just over there." Riley walked up the ramp to the fixed pier, and over to the far side of it. "Home sweet home." She gestured to the forty-five-foot Cruiser Craft.

"You live on a houseboat? Cool. I didn't even know they docked pleasure boats here. I thought it was all commercial."

"It is, but the place where my friends had this docked, a few islands down the chain, charged a pretty steep monthly fee, so I checked around. Someone mentioned Sugarberry was more rural, less resorty, which suited me, or my finances anyway. It's quiet and off the beaten track, and, most important, they don't mind Brutus. We just sort of . . . fit in here. I am still close enough to the rest of the Gold Coast properties to make the staging job work out." She shrugged. "So, I kind of persuaded them to let me lease a spot, temporarily."

"How long have you been here?"

She smiled. "Little over a year."

"Nice. Nice friends, too. Portable house loan. Not a bad deal."

"Yep," she agreed, thinking how Greg and Chuck had, for all intents and purposes, saved her life. Or had certainly provided the means to escape her old one. She let go of Brutus's collar and grabbed the railing that ran along the side of the boat. "You can step onboard here, then walk around to the back." Brutus led the way, and when she turned back to grab the bags she'd put down earlier when she'd had to go dog chasing, she found that Quinn had already picked them up. "Thanks — you didn't have to do that."

"You didn't have to offer me dry-cleaning service," he countered, watching Brutus nimbly maneuver the narrow alley between railing and boat to head straight over to his big water dish for a healthy slurp, before collapsing under the aft deck awning in a boneless heap. "Looks like he's taken to shipboard living."

"That he has. I'm not sure how he'd have done on a different kind of craft, but this isn't so much different from life in a tiny Chicago apartment. Easier, actually. Certainly a far more direct route to being outside then a twenty-two-story ride down in a small elevator." She took two of the bags from one of his arms and he reached around her to slide open the back doors. She stepped through and into a tidy little dining area, but walked past it, straight to the small galley tucked just beyond it. She set the bags on the stubby little counter that formed half of the U-shaped space, then turned to get the remaining two bags, only to find Quinn had followed right behind her.

"Oh." She stepped back slightly, only there was nowhere to go. "Sorry. Didn't know you were right behind me. Thanks," she added, when he set the bags down on the counter.

"No problem." He turned and checked out the rest of the main cabin, which formed the entire back half of the boat. In addition to the tiny dining area and galley, there was a small living room space, complete with recliner chair, short couch, small desk, and an entertainment center that held a state-of-the-art flatscreen.

"Pretty cool use of space," Quinn said. "And very bright, sunny, with all the windows and the back being all glass."

"Thanks. It's actually surprisingly practical. I thought it would be harder to get used to, not that there wasn't a learning curve." Some parts of it more expensive than others, though she was mercifully and finally all caught up with the repairs now, and hoped the curve was complete. "Once you get used to it, it's kind of nice not having a lot of space you just clutter up anyway. Sort of makes you think more about impulse buys."

"I bet. Nice setup," he said, motioning to the flatscreen.

"Yes, well, Greg likes his creature comforts. The satellite dish is hooked up top off the fly deck."

"Ah, right," Quinn said, in a slightly smoother, though still friendly tone. "Greg."

Since his back was to her, Riley smiled, and briefly debated about letting him think . . . what he was thinking. But she was already feeling bad about letting Quinn believe his assumption about her relationship status was true. Subterfuge of any sort was not her thing.

"Greg and his partner, Chuck, own the boat, though they've used it a whopping two times since making the impulse buy almost five years ago. Greg is a self-admitted gadget guy and Chuck indulges him because, well, he can. They both can. They're the most highly sought after food photographers in the country."

"Ah," was all Quinn said. "Well, these are

some nice toys." He stepped a little bit out of the galley as he continued to look around the cabin.

Not enough to let her squeak by, but enough so that she had a prayer of getting her equilibrium back. Even her first few nights of bad storms while living aboard hadn't made her feel as off balance and light-headed as being in close proximity to Quinn Brannigan did . . . right in her own galley.

"I take it you worked with them, back in Chicago?" he asked.

"I did, yes. In fact, we were assigned to the same project my first time out of the gate. They're known for being rather . . . outlandish, I guess is the best way to put it, and not a little eccentric. But, for whatever reason, they took a liking to me and, well, they became mentors of sorts, certainly helped shepherd me through the earlier trials and tribulations of getting into the frenzied world of print work. I owe a great deal of my success to them."

"So . . . you worked as a photographer, then?"

"Oh, no, sorry. I worked with them as a food stylist."

"Makes sense. I'm sure you were very good at it."

"I did okay for myself." She braced herself for the inevitable question of why she'd made such a huge geographic and career change.

Instead, he turned around, neatly boxing her right back in between counter and appliances again. "I don't know how your friends had the place decorated, but I can already see your influence."

Surprised, she momentarily forgot about her sudden need to escape. "You can? I haven't really done that much." With her various learning curve catastrophes and the sporadic nature of her job assignments, she couldn't afford to.

"The throw pillows on the couch — I'm thinking those are you. You like rich jewel tones. You also have some of the same kind of prints on the wall here that are in the bungalow." He smiled. "Give me a few more minutes and I could probably list a half dozen other things, but those were the first two I noticed."

"I'm sure you could." Suddenly she didn't feel so bad about letting him think she was involved. He had away of making her feel so . . . tended to. The center of his attention. His interest in her always seemed so . . . paramount and honest. Clearly she needed all the help she could get in regaining her perspective where he was concerned. "I, uh . . . let me get that towel for you."

He shifted slightly, to keep her from passing. "Wait."

"What?" She wasn't sure why he was making her so nervous. She'd already convinced herself that the "moment" she'd sworn they'd had — the whole cupcake thing — had just been her overactive imagination kicking in after the treadmill trauma had lowered her defenses.

He smiled, and there was a bit of a daring twinkle in his eyes. Just what she did not need him to be . . . more devilishly handsome.

"Was I right?" he asked.

"About — oh, the pillows, and . . . yes. Yes, you were. Apparently you weren't kidding about having an eye for detail."

"No. I wasn't kidding."

She was almost sure there wasn't some underlying . . . tone, in his voice, just then. She had no trauma to blame it on, unless she considered Brutus's belly flop off the pier a trauma — which she didn't. So . . . "Towels," she repeated, almost desperately. "If you'll just —"

Quinn slid easily to one side and immediately began walking around the cabin as if nothing had happened. *Because noth-*

ing had happened, her little voice supplied, a tiny bit waspishly.

She was a complete ninny. An apparently sex-starved, hormonally overloaded, reality-challenged ninny. It confirmed her earlier suspicions that she'd romanticized the rest of their time together as well. And that meant the faster she got him off the boat, the better.

"I'll be right back." She quickly ducked down the narrow passageway to the master stateroom. Another, smaller stateroom with two twin beds was opposite the master. Another space above deck, something called a cuddy, was where people could also sleep, if they lay flat on a floor mattress and didn't sit upright. Greg and Chuck had never entertained anyone on the boat but her, and she was hardly planning to have sleepover company, so she'd used it as storage.

Her thoughts went straight from sleepovers to the man presently inhabiting the main cabin. She felt more than a little ridiculous, letting herself get caught up in the nonsense she'd let herself believe, to the point that she'd lied about something — by omission — but that didn't even matter. Considering the fact that, on her best day, she'd be unlikely to attract a man like Quinn, it was rather pathetically comical she'd ever allowed herself to entertain such an idea.

She could blame that on the cupcakes, too, but it was time to put the blame where it resided.

On her, Riley Brown, klutz extraordinaire with the proportions of a sturdy English peasant — which was her heritage. Men like Quinn Brannigan, a studly Southern gentleman with crazy good genetics and a healthy dose of sexy Irish ancestry thrown in, didn't generally get the hots for peasants.

She rummaged in one of the roll-out drawers under the queen sized bed anchored into the space, requiring a step up in order to climb under the sheets. The step up provided the storage underneath, which essentially made up what would have been a dresser and a walk-in closet in a regular bedroom. She grabbed the remaining two clean towels and reminded herself — again — she really needed to get to the laundry. One of the things about living aboard she'd learned right off was the constant salty spray in the air was hell on clothes, skin, and hair. She did her best to keep up with at least two out of those three, but was forever behind on the laundry.

She slung the towels over her shoulder and slid the drawer back until it latched shut, then turned around just as Quinn was ducking down to step inside the stateroom door.

She squealed in surprise. Okay, yelped might have been a better description.

He immediately raised his hands, palms out, in front of his chest, "I swear, I don't make a habit of sneaking up on people. I'm sorry. I was just —" He took the towels from where she was clutching them in both hands, and slid them free. "I thought I could help, so I could leave you to get on with your day. Not to mention I'm sure you'd like to change, too. In fact, let me duck back out and —"

"No, that's okay, really," she assured him. "I'm sure you'd like to get going, too." The open space in the stateroom not occupied by the bed was narrower than any other space onboard, except maybe the shower. At the moment, it felt about a hundred times smaller. And a million times more intimate.

"There's two towels. Use one to dry off if you'd like, and take the other for the car." He really did fill the space right up, including that space she'd so recently cleared out in her head. "I'll, uh, just get out of your way and let you clean up."

She gestured to the tiny bathroom as she stepped past him. "Sink is through there if you need it." Greg had kept insisting she call it the head, but she just couldn't; it sounded like a guy term. She had managed to get the big three — cabin, galley, and stateroom. But don't ask her about aft and starboard, and all of that. She didn't see why they just couldn't say front and back, left side and right.

His voice halted her just outside the door. "You wouldn't by any chance have a T-shirt I could borrow, would you? Promise I'll get it back to you along with the towel." He smiled. "Polo shirts hold a lot of water, as it turns out." He was holding the hem edge of the stretched-out wet shirt in a ball in his cupped hands. "I'm dripping on your floor. I'm sorry."

"It's made to get wet," she said, somewhat absently, briefly transfixed by the way balling up the front of his shirt had managed to pull tight the fabric over his chest and the sleeves. She couldn't believe his claims that he was ever too scrawny. His shoulders and arms alone . . . made her want to fan herself. "Shirt," she said, belatedly remembering what he'd just asked her. "Right. Uh . . . I don't know." She turned back and started pulling out drawers and fishing through one, then another, still seeing the outlines of his broad shoulders and bulgy biceps in her mind's eye.

She wasn't finding anything. It wasn't like she was some perky little size six, or eight, but none of her T-shirts would fit his bigger-than-life, archway-filling frame. Not to mention he'd look ever-so-cute in melon pink sorbet or sherbet orange. From the corner of her eye, she caught him glancing around the stateroom, much as he had the main cabin, and it struck her that if she were, indeed, in some kind of committed relationship, as she'd allowed him to believe, wouldn't it stand to reason she'd have at least one or two of her partner's big ol' manly-man-sized T-shirts laying around? Left behind after their latest round of rambunctious, three-times-a-day, crazy-hot boat sex?

Possibly, she was just projecting. Then she remembered. She did own one oversized man's shirt after all. "I do have one that might work. I just need to get around to the other —" They once again did their do-si-do so she could squeeze past him and his shirt of amazing balled tightness, to get to the foot of the bed, where there was one more, wide drawer in which she stored her off-season clothes. She dug under the top few layers of long-sleeved Henleys and sweaters. "Here," she said triumphantly as she slid out a clean, but very old and worn, oversized White Sox baseball jersey. She shook it out, then tossed it to him. "That might work." He didn't have to know it was one of her sleep shirts. Let him think what he wanted. Not that it mattered, but it was a point of pride that he believe she was actually capable of having a man living onboard who would leave old jerseys strewn about.

"Thanks." He snagged it in one of those big hands of his. One of those same big hands that had framed her shoulder back in the kitchen of the open house — well, his bungalow, she supposed it was now. And again, on the stairs, and . . .

"Sure," she managed, her throat tight and dry all over again — because she was an idiot. She ducked her chin slightly as they did one last do-si-do. "I'll just be in the galley, putting stuff away. No hurry on getting the shirt back. Actually, if you want, you can just leave it at Lani's shop in town. I can pick it up next time I'm in for club night."

"Because coming all the way out here would add so much time to the trip."

She heard the dry, teasing note in his voice, knew there was no underlying message, just amusement. But tell that to her hammering heartbeat.

Before she could think up a suitable response, he said soberly, "I can leave it at the bakery, Riley, no worries. But, just so you know, I wouldn't have dropped by unannounced. I appreciate the loan. I'll leave it and the towel in town with Lani."

She felt foolish for trying to play it oh-so-cool, instead being oh-so-ridiculous. "I appreciate it." She turned back to the door, escape attempt number two the next thing on her immediate agenda.

"What's club night?" he asked.

She'd made it to the passageway, and debated pretending she hadn't heard him, then paused. She'd like to think she really wasn't that ridiculous. She braced her hand on the doorway as the boat swayed and dipped, then gripped it tightly after she turned back. It was that, or prove just how ridiculous she really could be, by face-planting at his feet. The same bare feet that were covered with the wet shirt he'd just pulled off.

She should turn back around. Decency demanded it, despite the fact that men on Sugarberry went shirtless more often than not this time of year. It was just . . . none of the men on Sugarberry looked like this. For that matter, none of the men in Chicago did either. And before she knew it, she wasn't turning around at all, she was staring. Gawking.

Giving herself lecture after lecture as she let her gaze travel ever-so-slowly up his still wet, khaki shorts-clad legs, to the belted waist and the expanse of flat, very male and muscular bare skin that extended upward from there. There was a dark, sexy swirl of hair patterning across his pecs, then arrowing down, oh so tauntingly, until it disappeared behind the buckle on his belt. She about swallowed her tongue.

Even being in imminent danger of death by choking apparently wasn't enough to abort the rest of the full-body sweep. He had his arms over his head as he was pulling the shirt on, so she got to watch the riveting display of pectoral and shoulder muscles at work and play. Then, like the curtain at the end of a performance, the Sox jersey fell down into place over all that gloriousness and the show was abruptly over.

Like a tractor beam of shame, her gaze lifted that fraction higher until it locked right into his. It was probably just the dim shadowy interior of the stateroom that gave those crystal blue eyes of his the dark, dangerous glint she saw there. Surely, that was it.

"I'm sorry," he said, though not exactly sounding at all put out. "I thought you'd turned your back."

"You asked . . . something." It was a damn good thing she'd already come to terms with the very — very — different leagues the two of them played in. If she'd ever allowed herself to seriously think about what it would be like to get naked with him, that little display had just guaranteed she would never — ever — be disrobing in front of this gorgeous specimen of man.

Yeah, she thought. Good thing she'd cleared that up.

"You have a club thing? At the bakery?" He smiled. "If it's a secret society, complete with a special handshake, forget I asked. I was just trying to think what kind of club meets in a bakery."

Was he seriously making small talk? "We, uh, that is, a group of us get together and . . . we bake. Cupcakes."

"To help the owner — Lani, right? To help her out with stock?"

"No. Just to bake. It's like . . . you know how guys have poker night? We have bake night. Lani teaches us stuff. She used to be a pretty big deal of a pastry chef in New York, and her husband is —"

"Baxter Dunne. I know." Quinn smiled

when Riley sent him a questioning look. "Scary Lois name-dropped him as a way to sell me on the finer points of Sugarberry's hidden celebrity allure."

Riley found herself smiling at his continued use of the dreaded nickname. "Anyway, we learn, enjoy each other's company, share what's going on." She managed a smile then. "And donate a lot of sweet stuff to the Senior Center, the Moose Lodge, and other unsuspecting groups all over the greater Savannah area."

His smile flashed wider and the exponential speed at which Riley's pulse rate zoomed told her it was time to end their little chit-chat.

"Sort of like a book club for bakers?"

"Exactly. And you don't have to read the boring stuff you'd never normally —" She broke off, then shook her head. "Good, Riley." She looked at him. "I didn't mean your books. I meant the stuffy ones that book clubs think they should be reading because someone, somewhere said that reading dysfunctional stuff about miserable people where it always ends badly somehow makes you a better person. I never figured that one out. I want the book club where everyone reads fun fiction." She smiled again. "Yours would fall in that group."

He sketched a little bow. "Thank you. Much appreciated. And if it makes you feel any better, I don't get highbrow, stuffy literature, group-read think, either. Well, that's not true. I understand why the genre exists, just not why there aren't at least an equal number of reading groups engaging in discussion about more popular fiction. I mean, it's called popular for a reason." With that, he bowed again. "Allow me to step down from that particular soapbox. You don't want to hear me pontificate."

"Actually, it's refreshing and relieving to hear you say it. I thought it was just me being shallow and superficial." Riley squeezed her eyes shut. "I really need to stop talking. You know I didn't mean that your books were —"

"I know what you didn't mean."

Her eyes flew open. The voice was much closer. In fact, he was standing right in front of her, just inside the door. The door she belatedly realized she was blocking.

"Thank you for the shirt," he said amiably enough, but his gaze was searching hers.

For what? she wanted to shout. "I'm sorry my dog is a bit . . . exuberant." She was completely hung up on that deepening sea of turquoise blue.

"Please let . . . whoever he is, know that I

said thank you as well."

"What?"

He plucked at the jersey. "The owner of the shirt."

"Oh. Right. I . . . will."

"Will you tell him one other thing for me?"

Riley nodded, held there by the steady gaze, the deep voice, that hint of accent . . . and the way he made her feel like the only woman in the universe.

"Tell him he's a very lucky man. And that I hope like hell he knows what he's got here."

"Got? Oh, you mean . . . the old White Sox jersey? It's not a real —"

Quinn grinned then, and she added *dazzled* to the list. "You, Riley," he said. "He's got you."

"Oh. Right." She wished she could somehow be at least slightly less banal. But that was not her karma. Not around him, at any rate. "I — thank you."

He kept smiling.

"I should let you get out of here." But turning around and having him follow her down the snug passageway . . . that she didn't need. "I'm — I think I'm just going to trade places with you and change out of my wet — uh, change. My clothes."

His eyes had flashed on the word wet for

141

the briefest of seconds, and she found herself holding her breath. For what, she didn't know, but there seemed to be some kind of anticipation . . . building. Surely that wasn't all in her mind? But then he backed up, slinging the spare towel around his neck, and the damp one, along with his wet shirt, over his arm, which he swung wide, gesturing her inside. Ever the gracious Southern gentleman. His Grams would be so proud.

Riley tried not to let that depress her.

"I'll launder and bring both towels back, if that's okay."

"You really don't need to." Against all odds, she managed to not trip over herself or in any other way cause further embarrassment as she got out of his way and let him out of the room. It was something, anyway.

"I don't mind," he said, as he stepped into the passageway.

She stopped him with a question. "Why were you down here?" she blurted out. "At the docks, I mean?" *Good God, Riley.* He was one step and a hop away from being back on the pier, on the way to his car.

He turned back, and paused in the door opening. "I spent my summers here as a teenager, fishing, working for my grandfather. He moored his big trawler on these docks."

Her eyes widened. "Your family is from Sugarberry?"

He shook his head. "Extended family on both sides are from New England, then Ireland the generation before that. My grandparents moved south out of consideration for my grandmother's health issues. Dad was born down on the Gulf. My grandparents moved here to Sugarberry after my father had gone off to college, married, and started a family, which began and ended with me."

"Why Sugarberry? The Gulf would seem a more prosperous place for a fisherman."

"Looking for less challenging competition as my granda got older and my grams' health was worsening. My father's career ended up keeping us around D.C.; work keeps him there still. So, I guess I'm something of a mutt, of sorts, geographically speaking."

"Your grandparents, they're gone now?"

"Yes, long time. Their house here is gone, too."

"I'm surprised with the way island lore is passed around down here, that there aren't stories about the famous writer's grandparents."

"My grandparents were both gone before I'd published my first book. I doubt anyone would have made the connection after the fact."

Riley smiled. "You seriously underestimate the depth and breadth of the local gossip mills. Your mom and dad are still in D.C.?"

He shook his head. "Actually, my mom passed when I was thirteen, which was right around when I started spending summers here. Kept on with it every summer until I was in my junior year in college. I had an internship that summer, in journalism, which was where I thought I was headed at the time."

"I'm sorry about your mom."

"Thank you. My dad . . . well, he had a pretty hard time of it. But it ended up giving me the gift of time spent with my grandparents, for which I'm forever grateful."

"He must be proud of your successes. Your dad, I mean."

Quinn smiled, but for the first time, Riley noted it didn't quite reach his eyes. "Yes, he is. Well, I won't make you stand around in wet clothes any longer. Do you need any help unloading that stuff? From the bags we carried on board?"

"Oh, no, that's okay. I've got it." Surprised to realize that their short chat had relaxed her once again, she was relieved when her smile came naturally, with no dry throat or heart-pumping side effects. "It would take longer to tell you where it all goes."

"Okay then, I'm officially getting out of your hair." He turned to go, but she stopped him one last time.

"Thank you, Quinn."

"For?" he asked, leaning back to look through the open doorway.

"Sharing. I'm sure you get asked endless curious questions about your past. I just . . . I appreciate hearing about it. I'm glad you had the chance to connect with your grams and granddad."

"Thank you. I'm not usually all that keen to talk about it, but this was nice. It felt . . . normal. I appreciate that."

"Good." Her smile spread. "I feel less guilty for being nosy, then."

"Nothing nosy about making neighborly conversation."

She laughed. "You might want to rethink that before stopping in at Laura Jo's diner or Stewie's pub."

He grinned. "So noted."

"Be careful getting off the boat. It's tied securely, but it still bobs."

"I will." But he stood there a moment longer, then another moment still. "Good-bye, Riley."

"Bye," she said, thinking he'd made that sound rather permanent. Wishing the idea didn't make her so sad.

She heard him talking as the rear glass door slid open, presumably to Brutus, and quickly shrugged out of her wet shirt and bra, pulling on the first thing she yanked out of the open bench seat. She frowned as she heard something — or, more to the point, someone — on the outside stairs that led to the upper fly deck. The weight of the steps were heavier than any noise Brutus would make, not that he could climb the ladder anyway. She figured, given his earlier curiosity about the boat, Quinn had probably decided to take a quick peek up there, which was perfectly fine. It was another guy thing. A fixation with all things transportation. She certainly didn't mind.

But as she pulled her hair from under the back of her shirt and grabbed her heavy comb, she found herself spending a moment or two wondering what it would be like to have someone else's footsteps echoing in her living space again.

She entered the galley just in time to see Quinn hop from boat deck to pier, and watched him, thinking about all kinds of things she had no business thinking, but

146

mostly about what he'd said about her when she'd thought he'd meant the old jersey.

Then she was sliding the rear door open, almost falling over Brutus, who was sitting like a sphinx, watching his now-beloved Quinn walking away, leaving him behind. If she hadn't been so busy gathering the courage to follow up with one final question, one she knew would plague her overactive mind otherwise, she'd have been a little wistful about Brutus's obvious bout of lovesickness. He'd never once, as far as Riley had ever seen, looked after Jeremy that way. She rubbed his head. "I'm sorry, too, big guy," she said, admitting that much was true. "Quinn," she called out, before she lost her chance. "Wait. Can I ask you one more thing?"

He turned around. If he was surprised, or annoyed, he surely didn't show it. His smile was as easy and amiable as ever. "Sure." He raised his voice just slightly to be heard over the sudden whip of wind, despite only being a few yards down the pier.

She walked to the side of the boat and looked up at him as he moved a few yards closer. "You said you hoped my . . . um . . . partner, knows what he's got. I know now that you meant me, but I still don't know what you meant. Not specifically. I realize

147

you were probably just being polite and charming, but on the off chance you meant it . . . can I be horribly gauche and ask what is it you think he's got in me?"

A slow smile curved Quinn's lips, and even with the short distance between them, there was no doubt the warmth in it invaded every speck of those crystalline eyes. "A woman who can ever-so-sincerely ask that very question . . . and honestly not already know the answer."

And with that, he turned and walked away.

Brutus's head bumped her hip as he ambled over to sit beside her. Riley draped a hand over his neck, rubbing his still-damp fur as she watched until Quinn was no longer in sight.

"I wish I knew what he meant by that," she told her faithful, currently sorrowful companion. "But maybe it's just as well I don't."

CHAPTER 6

Quinn wanted her so bad he could taste her. He'd written books around the theme of forbidden fruit, but he'd never once been tempted by it himself. Yet, he couldn't seem to get Riley Brown out of his mind. Not to mention her lingering impact on other parts of his body. All he had to do was walk into the damn breakfast nook and he got a hard-on. It was insane.

Quinn flexed his grip on the handle of the paper shopping bag he carried and glanced up at the shop signs as he walked past the row of stores circling the small square in the middle of the tiny town of Sugarberry. Other than the docks and Biggers' place down on the pier, it was the only commercially developed area on the small island. Even with houses lining the streets extending out from the square, and those scattered along the loop road that circled the entire island, it was still largely marsh-

149

land, dunes, and beach.

The streets that weren't paved, or set with bricks as they'd briefly been in some generation gone by, were most often composed of hard-packed sand and dirt, with a healthy layer of crushed shells ground in for good measure. The town itself was an odd amalgam of rural Southern charm and the more bohemian lifestyle often found in island culture. Sugarberry was only connected to the mainland by a single causeway over Ossabaw Sound, and even that was a relatively new development. As a teen, he'd had to take a ferry over. He couldn't recall seeing any ferry signs now, so maybe it didn't exist at all anymore. Understandable, though sentimentally speaking, somewhat disappointing.

Quinn also noted some of the shops had changed ownership over the years. More surprising were the ones that still remained the same, all these years later. There was some comfort in seeing the town square was still much as he remembered it. The grassy park in the middle, with the large fountain at its center. That much hadn't changed at all.

He spied the colorful and whimsical sign for Cakes by the Cup and slowed his steps. Hopefully just the sight of the cupcakes wouldn't have the same effect that thinking about them in the privacy of his own home had. Maybe he should have considered that before deciding to drop by. He'd come to Sugarberry with problems that needed solving. Thus far, the problem that was Riley Brown was preventing him from getting on to anything else.

After another fruitless morning alternately spent staring at his computer screen, or at the waves crashing against the dunes behind his bungalow . . . or her baseball jersey . . . he decided it was time to drop the damn shirt and towels off and cut the strings once and for all. Not that there were any real strings left between him and Riley. He could have dropped the stuff off at any time over the past week and that would have been that.

The borrowed items had made it from the dryer to the back of the chair across from where he sat to work. The really pathetic part was it wasn't even her damn jersey. Worse, it likely belonged to the man who got to see her in it. Nightly, for all he knew. But that wasn't what he'd been thinking about as he'd pondered the shirt.

It was the only tangible thing of hers still in his home. The bigger issue was how much he felt her presence without any tangible representation. How someone could have imprinted herself so viscerally into his thoughts, in a space they'd shared for less than an hour, he couldn't say, but he felt her there all the time. In the Florida room, the kitchen, the foyer, the breakfast area . . . his shower. And he didn't want to. Not any longer. He hoped the act of getting rid of the shirt and towels would somehow symbolize the total disconnect he needed to achieve so he could get on with more important matters.

"Right," he said under his breath while jiggling the bag in his hands, still staring up at the sign and not entering. Yet. "Good luck with that."

It would be one thing if it was just the farm girl freckles sprinkled across those often blushing cheeks, or that mouth, those lips, all abundant and beckoning, like ripened fruit begging to be suckled and savored, or the siren curls of gold that made him want to tangle his fingers in them, or the God-given curves that filled out her lush body. A body made for a man to sink himself into, to find pleasure in, and to pleasure in return. She was all fresh-faced innocence mixed with pure, molten carnality, in one unexpected package.

And yet that wasn't what made his body

behave like a randy fifteen-year-old. Or certainly not all of it. It was the direct talk despite the pink cheeks, the vulnerability so clearly present in her big brown eyes despite the dry, often acerbic humor. She spoke confidently about her work, yet was openly self-deprecating. There was the natural openness, her vibrant buoyancy, the inquisitiveness that had her sincerely asking about his family. And, most perversely, it was the way she moved through the world like a woman on a mission, but was a bit of a goofy klutz. She accepted those shortcomings with humor, which was its own brand of dignity, and also happened to be endearing as all hell.

She was unique and fascinating and he wanted to know more, to talk to her, to watch her move, to find out what she thought about . . . everything. She would be a woman with opinions. He wanted to know them all, to debate them, to laugh with her, kiss her inevitable boo-boos . . . then make wild, passionate love to her, and revel in all she would be capable of giving in return.

His hands tightened on the handle of the shopping bag until his knuckles hurt. He forced himself to relax his grip, the tension in his neck and shoulders, and all the rest in between. Maybe even more, the part between his ears.

She'd come into his orbit less than ten days ago, had crossed his path only twice in that time . . . so how was it that he'd found himself where he was? Maybe he was so wrapped up in the direction his book was taking him that he was projecting raw emotion on her. Or maybe he was merely using her as a distraction to keep him from thinking about the bigger thing, the major issue he'd come to Sugarberry to resolve.

But he didn't think so. He really, truly didn't want any distractions. He wanted to figure things out, make some hard, very serious decisions. Taking on new problems had been nowhere on his agenda.

It didn't matter why she fascinated him. Couldn't matter. What mattered was finding his way past the initial little buzz of fascination and getting back to his original purpose.

He pulled open the door to the bakery and stepped out of the sultry midday heat, into cool air redolent with the rich, buttery scent of baking cakes, the darker pull of melting chocolate, and an unknown variety of other treats that combined to make his mouth water. It was a decadent, multi-faceted assault on his senses and he couldn't help pausing to breathe it all in.

"Well, hello there, young man. Something I can do for you? Our fun special today is the Dreamsicle cupcake — mandarin-orange-soaked cake, a cheesecake filling, and orange whip on top. Our indulgent special is a truffle-infused chocolate pumpkin and ginger cupcake with mascarpone and cream cheese frosting."

Quinn hadn't initially noticed anyone in the shop when he'd first entered, so the friendly welcome caught him slightly off guard. "They both sound fun and indulgent to me," he said, running his gaze along the taller counters to the gap where a much lower counter held an old-fashioned, antique cash register.

It was there, behind the oversized register, that he finally spied the tiny bird of a woman. Her white-blond hair was set in a beehive of perfectly formed, meticulously preserved curls . . . and she was wearing what appeared to be an apron featuring a puffy white horse with purple neon mane and tail, over what otherwise appeared to be a sensible blouse. Pearls circled her neck and were clamped to fragile looking earlobes. He smiled, charmed and a bit flummoxed.

"You look like the indulgent type to me." She eyed him up and down. "Perhaps a mixed set? We have our standard menu as well, each and every flavor combination guaranteed to make you sigh in pleasure with every bite. Can I fix you up a box?" Her blue eyes twinkled merrily as he stepped closer to the counter. "Well, my, my." Her eyes widened as she got a better look at him. "Look at you, all grown up." Her gaze skimmed over him and up until their eyes met. "You're Gavin Brannigan's grandson, am I right?"

Quinn grinned. Apparently she wasn't done surprising him yet. He couldn't recall the last time anyone had recognized him for being a Brannigan first, and anything else second. "I think that's the nicest thing anyone has said to me in quite some time," he told her sincerely. "Yes, I am Gavin's grandson, Quinn. It's a pleasure to be back."

"I remember you from those summers you used to come down to fish with your grandpa. Didn't come around town much while you were here." A hint of scold was there, despite the merry twinkle, as if it were still something of a personal affront, all these many years later.

Given what he knew personally about some Southern sensibilities, especially in small towns, that wouldn't be entirely out of the question.

"Granda Gav kept me quite busy, sunup to sundown. On the rare occasion we didn't head out, Grams had a long list of chores for me to help her with." Quinn grinned. "I would have much rather been sampling the penny candy in those jars on the counter of Caner's Hardware, but I never had the time."

Her smile said he was forgiven and likely always had been. He suspected the pint-sized oldster just enjoyed being feisty. Of course, if he made it to her age, he hoped he'd enjoy indulging in a bit of that himself.

"He was so proud of you. Talked about you all the time. Track star, I seem to recall. Or something like it." She eyed him again, and the twinkle took on a clearly more feminine spark. "I must say you've filled out — and up — quite a bit, since those days."

"Yes, ma'am," he said, still smiling. He hadn't thought, given what little time he'd spent mingling with the locals, that anyone would really remember him. "I believe maybe I have. You, however, look exactly as I remember you, and as lovely as always. Mrs. . . . Liles, am I right?" He reached way back, proud and relieved that he was able to pluck the name from the flotsam and jetsam comprising his vast stores of beloved Sugarberry memories. "I remember you used to

157

come down to the docks and buy fish for your husband's supper."

She beamed and the warmth in her eyes lent her rouged cheeks some natural color. "Why, aren't you a charmer! And please, you can call me Alva."

"Why, thank you, Miss Alva. I'm honored." He'd always considered himself a polite gentleman, but it was amusing and maybe a bit poignant how swiftly the Southern rules of etiquette his Grams had taken such great pains to endlessly nag into him rose straight back to the surface, almost as if they were second nature. "And how is Mr. Liles?"

"Oh, my Harold passed on some time ago." Her smile didn't fade a bit as she spoke of him, but rather an affectionate spark flickered to life instead, tugging at much the same place in Quinn's heart that his grandparents' affection for one another always had. He knew that look well.

"We had a good life, we did," she said, a bit mistily. "Still miss him. Old coot."

Quinn's smile softened. "I'm very sorry to hear of his passing, and yes, I'm sure you do."

"You know," she said, sparking right back up again. "We were just talkin' about you at last week's bitchy bake."

Quinn's gaze had begun to drift toward the amazing works of cupcake goodness lining each of the display shelves, but shifted straight back to hers at that. "The — I beg your pardon, the what?"

"Every Monday night after we close, a bunch of us girls, and Franco, of course, get together, and we bake and we bi—"

"Right," he said, smiling because it was impossible not to. "I think I get the drift."

"Now, what happens in Cupcake Club is supposed to stay in Cupcake Club" — she lowered her voice to a more conspiratorial whisper as she leaned across the counter — "but I don't think it's really talking out of school to mention that you've been the hot topic the past two weeks running." She straightened and primped her hair, smoothed her skirt, as if nothing untoward had happened. "And now, here you are, paying a visit to our little shop, so I've a feeling that streak might just continue."

Despite the fact that bit of news was a little disconcerting, he found himself still smiling. "Well, I can't imagine there's anything of interest to discuss, but I appreciate your letting me know."

"Oh, don't sell yourself short. You're successful, talented, famous, and very good looking these days."

"I, uh, well, thanks." He tried gamely not to chuckle. Alva Liles had had something of a reputation for being a firecracker back when he was a kid, though he couldn't recall much of what was said specifically. He hadn't paid a lot of attention to local gossip and his Grams wasn't one to wallow about in it, either. But it appeared that nothing much had changed since then. "I appreciate any good word you can put in for me. In fact, that's kind of why I'm stopping by today."

Her expression fell a bit. "Not to buy cupcakes? You really must give at least the chocolate buttercream a try. Although, if you want my personal opinion, it's the red velvet that really steals the show. Lani's recipe is the moistest you've ever tasted. Add a cold glass of milk and you'll think you've been transported to heaven."

Do not think about cupcakes transporting you to heaven, he schooled himself. Heaven and cupcake in the same mental place made it all but impossible not to think of Riley, a certain breakfast nook, and many subsequent showers. "Actually" — he gamely kept the conversation moving forward — "I had the chance to indulge in Mrs. Dunne's amazing cupcakes a week or so ago. Heavenly is a good word, indeed. I came by today

to return some things I borrowed from Riley. Miss Brown," he corrected. "She said it
was okay to leave them here with you. I
hope that's all right." He lifted the paper
bag.

Alva eyed the bag, then him, with a considering gaze, for a moment or two longer
than was comfortable.

"If not, I can . . . come back another time.
Perhaps when Mrs. Dunne is here?"

"Oh, Miss Lani is here. She's back in the
kitchen. And no one calls her Mrs. Dunne,
though it is exciting, her marrying Baxter
and all. He's a famous pastry chef, too,
don't you know. It's been all the talk for
ages now. You'd think we'd be used to it, all
the fuss, with him living here, and filming
his fancy TV show right over in Savannah,
but then his cookbook came out last month,
and, well, it's brought a whole new round
of attention. We're actually getting phone
calls for long-distance orders, can you
believe that? From all over the country.
Personally, I think it has a lot to do with the
fact that they're just so darn cute together,
not to mention so talented." She placed a
hand to her heart and sighed. "We're real
proud to claim them both."

"I'm sure you are, as well you should be."

She proudly pointed to the shelves behind

161

the counter. "We have signed copies of the cookbook for sale, if you're interested."

For all the sincere pride she had, he hadn't missed the bit of a gleam amid all the twinkle, and had a feeling she might be one of Lani's more successful salespeople.

She eyed him up and down again. "Of course, now that you're here, we have something new to talk about."

"I assure you, there won't be much to say. I'm just here for some peace and quiet, working on my next book."

"Well, we're really happy to have you back. You're a Brannigan, so, of course, you're family here. Your grandparents are missed in these parts. Miss Annie made the best cobblers for our fall festivals, and Gavin could always be counted on to contribute to the big annual fish fry we had as part of our Independence Day festivities. Put in quite a good performance as part of our Christmas caroling group, too. Fine voice he had, solid baritone. Do you sing?"

"Ah, no, I'm afraid I don't." Quinn hadn't known about his grandfather singing carols, though he could well imagine it. It occurred to him some of the older locals on Sugarberry could probably share numerous stories with him about his grandparents, adding to his own memories. He was excited to

162

spend some of his time pursuing exactly that.

"Course, you could have come back sooner," Miss Alva went on to say. "We'd have kept your privacy private."

"You know, since coming back, I've wondered why I didn't come back sooner. My memories here are all good ones."

"Well, now you've got that fancy place and all, don't know what more you could want." She leaned forward and dropped her voice again. "You're not planning on having any of those wild celebrity parties, are you?"

He covered her hand with his own. "I can assure you, that's not anywhere in my plans."

She looked relieved . . . and a little disappointed.

Quinn swallowed the urge to grin. "And the house, yes, it's very nice, but I'd have been at home in my grandfather's old place, if it were still there."

"Real shame when the storm took it out. But Ted Rivers, the man who owns the property now, has done it up real nice. You should go over, say hello. He'd get a kick out of showing you around. Course, the rest of us will never hear the end of it, but it might do you good, visiting what was once the family home."

Quinn grinned. "I've been by, but haven't said my hellos. Didn't want to disturb anyone. Maybe I'll go ahead and do that, then. Thanks."

She gave his hand a little pat before he slid it away. "We're all glad you're here, and I'm happy to be the one to welcome you back." The merry twinkle appeared in her eyes again, the one that looked innocent enough at first glance . . . but made the back of his neck itch a little.

"So, can I just leave this with you?" he asked, offering her the bag.

"Certainly. If Riley asked you to leave it with us, you can be sure we'll see that she gets it." Alva took the bag, set it on the counter between them. "Of course," she added with such studied innocence his neck immediately started itching up a storm, "if you just hang around a few more minutes, you can give it to her yourself."

"Oh," he said, trying, and failing, to find the appropriate facial expression or response to that bit of information. His heart had instinctively leaped at the news, which was why his mind had immediately started running through the very long list of reasons why he shouldn't wait. "Well, I don't want to be in your way, or hers, so, if you'll just make sure —"

"Nonsense," Alva said, and he realized the twinkle-twinkle meant danger-danger. She was at full sparkle, and he knew damn well those wheels were turning up there under that scrupulously sculpted beehive bonnet. "In fact, you could help us out while you wait. Lani is back there right now, testing out a new recipe, and she's always wanting feedback. I'm sure she'd love to have your opinion." Alva beamed. "Play your cards right, maybe we'll name it after you. Our newest island celebrity! Or should I say our latest? Maybe you and Baxter will start a trend. Though I certainly hope it doesn't mean more house renovations. No offense. But we like to keep things simple around here."

"None taken. Simple has always been good enough for me. And please, pass along my hellos to Miss Lani, but I should really be getting —"

"Just wait right there. Now don't you move." Alva pointed a finger. "Miss Lani," she called out as she headed to a swinging door leading to the rear of the shop. "You'll never guess who's dropped in for a visit. Come on out and say hello, if you can."

Quinn shook his head and smiled. Wily, that one was. It would do him well to remember it. Since there was no escaping

165

without appearing rude, which he wouldn't do for a multitude of reasons, he took a closer look at the shop. And hoped like hell he'd manage to get out the door before Riley made an appearance. More time with her meant more things he'd be able to recall about her when he least wanted to. Danger, danger, indeed.

He glanced away from the cases of cupcakes. More temptation was the last thing he needed at the moment. His attention was drawn to the framed photos lining the front wall on either sides of the front door. On one side was a black-and-white picture of the bakery in a former incarnation. Judging from the car parked out front, he guessed the photo had been taken sometime in the late 1930s or early '40s. Beneath that was a bright, cheerful photo of the shop on grand opening day with a beaming woman he assumed was Leilani Dunne — or whatever her name had been then — standing arm in arm with an older gentleman wearing a local sheriff's uniform. He knew from Riley that would be her father. Leyland, he thought he recalled her saying.

Smiling, he took in several more *then* and *now* photos taken around the town square. The older photos were all from the same era as the old bakery photo, before either his time on Sugarberry or even his grand-parent's time. He thought for all the progress that had come to the small island over the years, keeping it a thriving community, not much seemed to have changed regarding its charm. The pace was slow now, as it had been then; the islanders were a close-knit community, yet welcoming to new arrivals. They had sustained a self-sufficient, modest economy that didn't rely on the tourist trade as most of the other, more populated islands in the chain did.

He'd noted the signs in the window of Laura Jo's diner that Wi-Fi was available, and the GO GREEN! flyer encouraging islanders to attend the meeting at the community center on proposed steps to keep the island environmentally friendly. And another announcing the upcoming annual fall festival coming in October, complete with a variety of carnival races and contests anyone could enter, and a pie-eating competition. So, progressive, yet protective of their more traditional, if not old-fashioned Southern sensibilities and way of life.

He shifted over to the other series of small photos, framed and mounted in a mosaic pattern on the other side of the door, tucked into the narrow strip of wall between the doorframe and the big display window.

Some were in color, some black and white, but they were all current, he thought. All were scenes taken from various points on the island outside the immediate town square. There were some from the docks, which he recognized, but most were dunes, sand, beaches, or marshes. He had similar prints in his bungalow, though most were somewhat larger. There were small ones, too, tucked into alcoves and used as accent pieces on various walls here and there throughout the place. Riley had had some on her houseboat as well. A local artist, he thought.

He slid his hands into his back pockets and rocked slightly on his heels as he let the photographs' natural beauty draw him in. The photographer had captured the serenity and the wildness. He could actually hear the waves, and feel the breeze that moved the dune grasses, smell the salt and brine in the air.

While the town photos had captured the people, the community, these captured the uniqueness of Sugarberry. For all that it was simply another small Southern town in so many ways, it was also an island community, with all the distinctive elements that set it apart from any other town or place.

"They're good, aren't they?"

Quinn glanced over his shoulder to find a pretty brunette standing behind him . . . sporting an Alice in Wonderland apron. He smiled and turned. "Yes, they are. Hello, you must be Leilani Dunne. Your cupcakes are incredible." He put out his hand. "Quinn Brannigan."

"Thank you!" She took his hand in a firm, quick shake. "Yes, Mr. Brannigan, I know who you are. Though may I say that while the photo of you on your books is quite good, you're a great deal more . . . charismatic, in person."

His smile deepened. "Very kind of you." He nodded toward her apron. "I noticed Miss Alva's apron, too. I like the whimsy. Suits the place."

She beamed, maybe flushed just a bit pink. "Thank you. I've collected them since I was little. It's been fun to have someplace to trot them all out."

She lifted up a tray with cubed pieces of cake arranged on it. A brown-flecked cake with melted caramel oozing out from the center. "I'm working on new recipes for the fall festival. These are my reverse caramel apple in spiced cake, with the caramel on the inside. Care to try a bite and give me an honest opinion?"

"I think I'm sold just looking at them, but

certainly." He took one of the toothpicks, pierced a cubed piece, and cradled his free hand under it to catch any of the drizzling caramel.

"Still warm, but okay to bite into," Lani said.

He popped it in his mouth and immediately closed his eyes as the flavors of apple, cinnamon, nutmeg, and creamy caramel burst and melted on his tongue at the same time. He groaned, just a little.

Lani laughed. "Okay. I think that's all the opinion I need. These go on the DEFINITELY CONSIDERING IT list."

All Quinn could do was nod.

Lani started to turn away, but not before Quinn shot her a fast grin and speared one more piece. She laughed and carried the sampler tray over to the counter.

After another moment spent contemplating how one bite of anything could be so decadently delicious, he said, "Would you happen to know who the photographer is who took the beach scene photos? I think I have some by the same person in my bungalow."

"I do," Lani said, then lifted the handled bag sitting by the register.

"Good. I'm interested in buying some prints." He pointed to the bag. "That's for

Riley. Uh, Miss Brown. Towels and a shirt I borrowed after Brutus and I did a little dance on the docks. All laundered and clean."

Lani laughed. "We heard about that. Brutus really is just a big lump of love."

"So I keep hearing," Quinn said with a smile. "Will you make sure she gets that? She said it was okay to drop it off here. I hope you don't mind."

"Not at all, I'd be happy to, but you can just give it to her yourself."

"Oh, that's not —"

Lani inclined her head in a nod toward the front of the store. "She's coming in the door, as we speak."

Quinn, still standing in front of the door, turned just as Riley passed by the big front display window. "Right."

"You can talk to her about the prints, too."

Quinn glanced back at Lani. "She knows the photographer?"

Lani smiled as she bumped the swinging door to the kitchen open with her hip. "She *is* the photographer."

CHAPTER 7

Riley pulled the shop door open and stepped inside just as Lani was pushing through the swinging door to go back to the kitchen. "Hey," she called, and Lani paused halfway through. "I'm here — I just had to come in the front. Shearin's produce truck is blocking the back alley. Again."

"I saw." Lani smiled. "Alva went over to talk to him."

Riley smiled back. "Really," she said with heightened interest. "Did she take her apron off this time?"

Lani nodded. "And refreshed her lipstick."

"Ah, taking one for the team. Admirable. Poor man won't know what hit him."

"I know. Poor Sam. Here he's been angling for one of Alva's home-cooked meals for as long as I've had the shop open, and she just isn't interested."

"I know. She told me Harold ruined her for all other men." Riley sighed and fanned herself as she said it.

"I know," Lani said. "Have you ever seen a picture of Harold?" Riley nodded and they indulged in a short burst of laughter.

"It is sweet, though," Riley said.

"All I know is if she can get Sam to stop parking his truck diagonally across the alley every time he makes a delivery, I'll cater a dinner for him myself."

Riley wiggled her eyebrows. "Somehow, I'm not thinking Sam is going to want extra company. He only has eyes for Alva."

Lani laughed. "Despite what she says, I'm not so sure Alva minds as much as she claims to. Hey, could you flip the sign for me? But leave the door unlocked, just in case. Franco isn't here yet, and Charlotte phoned and said she'd be in at some time tonight."

"Really? They're back?"

Charlotte and Carlo had gone back to New York so she could meet his giant, extended Puerto Rican family.

"That's great! Did she say how it went? How did the big introductions go? Is he going to go back to New Delhi with her to meet her folks?"

"She didn't have time to say, but she sounded happy. We'll get the nitty-gritty tonight. If we have to drag it out of her."

"I'll help pull," Riley said with a laugh. She piled her toolbox and quilted tote on the counter, then leaned down and took an appreciative sniff of the sampler plate. "What's on the tray?"

"Oh, right. I forgot I put those there. Inside-out caramel apple." There was a little quirk to her smile. "You'll all get to taste test tonight. I just brought them up front to get an outside opinion from a new customer."

Recognizing the quirk in Lani's smile, Riley's grew more bemused. "Really. Anyone I know?"

Lani motioned to a point behind Riley. "I believe you may have met once or twice." Then she pushed the rest of the way through the door. "Don't forget to turn the sign! He's distracting like that," she called out as the door swung shut behind her.

Riley frowned, completely confused, then popped a tester cupcake cube in her mouth, and promptly forgot everything else as she groaned in abject appreciation. She remained where she stood, enjoying every last bit of the entire flavor experience, then sighed in pleasure before turning to get her stuff. "Oh, right. The sign." She turned back to the door, only to jump back a half step, then stop dead in her tracks.

Quinn lifted his hand and gave her a short wave.

"It's like you were put on this earth to give me repeated heart attacks," Riley said, dropping the hand she realized she'd clasped to her chest like some fluttering heroine in a sultry, Southern drama.

"I didn't want to interrupt, that's all. Sounds like an exciting evening ahead. I didn't realize it was closing time. I can see myself out."

There hadn't been a trace of sarcasm in his voice, so she kept her tone politely casual as well. "We close early on Mondays, at six. It's usually the slowest business day."

"We? Do you moonlight for Lani?"

"No, I just — we're family here. Of sorts."

"Right." He smiled. "So this would be bitchy bake night, then."

Riley rolled her eyes, but couldn't help laughing. "I see you've met Miss Alva. She does help out in the shop from time to time."

"Wise choice. She's a good salesperson. I don't know any of the other members she mentioned, but it sounds like you've assembled quite the group. Sounds like fun."

Riley lifted an eyebrow. "It is — if you enjoy baking, anyway. Somehow I don't see you frosting little cakes, but —"

"My skills are many and varied," he said. "But, you're right. The only thing I ever baked was biscuits with my grandmother, and that was ages ago. I'm not sure being the designated biscuit cutter really qualifies me even as that. I had to stand on a stool."

Riley's smile warmed, even though she was determined not to soften toward him. She needed to stop thinking about him. All the time. He needed to stop being charming. And memorable. More Quinn Moments she definitely did not need. And right before Cupcake Club, too. She needed him gone before Franco and his all-knowing eyes and ears strolled in. "I think that sounds rather sweet, actually. I'm sure she loved the help."

"She did. It's a good memory. Actually, when I walked in here and took in how good everything smelled, it brought back all kinds of memories of being in my grandmother's kitchen over the years. Many that I'd forgotten."

"Scent is a powerful trigger," Riley said.

"Yes," he agreed, and somehow those crystal blue eyes of his grew fractionally darker, and a lot more focused. "It certainly is."

Riley felt her skin come alive, but not in an embarrassed flush this time. More like a

176

sudden, intense awareness. Their parting conversation the last time they'd crossed paths echoed through her mind. *A woman who has to ask what she's worth . . . without already knowing the answer.* Or words to that effect.

"How did you and Lani come to know each other?" he asked.

"Why?"

His smile spread to a grin. The kind of grin that did nothing whatsoever to help her maintain her equilibrium.

"Just making conversation, that's all. I'm a writer. We want to know everything. I like knowing more about people. I enjoyed the things you shared about some of the folks here, who've come to be your friends."

Yet another reason she needed to get him out the door. "I, uh, well, there's not much to the story, really. I had just moved here, and I was exploring the town square, checking out all the shops." She edged past him to flip the sign. "While working as a stylist for *Foodie* — that's the food magazine I was on staff with back in Chicago — I'd heard about Lani's shop, and the whole story with Baxter bringing his show here to woo her and . . ." And she'd thought it ridiculously romantic. But she wasn't going to share that with Quinn. "So, I made a point to stop in.

We're both tied to the same industry, or were anyway, in my previous life, so I wanted to say hello. She was in the kitchen, so I poked around while waiting for her to come up front, and, I guess I found myself rearranging things — just a little."

Quinn lifted a brow. "Rearranging things? Like the displays?"

"Her window treatment was all wrong. The cases were good, but they could have been improved, and the shelves behind the register weren't really being put to the best possible use." Riley smiled and shrugged. "I can't help it. I'm a stylist. It's how my brain works. Anyway, I was just sort of moving things around a tiny bit in the big display window, nothing major, just . . . little adjustments, waiting for her to come out."

"And she caught you, red-handed? Or cake-handed, as the case may be?"

Riley laughed at that, and felt the guard she'd tried to keep up collapse like so many cupcakes on a three-tier crystal display stand. "More like frosting-fingered. I sort of knocked one of the little signs over and it snagged the display tablecloth and —"

Quinn lifted his hand. "I think I've witnessed this first hand."

Riley did flush then, but it wasn't so embarrassing anymore. He knew about her klutz tendencies, and apparently found them amusing, or at the very least not off-putting. She found herself laughing as she once again owned her shortcomings, and he laughed along with her. Of course, defenses down, their gazes happened to catch, as they always seemed to do at some point when they were together and . . . *dammit,* she was sucked right back into another one of those moments.

At least they were moments to her. She'd swear they were for him, too. That whole deepening blue thing happened as his pupils expanded, and her throat went dry and her palms grew damp. Their laughter faded, but somehow, the goofy smiles did not, and for some reason she couldn't explain, that made the moment even hotter, more intense, than all the previous moments combined. Maybe because they had a shared history, now that they knew more — and liked more — about each other.

"Anyway," she managed, pushing gamely past the sudden tightness in her throat, "I apologized for the wreckage, explained what I was doing, and made a few suggestions. We got to talking about my background, and we knew some of the same people." She lifted a shoulder. "It happened to be a Monday, in fact the shop should have been closed. She'd just forgotten to flip the sign, which was why she'd been in the kitchen as long as she had. Some of the gang started showing up, and she introduced me around, and somehow I found myself back in the kitchen, and . . ." She smiled and shrugged.

"Baking happened," Quinn finished.

"It did, indeed. I've been part of the bitchy bake group ever since."

"I would imagine it's been a nice tie-in, between the work you do now, and what you did before, working with food and all. Why the change?" he asked. "And the migration?"

Her defenses down, Riley wasn't prepared for the question. Something of that showed on her face, and he lifted his hand to halt her response. "You know, none of my business. Even writers don't get to know everything. I didn't mean to pry."

"Fair's fair," she said, "I asked about your family and history here." Riley smiled briefly . . . but didn't exactly get around to answering the question.

"Do you enjoy what you're doing down here? Staging homes? I guess it's a much grander scale than styling food, bigger platform, bigger challenge. Bigger payoff?" He held her gaze for a moment, then let out a short, self-deprecating laugh. "I'm doing it again."

She couldn't help it, she laughed, too. "You just can't help yourself, can you? If you were a cat —"

"I know," he said with a fast grin. "I'd be dead right now. Usually I'm less impulsive about it, but what you did in Chicago, what you do here . . . I find it all fascinating. We're both in creative fields, but so very different in what we draw from, how we build our respective scenes, so to speak." He shrugged. "It's compelling and interesting and makes me want to know more."

"Well, I'm flattered," she said.

But it wasn't by accident that she changed the subject. "Lani said you were a new customer. Did you come by to pick up some cupcakes? They are addictive."

He hesitated, then said, "Actually, I was just dropping off the towels and your shirt." He pointed to the shopping bag, still sitting on the counter by the register. "All freshly laundered, good as new."

"Oh, thanks. Although nothing can make that jersey good as new again." It had been bugging her, the whole subterfuge thing, so she added, "I've had it since I was in high school." She smiled. "But I appreciate the effort."

Quinn's smile returned, too. The kind with

crinkles around the eyes and that honest warmth filling them. "High school, huh?" He exuded all that charisma as naturally as most people breathed air.

"Actually, it's Tommy Flanagan's jersey." Her smile turned dry. "I'm just not as good at returning things as you are."

"High school sweetheart?"

Riley laughed at that. "Only in my desperate little schoolgirl dreams. Tommy was the football quarterback, debate team captain, and senior class president, all rolled into one."

"I hate him already," Quinn said.

Riley grinned. "He made it hard to do that. He was the kind of guy everybody loved. But when it came to girls, he was the head cheerleader type, and well . . . I was definitely not that."

"So, how'd you end up with the jersey?"

Her smile turned rueful, and a tiny bit of heat infused her cheeks. "Let's just say the less than graceful moments you've had the pleasure of witnessing when you've been around me had their roots very early on in my childhood. By high school, I was a full-fledged dork. In this case, it involved a ridiculous attempt on my part to impress him with my pre-track warm-up skills — of which I had absolutely none, by the way —

and the very unfortunate timing of the track field irrigation system flipping on."

"Aw. I'm sorry. Though I'm sure you made a very charming drowned track dork."

She laughed. "I don't know that Tommy shared your vision, but he was a gentleman. My track suit was white. Opaque when dry, not so much when wet. When wet, it showcased the little yellow ducks on my matching cotton bra and underwear."

Quinn closed his eyes and shook his head, trying not to laugh.

"Don't hold back on my account," she told him. "I mean, any sixteen-year-old girl who has ducks on her underwear deserves what she gets." She waited a beat, then added, "Soooo sexy."

He opened one eye, caught hers, and they went off in peals of laughter. "I'm sorry. That's just . . . so wrong of me," he finally managed, wiping the corner of one eye. "I'm sure you were adorable in ducks." That sent them off all over again.

"Sadly, they were utterly me," she agreed, trying to catch her breath.

"Well, if it makes you feel any better," he said as they struggled to get themselves back under control, "we share track and field attempts to impress gone awry. I think I told you, I was a skinny kid in school. I really loved sports, but I was too small for football, and not tall enough at that point for basketball. Baseball wasn't my thing, so I went out for track. In the case of my brutal downfall, it was the state championship meet, my first year on the team, and I was going to impress Amy Sue Henderson, star distance runner from our crosstown rival, with my mad pole-vaulting skills."

Riley covered her mouth to keep the laughter from starting all over again. "And?" she said, the word muffled behind her hand.

"You know how you run down the lane, plant the pole in the pit, then launch yourself over the bar to the big mat on the other side?"

All Riley could do was nod at that point, tears of mirth already forming at the corners of her eyes.

"Well, I took off running, and made the mistake of looking over, midstride, to see if she was watching. And when I saw that she was, I got all hung up in those pretty green eyes, and it threw me off count. I planted the pole on the track, missed the pit entirely, tried to launch myself anyway —"

Riley covered her open mouth.

"— snapped the pole in half, and landed in a skinny, crumpled, disgraced heap in the pit."

Riley's hand dropped away. "Were you okay?"

"My body was fine. I would have sworn then, though, that my ego would never recover. Or my self-confidence."

"What did Amy Sue do?"

"Let's just say she wasn't raised with the same admirable traits as Mr. Flanagan. She and her teammates were highly amused."

"Bitch," Riley whispered.

Quinn grinned. "It was painful, but a lesson was learned that day."

"Which was?"

"Run softly and be careful where you plant your big stick?"

Riley spluttered a laugh. "I can't believe you just said that."

"Sorry." A mischievous twinkle glowed in his blue eyes as he laughed along with her. "Actually, I learned to be more realistic in my goals. On and off the field. And to stay focused on the more important ones."

"How did you get yourself back in the meet? I mean, could you?"

"I stumbled through the three other events I was in. It's mostly a mortifying blur. Unfortunately there was no Hollywood ending where I went on to dominate in all the other disciplines and take home multiple golds. But by the time track season rolled around the following year, I'd gained some size along with a lot of height. I worked really hard, and I got pretty good at it."

"Decathlete, you said. That's impressive."

He shrugged, his smile self-deprecating and far too endearing because of it. "By my senior year. Maybe I was just trying to prove myself to the Amy Sue Hendersons of the world."

"Maybe." Riley understood the feeling. "Maybe we're always doing that, in one form or another."

His expression sobered a bit, and their gazes connected again, but, for once, he didn't probe, didn't push. And she was more grateful than he could possibly know. The whole fiasco with Jeremy had brought a lot of her insecurities crashing back, and though she was dealing with them, it was still a sensitive topic.

Quinn turned and nodded toward the photos framed on the wall by the door. "Lani tells me this is your work."

"It is," she said, thankful for the shift in topic once again.

"They're really good. I'm assuming the prints in the bungalow are yours, too? And obviously, the houseboat. I guess I should have put it together."

She shrugged. "I don't see why you would have."

"David handled all the paperwork for keeping the furniture and things, but I did go over the inventory list to make sure we hadn't missed anything. I didn't see you listed as a lease or buyer contact."

"Since most of my jobs are somewhere along the chain of barrier islands, I use my prints in some of the houses I stage."

"So, were some of the shots taken on the other islands as well?"

She glanced at the photos that Lani had chosen for the shop. One in particular was a small print of a picnic table in the wilderness park just down the road from Lani's place. It had played an important role during Lani's courtship with Baxter. She'd talked about it once at Cupcake Club, so Riley had done some exploring, found the place, and shot it as a gift for the couple's first anniversary. A larger print of the same shot, matted and framed, hung in their home.

"Occasionally, but these were all taken here." Various other memories flitted through Riley's mind, of time spent wandering with her camera. Brutus often forged the way. That made her smile. She had albums full of photos of him, discovering

187

his place in island life, too. "Taking them was a large part of how I came to fall in love with the island," she murmured, then realized she'd spoken the musing out loud.

"I can see why." He came to stand beside her.

She kept her gaze fixed on the prints, but there were a lot of other images crowding her mind. None of them framed and on the wall.

"I didn't mean to keep your work from you," he said. "I'm guessing you usually take your prints back down after the homes are done being shown. If you want me to return them, I will." He shifted his gaze to her. She could feel it, like a warm caress. "But I'd prefer to keep them, or at least some of them. I'll get David to work out whatever compensation —"

"They can all stay. No compensation required." She wished like mad every little glance and word from him didn't affect her so acutely.

"Well, if you ever need them for a job —"

"I'm good," she assured him. "I have plenty. And I'm always taking more."

"Thank you. I appreciate it. They're a big part of why the bungalow feels . . . right to me." He made a soft snort. "How's that for a descriptive turn of phrase?"

She smiled. It made perfect sense to her. "I'm glad you like them."

"Does Lani sell your prints? Are they for sale, I mean? If so, I'd —"

Riley shook her head. "These were gifts to her, mostly because she kept bugging me about them after seeing a few I'd put up on the houseboat. She's offered, many times in fact, to put more in here on a commission basis. But I don't want to . . . I don't know, commercialize the work, if that makes any sense. I take them because what I'm looking at makes me want to capture it, for my own pleasure. If I think it will move someone else, then I give it to them. But that's all the satisfaction I need or want, really. It's just something I do for myself. A hobby, I guess. I don't want it to be work."

"Well, as hobbies go, it's a spectacular one. If you ever change your mind, the offer stands."

"Thank you. I'll keep it in mind."

"What about the older prints?" he asked, motioning to the black and whites on the other side of the door. "There are some of those in the bungalow, too."

"Lani came across them when she was cleaning out this place after buying it. It had stood empty for some time and there were boxes of stuff left behind long ago."

"Nice find," he said. "I like the historical bookends. Old and new, then and now. So the older prints in the bungalow, they wouldn't have come from here?"

"No, they didn't. I don't know how much you know about the place, but the bungalow had been unoccupied for a very, very long time. The older gentleman who owned it had apparently used it as a summer place decades ago. He had been in ill health for many years, and left it to sit, mostly neglected. When he passed away a few years back, his executor put it on the market. Two investors finally bought it, had it completely renovated and updated, and really made something of the place, as you've seen. It's quite a showpiece, especially here on Sugarberry. The pictures you have were either already on the walls, or found in storage boxes. Fortunately, the new owners didn't ditch them. I found them stacked up in one of the upstairs bedrooms, and decided to use them. So, they go with the house."

"That they do," he agreed, though she knew he understood she'd meant they were conveyed with the lease agreement. "Your work complements the vision of whoever took them. Your viewpoints are much the same. Kind of interesting, when you think about it. Two people whose paths never crossed, from different eras, both moved by the same setting in much the same way, both documenting it in their own way."

She smiled at that and found herself nudging his arm with her elbow. "You're such a writer."

"Storyteller," he corrected. "And yep, I can't help it. That's how I see things, I guess. How I document what I see. I think about the story that goes with them, or that might have gone with them. If I were telling it."

"Have you always known?" she asked. "About being a storyteller?"

"Um . . . my understanding of the calling developed over time, but looking back, there were clues all along. What about you? Have you always had an eye for setting? Either behind the lens, or staging and styling the things in front of it?"

She smiled. "I was forever rearranging my stuffed animals and I set a mean tea party table, even as a five-year-old, so . . . yes, you could say that."

He grinned at that. "Did you head straight into that field?"

She glanced up at him again. "Yes, Curious George, I did."

He laughed. "I've gone from dead cat to curious monkey. But I'm done apologizing.

I can't help it. The subject matter is very interesting to me."

"Interior design?"

"No." His gaze landed very squarely on her own. "The woman doing the designing."

She hadn't been prepared for that. For the intensity of his gaze. Or the way it tied her tongue right up.

"Bonsoir, ma petite bakers," Franco called out as he sailed into the shop. "Oh." He stopped short as he almost stumbled straight into them. "Didn't see you there." He ran his gaze openly over Quinn. "Well, 'allo, *Monsieur* . . . Brannigan, I presume?"

Quinn kept his gaze on Riley's for a fraction of a second longer, then glanced up at Franco. "Quinn," he said. "Please."

"Franco." He stuck his beefy hand out and they struck a quick shake. Franco glanced between the two of them and Riley could see the struggle between the knowing smile and the frown of concern.

"Lani is in the back," Riley said. "Alva is next door." She wiggled her eyebrows, hoping to distract him. "Dealing with Sam. And Charlotte is back! She'll be in tonight."

Franco clapped his wide palms together. "A tasty evening menu, for sure." He kept his gaze straight on Riley's. "Will you be

192

joining us?"

"I will. Quinn — Mr. Brannigan, was just dropping something off for me."

"Ah, the borrowed shirt," Franco said, his openly curious gaze moving back to Quinn. "I see."

"I've taken up enough of your time," Quinn said to Riley, then looked at Franco. "A pleasure to meet you." He turned back to Riley. "Thank you for the loan, and for indulging the dead cat. And the curious monkey. Both are greatly appreciative."

She couldn't help it, even with Franco sucking in every blink, she grinned. "Did I have a choice?"

"We all have choices." He smiled at them as he sketched a slight bow, and let himself out.

Riley immediately lifted her hand, blocking Franco's handsome face. "Don't start. Do not even start. I can't. Okay?"

She looked up, expecting to find either a pout or a devilish smile. Instead, his expression was completely unreadable. It was so unlike him, she wasn't quite sure what to think of it.

"Okay." He put his hand at the small of her back and guided her to the counter where her baking tote and toolbox still sat.

"That's it? Are you feeling all right?"

"Better than I have in a very long time." He surprised her by leaning down and planting a kiss on top of her head. "Just remember, I'm always here if you need me."

She surprised them both by turning and hugging him tight. "I know you are." She looked up and smiled. "I'm a lucky girl."

He leaned down and kissed her nose. "You don't know the half of it, honey." They laughed as they headed to the kitchen.

CHAPTER 8

"It's coming along fine," he lied. Quinn tucked his cell phone between his ear and shoulder as he shifted gears and pulled his Carrera into the narrow, crushed shell and gravel lot behind Laura Jo's and parked. He didn't immediately get out, wanting to finish the call with his editor first.

It was already humid and, even though the calendar had finally turned the page to September, he knew the day would be a scorcher. At the moment, there was a steady, early morning breeze. It carried the rich, mingling scents of sizzling bacon and fresh roasted coffee wafting out the screened kitchen door, straight through the open windows of his car, making his stomach grumble in appreciation.

He'd started something of a habit, indulging himself with a hot breakfast a few mornings a week. Those delectable smells didn't begin to promise what they actually delivered, providing another reason to end his call as swiftly as possible.

"Good, great! So . . . can you give me a delivery date? Pretty please," Claire begged. "Just so I can keep the wolves at bay. They're starting to circle."

"I'm sure they are, and I'm sorry for that. I am. But it's not like we're behind schedule."

"I know, I know. We just usually have a publication date all picked out by now. Can you give me even a whisper of a general idea?"

Quinn sighed. He'd known the pressure would start sooner rather than later, but he hadn't expected the Big Push this soon. He should have, he supposed. With the industry struggling to find its way in an era filled with new gadgets and an ever widening variety of publishing formats, all the New York publishing houses were feeling the pressure to do whatever it took to ensure their upcoming release lists remained strong and vital. He was at the top of his publisher's list in that department. An announcement of a new release from their best-selling author would go a long way toward quieting the wolves, from the publisher, to the distributors, and on down the chain, to the most important element . . . the reader.

No one was more keen on satisfying that particular link in the chain than he was.

"Claire, as soon as I feel I can give you a target, you'll be the very first to know. You know I'm consistent, I'm never late, and I don't let you down. So just tell everyone to calm down. They'll have another Brannigan title for next year's schedule. Sitting on my shoulder is not helping the process."

"I know, I know. You know I wouldn't be making a peep unless I really had to," she said, all contrition now.

"I do. Just glad we're on the same page. I'm looking forward to some uninterrupted writing time," he added pointedly.

"Of course," she said, though they both knew his uninterrupted time had been officially marked as limited now. "So, how is it down in Georgia?" she asked, which translated into *Is migrating to the middle of nowhere making you write any faster?*

"It's great, actually. Better than anticipated."

"Good, great!" she said, overly excited by the news. He knew she'd take that and run with it. *He's on a roll!!,* she'd tell them.

"Always good to talk with you, Claire." He seized the chance to end on an enthusiastic note. "I'll be in touch." She should hear those words as *don't call me, I'll call you,* but they both knew she'd ignore them.

"It's good to touch base with you, Quinn." Sincere affection mixed in now that her official duties were complete. "You know, if you want to send me a partial, so I can start the marketing ball rolling —"

He rolled his eyes even as he smiled. Claire, after all, would always be Claire. Her professional duties were never really complete. He didn't fault her for continuing to push. Her bulldog-in-a-poodle-suit tenacity was what made her the successful executive editor she was. It worked to his advantage when she was fighting in-house to get him every possible edge in promotion and placement.

There was sincere warmth in his voice when he continued. "You know I don't write that way. I'm all over the place until the book is finished. That hasn't changed."

She laughed. "Can't fault a girl for trying. Besides, you know at heart I'm just a fan who can't wait to see what you're up to next."

If you only knew, he thought, feeling a different tug in his stomach.

The shame of it was, Quinn knew her statement to be utterly true. In addition to being savvy about marketing, branding, placement, and the business side as a whole, she was keyed in on an intimate level with his work. She didn't just get his work as it pertained to current marketing trends. She truly understood and enjoyed his stories purely as a reader. She was his target audience.

It was that very duality that made them such a good team. He valued her input on all things, especially on story, more than she knew. However, the politics of the game didn't make that easy to express. Over the past few months, he'd been sorely tempted to pick up the phone, wanting to pick her brain about the new direction the current work was pushing him toward. Not to get her blessing, or force the panic attack such a revelation might induce, but to discuss the work itself. More than current market analysis, that was what he needed to help him decide what to do.

The problem was, she played for both sides. A fact he could never forget. There was no way to talk with her about his idea, without simultaneously announcing the same news to his entire publishing house. He couldn't ask her to keep it a secret until he decided, and he wasn't ready to make any kind of public announcement yet. It was the same reason he hadn't bent the ears of any of his fellow authors. Not that he couldn't trust their discretion, but this was not a typical brainstorming session. The idea that someone so successful in one genre was even contemplating switching it up would be too juicy a tidbit to keep under wraps. Especially in the current writer-eat-writer economic environment.

If and when he decided to change it up, he'd need to control the big reveal as best he could. He'd have to tell Claire immediately. It would be career suicide, on many levels, to just spring the manuscript on her, fait accompli, then let the chips fall where they may. But when — and if — he did tell Claire, he needed to be damn sure of what he was doing, so he could defend the book as thoroughly and enthusiastically as possible, ensuring to the best of his ability that it would be well received, with everyone on board his new train and thrilled to be there.

"We'll talk soon," Claire was saying.

Once again, he bit his tongue and kept his tumultuous thoughts to himself. "I know we will," he said dryly, accepting the inevitability of that. "Take care." His smile faded as he clicked off the phone. He groaned as he slid his sunglasses off and hooked them on the rearview mirror. The dragons were officially breathing fire.

Climbing out of the car, he pushed the aggravation away, focusing instead on the pleasures of Laura Jo's bacon and egg sandwich, the world's best coffee, and the friendly smiles and hearty welcomes of the locals who also made the diner part of their morning routine.

He'd wondered at first if he was making a mistake, if bumming around the island would end up inviting more distractions than he already had. Thanks to a small write-up in the local paper announcing he'd leased the old Turner place, and mentioning his ties to his grandfather and the island, everyone knew who he was, even those who'd never heard of him three or four weeks ago.

Although his ties were tenuous at best, it was precisely that connection to Sugarberry that had made him an instant local to the other islanders; welcomed, accepted, and, other than a nod and a friendly hello, largely left alone to his own devices. He appreciated both. More than he could have imagined. They also took a sense of pride and ownership of his accomplishments — local boy makes good — which could have come off as a bit of latching-on, but felt like a warm, supportive embrace.

He hadn't realized how un-embraced he'd

felt, or just how solitary a life he'd led over the years. He considered himself social, and involved. He did charity work, played a round of golf with a few fellow writer buddies when he could. David and Finch were always about or in contact, and there was rarely a time when he wasn't traveling to see places he wrote about, or tracking down, meeting, or talking and listening to the broad range of people he interviewed and came to know while doing research for his books. He'd have said he had a full, vibrant, interesting life.

Yet, in a very short time, the span of a single month, the whole island had become as comfortable to him as his bungalow had been the moment he'd set foot in it. It felt like home. Or certainly a place he'd like to call home. Even with the monumental decision he had to make, he couldn't remember ever feeling so . . . grounded. Centered. As if rooted, toes in the sand, island breeze on his skin, and the quiet, loyal support, so good-naturedly offered up by everyone around him . . . he could free the rest of himself up to think, to ponder. To plot and plan — which would be ever-so-glorious . . . if he could just decide which version of the story he was going to tell.

His problem wasn't that he didn't know

what to write next. He wasn't blocked. Quite the opposite. There were two stories dueling for supremacy in his head. The one he knew he could write, because he'd written it, or some version of it, a dozen times before. The one he knew, hands down, was a solid, marketable, exciting idea that would produce a great story once it was all done and told.

And the other one, the tantalizing one, the one luring him down a path that was dark and shadowy, where there was no rich experience, accumulated knowledge, and certainty to fall back on. That story was all but bursting inside his head, luring him like a seductive siren. Promising heat and fun and heady anticipation, even though he knew there was a better than average chance his career would end in one huge, crashing, explosive ball of flames.

The only real question was . . . did he risk the flaming ball of destruction for the chance to achieve what might be a slow, steady burn? One that could keep him in a heady, exciting place for many years to come?

"I wish to hell I knew," he muttered as he climbed the short set of steps to the rear door of the diner. He'd needed to escape the four walls of his house . . . and the four sides of his beckoning computer screen. *Write what you know . . . make everyone happy . . . keep your day job.* Those were the words echoing in his ears when he sat down to work. As was often the case of late, it had driven him straight out the door through the dunes and to the beach.

But a long, limit-testing run or punishing sea swim hadn't done a damn thing to silence the voices . . . or convince him to embrace them. He knew the creative process was unpredictable at best, so he remained hopeful every time he set off down the sand, that the epiphany would come, that some thought or idea would signal to him why he should turn his back on the seductive siren call torturing him, and stick to the steady reliable companion he'd worked so hard to cultivate. To believe in. To trust. He'd already achieved that with his publisher, his editor, and most important, his readers. Was he tossing those relationships away, like a sorry bastard who cheated on his spouse?

But that wasn't even half his problem. Half his problem — hell, it felt like all of his problem — was those long runs that were supposed to promote clearheaded, rational thinking . . . did nothing of the kind.

No sooner would he settle into a nice loping stride than his thoughts would trip away from the dialogue his characters should be having to echoes of other conversations, real ones, of laughter shared and insights revealed . . . and a pair of devastating dimples bracketing a mouth he'd spent far — far — too much time wishing he'd already tasted.

What should have been a brief, inconsequential run-in at the bakery the previous week had turned out to be neither brief nor inconsequential. Every time he was with her, he learned more . . . and the temptation grew. He'd first told himself he was using his attraction to distract himself from the confusing and challenging choices he had to make. It wasn't the first time his head had been turned. He'd been writing long enough to see a distraction for what it was.

Riley Brown was in a whole new category. He couldn't truly imagine that he'd ever forget her.

Quinn opened the screen door to the kitchen and gave a small salute and smile to Laura Jo and her line cooks, who were busily plating and serving up dishes, sliding them across the top of the half wall that divided the kitchen from the front diner counter and the tables lining the walls beyond it. He'd come in through the kitchen door by mistake his first time, thinking it was merely the rear entrance, since that was where the parking lot was. But he'd learned most everyone either lived within walking distance, or worked around the town square, so they came on foot. A few tourists or island wanderers would park along the curb out front, in the few spaces available. Typically, the other cars in the rear lot belonged to Laura Jo and her staff.

She'd thought he was sneaking in due to his celebrity status, which had made him laugh. Despite his sales numbers and his smiling face plastered on book jackets around the globe, he was like the rest of the best-selling authors out there — household names no one would recognize in person.

At best, he got the "where do I know that guy from?" look or a head scratch. It was amusing when Laura Jo had seated him discreetly in the back of the restaurant, right by the kitchen door, thinking he wanted privacy, and then had snuck samples of all kinds of heavenly goodies to him. He'd appreciated her sensitivity even if, normally, it would be unwarranted. With Sugarberry being so small, and folks knowing everything about each other's business, he'd accepted the privacy she'd offered, simply for the chance to think and plot without interruption.

But on Sugarberry, there really was no such thing as privacy, no matter where he sat. On the other hand, because he'd been so quickly and warmly adopted by the islanders, rather than finding their smiles and jovial hellos and hey, how are yas intrusive or suffocating, he found them welcoming and heartwarming.

He felt like the Norm character from the iconic *Cheers* television program, with everyone raising a mug or tossing out a friendly hello whenever he wandered in. Sometimes the islanders engaged Quinn in conversation, other times they'd leave him to his thoughts, but he was always greeted warmly and openly. More surprising to him was that, rather than sit back and keep to his own thoughts, or observe and listen, he found himself actively engaging in the conversations that sprang up around him, as most of the other diners did, everyone talking over each other and any number of conversations converging, dividing, then converging again. He'd immensely enjoyed the give-and-take, learning more about his new neighbors, and finding himself sincerely and actively getting caught up in their lives.

He still used the back entrance, though more as an amusing tradition, one he and Laura Jo enjoyed . . . and he still took the rear table by the kitchen door. Mostly because Laura Jo still spoiled him with tasty tidbits.

He pushed through the door to the diner that morning and was greeted by a wave of "Hey," and "Mornin' " and nods or coffee mug salutes all around. He gave a short wave and a smile to everyone, then settled in at his table, which already had a well-thumbed copy of the *Daily Islander* on it, even though it was barely past nine in the morning. He'd also discovered islanders were an early rising lot, and knew he was easily the fifth or sixth occupant of that table that morning. Not being a morning person, his leisurely mornings were one of the things he enjoyed best about writing for a living. That had shifted a bit since his arrival on Sugarberry. He wasn't entirely certain why, but when the sun came up, he generally followed close behind it.

He was getting more regular exercise now than he ever managed in the city . . . which he was doubly thankful for. He'd relearned the joys of the slower-paced, Southern lifestyle . . . most especially as it pertained to the utter pleasure to be found in lingering over a well-prepared meal and a good cup of coffee. To that end, he settled back in his chair, the tension from Claire's call already easing out of his neck and shoulders, then smiled broadly as he picked up the paper and realized it was Thursday.

Miss Alva's advice column ran on Thursdays.

Laura Jo popped out with a fresh cup of coffee, two creams, one sugar, which wasn't at all how he'd taken it in his former life, but how he always had his coffee now. "Thanks," he told her, wondering how he'd ever enjoyed the brew bitter and black. "That bacon smells incredible."

"Good. You're about to get some with an egg, sunny-side up, on two slices of grilled toast."

Quinn closed his eyes in anticipation. "My heart and soul thank you, even if my arteries do not."

"Come now, a finer specimen of a man I don't recall I've ever seen. Except, of course, for my Johnny. Rest his soul."

"Of course," Quinn agreed with a smile, "and thank you kindly." She spouted some version of the same sort of flattery every time he came in, and he was quite certain did the same with every other customer as well, sounding just as sincere, which was a large part of her charm. And why his cheeks warmed right up, every time.

"I'll be right back out," she said with a wink.

He grinned and shook his head, taking another sip of the sweet, creamy, aromatic brew as he flipped the paper open straight to "Ask Alva." The column was purported to be an advice column, but was, in fact . . . nothing easy to label. Folks did send in letters, and they did ask her advice, but that only seemed like a flimsy excuse to gossip about everyone on the island. She didn't name names, but there was no doubt to anyone who lived on Sugarberry — which comprised the entire readership of the daily paper — whom she was referring to as she spun her tales of "advice." She always managed to include a colorful story about how someone of her acquaintance had once done something similar to someone else. The end result rarely was a flattering portrayal, but was always told in such an entertaining manner, it never left a bad taste. Well, other than perhaps to the person being scolded for their bad behavior. But since they generally appeared to deserve it . . . Quinn didn't judge himself too harshly for being amused.

It did make him wonder why anyone would send a letter in and assume they'd retain any sense of anonymity, which led him to suspect the actual validity of those letters . . . but as a born storyteller, he'd immensely enjoyed the few columns he'd read thus far and settled in with the happy anticipation of another round of entertaining anecdotes over breakfast.

Laura Jo popped out a moment later and slid a steaming plate in front of him. It was like a mini buffet for one. He loved the South. In addition to the egg and bacon grilled sandwich, there was a side of pan-browned, hashed potatoes, a small bowl of buttered grits, and what he knew was going to be a melt-in-your-mouth flaky, buttermilk biscuit. Add to that the little bowl of apple butter, another one of sausage gravy, and a second mug of coffee to replace the one he'd already drained, and it was his own personal definition of the "great and grand beyond" — which was where it would likely send him, if he kept eating like this, he thought with a chuckle . . . then dove right in.

When Laura Jo stopped by to top off his mug again, Quinn looked straight into her lively gray eyes. "Will you marry me?"

"Well, now that my sweet Johnny has met his maker . . . I am available," she responded, without missing a beat. "Of course, I'll expect you to take me away from all this."

He gave her a look of mock horror. "Why would I want to do that?"

She leaned down and propped her ample frame on the table with one hand, while the other expertly kept her serving tray aloft. "If I can put out that food you're devouring from my little, sorry excuse of an aging kitchen where half the stuff don't work unless you kick it, pound it, or swear at it, imagine what I could whip up for you on that brand-new Viking I hear you have." She fluttered her lashes as she straightened. "I'll consider that your dowry."

Quinn laughed outright, then took her hand and kissed the back of it. "Take me, I'm yours!"

She tugged her hand free, then swatted him with the towel she kept tucked in her apron pocket, but not before he spied the bit of pink in her cheeks. "Scoundrel."

"Saucy temptress."

She laughed even as she snapped the towel at his leg and stepped back toward the kitchen. "Just because you have a way with words, don't think you can woo me."

"Good thing Johnny's not around, or I'd have to tell him to keep an eye on his back," he called out as the door swung shut behind her. Still grinning, he continued his meal with renewed energy, like a man starved, knowing it wasn't so much his belly but his battle with indecision fueling his need for biscuit-and-gravy comfort. There were few forms of comfort more satisfying than a home-cooked Southern breakfast.

His mind immediately skipped from Alva's sermon on the evils of coveting your neighbor's wife and how she once knew a certain tackle shop owner who should really have kept his bait on ice . . . to a different kind of comfort food. Riley Brown came directly to mind, full lips parted, blouse opened, with chocolate frosting smeared all over her —

"Well, look who's up early and eating like a man should first thing in the morning."

Quinn startled guiltily from his little reverie, so much so that he rattled the table and almost knocked his coffee mug over. He quickly steadied everything, then looked up to find all five-foot-nothing of Alva Liles smiling straight at him. "Good morning to you, Miss Alva. What has you up and about this fine morning?"

Quinn shifted uncomfortably in his seat, thankful for the linen napkin covering his lap, certain that, like his body's current condition, his thoughts would somehow broadcast themselves like a neon sign. But that was Alva's influence on folks.

Eighty-three or not, ol' eagle eye immediately spied the column he'd folded the newspaper to. She beamed. "Are you enjoying today's column?"

"I am. Always do," he said, happy and thankful to direct his thoughts away from Riley and on to anything else.

As if Alva had some kind of Vulcan mind meld with him — the more he got to know her, the more he wasn't too certain she wasn't at least part alien; it would explain so much — she took the seat across from him. "Can I ask you a nosy question? And you can just tell me I'm an old busybody who should mind her own business. I won't take offense."

Quinn, who couldn't imagine anyone saying that to Alva's face — certainly not him — simply nodded. And braced himself.

"I was wondering if you were . . . involved. With a woman, I mean." She placed her tiny, birdlike, blue-veined hand on his arm, and gripped it with surprising strength. "I don't want any details, you know, just a simple yes or no. Are you available?"

Quinn instantly thought of Riley again, and was surprised. More from panic than plan, he flashed Alva a grin and covered her hand with his own. "Why, Miss Alva, are

214

you askin' me what I think you're askin' me?"

She swatted at him much the same way that Laura Jo had. And blushed much the same way, too, he noted, charmed by the notion that anything could make the tiny octogenarian blush.

"Now, now, Mr. Brannigan, what kind of woman do you take me for?" She smiled at him, that devilish twinkle back in her eyes. "On second thought, be the gentleman I know you to be and don't answer that."

He laughed, and her eyes twinkled.

"So" — she said, not letting him off the hook.

"Is this going to end up in your column?" he asked.

"That depends. Are you asking for my advice?" She leaned a bit closer. "Perhaps you'd like some guidance on how to approach a certain someone who might have caught your eye?"

He saw the speculative gleam behind the deceptively sweet twinkle. In his head, he heard the *danger, danger* sirens go off, but somehow managed to smile. "I'm usually pretty good at that sort of thing, once I set my mind to it."

Alva slid her hand free, and thanked Laura Jo for the mug of coffee she slid in front of her before trotting off once again with a full tray. "Well, then, I suppose the only other question left is . . . what are you waiting for?"

Quinn was amused by her endearing question. Speculation and potential gossip fodder aside, he knew her interest was sincere. Perhaps not so much on his behalf, as that of her fellow Cupcake Club baker.

"I wasn't so much waiting as being respectful," he said, not bothering to confirm they were talking about Riley. Alva was no dummy. Other than Laura Jo and Miss Alva herself, Quinn hadn't spent any real time chatting with any other woman on the island.

"Well, that's a measure of what a fine Southern gentleman your mother raised you to be —"

"And grandmother. My mom passed when I was young, and Grams picked up the project from there." He smiled. "And what a project I was. But I'd like to think they'd be proud of how I turned out."

Alva's smile was warm. "I'm more than certain of that. But I'm not entirely certain what it is you think you need to respectful of?"

Quinn was amazed he was even having this conversation. He was always the questioner, the seeker of information, never the one being questioned. "Well, not to speak out of turn, but, assuming we're talking about Miss Brown, I was being respectful of her current relationship."

Alva's carefully penciled-on brows — works of art in and of themselves — furrowed delicately, though her magnificently rendered bouffant of blond and silver curls didn't so much as quiver. "What relationship?"

It was Quinn's turn to frown. He didn't think it was possible that anyone on Sugarberry could have a relationship that wasn't known to the rest of the population. Especially the member of said population currently seated across the table from him. But Riley did a lot of work in the lower islands, and it was quite possible that she was able to keep her private life discreet and at a distance. She was from the city, too. Perhaps she wasn't comfortable conducting her romance in a fishbowl.

In that case, he definitely didn't want to be the one to out her to her friends. He gave Alva a half-abashed smile. "Perhaps it was simply her way of letting me know she's not interested. Please, don't mention it to her. I appreciate her kindness in letting me down gently."

To his dismay, Alva's frown didn't ease, nor did the speculative gleam in her eyes diminish.

Wonderful. Now what had he done?

CHAPTER 9

Riley plopped her tool bag and supplies on the worktable next to Charlotte, then gave her a quick hug. "If it's any consolation, boys are dumb."

"Hey now," Franco said, stationed at the table just behind them.

Riley looked over her shoulder at him and made a kissy face. "Not you, my sweet baboo," she crooned, "never you."

"Damn straight." Delivering the words in his full-bodied, Rambo-from-the-Bronx voice, he then executed a perfect curtsy and twirled around back to his table. "Carry on, ma petite mes amies."

Charlotte rolled her eyes, but she offered Riley a short smile. "Why does it have to be so complicated?"

"Because your fiancé is Puerto Rican and you're from New Delhi. Even though the two of you are poster children for the rainbow coalition, your parents are from different cultures and different generations. Take heart, Carlo's folks loved you."

"As a business partner and potential career stepping-stone for their son, yes. As his wife? Don't fool yourself, Riley." Charlotte laid her hand on Riley's arm. "We knew it would be far from easy. With that as a given, our visit to his family went very, very well. I think that's why I was so surprised to hear they have no interest in meeting my family when they come to visit next month. I thought I was being accepted into the family circle, but I was just being accepted into the one-of-Carlo's-nice-friends circle."

Riley frowned and lifted up Charlotte's left hand — the one with the beautiful diamond and antique platinum setting adorning her ring finger. "They do know you're engaged. Wasn't this his grandmother's ring? I'm sure they didn't miss that."

Charlotte looked away, but only for a moment. Riley tightened her grip on Char's hand when she tried to tug it free. "Tell me you did not take this ring off when you met his folks."

"Okay, I won't tell you. We wanted to test the waters first, see how they liked me. We were going to have a little dinner party later on, and make the formal announcement to them then."

"Your parents know, right?"

Charlotte shot her a dark look. "Why do you think they're traveling here? They didn't come to see me graduate from culinary school. They didn't come to see me accept any of my awards. But I announce I'm engaged, and suddenly they're booking flights. I honestly didn't think they'd care."

"Really?"

Charlotte squeezed Riley's hand, then let it go. "We haven't been any kind of actual family for a very long time. I don't know why they're suddenly being traditional about things. Possibly they want grand-children. I haven't a clue. But it won't change things between Carlo and me, no matter how horrid they are. And they will be horrid. At least I'll defend him to them, if it should come to that. We're not asking them for anything to do with the wedding, or anything else. Neither are we asking anything from Carlo's family. So there's no dependency on either side. I just wish . . ."

"That he'd been as willing to face the fire as you are?"

Charlotte nodded. "It's unfair, I know. He's close with his family. All five million of them — which is why I left it to him to handle however he saw best. But now . . ."

"Now you want him to stand up for you."

"At least stand with me. He's . . . waffling. Not about us, but about how to blend me into his family. He doesn't want any strife, and I know that's not possible."

"You don't think he'd end things with you because of family pressure, do you?"

Charlotte shook her head, but her eyes told another story. "I wouldn't think so. Or I hadn't. Before. Everything has gone so well. Amazingly well. It's truly like a fairy tale. Not that it hasn't taken a lot of work on both our parts. We work together now, and live together. All that togetherness brings many challenges, but they're the kind you want to tackle, relish tackling, and figuring out. Because the reward is so worth it. Worth ten times more. A hundred. Any number to infinity. We both know what we have is special. We've been around long enough, dated enough, hurt enough, and loved enough, to know that this kind of relationship comes along once in your life. We're not going to mess this up. Do you know what I mean?"

"I do, yes, very much." Riley, moved by Charlotte's avowal, answered without thinking.

Charlotte took both her hands. "I suspected so. Will you tell me?"

"Us," Franco chimed in, not even pretending he wasn't hanging on their every word.

"What happened to your fairy tale, Riley?" Char asked. "It wasn't long ago, was it? Is that why you came to Sugarberry?"

Regrouping quickly Riley turned Charlotte's hands over in hers, squeezed back gently, then let go. She turned away to fiddle with her tools, but wasn't paying any attention to what she was unpacking. "You're in a really good place, Charlotte. You and Carlo. You're so lucky. Even better, you both know how lucky you are." Riley sent her a brief glance. "Hold on to it, do whatever you can to nurture it. Don't take it for granted. I know you're struggling right now. Talk to him. Honestly. Openly. Tell him what you're feeling. Don't make him guess and don't sweep it aside."

Franco came around the table and gently pulled her against his side with a brawny arm over her shoulders. "You should take your own advice, *ma belle.*"

Riley snorted, but it caught on a sob in her throat. "You don't have to tell me that. Trust me, if I ever get the chance again, I will."

He turned her to face him and Char joined in their little circle. "You have the chance now. That rule doesn't just apply to partner relationships, but to friendships as well. Both require trust and commitment, after all."

Riley blinked away the sudden sting behind her eyes. "You're right. Don't think I don't love and appreciate both of you. I know I'm new to your group, that you both go way back with Lani, but —"

"It's not about time spent," Franco said. "Paths cross, some briefly, and others stay connected forever. Ours will."

"Thank you," Riley said, deeply sincere. "You all don't know how much your friendship has meant to me."

"You have friends back in Chicago," Char said. "Have you at least been talking with them?"

She looked first at Char, then at Franco, then down at her hands. "I do. A very few. But . . . not like the three of you are with each other. It's complicated."

Riley had long ago shared with the group that both her parents had passed away. She'd never really known her father, who'd died in combat when she'd been barely a toddler. Her mother, in the same branch of the military, had died of complications from pneumonia when Riley was in college. Hers had been a nomadic life. Her mom was often gone and Riley stayed with this family or that one on whatever base they were stationed, until her mom returned. There had been nothing traditional about her upbringing, but it had been the only life she'd known. She'd been independent very early on, and hadn't thought that was so bad.

While her life had prepared her to fight her own battles and fend for herself, it had taught her little to nothing about how to put down roots, much less make and sustain lasting friendships. She had no immediate family, just a string of cousins scattered all over that she'd never really known or been particularly close to.

Char one-arm hugged Riley, too. "I've been going on and on about my bliss, then whining about little things. You must think me a ridiculous fool."

"No, I think you're madly in love and you want to hold on to that forever. You should want that." Riley looked at Char. "And you will hold on to it. So will Lani and Baxter. You guys are doing it right."

Franco gave her a supportive smile, but there was sadness in it. "Not all of us get a real chance to fulfill our dream." He was referring to the painful end of his relationship with Brenton.

"Exactly." Riley still hoped she could escape without rehashing the entire humiliating ordeal of Jeremy.

But Char pulled up a work stool and Franco pulled up two more. "Sit," he commanded. "No one else will be here for at least an hour. Alva is helping Lani cater the Kiwanis community garden fund-raiser, and Dre isn't coming tonight."

"I know, she told me her fall semester schedule is still all screwed up." Riley smiled. "I'm so proud of her. It's her last year."

"We are, too." Char rubbed Riley's arm. "You don't have to share if you don't want to."

Franco shushed Char with a *"shh"* and a glare, then gave Riley his most earnest and supportive look. "You'll feel better. You remember how long it took you all to pull the story out of me —"

Char snorted. "Right. I believe it was, oh, approximately sixty seconds after you came storming in the back door." Then she relented and rubbed his arm, too. "And it was horrible. We were all devastated for you. You know that."

It had been horrible. And no one had understood the depths of Franco's pain brought on by that kind of devastating blow

226

more than Riley.

Franco had moved to Savannah from New York to stay with his newly committed partner, Brenton, a PA on Baxter's cooking show. For Franco, Brenton was the love of his life, and everyone who had seen them together would have agreed the feeling was mutual — right up until ten months ago. Franco had surprised Brenton on set to celebrate the anniversary of the purchase of their condo where they'd first lived together as a couple, only to discover Brenton locked in an embrace with another PA — a female PA, at that — in the prep kitchen.

It had shattered his entire world, and the whole Cupcake Club had suffered right along with the brokenhearted Franco.

"I know you were, and it meant the world to me." Franco looked back at Riley. "Trust me, honey." All traces of France were gone. "Never underestimate the power of collective disdain and loathing on the one that done you wrong. It's so much better than a pity party for one."

"I know, I just don't want to dwell on it anymore. I've moved on. Rehashing it won't help me now. A group bashing session would just feel . . . petty."

"Did you think I was petty for wishing bad things on Brenton?" Franco spit the name out like he'd just tasted something bitter. "Or worse, yet, pathetic?"

"No, no, not at all. But it had just happened to you. It's expected when you're raw from being so badly hurt. It's been almost two years for me. I have no excuse."

"That depends," Char said. "What did he do?"

"Why do you think he's the one who did anything?"

Char and Franco gave Riley a quelling look, then Char added, "It doesn't take two years to get over it when you're doing the dumping."

"Maybe I deserved it," Riley pointed out.

Instead of admonishing her, Franco stroked her hair. "Oh, *belissima,* is that what you think?" It was such an instinctive, heartfelt gesture of comfort, hot tears instantly gathered in the corners of Riley's eyes. "Bastard," he added, with just the right amount of French-accented disgust to make her go from the verge of tears, to half-snorted giggle.

"Well . . . he is that," she agreed. "But it sounds so much better when you say it."

He hugged her again, then pumped his fist in the air. "*Solidaritie!* See? I told you, ees much better, this beetching with friends." All he needed was a French flag to fly over his head.

"Will you tell us what happened?" Char asked.

Riley sighed. Somehow, telling them didn't seem all that bad. Maybe Franco was right. When you knew the people you were sharing difficult news with would have your back, no matter what . . . telling became almost a relief. Determined not to get sniffly again, she took a breath, squared her shoulders, and smiled at them. "You know, maybe if I'd spent my time cultivating true friendships and not just work relationships, things would have turned out much differently. But I had no time for real friends. I was too obsessed with the amazing bliss that was my relationship with my fiancé."

"Possibly. I know it's helped having all of you keeping me grounded when I feel like I'm floating five feet off the ground." Charlotte smiled dryly. "I was never a floater. Ever. In fact, I was always the lead balloon in the room. If you'd told me I'd ever be in this situation, a ring on my finger, and fighting mad about families blending and still wanting this partnership so badly, the cynic I used to be —"

Franco snorted.

Char elbowed him, not gently. "And am not any longer, would have had a very good, very long laugh. In fact, it's a good thing I met Carlo about the time Lani and Baxter figured things out, because I don't think I'd have been the friend she needed, otherwise."

Char made a face at Franco, who bussed her noisily on the cheek, making her smile sincerely. She looked at Riley then, with all that honest affection still clear in her dark eyes. "I shamelessly need you to help me navigate this, so please let us help you navigate, too. Even if it's in the past, some waters stay dark and run too deep, until you cross them and realize it wasn't so bad a crossing after all."

"Maybe." Riley was heartened by the steadfastness she saw in both their faces. She huffed out a sigh. "Okay. His name is Jeremy. He's a journalist, a very good one, magazine articles mostly, and a trained chef, so his work was all food oriented. We both worked for *Foodie.*" Char and Franco knew that was the magazine she'd styled food for back in Chicago. "It was love at first sight. We were disgustingly inseparable when we weren't dragged apart by work, which wasn't often, but you'd think we'd been cast off to the desert for months after just a day spent apart. Yes, our bliss was that disgusting. I knew I was, hands down, the luckiest girl in the world. He made me feel like the only woman who'd ever existed in his."

I'm not going to sound wistful, dammit. "It's funny, you know. I don't miss him. Not the man, anyway. What I miss is how I felt when I was falling in love, knowing that the person I loved was falling, too. Being around you all, even listening to Alva share her stories about Harold . . . that's the part I wish I still had, that sense of being connected to someone in the way you can't be with friends or family, no matter how strong the ties. I don't miss Jeremy, but I do miss having that one person who is all the things your nearest and dearest can be . . . who is the one no one else can be. Your lover. Your mate."

Out of nowhere, an image of Quinn's sexy, smiling face popped into her thoughts. She blinked it away, disconcerted, and tried to stay focused on the story. She'd been struggling to kick him out of her fantasy life since he was not going to be in her real one. It couldn't be healthy to allow herself to daydream about what might have happened with that cupcake in the breakfast nook . . . if she hadn't been sweaty and scratched up, with random foliage sticking out of her hair. Or, on the boat . . . when they were both drenched and smelling like wet mastiff.

Surely it was a bad sign when she could

make a fantasy out of even that.

"Riley?" Char touched her knee. "If it's too painful —"

"What?" Riley snapped out of her reverie. "No, that's not it. It's just like I said. I miss the feeling of it. Of being in love."

"I know." Real sadness tinged Franco's voice.

Riley leaned her head on his arm. "I know you do. And it sucks to have it taken away. Ripped away, really. Especially when you don't see it coming."

"Oh." Char spoke softly. "I'm so sorry."

"I was, too," Riley said, simply and honestly. She glanced at Franco, who was nodding. He might not have been involved with Brenton for a fraction of the time she'd been with Jeremy, but none of that mattered if you'd gotten to the part where you trusted the person you were in love with to take care of that special bond. To treat it with the dignity and respect it deserved, even if the bond was going to be broken. "It's not that I couldn't have gotten past it if we'd fallen out of love, or had problems we simply couldn't surmount. Even if only one of us was having those issues. But when one person wants out, there are ways to end things, and ways not to."

"Hear, hear," Franco said, a bit of mad

edging out the sad.

"Did you know he was — that he wanted out?" Char asked.

"Not a single clue. I mean, in retrospect? I realize ours was not necessarily the utopian bond I'd imagined it to be. But we weren't arguing, or having any concerns or stresses we didn't always have. We were happy, in that settled way you are when you've been together a long time. None of our co-worker friends, who were with us for long hours every single day, noticed or knew anything was off. No one suspected, least of all me."

"When you love someone, and are loved in return, you trust each other to respect your relationship," Franco said, mirroring her thoughts exactly. "You become the easiest one to dupe, because it would never occur to you to think otherwise."

"Exactly," Riley said. "I get that I was easy to fool . . . but how do you look your best friend in the eyes, and play them for that fool? Knowing you're doing it? That I will never get."

"Me, either," Char said. "I've never experienced that kind of betrayal, because until Carlo I never allowed myself to be vulnerable to anyone. But I've watched it so many times. Breaking up seems hard, not wanting the scene, the drama, but the alternative, is so . . . cowardly."

"That's the other thing," Riley said. "On top of being bludgeoned with the revelation that the person you loved and thought the world of clearly didn't hold you or your love in the same esteem, you also have to admit he's a lying, cheating bastard. In one swoop, Jeremy destroyed every single attribute that made me fall in love with him in the first place — which made me feel even more ridiculous. On top of being sad, and horrified, and heartbroken because I chose to love a man who was capable of doing that I ended up wondering how much of an idiot am I. How did I not know he was capable of that?"

"How do any of us know?" Charlotte said. "We're each evolving all the time. I'm a great testament to that. I was always attracted to men who would certainly never love me back the same way. Self-inflicted relationship sabotage. But we do grow, hopefully in a positive way. I believe that I have. But sometimes it's not positive growth. Life brings new things, new experiences, and a gradual building of events can change people from who they were before."

Char squeezed Riley's arm again as she continued. "But that's just the thing, Riley. You came through it, and you can look yourself in the mirror, and know who you really are. A woman capable of loving fully, with all her heart. Capable of giving herself completely to someone, and cherishing the sanctity of that bond. Jeremy also gets to look in the mirror and see exactly what kind of man he turned out to be."

"Not that he'll ever allow himself that kind of honest assessment."

"You never know what lies in store for him. I'm a great believer in karma. But even if he never holds himself accountable, look at it this way, at least you're no longer accountable for him. Or to him. You're free of his selfish, cowardly, thoughtless acts. Free of having anything to do with his damaged self. You fell in love with something good. It's not your fault he allowed himself to sour into something bad. No matter the dynamics, everyone can choose how to handle life's hurdles. That's how he chose to handle his. Better you knew before something really important happened. Like marriage. Illness. Hardship. *Children.* He deserved to lose you. And you deserve someone who would do anything not to."

"I love you," Franco blurted out, and hugged Charlotte hard. "That was beautiful. That will stay with me forever, I think. I hope. So wise."

"It's simply how I see things now. I couldn't have said those things even two years ago — which is a testament to my growth," she said tearfully.

"Thank you." Riley sniffled, not even trying to stop. "I — that helped me, too." She laughed through the tears. "It really did."

"Good." Charlotte smiled. "You know what, putting all that into words helped me, too. I know now what I want with Carlo. What the 'small stuff,' as you call it, is . . . and what's worth waging war for. So, thank you, too."

They shared smiles for another moment, then Franco pulled them both in. "Group hug." They hugged and laughed, and there was more sniffling. Setting them back on their stools, he crossed his legs and folded his arms over his knees as he swung to face Riley. "Okay, Dr. Phil is over. Now it's Oprah time. What did the rat bastard do? And where can we hunt his ass down?"

Chapter 10

Riley burst out laughing, and so did Charlotte. "Say it again," Riley urged Franco. "You know."

"Bastarde!"

She grinned. "I know it makes me seem small, but I don't think I will ever tire of that."

"I'll have shirts made," he said. "We'll get Dre on board."

Riley's laugh turned to a groan. "I can only imagine what she'd do with it. Goth bastarde!" Riley pumped her fist. "You know, though, that might work," she said thoughtfully. "A few tasteful skulls, some blood . . ."

Char shuddered, but they were all laughing.

"No more ducking," Franco said. "You've come this far, just air the rest of your laundry, missy, and we'll be all done with it."

"It was the sitter," Riley said bluntly. Surprisingly, there was a twinge of sadness, more than a twinge of anger, but an even bigger one of disgust. "We were together seven years . . . and he dumped me so he could boink the hot sitter."

"Seven years? That's a long time, *mon amie*. I'm so sorry."

"Yep, the better part of my adult life, up to that point."

"We're going to need to add a few more lines to those T-shirts," Franco said, making Riley smile, and nudge him again.

"You know you want to."

"Oh, I do. Bastarde," he said again, in a growling, hissing kind of way.

"Oooh, I like that one, too."

"Wait," Charlotte said. "Did you say the sitter? You had — he had, children?" She looked appropriately aghast.

"Thank God, no. I can't imagine how awful it would have been if he'd dragged children through all of that. I was a fully grown adult and it leveled me. She was the dog sitter for Brutus." Riley smiled. "I remember the day I got Brutus. I knew Jeremy would kill me when I brought him home from the pound. He was a bit of a neat freak. Jeremy, not Brutus."

"Brutus was a pound puppy?" Franco asked.

"Is that really surprising?" Riley asked dryly.

"Well, when you put it that way . . ."

"Some family got him as this adorable big lug of a puppy, then he grew into a mammoth lug of a dog and they couldn't handle him, so off to the pound he went."

"Why were you there? Did you two want to get a dog? From what you've told us about your schedule when you were a stylist —"

"No, we'd never even so much as breathed a whisper of it. We'd talked marriage, we were engaged then —"

"You were engaged?" Charlotte asked. "It just keeps getting worse."

"I know. We dated for two years, then moved in together, got engaged about eighteen months later, but never could set a date because our schedules were so crazed. But that didn't matter to me. I've never been the type to dream about my Big Day."

"Me, either," said Charlotte. "Probably because it was all my mother talked about. I was betrothed at birth to a boy from a very good family and my whole life was geared toward the Big Day, as you call it. I couldn't wait to get out."

"I've always dreamed about mine." Franco sighed wistfully. Riley and Charlotte smiled, but Charlotte took his hand and squeezed it.

"If it helps, you're more than welcome to plan mine. Of course, you'll have to deal with two families hell-bent on making sure it never happens. We should just elope." Charlotte's eyes lit up, but it was short-lived. "His family would really never forgive me then. He has all sisters. Five of them."

"Yikes," Riley said. "Well, we had no pressure either way. We had a life together. I was where I wanted to be, with the man I loved. I had no family hounding me to set a date, and his parents spent most of their time bickering despite being divorced for more than twenty years." She shrugged. "We both knew we wanted kids, somewhere in the distant future, so I figured marriage would happen when it finally mattered. At the time, we loved our jobs, loved the lives we had, so . . . children were not imminent. We were both in agreement on that. I knew he'd always had dogs growing up, and I'd always wanted one, so I guess whenever we did have that hazy future family, I always pictured a dog in it. I suppose I figured Jeremy would, too."

"But this wasn't some hazy future time,"

240

Franco said.

"Well, yes, true. That was the day, or one of them, when the future stopped being quite so far away. I mean, it has to happen at some point, right?"

Charlotte's eyebrows climbed. "You just . . . came home with a dog? A very large dog?"

"No, no. I wouldn't have done that. It was going to be a monumental change, so I talked with Jeremy first. It was rare that I asked for anything, really rare, so Jeremy had a hard time saying no to me about it. Even then, I wouldn't have insisted if I thought he was really against it. He seemed more concerned about the logistics, though, than about having a pet, so I asked, if I could get all the care and feeding issues worked out with our schedules, would he be on board, and he agreed. In fact, once I did get it figured out, he was excited about it. I was the same kind of marshmallow with him when he really wanted something, and he had taken advantage of that fact, many times."

"You two were disgusting," Charlotte said.

"Back in the day, yes. But you're one to talk," Riley shot back.

"So . . . did he love Brutus on sight as you did?" Charlotte asked.

"And you never said, but why were you at the animal shelter in the first place?" Franco put in.

"Mrs. Stroeheimer. In 4B. Her cat was forever getting out, getting into scrapes, and usually ended up in lockup at the local shelter. They all knew him there, so they'd call her up and I'd take her down to pick him up."

"Why didn't she get him fixed so he'd stop fighting and well . . . catting about?" Charlotte asked.

Franco groaned at that. "Women always want to cut off a man at the —"

"If it kept him from catting around," Charlotte said, looking him dead in the eyes, "then, perhaps, yes."

Franco considered that, then nodded. "You may have a point."

"Oh, Mr. Bumpers was fixed. He just liked to fight. Usually over Dumpster food. It had to be some sort of king kitty complex, because Mrs. S. fed him like royalty. He didn't need to dive for food, much less fight over it. Anyway, whenever we went down to spring him from lockup, I usually waited in the car, but that day she was feeling a bit lightheaded, had complained of being a bit dizzy, so I helped her inside."

"And then, the Hallmark moment."

Franco fanned his hands out in an arc as he hummed a tune, then clasped his palms under his chin.

"Maybe not quite like that. I knew it was a mistake to go inside the minute I stepped through the door. I can't stand misery — I mean, who can? — but it wrenches me. I know I can't save them all, and that there are many animals out there in that same situation. But I also knew I could reduce that number by at least one."

"And there was the childhood dream," Char added.

"Exactly."

"But wasn't there some small, lap-size dog that needed rescue?" Franco asked. "You lived in an apartment in the city, right?"

Riley nodded. "A tiny one. Yes, there were dozens of other dogs, all of them smaller than Brutus, of course."

"Of course," Char and Franco said together. Neither of them was really an animal person, but they had taken to Brutus. Eventually.

"He was lying in a run in the back, chin on his paws, not even trying to get my attention. It was as if he knew there was no point in it. The shelter was in the middle of the city. Who was going to be looking for a dog his size? He was just so . . . defeated."

"Oh boy," Franco sighed.

"Exactly, right? I didn't have any intention of adopting any of them, though I admit at that point the seed, at least, had been planted. When that hazy, future day came, I knew right then I'd adopt rather than buy. But when they brought out Mr. Bumpers, I asked about Brutus. I was worried for him. He wasn't even trying. I had such a feeling of . . . dread for him. I guess I expected something like that same attitude from the woman who worked there, but her face immediately lit up and she went on and on about what a doll he was, how charming he was, and how they all loved him to pieces and he was such a gentle giant."

"Sucker born every minute," Franco said, shaking his head. "She was envisioning how much more dog food they'd have to spread around."

"Come on," Riley said. "You know him. That's exactly how he is."

Char and Franco shared a look, then nodded toward her. "Of course he is," Char said, in the same tone one would use to placate the mother of an unruly child.

Riley stared them right back down. "Then I saw the sign that said they only hold dogs for sixty days. This was not a no-kill shelter. And I noticed on the card next to Brutus's cage how long he'd been there." She gave them a solemn look. "Just a few days shy of two months."

Char's and Franco's expressions fell at that.

Riley nodded. "I know. But, even then, when I left, I wasn't planning on anything. When Jeremy got home, of course I told him all about taking Mrs. S down there, and, well . . ."

"You took Brutus home the next day."

"I got him a stay of execution the next day. There was a lot of advance planning required. We brought him home ten days later. We had to pass a home inspection and interview."

"Seriously?" Franco asked. "I'm surprised they didn't drag him out and stuff him in your car before you could change your mind."

"It's the law. Anyway, I thought for sure they'd turn us down for being apartment dwellers, but it turns out mastiffs aren't all that athletic or physical. They don't like to do more than take a short walk, maybe chase a ball in the park, but that's about it. So, we were approved."

"Who ended up hiring the dog walker? You or him?" Char asked.

"I did." Riley sighed. "I know. Can you

believe that? But Jeremy was too busy and he trusted my judgment."

"He did a hell of a lot more than that," Franco muttered.

"To be honest, I never thought of him in context with her. For all I knew, their paths would never cross. I was more worried that she couldn't handle Brutus."

"You liked her?" Charlotte asked, her mouth all pinched up as if she'd just tasted something really, really sour.

"Sure. If you can really like super perky, five-foot-nothing, ridiculously fit, zero-body-fat women with thick, television-commercial-worthy straight glossy hair, perfect teeth, and a Lithuanian accent I found challenging to understand. As I found out much later, Jeremy apparently found it mysterious and sexy." Riley looked at Char. "So, tell me, how bad is my karma going to be if, even before everything happened I admit I pictured her aging like Mrs. Pachulis in 2A? I'd seen photos of Magda when she was younger and she was quite the looker. At seventy-five, not so much. She had this big, pointy mole, right here." Riley pointed to the side of her chin. "Is it small of me to picture Camalia with a big hairy mole? At age twenty-three?"

"Not small," Charlotte assured Riley.

"God, she's only twenty-three?"

"Bastarde," Franco hissed again.

"Now. She was only twenty-one then. Maybe that's it," Riley said. "I made it happen because of my less than charitable thoughts. It was karma coming to get me."

"You don't honestly believe that," Franco said.

"No," she admitted, "but it did cross my mind that day. It was New Year's Eve —"

"New Year's Eve? Seriously?" Charlotte asked.

"As a heart attack," Riley responded. "Which was what I almost had. I ended up coming back early from the mani-pedi-massage Jeremy had booked for me as my Christmas present. I skipped the massage because they were running behind, and we had a huge industry shindig to attend that night, lots of power players. We were really amped for it, so the last thing I needed was to be a limp, relaxed noodle. I rebooked that part, thinking it was something to look forward to after all the holiday stuff."

"You're not saying he got you a spa day, specifically for you to use on New Year's Eve in preparation for this big party, so he could . . ."

Riley nodded. "Oh, that's exactly what I'm saying."

"And then you skipped the massage." Franco sighed and stroked her arm. They could see the train wreck that was about to happen. "You had no warning."

She shook her head. "Nope. I even stopped on my way back to pick up something to wear under my dress to surprise him. Only, I was the one who got the surprise."

"I'm so, so sorry," Charlotte said.

"Me, too," Riley said. "They were both naked. Right on my dining room table. With Brutus watching. I was jealous of her effortless perfection. We'd even made jokes about it, like couples do about people. She was so young, more than ten years younger than he was. He talked about her like she was a kid."

"Because she was a kid."

"I know. And he was madly in love with me, right?"

"Maybe it was just crazy temptation. Like you said, boys are dumb," Charlotte offered.

"I don't know if I could have forgiven that either. It would have been easier, I guess. But that wasn't it. They didn't even know I was there, because they were so . . . enthusiastic."

"Oh, dear," Charlotte said.

"I threw my Victoria's Secret bag at her.

Clipped her on the cheek. She may never have a hairy mole, but she'll probably have a little scar to remember me by."

"That's the least of what I'd have thrown at her," Franco said.

"They were startled, of course." Riley blew out a heavy sigh, prepping herself to go through it one more time. "Jeremy was contrite — not so much because of the cheating, but because I'd caught them at it. He had the nerve to be worried about covering her up, about her modesty. On my dining room table — *my* table — and he was more worried about me seeing her naked than —" She broke off, composed herself. "Once they were adequately covered, Jeremy proceeded to apologize that I'd found out that way. I asked how long it had been going on. He didn't answer, but he put his arm around her — not me. He never even touched me, or tried to —" She stopped. Reliving that exact moment didn't make her mad, it just broke her heart all over again. In that one moment, her entire life, everything she thought she had, thought she was, believed, and trusted in . . . fell apart. "He told me he loved her. And that he'd been trying to find a way to tell me, for a whole year. A whole year, and he couldn't find the right time to say, 'By the way, I'm boinking

Camalia all over our apartment. Happy New Year.' " She stifled the sob clutching at her throat, pissed with herself for letting it get to her again. "They wanted to keep Brutus."

"Oh, honey." Franco stood and pulled her into a bear hug. "Now I am going to shoot him dead."

"I told Jeremy if he so much as laid a finger on Brutus, I'd cut parts of his body off and feed them to Mr. Bumpers," she said, muffled against Franco's chef coat. "While he watched."

Charlotte rubbed her hand on Riley's back. "I'd have held him down for you."

Riley gave a watery laugh and shifted from Franco's hug back to her stool. "My mad didn't last long, at least not right then. It took a while to get back to that. I was just . . . so devastated. Before that, I didn't know what it felt like to be heartbroken. It's this huge, clutching chasm in your chest. All the time. I wanted to get past it, to move on. To get mad again." She half sniffled, half snorted. "And I did. At least the mad part. I used up all my sick leave and my vacation time because I couldn't face the chance of seeing him at work."

"Oh God. You still had to work together."

"I didn't know what I was going to do.

But I had to go back or risk being fired and I loved my job."

"But you ended up leaving Chicago," Charlotte said.

Riley nodded. "I lasted five months, three days, and one hour. And I'm proud of that. But even I can only take so much. No career, no matter how hard you've worked to achieve it, or how much you love it, is worth everything. No matter how much you deserve to think you shouldn't have to lose that, too, there's only so much you can do. Sometimes, you just don't get to win."

She slumped on her stool. "The first day I went back to work, I was freaked out about getting through the day without falling apart, not knowing what I was going to do when I saw him — it had only been two weeks — and I was still raw. Just . . . raw. Like a giant exposed nerve. I was a walking disaster. I had no business trying to do anything for a client, but I knew I couldn't sit at home and think about chopping my dining room table into kindling and setting it on fire, in Jeremy and Camalia's front yard. That probably wasn't healthy."

Drawing herself up, Riley took a steadying breath. "What I hadn't counted on was arriving at work to find out Jeremy had never missed a day. In my absence, he had actually gotten Camalia hired."

Franco and Charlotte gasped.

"Apparently Miss Perky Perfection had graduated with her degree in journalism right before Christmas. She was going to work with us, right in our department. Not a single person had thought to call and warn me — not that I had been taking calls. When I walked in, there they were, all gathered around the meeting table, drinking coffee and laughing. Laughing," Riley said, as if the concept was so foreign to her, she simply couldn't fathom anyone wanting to do it ever again. Of course, that was exactly how she'd felt at the time. "I was this pathetic, shattered shell . . . and there they were, all happy and . . . laughing. With my friends. Our friends. Well, our co-workers anyway. How could they? You know?" She laughed, but it was hollow. "The laughter died as one person spied me in the doorway and slowly everybody turned and stared at me. I don't know which was worse, the look of regret on my co-workers' faces, or the pity on Jeremy and Camalia's. Humiliating doesn't begin to cover it."

"And he's still anatomically intact?" This came from Franco. "Because I might have had to . . . do some rearranging."

"I don't really remember the next few

252

minutes, but everyone started to walk toward me, like they were going to what? Hug me? Say they were sorry? One guy — Ted, from graphics — lamely apologized and said he thought I knew. I think I laughed, before I turned around and fled. Just . . . ran out."

"But you went back," Char said. "My God, how?"

"You know, I don't really know. I was like a zombie, but I felt I had no choice, and that by plowing through, I was being the bigger person, the better person. But I sure didn't feel bigger or better. In fact, it was probably the unhealthiest thing I ever made myself do. It was like working in a toxic cesspool every day. I didn't trust anyone there, no one —"

"Of course you didn't, they all betrayed you."

"Why did you finally leave? What happened?"

"Oh. I found the announcement. By accident, someone left it on the conference room table. Or maybe it wasn't by accident. I don't know, don't care."

"Announcement of what?" Char asked.

"Jeremy and Camalia's wedding."

"Five months later?"

"Well, you have to remember, for them, it

had been more like a year and a half."

"Still. You'd been engaged longer than that."

"I guess the future wasn't as far off and hazy for them. Whatever. If I thought the looks of pity I'd been getting up to that point had been gross, I could only imagine where it was going to go from there. Not to mention the endless talk of wedding dresses, wedding cake, photographers, and food —" Riley made a sound of disgust. "That was it. I surrendered. I saw the future and wanted no part of it. I walked straight to my office, dropped the announcement in the shredder, packed up my tools and whatever I could haul out on my person, and left. Didn't say good-bye to a single person."

"Can't blame you," Franco said. "Then what did you do? How did you quit?"

"I sent in my resignation by e-mail. And told them to go to hell when they didn't even try to get me to stay but offered to give me good references. I was damn good at my job, the best stylist they had. I didn't need their damn references. They should have at least pretended they wanted me to stay, though I wouldn't have. They just . . . chose Jeremy, I guess." She shook her head. "No one picked me. I know that sounds so . . . pathetic."

Riley lifted her shoulders, then let them slump. "I lasted one whole day at the apartment, but I'd wallowed enough by then and even I wasn't that pathetic. I packed some things, got Brutus into my car, and we drove east. I had two friends, Chuck and Greg, who I'd worked with on several shoots earlier in my career. They'd become mentors and friends to me. They'd looked out for me, professionally, and I knew they'd probably help me figure out the next step. At that time they were living in the Hamptons, so I called them and they invited me out, told me I could stay as long as I wanted. They had a houseboat they were always planning to wander the ocean blue on, though they never did. I don't remember who first had the idea I should live on it, but I do know there was a lot of wine involved. Anyway, Chuck has an uncle who lives on Jekyll, so that's where they had the houseboat docked. I couldn't afford to keep it there, so I had it moved up here, thinking I'd stay until I figured out what I was going to do next." She smiled then, pushing the ugliness away. "And here I still am."

"We choose you," Franco said. "I'm glad you're here."

"I am, too," Charlotte agreed.

Riley took a deep, deep, breath, and let it out slowly. It felt good. Cleansing. "Okay, so that's it, right? I don't ever have to talk about this again?"

"Non, mon amie, of course not," Franco said. "Unless you need to bash him. Then we'll all jump in and help. With great enthusiasm."

She grinned. "Thank you. And thanks for dragging it out of me. For obvious reasons, it's not something I like to talk about or even think about, but it's good to have it all out there. I'm happy here. Truly happy. I choose you all, too."

"Do you miss Chicago?" Charlotte asked.

"At times. Not so much the city. I've truly embraced island life. I love it here. I'm at peace here, and, more important, I feel like I fit in. I don't think I realized how much I didn't fit in, in the city. It was the job that took me there, and my life with Jeremy kept me there. Magazine life is pretty bohemian in a lot of ways and I loved so much of it, but I didn't really fit in with the movers and shakers, suit and tie stuff. Here . . . I'm accepted for who I am. Maybe because I can finally just be myself, I've figured out how to have — and to be — the one thing I've never really had in my life." Riley smiled at them. "Friends. True friends."

Charlotte nodded. "You do. I'm glad you know that. We've always been in your corner."

"I know, and I should have confided sooner, it's —"

"No, that's no one's business but your own," Charlotte said. "But I'm glad you felt like you could finally trust us enough to share. It makes sharing back that much easier."

"Not that it's a real struggle for us," Franco said dryly, earning a nudge from Charlotte.

"We've had each other for a very long time, so we're used to it," Charlotte said. "Do you miss your work, styling food?"

Riley nodded. "I do. A lot, actually. That was the one thing that did fit me. I think that's why I love getting together with you all so much. Jeremy and I were big foodies, too, so I guess I miss that part a little bit, the restaurants, trying new chefs, new dishes. Working at *Foodie,* there were always events and things. I miss that part. Not so much the social game, or the power plays, but the food. It's always been about the food for me."

"You'll have to come into Savannah for more than just shopping," Charlotte said. "Carlo is an amazing chef, and between us we've already met many of the local chefs and industry people. I think you'd really be surprised by the level of sophistication in their food. We go out all the time, doing exactly what you said, tasting, trying new things, getting inspired. We'd love to have you join us."

"Thank you," Riley said, loving the idea, but not so sure she wanted to be the third wheel to the giddy couple.

"I'll invite myself along," Franco said, so good at picking up on her every mood. "We'll double-date."

"Deal." Rather than feeling as if she'd given a chunk of herself away, Riley felt she'd received a very big gift. She knew her new friendships had been cemented with the exchange of trust.

She supposed the next thing would be figuring out where she wanted to go with her other relationships. Of course, Quinn's sexy grin popped to mind, but this time she didn't automatically try to block it.

Was it time to hang out her dating shingle again? She smiled, and tucked the thought away to ponder later. She'd done enough emotional dredging for one day.

"Let's make some cupcakes," she announced. "I could use something decadent and sinful." As they fell into the rhythms and patterns they'd established over the months of baking and working together, she realized she was happy. More important, for the first time in a very, very long time, she felt . . . hopeful.

She had no idea what the next step on her path would be, but she figured hope was a pretty vital ingredient to have. And, for now, that was enough.

CHAPTER 11

Hannah looked up, grooming brush in hand, as she heard the footsteps entering the stable. She stroked the mare's neck and mane, more to gather herself than to settle the startled horse. She should be more surprised to see him again. Maybe, in some part of her, she'd always known she would. She took a step away, and faced her intruder. "What are you doing here?"

If the lack of a warm welcome bothered him, he didn't let it show. Not surprising. "To be honest, I don't know."

"Then, perhaps you should head on out. Come back when you do know."

He cocked an eyebrow at that. "Is that an invitation?"

She allowed herself a moment to drink in the sight of him. It had been, what . . . five years? Six, now? It might as well have been twenty, for all that had happened in their lives since.

It might as well have been yesterday, given the way her heart was pounding. "I don't know what it is," she said, deciding honesty was the only way to handle this. Handle him. "What made you drive all the way out here? Did something happen on an old case?" She didn't bother asking how he'd known where to look for her. He'd once been the best detective the Denver police department had ever had. Colorado was a big place, easy to get lost in, which was precisely what she'd done after leaving the medical examiner's office over half a decade ago. But if Joe St. Cloud wanted to find someone, he usually did.

"I'm not with the department any longer."

"I know," was all she said, and found herself enjoying the way his eyebrow lifted again. She'd surprised him with that. Good.

He walked closer then, and she had to work at not taking a physical step back. It would have been better — smarter — if she could have taken an emotional step back. Just as she'd done the entire time they'd worked together.

"Some things you can walk away from and never look back." He stopped right in front of her. His piercing blue gaze, the one she'd seen pin down the most heartless killer and make him beg for mercy, pinned her now. "Other things . . . not so much."

Quinn abruptly closed his laptop. *Dammit.* He'd promised himself he'd stop doing that. Stop giving Joe and Hannah a voice, until he figured things out. But he'd been doing exactly that. He shoved away from his desk. A good hard run, that's what he needed.

Because today was going to be D-Day. Decision Day. He couldn't put it off any longer.

Already in running shorts and a T-shirt, he put thought to action and headed straight out the back, through the dune trail. Kicking off his flip-flops, he tucked them between the blades of a palmetto bush so they wouldn't blow away. He wasn't coming off the beach until he'd committed himself to figuring out the lives, and eventual epic love story, of (maybe retired) homicide detective Joe St. Cloud, and (maybe former) forensic analyst and (now full-time?) horse rancher, Hannah Lake.

Quinn had been on Sugarberry for thirty-six days. October loomed less than a week away. He'd taken reams of notes and plot-

ted out both versions of the story, wanting
— needing — one of them to grab him and
not let go. Problem was . . . they were both
good. Any other time, he'd have had his
hooks deep into the homicide detective and
forensic analyst partnership, pushing, dragging, propelling them through the paces of
another gritty, grisly string of murders . . .
and letting them burn off the tension and
screaming stress with steamy hot, bodies-
up-against-the-wall and down-on-the-floor,
mind-blowing sex. He knew exactly how
he'd tell their story, how they'd work together, play together. He liked these two. A
lot. And they were going to like each other
a whole lot more.

It was why the other story idea kind of
pissed him off. He should already be knee-
deep in brain matter and severed body
parts, relishing the difficult path he was going to force those two down, if they had any
hope of solving the murders. He'd even
started the opening chapters, more than
once.

But snatches of other dialogue, the kind
that happens long before a partnership is
solidified, kept whispering in his head. Images, ideas teased and tantalized. His capti-
vation with the two people he'd created
grew by leaps and bounds . . . but in the

reverse direction. His characters usually had a backstory, how they'd come to be who and what they were as the story opens. His problem was, the backstory was as tantalizing as the current one he'd had in mind for them. So much so, his mind kept going there . . . and sticking around for awhile.

The more he thought about what they could give each other, the more tantalizing that story became. To him. Question was . . . would anyone else care? He simply had no answer for that.

Quinn started off down the beach right along the water's edge, enjoying the feel of the cool, wet sand under his feet. The nights were cooler, but the days were still climbing to a pretty blistering average temperature. He enjoyed the chilled feeling he got while running on the cold wet sand, knowing it would be too hot to walk on barefooted, much less run on, by mid-afternoon.

The high tide was ebbing as the sun rose slowly above the horizon. New day. *The* day. There wasn't anything else his two characters could teach him, say to him, or persuade him to do. He had to pick. Would the murders be the story, and their past history already defined? Or would the murders be their past history, and their coming together define what happened next?

He'd settled into a particularly punishing pace, when out of nowhere, something clipped him hard on his right hip, sending him careening left, across the remaining narrow strip of sand, and into the water. He managed to catch himself before he went face-first into the surf, but not before getting soaked by an incoming, late-breaking wave. It was only as he shook the water from his hair and wiped his face that he spied Riley, about ten yards down the beach, running toward him.

Them, actually. Just above the safety of the waterline, Brutus had planted his massive, muscular butt in the sand, and was presently drooling all over an impressively large hunk of driftwood clenched in his mighty jaw.

"I'm sorry. I'm so sorry!" Riley called, out of breath from the run. She stopped at the water's edge in front of him, and tried to say something else, but ended up putting her hands on her thighs as she bent over to catch her breath.

"I'm starting to sense there's a pattern where water and Brutus are involved," Quinn said as he strolled from the waves swirling around his calves and walked toward them. As soon as his bare feet hit dry sand, Brutus dropped the driftwood right on top of them, then looked up expectantly, tongue lolling.

Wincing, Quinn bent down and hefted the log off his toes, then turned to loft it into the surf, only to have Riley spring into action, and grab his arm at the last second. "No, wait! Don't throw it in the water." Her voice was almost back to full strength.

Quinn turned to face her. The moment he'd realized who was running down the beach, his heart had literally leaped in his chest. Leaped. He felt foolish. And giddy.

Her cheeks were flushed, her eyes sparkling, and her blond curls danced about her head in a happy halo. Her lips were moving as she said something, but he was too busy corralling every ounce of his control to keep from hauling her into his arms, right up against his drenched frame, and kissing her until she lost her breath all over again.

"He's afraid of the water," she was saying when he finally conquered the beast of temptation.

"What? Wasn't he the one who went for a swim last time?"

"That was different. He didn't exactly go in willingly."

"But he stayed in there and paddled around like a champ."

"That was the channel. No waves."

"Oh." Quinn said, as if that made perfect sense.

Tired of waiting, Brutus leaned in and head-butted Quinn on the thigh, then looked up at him again, eyes shining in anticipation.

Quinn staggered a step, leveling a look at Brutus. "Patience, buddy."

Riley chuckled. "If this were a cartoon, there would be little hearts and birds floating over his head right now."

"I'd hate to see what he does to his enemies." Quinn flexed the sting out of his toes. He took a few steps farther up the beach, then turned to look down the shoreline. Brutus scooted around on his butt and followed Quinn's every move. "Don't get up on my account," Quinn told him, then cocked his arm back and did his best to launch the log as far down the beach as he could, which was maybe twenty or twenty-five yards away. It was a big log.

As he'd done in Quinn's backyard, Brutus watched the sailing hunk of tree without moving so much as a muscle, but Quinn noted he was tense and on full alert. As soon as the log hit the sand, Quinn expected him to explode like a coiled spring of action. Not so much. Brutus eased up off his haunches and sauntered down the beach at a slow trot toward his quarry.

Smiling, Quinn shook his head, then turned as Riley came to stand next to him.

"He follows his own drummer," was all she said.

"I can respect that."

She looked him up and down, which did absolutely nothing to support his struggle to keep his hands to himself. "I'm really sorry. You're all wet. Again. I swear, I didn't see you, then suddenly Brutus took off. He never runs, so I had no idea . . . but I should have known, I guess. The last time he took off, it was to run to you." She looked up at him and smiled. "Just another Quinn Brannigan fan, I guess. A really big fan," she added, as Brutus trotted back toward them, tree chunk clenched in his jaw.

"As long as he doesn't start his own fan club, with more just like him, I think I can handle it."

Riley laughed. "When I came around the bend and saw you running, I called out and tried to warn you, but with the wind and the waves, I was too far away. I tried to catch up, but you were running like . . . well, like the hounds of hell were on your heels."

"If I'd only known," he said, and they laughed.

"I'm really sorry."

"Don't be. I'm sorry I made you run."

"That's okay, clearly I could stand to do more of it." She grinned, and her already wind-pink cheeks pinkened a bit deeper.

It wasn't the sort of thing he'd have thought would be a turn-on, but with her, the blush did amazing things to his circulation, too . . . just a bit farther south.

Brutus dropped the log on Quinn's feet, again. Quinn tried not to flinch as he bent down and scooped up the log again. "You're a menace," he told the dog. "Here you go."

"He'll want you to do that all day if you let him," Riley warned.

Quinn launched the log anyway. "How exactly do you not let him do whatever it is he wants?"

"Just rub his head, scratch his ears, and tell him you're all done. He'll understand. He's just a pussycat, really."

"Right. I can see that about him." Quinn started to walk toward the dog as Brutus got closer to the driftwood, and Riley fell into place beside him.

"I'm sorry we interrupted your run. You looked very . . . dedicated. Let me get Brutus and we'll leave you to get back to it."

He wasn't going to tell her that running in clothes soaked in salt water and sand was probably not the best idea if he wanted to keep his skin intact. "That's okay, I don't mind. I was just . . . running from frustration, really."

"Was it helping?"

He chuckled. "No, but at least it felt more productive then sitting and staring at my computer screen."

"Oh. Are you having problems with the book?" She waved her hand in front of them. "That's none of my business. Sorry."

"Don't be. Dead cat." He winked at her when her gaze flew to his, and they chuckled. "To answer your question, no, I'm not having problems coming up with the story, I'm having too much success coming up with a story. That's the problem."

"Too much story is a problem?"

They caught up with Brutus, but rather than plop the log in the sand again, he kept it and fell into step in front of them, leading their procession down the beach. Quinn kept walking . . . and so did Riley. He decided, sandy wet clothes or not, it was a much better way to spend the morning.

"Too *many* stories is the problem."

"Huh. I guess I never thought of that. I always pictured writers bent over their keyboards, struggling to come up with the perfect line, the perfect way to set the next scene. I guess it never occurred to me you might have too many ideas and have to figure out which one fits the story best."

"Well, you're right. That's generally not the problem. You have it more accurately with your first assessment." He slowed his steps and shifted his gaze to her. "In this case, I actually have two story ideas for the same characters and I'm struggling to figure out which one to tell. Both are good, both compelling, and I don't know which one better serves them. And me."

"Can't you give one story to a new set of characters? And write both?"

"I don't work that way, but I did consider it. In this case, however, they simply are these people with these stories. No one else's. There are two different universes I can have them inhabit, either one of which they'd rock, but they can't inhabit both, and the universes can't collide, not as I have them, in my head. They compel me in a way no two characters ever have before, at least not before I've even begun. They're important to me now that I've spent so much time with them in my head."

He chuckled. "It sounds a little crazy, or a lot crazy. Normally I have a general feel, then dive in and get to know my protagonists as I go. But I know these two better already than I do most characters at the end of five hundred pages. They are fully fleshed out, developed people who feel as real to me as any characters I've ever devised. I can't let them down by giving them any less than a rocking, compelling, engaging, and fulfilling story that lives up to the epic potential they have."

"Wow."

"Exactly." He laughed. "No pressure."

"No one else can solve the crimes in these stories but them? And the stories can have nothing in common?"

"In my head?" He grinned. "No. I have to pick one. I feel like it's Sophie's Choice or something. Once I commit, that is their story. There's no giant erase, and start over. It's who they become. To me."

"Why can't you make it a series or something?"

"I thought about that, but that won't work, either. The stories put them together at two different times in their lives. They can have one life, or the other, but they can't have experienced both, not together." He slowed his steps, paused a moment, then stopped walking altogether. "Can I ask you something? Hypothetically?"

She turned to look up at him, then shifted so his body blocked the sun from her face. "Sure."

"And can I trust your discretion?"

She frowned slightly. "Of course. Why?"

"First, let me ask you this. And be honest. Brutally, if needed. What is it that draws you to my books? I mean, when you sit down to read, what's the thing you hope to find, the element that makes you anticipate the story most?"

"That's easy, though you might not be happy about it. It's the relationship between the two leads. Always."

He folded his arms. "Really?"

She smiled and lifted one shoulder in a half shrug, as if to apologize. "Really. I know you're a crime novelist and you do an amazing job with all the gritty, gory stuff, and I'm sure most people read your books to get their murder mystery suspense fix. But, since you're asking me, I can only tell you that I put up with the gory, grisly stuff so I can get my relationship fix from the leads. You always have such powerful couples and they're so unapologetic in their commitment to one another. I love that." Her smile turned dry. "Gee, aren't you glad I'm the one you asked?"

"Actually, I am." He started walking again, his mind spinning in a new direction. "You said unapologetic. What is it that couples who love each other should apologize for?"

"Absolutely nothing," Riley said. "That's what makes your books so great. You totally get that. Despite all the tragedy they live with every day, they're allowed to be happy. Most books — mystery books, anyway — have the lead detective, be it man or woman, leading some miserable or deeply conflicted life and they're never allowed to get the girl — or guy — and live happily. Or if they are, it's short-lived and their new love must die or dump them, so they can go back to being an even more tragic figure. I enjoy a well-told mystery, and I like trying to figure out who did it, but isn't it bad enough that some poor soul, or souls, died and some horrible monster is on the loose, without making the lead guy who catches him miserable, too? I mean, after a while, it's just depressing. And hopeless. Like, we caught the bad guy, so everyone can sleep a bit more easily, except of course the guy who did the catching, who is still deeply conflicted and wretched." She shrugged again. "I guess I don't get why it all has to be so dysfunctional and tragic, in the guise of making it more like 'real life.' " She punctuated the last two words with air quotes. "Real life has joy and love and happiness, too. And fun, and humor, and . . . well, you get my meaning. I love that you show the gritty, all-too-real side of what can happen in this world, what human beings are capable of perpetrating . . . but you show both ends of that spectrum. Maybe it's the balance, or the contrast, that makes the horrible things that much more horrible. When characters love like your people do, you — meaning me, the reader — are that much more petrified something bad will happen to them, too. That would be just too tragic. So it makes my heart pound harder when you put them in jeopardy than when some sadsack detective puts his neck on the line." She stopped walking. "I'm sorry. I'm probably sounding like a crazy stalker fan, and you just have your couples in love so they can have hot sex." She grinned. "I like that part a lot, too."

Quinn grinned back. "I'm glad. So do I. To answer your other question, no, that's not the reason why I develop my crime-fighting couples the way I do. I do it . . . well, for exactly the same reason you enjoy it. I'm glad to know readers are getting that. Well, one reader anyway."

"Oh, I'm sure it's a whole lot more than one reader. I think that's why your stories have such universal appeal. I don't know what the breakdown of your readership is by gender, but I bet you have pretty deep hooks into both groups."

They walked down the beach in companionable silence, Brutus still leading the parade, as Quinn's thoughts eddied and swirled.

"So . . . what was the hypothetical question?" she asked.

He glanced up. "Oh, right. Actually, I think you already answered it."

"Oh." She looked a bit deflated. "Okay."

"All right," he said, grinning, "here it is, but again —"

She made a lip-locking motion with her fingers, then threw the imaginary key away. On impulse, Quinn darted out a hand and made an air grab, as if catching the imaginary key. He curled his fingers into a fist, and smiled at her.

She smiled, too, and her cheeks warmed again. He got all caught up in watching her pupils expand and her gaze drop to his mouth, before she looked away, back to the shoreline in front of them.

And the question just popped out easily, without hesitation. "Would you be interested in reading a book from me that might leave out the grisly, gory, psycho killer part?"

She stopped walking again, and turned to look up at him. "Yes." She said it instantly and decisively.

And it was exactly what he'd wanted her to say. "Okay," he said. *Okay,* he thought. They started walking again. He expected her to pepper him with questions, but she didn't, respecting his silence and need to think as they continued on down the beach.

Brutus suddenly made a turn up the sand to where a cluster of trees provided a swath of shade, and plopped himself down under them.

"I think he needs a break," Riley said. "This is a lot of exercise for him. I know he looks big and strong, but a lot of extended motion is hard on his hips and back."

Quinn nodded and followed Brutus's path up the sand. "I think there's room here for all of us."

"You don't have to wait, you can —"

Quinn sat just in front of the shady part, so the sun beat down on the damp front of his clothes. He smiled up at Riley, then patted the sand next to him.

"Okay." She sat down next to him. Past the edge of her loose-fitting, knee-length, light tan khaki shorts extended the whitest legs he'd ever seen.

"Do you want to sit in the shade?" he asked.

"What?" She noticed where his gaze had

gone. "Oh, no. I have like 4000 level sunscreen on. The only way I'd tan is if all my freckles converged, and since that would just be oh-so-lovely, I opt for the Casper approach."

He looked at her. "I think you have beautiful skin. So you're probably the smart one."

He knew the skin in question would turn bright pink at the compliment, and she didn't disappoint him. Feeling utterly content and happy, he smiled and turned his gaze to the water, but not before noticing the bright pink toenail polish she sported . . . and the delicate silver band circling her pinky toe.

Just like that, his body leaped to life all over again — with a vengeance — causing him to cross his ankles and shift his weight in the sand. Sitting more upright, he plucked his damp shirt away from his skin so it hung looser.

Riley wore a melon-pink tank top covered with an unbuttoned, short-sleeved pink, orange, and white plaid camp shirt. Her loose-fitting shorts rode low on her hips, drawing his eye when she'd walked toward him earlier. The whole outfit was perky and cheerful and suited her blond curls and ready smile. Styled more for comfort than to show off her figure, it certainly wouldn't be deemed overtly sexy. Nor were her freckles and pale skin. Not overtly.

Yet, something about the feminine tipped toes, and the earthiness of that tiny band of silver, combined with the comfortable way she dressed and the even more comfortable way she inhabited her lush, curvy body . . . pretty much drove him mad with the need to pull her under him . . . and find out what was beneath all that cotton and color.

He dug his fingers into the sand and wondered again about Alva's remark regarding Riley's availability. He'd thought about that more than once the past week or so. Many more times than once. And had come to the conclusion that it ultimately didn't matter. If she was unattached and he'd just assumed otherwise, she'd let him run with that assumption. Meaning she was okay with his believing it. Obviously, she did not want to let him to get any closer.

He'd decided to respect that, and her, and just get the hell over it.

But that was decidedly more challenging to do at the moment.

Quinn decided to simply keep his focus on the sound of the water, the feel of the sun soaking through his damp clothes, warming his skin . . . and not on his simmering awareness of the woman sitting beside him.

Right.

"So," she said at length, "and you don't have to answer, but following your hypothetical question . . . is that the problem you're having? You have a murder mystery story for your couple to solve . . . but you also want to just spend time telling your couple's story? No murders. Is that it?"

He shot her a quick glance, intending to look straight back to the water, but he instantly got caught up in the sincere, direct gaze she'd aimed his way, and he replied without thinking. "I think their love story would be less than it could be if it came before they grew into the characters they are now. It's not the right time for them to have the love story I know they'd have later. But later . . . there are no murders to solve because he can't deal with any more death. They will have solved all the ones they're capable of."

"I get it now. So it really is either or. They either love each other while fighting crime . . . or find each other after they've fought all the crime they can handle and fall in love then." She sighed. "I can see the dilemma. Either way, they are who they are right now. So now is when it has to happen."

"Exactly." He felt as if an enormous pressure had been removed from his psyche. It wasn't a solution, but it was a huge help to know someone at least understood the dilemma. "Thank you."

"Why? I didn't do anything."

"You got it, and that's more than I'd hoped. I had begun to think I'd gotten so far into the forest I'd totally lost all perspective on the trees."

She shook her head. "I don't think so. You just want to do them justice. And you don't know which way will do that best." Riley shifted in the sand and rolled to one hip so she could face him more directly. "I will say this. I really do love your suspense, purely for the complex plots you come up with. I can rarely ever figure out all the twists and turns. But . . . and I mean this as a compliment, there are times in every single book that I wish I could spend more time with your characters, away from the crime stuff. Of course, that's not what the story is about, so there is no time for that. I understand that it wouldn't make sense . . . but I feel a little left out, every time. Not let down, really, because your books are always wildly satisfying, but . . . maybe you know what I mean."

"To be honest, I always thought the balance was right where I wanted it. I liked contrasting big love against big tragedy, but I was always comfortable with the balance."

"So, why are these two different?"

He lifted one shoulder. "I don't know. I really don't. They just are. I see them, I listen to them, and there's just so much more to tell. I've tried to relegate whatever brought them together to something that's already occurred when we meet them, and I know they'd do a hell of a riveting job as my crime-fighting duo for the murder mystery I want to tell . . . but I just — I couldn't make the balance work for me. I feel like it wasn't right, or fair to them. I wasn't giving them all I could allow them to have, when I know they are capable of having so damn much more."

"So, doesn't that answer your question?"

"What do you mean?"

"If telling their story that way feels like you're letting them down . . . then you probably are."

"Okay, but following that . . . if their careers are done, over, for whatever reason, and it's from those ashes that they come together . . . if I'm not giving them anything else to do, and there aren't all those other extra crazy twists and turns . . . does it become dull and not so passionate and epic after all? Do I need that contrast of murder and mayhem in order to make their love story compelling? This would be a huge departure for me, so I have no sense of how it would fly. If I'm going to make that huge leap, risk pissing a lot of people off, then I feel like I have to be damn sure I know what I'm doing, that I can pull it off, make it work."

"Well, I'm the wrong person to ask, because that story seems just as compelling to me as the thriller. Mayhem that scares the crap out of you doesn't have to include murder. There are many terrifying things out there. I think falling in love is dangerous territory for two people who are a little flawed, and a whole lot damaged, to find themselves suddenly traversing. Especially just when they thought it was safe. You know? They walk away from the murder and mayhem, the bullets flying, because they can't risk it anymore . . . only to find they haven't ever risked the thing that puts them in the most personal danger they've ever been in. Murder happens to other people, and they pick up the pieces. But what if the pieces might be theirs? And the bullet they end up dodging is coming from a shooter they never saw coming? Because there are no more shooters, right? Except . . . uh-oh."

She smiled. "We know the shooter is out there, just like in the murder mystery. *We* — meaning the readers — we see the bullet coming, we see the big looming threat that is going to be them being tempted by each other, them falling in love, but they don't. They're going to be completely blindsided by that shooter. I don't know how much more on the edge of your seat you can get than that. If, at the eleventh hour, they screw it up, and they don't figure out how to conquer the shooter — who is love — they're the ones who lose it all. Can't risk much more than that."

"Well," he said thoughtfully, "when you put it like that." He grinned, but there was already a swirl of thoughts literally bombarding his brain. He finally — finally — felt that inexplicable knot in his gut, that snap, crack, and sizzle that made his fingers twitch to type, that sent his brain to racing . . . that *thing* that told him he'd found it.

He'd contrast the cases they'd solved in their respective pasts, the very ones he'd have had them solve if he'd gone the other way, against the danger they now found themselves in when pitted against each other, fighting against an entirely different kind of mayhem, just as Riley said. The mayhem that comes internally when two people are fighting against falling in love. He could even plot it like a murder mystery as they discovered the clues and, ultimately, solved the case. The case being coming to that place where they could commit to loving one another. Maybe they'd crossed paths professionally — no maybe about it, they had — so there would be some joint knowledge of their respective pasts. They applied what they knew, what they had discovered, in completely different ways. They'd struck sparks before, good and bad, but it's only with all the rest done that the real conflagration would begin.

"So, do you get what I mean?" She looked at him uncertainly.

"Not only do I get what you mean," he said, the excitement juicing him up higher, faster, "I can write what you mean. And, going one better, I can sell what you mean." He grabbed her face and planted a big noisy kiss on those big, juicy lips, then hooted so loudly he startled Brutus into looking up to see what all the excitement was about. "Oh my God, Riley. You did it. You nailed it." His hands still framed her face. "*Nailed* it!"

He scrambled to his feet, pulling her up

along with him, straight into his arms. He spun them around, laughing, sounding like a wildman. The relief was so profound, he hooted and spun her around again. "You saw the trees. You saw the whole damn forest."

Her eyes were wide, like huge pools of melted chocolate, as he set her feet down on the sand, but he kept his hands on her arms. "I can't believe I didn't get it," he said, laughing again. "But you have it perfectly and exactly right. It fills the exact same bill, but with entirely different stakes, scarier stakes. Why didn't I see that? It's both, and it's more. So much more. You're a genius."

"Oh, it was nothing," she said, but she was as breathless as he was, and she looked just as dazzled and excited as he felt.

She grinned, and her eyes lit with that always present light that seemed to be constantly inside her. Her lips parted on a breathless laugh, drawing his gaze . . . and his attention.

The sizzle in the air changed abruptly from exuberant celebration and relief, to something decidedly more . . . elemental.

His hold on her arms gentled as he realized his excitement had him gripping her rather intently. He rubbed his fingers absently over the place where he'd held most firmly, but his attention was drawn from parted lips to darkening eyes, then back to her mouth again. "I've thought a lot about what you would taste like," he said, giving up entirely on censoring himself. He was giddy for all sorts of reasons, and it was just too damn good. Too damn good. Mayhem, indeed. "And I kissed you so fast, I didn't even get to savor it."

He saw her throat work. "Is there a rule about do-overs I don't know about?" She tried for casual humor, but the way she was looking at him was anything but casual.

That was also damn good . . . because he'd hate to be the only one feeling this way. "The only rule I have is that I don't kiss someone who is regularly kissing someone else." He smiled. "Spontaneous kisses of profound gratitude notwithstanding."

"I like that rule."

"Good," he said.

"Yes, it is," she agreed. "Very."

"You're not going to make this easy, are you?" But that was okay, because he was done worrying about easy. "Down at the docks that day, by your boat, you said you were involved with someone."

"No, I didn't."

"Okay, you're right." Fair was fair, after

all. "I said it. You didn't correct me."

"I . . . thought it would be easier that way."

"Easier for who?"

"Me. I didn't think you would really care one way or the other."

That pissed him off a little, because it wasn't true, and because he was pretty sure it was herself she was judging and finding lacking . . . not him. "But you did. Care, I mean."

"I like you. And I'm a sucker for caring about people I like. My defenses in that area stink, and, try as I might, there doesn't seem to be much I can do about it." Riley held Quinn's gaze for a long time, then said, "Can I ask you something? And I want an honest answer. Be brutal if necessary," she added, echoing his earlier request.

Normally he would have grinned, but the stakes felt suddenly high. Really high. And decidedly personal. He frowned. "Okay."

"You've been struggling to figure out your book. I'm guessing from your profound gratitude it's been more than frustrating. Maybe even a little frightening. And you've come here, to Sugarberry, because you wanted some time to focus on that. And . . . well, I'll be honest, I've followed you a little bit in the media, and I know half that stuff is made up, and the other half probably grossly exaggerated, but . . ." She trailed off, then said, "I guess I want to know if this interest you say you have in kissing me is based on a sincere interest in getting to know me."

She paused, and he realized this was harder for her than she had allowed him to realize. "Or because I'm here, and convenient? Because I'll be honest," she added, not letting him reply, "I don't strike me as the kind of woman you'd normally go for, and that's fine, no judgment, no harm, no foul. I get the attraction of hassle-free convenience. I'm probably the last person you'd see as a threat to complicate things. It's just I stink at that kind of thing. I wish I didn't, because it would most likely be a wonderful way to spend some time. I just . . ." She lifted her shoulders, then let them drop, along with her gaze. "It's not a good fit for me. It's not what I would want, or choose."

He started to say "me, either," with absolute sincerity, except, the truth was, she'd pretty much described exactly how his relationships had gone. He'd done that very thing in the past, enjoyed that exact kind of easy, breezy, no-demands relationship. Too many of them, in fact. He'd told himself if they were meant to be more, they would be.

But how often had he set them up, subconsciously, or chosen women, specifically, knowing the chance of getting tangled up was unlikely to happen? He'd never wanted to hurt anyone, least of all himself.

He was pretty sure the "me, either" response absolutely applied. It was just . . . why would she believe that? Why did he?

"No, I wouldn't think you would," he said, instead.

She looked up. "But you would," she said, not quite making it a question. "Choose that."

"It has been a choice I've made in the past, yes," he said, giving her — and himself — the brutal honesty she'd asked for.

She looked disappointed. But not nearly as much as he was in himself. She wasn't wrong to feel the way she did.

"But I am also being honest when I tell you that's not why I said what I did. To toy with you, or play you. I said it because it's true. You couldn't be more wrong about your ability to complicate things. You drive me crazy. You're forever in my thoughts. That wasn't something I expected, not because it was you, but because that traditionally would not have been me. It just seems to be me . . . where you're concerned.

And I honestly don't know what to do about that."

She frowned, then smiled that dry smile, making one dimple wink out . . . all but begging him to get the full grin out of her. "So, then, I think I'm flattered. Maybe. I guess."

He grinned at her unexpected response. "You should be. Maybe. I guess."

They laughed, and the tension eased just a little. It was still there, simmering below the surface. It probably always would be, as long as it wasn't tended to.

"Thank you," he said, at length.

"For the story idea? No problem. Sounds like you'd already done all the heavy lifting. You just needed someone on the outside looking in to see where to place it all so it looked real pretty" — she grinned — "which, of course, is my specialty."

"It certainly is." He softened when he looked at her, despite the still sizzling sexual tension. "Maybe I should be brainstorming with stylists and stagers instead of other writers and my editors.

"But that's not what I was thanking you for. I meant for your frankness and your honesty. It's not what I want to hear, but it's what need to hear. I never want to take advantage . . . but I might have with you. I don't seem to have much control over what I'm thinking or what I want, where you're concerned."

She smiled brightly then — too brightly — and let him the rest of the way off the hook. "Well, now neither one of us has to worry about that." She patted his arm, in a friendly, end-of-conversation way. "It's good that we talked, and aired it all out." She started to ease out of his hold, and he was pretty sure if he let her, she'd have taken off back down the beach. Never to be seen again.

He tightened his hold instinctively, keeping it gentle, but not ready — maybe never ready — to let her go. "So . . . that do-over . . . it's off the table, too. I guess." It was a ridiculous thing to say, he knew that, but it was all he had left.

She looked at him, and her smile faltered — badly — even if the spark in her eyes did not. "Quinn . . ."

"I know. I just . . ." He trailed off. "I know," he repeated. "We don't always get what we want." He held her gaze, hard as it was to see the desire there, and know he couldn't act on it. "It just . . . God, this sounds like a corny line from some fiction novel," he said with a short laugh, "but it just feels wrong. Walking away."

"What does it normally feel like when you walk away?"

It stung, her presumption that he was always the one to do the walking. It shouldn't have, because she was right. But it did, because she was right. "That's just it," he said, feeling more exposed than he'd ever allowed himself to be before. "It normally doesn't feel at all."

Her expression sobered as she looked as intently at him, into him, as he was looking at and into her. "You . . . really mean that."

The corner of his mouth lifted. "I wish that wasn't so hard to believe. I'm not a thoughtless jerk. I don't set out to hurt people. I'm always honest."

"I never thought you were a jerk, thoughtless or otherwise. You strike me as exactly the kind of man who says those kinds of things all the time, because you don't want to hurt anyone. I think it's second nature for you to soften the blow, to say things that make others feel good about themselves, to take the blame all on yourself for things ending when they end."

"Maybe." He never really thought about it that way. "But I didn't keep you from walking away just now because I didn't want to hurt your feelings." He slid his hands down her arms, and tucked his fingers through hers. "I kept you from walking away because I really don't want you to go. It's as simple and as complicated as that. I don't have anything else to offer. There are no promises I can make, so it's a purely selfish thing, and I'd like to think I'm not a purely selfish guy. It's just . . . the truth."

He broke off, looked down at their joined hands, sighed, then made himself look at her again . . . and laid the rest of himself bare. It was the least he could do, the least she deserved. "You make me feel, and think, and want things that aren't typical for me. I don't know why, and I don't have the slightest clue what it would mean, or where it would go. You're probably right not to take that risk, right to turn around, and walk down the beach, and not look back. All I have is the truth that I don't want you to, that it's not what I would choose. For the first time, it will make me feel something, when you leave."

She held his gaze steadily, for what felt like an eternity.

Until, finally, he let go of her hand. "This isn't fair to you. You've told me what you want."

"No," she said, suddenly finding her voice. "I told you what I can handle. Or, more to the point, what I can't." She took his hand back in hers. "I never told you what I want."

His heart started pounding hard. He'd never reacted like this to anyone, had never felt such a simultaneous wrench of anticipation and abject fear. His characters had . . . but not him. He realized he hadn't come close to doing that feeling justice when he'd described it. He'd sure as hell be able to now. "What" — he had to stop and clear his throat — "what *do* you want, Riley?"

Her lips, the very ones he was dying for, curved slowly, followed by the wink of one dimple, then the other. The warmth of her smile infused her skin, and reached all the way to the very depths of her deep, brown eyes. "What I want, Quinn Brannigan . . . is that do-over."

"Riley —"

She put her fingers — trembling fingers, he noted — across his lips. "Just kiss me and put us both out of our misery, will you? We'll plot the next scene when this one is done."

"Well, when you put it like that . . ."

Chapter 12

Riley closed her eyes. How was it she'd ended up on a long, quiet stretch of beach, standing under an Indian summer sun . . . and asking Quinn Brannigan to please kiss her?

"Riley?"

She blinked her eyes open. *Oh, right . . . he hasn't actually kissed me yet.* And all of her bravado fled. "I knew it," she whispered. Not accusatorily, more dispiritedly.

The corners of his eyes crinkled as he smiled, and she wanted to think that was affection she saw in those blue eyes, sweetly concerned affection. For her. But what were the chances of that? She should have run when she had the chance.

"Knew what?"

"I'm either dreaming this, and right now is when I'm going to wake up, because that would so be my luck, or you're about to tell me some really good reason why you changed your mind."

"Why would I do that?"

"Because this doesn't happen for me. I mean, once upon a time, a long time ago, it happened for me, but I didn't know then what I do now. Granted, I haven't been trying, or willing to even give it a chance to happen again. In case you haven't noticed, I'm kind of a disaster, so what were really my chances anyway? I mean, what guy really wants someone who lives on a borrowed houseboat, and at any given moment is sporting at least three bruises and two Band-Aids, has a dog who, even though he means well, is kind of a one-person wrecking crew, and —"

"This guy." He cut her off by taking her face in his hands, and kissing her. Really . . . kissing her.

At first she just stood there, hands out at her sides, stunned into inaction, simply letting him.

Then he lifted his mouth just slightly from hers, enough to look her in the eyes. His still had those endearing smile crinkles at the corners. And there really truly was affection there . . . for her. "The reason I stopped before was because I didn't want you hiding behind closed eyes when we kissed for the first time. Now, kiss me back."

He urged her arms around his shoulders, then pulled her fully into his own.

"Oh," she gasped in surprise. When their bodies finally made contact, she breathed a much softer, "Oh."

"Exactly." Easing his mouth back onto hers, he said against her lips, "Kiss me, Riley,"

So . . . she did. She hadn't kissed anyone since Jeremy — a lifetime ago. So long ago she had no other point of reference from before him. She had no sense of what it would be like when and if she ever kissed someone again.

She'd been head over heels in love with the last man she'd kissed, at the time she'd kissed him, and had felt loved every bit as much in return. And that had all been a lie.

When Quinn tucked her more firmly against his body, all big and dry and warm from the sun, and coaxed her lips apart, then groaned in the back of his throat like a long, satisfied growl as he slid his tongue into her mouth, she could never have anticipated it would be anything like this. Because she hadn't known there were kisses like this.

Quinn's kiss was slow, and unhurried, exploratory and, well . . . fun. He kissed her like he had all the time in the world, and planned to take every advantage of it. What pulled at her, what tugged someplace deep she didn't know she had, was that it wasn't artful seduction. The sounds he made, the way he encouraged her to kiss him back, then took such clear pleasure in it when she did, told her he wasn't in any more control of how this made him feel than she was. It was heady and intoxicating.

Her body flamed, and muscles long out of use clenched and tightened in that blissful, achy way, as slow and steady need began to build. It felt good to know she wasn't broken. She'd certainly felt that way. Empty, switched off.

Everything was switched on now . . . and it all worked just fine. If she hadn't been so caught up in kissing him back, she'd have let out a little shout of triumph. Her own little hoot and holler of relief. If she'd felt empty before . . . a few of Quinn's kisses were doing a pretty good job of filling her right back up.

She slid her fingers into his hair, and urged him to go deeper. She was purely in the moment. She had no past, and didn't care about the future. Just that exact moment. She would be quite happy to stay in that moment forever. She wanted to remember everything about this.

Quinn lifted his mouth from hers, then

kissed the side of her jaw, then her temple, and pulled her into his arms, tucking her head under his chin. "That was . . ." He didn't finish, but the way his heart pounded under her cheek said it all.

Riley smiled against his chest. "It sure was," she agreed. She closed her eyes with the intent of going back over each delicious moment in her mind, willing it to permanent memory — the look in his eyes when he told her he wanted to kiss her, the taste of his mouth, the shape of his lips, the way he'd kissed her like tomorrow would never come. She wanted to remember every sensation, every feeling, to be relived whenever she desired.

Would there be others to store away? She had no idea, and Quinn had admitted he didn't, either. He'd admitted he didn't usually get involved, or get serious, or even know why he'd been interested in her. So, she'd take the one memory they had made, and hold it close. It felt good to have a sweet, wonderful memory to think about, and remember with nothing but joy. And that was enough.

A start, a first step up and out. Something.

Quinn tipped her chin up, shifting back so he could look into her eyes. "Thank you."

Surprised, she said, "For?"

"The do-over." They laughed. "Can I ask you something?"

"Of course." She liked — a lot — that he hadn't let her go. Staying like this, half wrapped around him, now that the mindlessness of their kiss was over, was . . . comforting. Like they wanted to linger in the moment a little while longer . . . before whatever happened next, happened.

That was nice. Really, really nice.

"Earlier, when you were releasing me from my apparently misguided desire to kiss you, you said a guy like me wouldn't normally choose you." He caressed her cheek as he said it.

She smiled up at him. "If you recall, you agreed."

"Much to my shame, if you also recall." He grinned then. "And which, I believe, we've now aptly disproved."

She liked that grin. It started that fluttery business all over again in her stomach. "Well, it's possible it felt like you might have, you know, enjoyed it," She teased him back, then smiled. "A little."

"So . . . let me ask you this. Strictly in the fair's fair category, when you kissed me back, were you kissing that successful guy on the back of the book covers? Or were you kissing me?"

She'd had no idea where he'd been headed, but that definitely wasn't it. In fact, the question surprised her. Greatly. Because he wasn't just teasing, or flirting. He was serious. She knew him well enough to know that — which, more or less, answered the question. She just wasn't sure how to explain that to him. "Well, it wouldn't be completely honest of me to say there isn't a certain surreal factor to all of this, because I have looked at your picture many times, and probably all of your readers feel some kind of connection to you from reading your books. It's an intimate act, in some ways, peeking into your mind like that, though one-sided since you don't get to peek back. And you telling me you wanted to kiss me . . . some part of me had a bit of a dork-out moment. Okay, a big dork-out moment. I'm human."

His lips twitched, but he was still serious when he said, "Riley —"

"No, wait, let me finish. I am a dork, at heart. We both know that. And that's just it. Straight off, you knew that about me. It's pretty much the only part of me that's been on display every time we've crossed paths. I never had a chance to show myself in a better light. So, when you kissed me, I had no doubt you knew exactly who you were kissing. I might not have believed you'd want to, but when you did . . . I knew it was honest, and real.

"You're exactly right. Fair's fair. You deserve to know what's honest and what's real, too. Unlike with me, initially what I had to go on with you was the book jacket guy, and book jacket guy always struck me as someone completely at ease with himself, who knows exactly who he is, is very comfortable in his own skin. Meeting you didn't change that impression. If anything, you enhanced it. So, at first, sure, I probably was superimposing the book jacket guy onto the actual guy. And if you'd kissed me the day we met, yes, I'd have been starstruck. I wouldn't have been able to help it. That's all I knew of you, all you were to me."

"But?" Quinn looked partly amused, but more curious . . . and maybe a little uncertain. "I can hear the *but.*"

"Don't worry, it's a good one. Well, it is to me. The day we talked on the houseboat, and again at the bakery, I felt I had gotten to know a little more about you, but it wasn't until today, walking on the beach, talking, that I felt I was meeting the real you. The uninhibited you, the writer, the man who is passionate about his work, focused, worried about it. Your work fascinates me. I could be ten dead cats and a dozen curious monkeys about it and still just scratch the surface. But that's more about me being a reader, a lover of your work.

"When *you* talk about your work, though . . . suddenly you're not polished and effortlessly charming guy, you're . . . I don't know, more real. Vulnerable, unsure. When you shared your frustration about the story, and how you've been agonizing over it, you're . . . well, it turns out you're a lot like me. You worry, you think too much, you spend a lot of time in your head, and you're way more concerned with doing something the way it should be done because that's what is satisfying to you, than just making everyone happy. I can't tell you how many photographers I drove absolutely bonkers with my insistence on getting the food styled and displayed just so for a camera shot. I had this idea in my head and I knew it would be the most tantalizing, mouth-watering presentation, and it mattered that I achieved the image in my head, or as close to it as I could. I'm the same way now with staging houses."

She smiled and shook her head. "So . . . you're kind of geeky about your work, like I am about mine. Beneath all the success and polish, good looks and charm . . . you're just a writer guy struggling to tell a story, a little off the beaten path, maybe a bit nerdy about it — which is great. I totally get that guy. And that guy, I might even believe, gets me, too. That guy I can almost believe would want to kiss dorky ol' me." She felt her cheeks warm a bit, but she said the rest of what she wanted to say. "So, when I kissed you back just now? That's who I kissed. That guy. You."

His expression was one of surprise, maybe even a little shock, and she was afraid maybe she'd insulted him. "I think that might be the best thing anyone has ever said about me. And it's good to know you like that guy" — he pulled her close again, so she had to tip her head way back to look into his eyes — "because that guy does get you, and he is exactly the guy who wants to kiss you. And maybe now I get that, too."

When he took her mouth, it wasn't gentle, or coaxing, or exploratory. It was that ardent, passionate kiss she'd thought about the first day they'd met, the one up on the big screen that happened when someone finally made that move, in that moment. Only way — way — better.

He didn't kiss and coax, he claimed. Even then, he wouldn't simply take. He wanted her to take him back, challenging her to a duel of tongues, of heat, trading his groan for her gasp, until she was close to begging him to just pull her down on the sand and get on with it already. Those newly invigorated muscles had long since gone from clenching to aching, and her fingers were digging into his chest, grasping at his shirt, wanting nothing more than to pull it off so she could feel the heat of his skin directly under her touch. She wanted to taste him, lick the salt from his skin, she wanted —

"Oof!"

A split second later, they were sprawled in the sand, but not in an amorous tangle of arms and legs as she'd hoped . . . more in a heap of tangled limbs courtesy of Brutus, who had his front paws planted on Quinn's chest and arms, so he could stare him down . . . and drool on him.

"Holy Cr— Brutus!" Riley called to the dog, when she got her wits back enough to realize what had happened. "I don't know what's gotten into him. He's not the protective type. He's never — Brutus! Get down! Off!"

She started to scramble to her knees, intent on dragging him off Quinn if she had to, when Brutus leaned his big old head down . . . and gave Quinn a huge swipe of his tongue, right across his face.

"Gah," Quinn sputtered, but pinned as he was, by Brutus and Riley, he couldn't do much about it.

Riley sputtered, too, but with laughter.

"Easy for you," Quinn said, still spitting. "You're not the one that just got slimed."

"Oh my God. I'm so sorry." Riley scrambled off Quinn as best she could without adding injury to insult, though he did groan a few times as she managed it. "But it is kind of funny."

"He's probably jealous," Quinn forced out from lungs half crushed by the weight of the dog's paws. "I get it."

"Get off him, Brutus," Riley said, breathless from her efforts and the laughter that kept spluttering out. "He's jealous, but not *of* you. I think he just wanted some loving, too." She, grinned as she tugged on Brutus's collar. "Come on, big guy. It's okay. Quinn likes you, too. Let's go find your stick."

Brutus didn't budge. He was still gazing at Quinn, tongue lolling, like a starry-eyed fan dog.

"Brutus!" Riley commanded, finally getting her wind and getting past her case of the giggles. "Off!"

Grudgingly, Brutus stepped off Quinn's

chest, then plopped his butt in the sand next to him, still staring adoringly.

"I've never seen him take to anyone like this, and so fast, not even Jeremy. Are you okay?"

Quinn rubbed at his chest, coughing a little as he sat up. "Who's Jeremy?"

Riley's mouth fell open, then snapped shut. Had she really said that out loud? She closed her eyes on a silent groan. *Wow. Idiot.* She opened them to find Quinn standing, brushing the sand off his shirt. Thanks to Brutus. Again. "My ex-fiancé."

Quinn stopped brushing in mid-motion to look at her. "Fiancé?"

"Ex," she repeated. "We broke it off the year before last. The beginning of the year before last."

"How long were you engaged?"

"Four years." She laughed then, but there was little humor in it. Nerves got the best of her, and she suddenly couldn't seem to shut up. "Who stays engaged for four years? And that was after dating for another three and a half. I didn't think it mattered. We were together, you know? But I should have known he was never going to stick with me, right?" She shook her head, then busied herself brushing the sand from her shirt and shorts, more to give herself something to do, and anyplace else to look but at Quinn's unreadable expression. "It's ancient history."

"Right," he said. "And how long have you been on Sugarberry?"

She looked up then, serious, too. "A couple years. Yes, the same exact couple years, okay? Do you really want the whole pathetic story? I told you I was a dork."

Quinn took a moment to give Brutus a hearty pat on the head and scratch behind the ears, then walked over to her and took her arms in his hands. His grasp was gentle, but firm, as was the look he was giving her. "Maybe. But you're also strong, funny, sweet, and kind. And sexy as hell. You're utterly and completely yourself at all times. That's one of the things I find most attractive about you. You're exactly who you are. Band-Aids, monster dog, and all. And I seriously doubt there is anything remotely pathetic about whatever happened back then, especially if it made you leave a job you obviously loved, to move this far away, to start over. Painful, hurtful, and probably a whole lot of other things, but pathetic? I doubt it. Unless maybe we're talking about him." He shrugged, but his gaze stayed, laser-like, on hers. "Just a guess on my part, but probably a good one."

She stared back at him, totally taken aback. He'd stood up for her, just like that. "You don't even know me."

"I do know you. You just got done telling me how much we're alike. I know you, Riley. At least I know that much."

"I — thank you. For saying that. All of that. It means a lot."

"I meant every word. That's who I kissed. And it has a lot to do with why I kissed. And want to keep kissing."

"I —" She broke off, looked away. "This . . . is a lot." Suddenly she felt vulnerable and shaky and not necessarily in a bad way — which just made getting the hell out of there so she could regroup and think all the more imperative.

"Is that bad?"

"No. Not at all. In fact, it's very . . . very good."

"Too good? Is . . . are you nervous? Because so am I, believe me —"

"Exactly. All the more reason to retreat, regroup a little. It's been a big day, and there's a lot swirling around here, and" — she slid her arms from his grasp and stepped back, brushing her hair from her face, though the wind kept blowing it right back — "I'm sure you want to get back to your book, now that you have an idea of what you want to do."

"It was your idea."

"It's yours now. So, maybe it's best for you to just go do . . . what you do. And so will I. And . . . we'll see. About what happens next. We'll just . . . see."

"Riley —"

"I just need a little space, okay?" She was trying not to panic, but this was too much. Way too much. It was one thing to kiss him, to fantasize about doing a whole lot more with him. But she hadn't counted on the whole emotional vulnerability part. She thought she'd have more time to figure that out, or at least how she felt about being so . . . so exposed to someone again. "I'm not running," she told him. "I'm — that's not me. But this is happening very fast. It was just supposed to be a kiss."

Quinn didn't say anything to that, and his expression was completely unreadable. She didn't know if he was pissed, disappointed, disgusted, or all three.

"It was," he said finally. "The best damn kiss I've ever had. And yes, I guess that is a lot. It is for me, too. And no, I didn't see that coming either. That bullet. But, unless you tell me otherwise, at some point, I'm going to want another kiss. I'm also going to want to know more about you. And want

you to know more about me — which is terrifying . . . and exciting as hell. You're not
the only one exposing your soft white
underbelly here. But . . . wherever that path
leads, I want to follow it. I have never been
that guy who wanted to know where that
path goes. But I want to know now. Because
I'm very definitely that guy with you. You
just have to decide if that's the guy you want
to know, too."

"Quinn —"

"It's a lot. It might be everything. So take
some time. Figure out what you want . . .
and what you can handle. I know what I
want." With that, he turned and took off
down the beach at a steady lope.

He didn't look back.

CHAPTER 13

"Well, the wolves are wary . . . but excited!"

"I'll take it. Just as long as you trust me that this is going to be amazing, we're good." Quinn pulled into his spot behind the diner. "I know it's a gamble, Claire, but —"

"Stop selling me and go write the damn thing. I'm on your side." She paused a moment. "You know, you're excited about your books and I know you put your heart into everything you write, and that this will be no different. But . . . I've never heard you quite like this before."

"I've never written anything like this before."

"I know, but there's something else. You have this . . . energy about you, or something. What are they feeding you down there, anyway?"

Quinn tried like hell to picture Laura Jo's bacon and egg sandwich, but his autopilot brain took him straight to Riley. "You and your nice, clean, marathon-running arteries don't want to know."

She laughed. "You're probably right. Whatever it is, keep doing it. I've never heard you sound this . . . well, happy. Settled. I'll talk to you later. And thanks for the due date. That helped a lot, in all corners."

"My pleasure. Truly." He signed off, climbed out of the car, and headed through the back door. Laura Jo wasn't in the kitchen, which meant she was out front serving. He nodded to Petey and Magro, then ducked through the door . . . only to find someone else was already occupying his regular table.

"There you are." Alva tapped on the table with the corner of her menu, clearly annoyed.

"A pleasure, Miss Alva," he said, the smile sincere. He had no idea what she was up in arms about, but he was certain he was about to find out. One thing about Alva, you didn't have to be a mind reader. "Mind if I join you?"

"You're usually here earlier," she said, by way of a response. "I've been here twenty minutes."

"I was working. Got on a roll." In fact, if

Claire's call hadn't disrupted the flow, he'd still be hunched over his laptop. "I'm sorry, but were we supposed to meet?" He took a seat across from her, still smiling. "If so, my apologies. I never like to keep a pretty woman waiting."

Two spots of pink bloomed in Alva's cheeks, but she was having none of his charm. The twinkle in her eyes ran more along the edge of dangerously glittering. "Well, you have an odd way of showing it. You know, men might like it when women play hard-to-get, but we women don't need any such foolishness. When we're interested, we're interested. Is that so hard a thing to comprehend?"

"No, not at all. I prefer the direct approach myself." Quinn was more confused than concerned, and his smile when he leaned forward and covered Alva's hand, came quite naturally. "Are you trying to tell me something of a . . . personal nature, Miss Alva?"

She snatched her hand out and swatted the back of his with it. "Of course I am. Why do you think I'm here? And if you'd stop fluttering those baby blues and trying to seduce me, I'd tell you about it."

He subverted his choke of laughter into a brief coughing spell, causing Alva to push her water glass to his side of the table. "Take a sip," she ordered. "And see if you can stop flirting for five seconds so I can say my piece."

"Yes, ma'am." Dutifully taking a sip, then another one, he put the glass down only when he was certain he could maintain a sober, considerate expression. She was a pip, though.

"Of course, maybe that's the problem," she said.

"The problem?"

"Oh, don't try and act all innocent with me. I'm sure you've left a string of broken hearts from Hollywood to New York City."

"Actually, I don't spend much time in either of those places. I have a place in Alexandria, just outside the nation's capital."

"Another town where sex is about power."

Quinn shoved the water glass away. He knew Alva could be a real pistol, but he'd never seen her worked up like this. "Speaking for myself, I don't trade sex for anything. But as long as the two people having it are satisfied with what's what, then I don't see the problem."

Laura Jo had stopped by the table just then, heard his comment, and suddenly got busy taking an order at a nearby table. He could see her straining to eavesdrop.

"What's this all about?" he asked.

"What it's about is you leading on our sweet Miss Riley Brown, then casting her aside like yesterday's newspaper. I don't need to know the details, but we're a close-knit community here and we stand up for each other. We had it in our hearts to stand up for you, too, but if you think, for one minute, that gives you blanket approval to just waltz in here and —"

"Whoa, whoa." Quinn covered her hand again. "Before I end up in your next column as the What Not To Do lesson, let's talk this over. First of all, no one has led anyone on. Riley and I are very direct people and I doubt there's been any kind of misunderstanding on where we stand. I'd be very surprised to hear she's said otherwise."

"It's not what she's saying," Alva said, a bit of the wind out of her sails. "It's what she's not."

"Well, that's a little different. Friends looking out for friends isn't a bad thing. Not at all. What makes you think whatever she's not saying has anything to do with me?"

The answer to that interested him more than it should. He'd spent the three days since their time on the beach all but umbilically attached to his laptop, partly because

317

Joe and Hannah's story was gushing out of him and he had the power to make them do what he wanted them to do . . . and partly because it kept him from hunting down whomever Jeremy was, and punching the son of a bitch for putting that look in Riley's eyes. Considering Quinn was a man who believed in using words rather than fists, that had been a rather surprising revelation. Mostly he'd kept himself tethered because it prevented him from doing something he'd actually regret, like trying to make Riley do something she didn't want to do. He'd pushed her quite enough. Maybe too much. The next step was hers to take. Or not. She knew, quite clearly, where he stood.

"Well, for one, the expression on your face right now makes me think it has something to do with you." All Alva's irritability was gone, replaced with a more curious gleam. "I don't want to speak out of turn, or break any confidences, but I will say we've been getting together weekly since she moved to the island over a year ago, and only recently she finally opened up about her life in Chicago. Her personal life, I mean. She's a happy, outgoing, smart, and capable woman, and yet she held that in for close to two years. Tells you something. That's all I'm going to say about it."

Quinn's expression was half smile, half frown. "I can't tell if you're encouraging me, or warning me off."

Alva smiled, and there wasn't the slightest bit of calculation in her old eagle eyes. Just honest affection. "I'm not right sure myself. All I know is leaving things simmering, whichever way they're to go, isn't the same as resolving them. Can't leave the house as long as you've got a pot still on the stove, if you get my meaning."

Before Quinn could comment, Alva's attention perked up and moved past his shoulder.

Quinn's neck tightened, as did other parts of his body. Had she spotted Riley? He knew they might cross paths at some point, he just hadn't counted on it being at Laura Jo's . . . with Alva playing chaperone, and half the island in attendance. Something told him Riley wouldn't be any happier being the topic of Alva's conversation than he'd been on the receiving end of it.

When he glanced over his shoulder, he saw that Walter, Dwight, and two more of their town council cronies had stepped up to the counter. Quinn looked back at Alva. The agitation was back if the stiff posture of her tiny frame was any indication, but she wasn't paying any attention to him.

"Something going on here?"

"I'm holding my annual invitational poker tournament. Maybe you've seen the flyers?"

Quinn nodded. "I have. And I think it's great. Grams, rest her soul, played a wicked game of gin rummy, but I don't know that she ever tried her hand at five-card stud." He smiled. "My bet is, she'd have been quite good at it."

Alva smiled. "You don't know everything about your grandmother." Her twinkle was back. "But it would be a good bet to make." She looked back at the foursome placing their coffee order. "Brodie Banneker has had a bee in his bonnet ever since the tournament I had last year, after the fall festival. It turned out to be quite the event, what with the whole secret auction fiasco, and Baxter making a guest appearance." She folded her hands over her purse, which was draped with her gloves, the epitome of senior citizen propriety. "Naturally, I wanted to hold a rematch."

"Naturally."

"Charlotte and her fiancé, Carlo, are going to cater. She's part of the Cupcake Club. They run their own catering business out of Savannah called Sweet and Savory. She does the sweet, Carlo does the savory. Baxter has promised another appearance.

He's going to give away a few of his cookbooks (signed, don't you know) and" — she looked particularly pleased — "don't tell a soul, but he's going to give away tickets to see a taping of his show, all expenses paid. Hotel, the works." Alva leaned forward and covered his hand. "Of course, I was thinking about asking you if you'd like to contribute in some way, maybe a few signed copies of your latest? I know you're here all hush-hush, working on your next project, but since everyone coming to the match knows you —"

He nodded. "I'd be more than happy to."

Looking very pleased, she said, "And while we're on that topic, I've been meaning to ask if you can make time to have a little talk with me. For my column?"

Quinn blanched. "Me?" The single word came out as a less-than-manly squeak. "Wh-why?" He thought he'd made it past the firing squad of one.

"Now, now, don't look like a boy with his hand caught in the church plate. I don't just do advice columns. Sometimes I do human interest. In fact, my launch column was about Baxter when he first came to film his show here, in Lani's shop. Turns out it was all part of his big plan to woo her — see, there's a man who doesn't sit around and wait for things to happen — and I got the scoop." She leaned forward again, dropping her voice. "I'd be so honored to get the scoop on your next book. I've asked around, but there's been nary a word on it. Seems like something hush-hush is happening. Am I right?"

Quinn briefly narrowed his gaze, and decided if the UN really wanted to negotiate world peace, they need look no further than Alva Liles. He didn't bother asking her whom she'd spoken to, doubting Riley had said anything, but not putting it past Alva to have called his publisher. Maybe they should ask her to find out where the missing seventeen minutes of Watergate tape had gone. Or where Hoffa was buried.

"As a matter of fact. I do have some interesting news. But I can't talk about it just yet."

He thought her carefully coiffed beehive might finally come unglued as she all but vibrated in her seat with excitement. "Well, that would be very kind of you. Very kind indeed." The sweetness and cream response didn't at all match the avid gleam in her eyes, but that's what made it so much fun. "You just say the word, and I'll have you over to dinner. I think chatting over a nice meal is far more civilized, don't you? I cooked for Baxter. All my husband Harold's favorites."

"That sounds civilized and tasty," Quinn said, making a point to chat with Baxter when he had the chance, and look up that first article in the *Islander* archives. That was the great thing about being a writer, he could pass off any snooping as research.

Alva's gaze had drifted back to the foursome at the counter, and her fingers clutched at her gloves a bit tightly.

Quinn was curious despite himself. "What is the problem with the poker tournament?"

Alva dragged her gaze back to his, annoyed all over again. "Well, this year, to avoid any . . . unpleasantness, I opted to make the tournament an invitational."

"And how does one get an invitation?"

"Why, from me, of course. It's my party."

"I take it Walter and other council members didn't make the cut?"

"The tournament is only open to women. And it's not Walter, it's Dee Dee Banneker's husband, Brodie, who's the problem. He used to be a deputy sheriff, now sits on the council. I didn't invite his wife. She was the instigator of all the drama last year. And, of course, since she's not coming, her best friend Suzette is making a stink about it — her son-in-law's the fire chief, also on the council — and not coming, either. Though I'd have let her if she'd asked." Alva leaned forward. "She's not much of a player, but she makes a mean ham salad. Win-win, really."

Quinn swallowed another snort of laughter. "So, what is the council doing about it?"

"Passing an ordinance to prevent me from holding the tournament in any public facility. I had it here at Laura Jo's last year, but I was aiming for a bigger venue this year, as I've invited a few more players. I'm not limiting it to the seniors this year. Lani May and Miss Riley, for instance, are both playing. But there aren't any private places with more space. Lani would have us, but we can't squeeze in there. I booked the Senior Center annex. It's a new building we added on last year." She patted her hair. "Due to a prior misunderstanding, I'm no longer allowed to book the center itself, but there was no rule about the annex and my money is just as green as anyone else's. Besides, most of the players use the center facilities all the time. Doesn't seem right to keep them from enjoying this event. Now they're saying I can't use it for a private event, but I don't think they can do that."

"So, you're fighting City Hall, as it were."

"I'm fighting Brodie Banneker and his ridiculous group of cronies. Why, I taught them all Sunday school when they were barely out of diapers. Taught their children, too. Seems un-Christian-like if you ask me. Keeping a Sunday school teacher from having a little party."

Quinn struggled to keep a straight face. "How many invitations have been issued?"

"Twenty-eight. Up from sixteen last fall."

He couldn't have said what provoked him to open his mouth. "Perhaps I can contribute more than a few signed books."

Alva suddenly lost all interest in the councilmen. Her hands were still clutching her gloves when she looked back at Quinn, but there was nothing innocent in those gleaming eyes. "Why, Mr. Brannigan. What do you have in mind?"

CHAPTER 14

"He did what?" Riley paused in the middle of scooping chocolate-pumpkin cupcake batter into rows of cute yellow and purple floral paper liners to look over at Alva.

"Who did what?" Dre asked from her perch on a stool across the room. She was preoccupied with her latest project: sugar-crafting.

"Alva just told us Quinn Brannigan is going to have the invitational poker tournament at the bungalow," Riley said.

"Cool," Dre offered, not looking up from the delicate sugar creations she was painstakingly building. Riley didn't know what they were, exactly, but they looked like exotic blown glass made entirely out of sugar.

Riley steered well clear, knowing better than to get anywhere close to that kind of fragile work. "Cool, yes," she echoed with feigned enthusiasm. "Awesome."

Alva kept a speculative expression on her face as she looked at Riley, so Riley went right back to scooping batter. She'd accepted Alva's invitation to the poker tournament back when Alva had first planned it, and there was no way to gracefully back out now. But the idea of the event being at the bungalow, spending time in Quinn's space . . . well, she didn't know how that made her feel.

Actually, she knew exactly how it made her feel. Confused, regretful, and annoyed at herself for feeling either when she very much wished she simply felt nothing. She *knew* she'd made the right call in not contacting him. She'd done what he'd asked. She'd figured out what she wanted, and, more important, what she could handle. And she couldn't handle Quinn. She just wasn't ready to take the kind of risk he was offering.

Maybe the way to look at the poker tournament at the bungalow was to treat it like a test, an assessment of her decision to continue on with the life she already had, to not take on anything more. If she passed, that meant she'd done the right thing. That the status quo was where it was best for her to stay. She'd spent the better part of last year going through the big giant test of living through the anniversary of every special date and holiday she'd shared with Jeremy. After seven years together, there had been many. This year, she'd been concentrating on making new memories and new special days. But shouldn't she have a few more under her belt before any of those new memories included someone who might put her through another "test year"?

She sighed. Maybe she could just get food poisoning or something and not be able to go. That sounded like more fun.

"I've abandoned the potluck idea after Beryl brought that torte dessert to the Independence Day picnic. Remember, the one with the exotic fruit that turned out to be poisonous?"

"We remember," Dre and Riley said in unison.

"I'm still trying to forget," Dre added.

"Aren't we all, dear. Especially Beryl. So I didn't want her to be embarrassed in any way. Charlotte and Carlo are officially on board for the catering. Isn't that fun?" Alva was clearly excited about the plans as she filled her pastry bag with whipped cream-marshmallow fluff filling. "And Franco has agreed to be our server for the evening."

Riley smiled at that. "That will get the party started."

"The ladies all adore him," Alva agreed. "It's the Gallic accent. Gets them every time." She turned one of her cooled cocoa cupcakes over and punched a hole in the bottom of the paper liner with the tip of her pastry bag, then squeezed a shot of cream-fluff filling into the chocolate cake. "And," she went on, picking up the next cupcake, poking another hole, "since we're holding it on private property, the town council and Brodie Banneker can bite my fanny."

"And a very nice fanny it is, Miss Alva." Baxter's handsome face creased in a wide smile as he entered the kitchen through the back door. He leaned down to buss her flour-coated and pink cheek. "Can I steal one of these?" He plucked the cake she'd just filled from her tiny hand, peeled the wrapper back and took a bite. He immediately closed his eyes. "The town council doesn't know what they're missing."

"My point exactly." Alva brushed at her apron and patted her net-covered hair . . . all while beaming up at him like a schoolgirl with her first crush.

In addition to the fact that Baxter Dunne was one of the industry's top pastry chefs, with a successful New York City patisserie, a best-selling cookbook, and a hit television show under his belt, he was also exceedingly tall and rangy, with a thick thatch of blond hair and sizzling hot electric green eyes. And he packed a lot of charm into that sexy British accent. They all had a little crush on him. Even Dre had stopped spinning sugar to gaze fondly at her idol. It was pretty much the only time Riley ever saw her soften up.

"Has anyone seen my lovely wife?" Baxter asked, strolling around the room and checking what everyone was working on. "Who is the lucky recipient of this week's labor?"

"Charlotte is taking all the cupcakes this week and distributing them to one of the children's wards at a hospital in Savannah," Riley told him. "The doctors and nurses will be happy campers, too, I think."

"Indeed. Lots of happy faces. That's good." He peeked over Riley's shoulder. "What are you teaching yourself this week?"

"Nothing yet, just baking the last of the cupcakes. Pumpkin-chocolate."

"Great flavor profile." Baxter nodded to the rack of cakes cooling to her right, and the bowl of chilled frosting. "What's the topping?"

"Cream cheese and mascarpone. I've never worked with Italian cream cheese, so I wanted to try." She shot him a dry smile. "This is my second batch."

"Let me guess. Overmixed it the first time 'round and the mascarpone curdled."

Riley nodded, raising a guilty-as-charged hand.

"Hey, that's what experimenting is all about." He took a small, unused spatula and scooped a dollop of the frosting on it, then scooped off some of that with a finger, which he tasted. "Creamy, well blended, no lumps. Quite good. You should let Lani sample this."

Riley laughed. "It's her recipe."

"Ah," Baxter said, with a chuckle. "Of course." His eyes warmed, as they always did at the mention of her.

The fact that he was utterly besotted with his wife made him all the more ridiculously hot, Riley thought with a little sigh. "She and Charlotte are upstairs going over details on a joint catering event they're doing in Savannah next week."

"Right, right. The charity thing. I'd forgotten about that. Delightful as always to see you ladies. Keep up the good baking." He sketched a quick bow, then ducked his head so he could go through the narrow door leading up the back stairs to the small apartment space on the second floor over the shop. It was partly used for storage, partly as an office, but still had furnishings from when it had been a living space. Dre, Franco, and Charlotte had all crashed there from time to time when their Cupcake Club sessions ran into the wee hours and they hadn't wanted to make the drive back over the causeway to the mainland.

Riley had just finished scooping out her last cup of batter when the sound of cheers from the apartment overhead echoed down to the kitchen below.

"Oh, fudge," Alva said, dismayed. Startled by the sudden sound, she'd squirted filling clear through her cupcake and shot it out the other side, where it had landed in a haphazard heap all over the rest of the cupcakes on the rack.

Riley, who had looked up at the sudden sound, glanced over at Alva's table. "Both a filling and a topping, all in one," she teased.

Alva, with a disgusted look at the pastry bag as if it were to blame, set the overfilled cupcake down to inspect the mess on the other cakes. "That will scrape off well enough, I suppose." She sighed, clearly not enthusiastic about the chore.

"I say spread out the squirted stuff over the top of each cake as a secret filling layer under the frosting. You can call them Alva's Surprise Cakes." This from Dre, who never broke her fierce focus on the crystallized . . .

whatever it was she was constructing.

Alva paused in mid scrape to ponder that. "Alva's Surprise Cakes," she repeated. "It does have a certain ring." She didn't say anything more, but Riley glanced over to spy the sly senior carefully shift her spatula so it smoothed rather than scraped.

Riley smiled privately as she carried her trays over to the oven. The only question was which new angle Alva would use to convince Lani to include the Alva's Surprise Cakes on the bake shop menu. Everyone knew Lani's cakes were Lani's cakes. She shared her expertise willingly, and even some of her standard recipes, but only her own recipes were used to keep the trays in the shop full. No guest chefs, not even her famous husband.

But that didn't stop Alva from trying.

Riley shot Dre a droll smile, knowing she'd intentionally put the suggestion out there for the pure entertainment value of watching Alva plot and plan. "Nicely done," Riley murmured as she turned back from closing the oven, her voice low so only Dre could hear.

Dre merely lifted her hands, palm to the ceiling, and pumped up twice, then went right back to work.

"Shoulders tight?" Alva asked her, catching the motion.

Riley swallowed a snort of laughter and purposefully did not look at Dre, who she knew would remain utterly expressionless. Another skill set Riley did not possess.

"You shouldn't stay hunched on that stool like that," Alva advised Dre. "Young people today simply aren't taught the life benefits of proper posture. Get to be my age, and you're thankful you can stand upright at all."

Riley scooped up her empty batter bowl, dumped the other utensils she'd used in it, and carried it all over to the utility sink. "Wonder what the cheer was all about?" she commented as she washed and rinsed.

Before anyone could respond, the door to the upper floor opened and Charlotte, Lani, and Baxter poured into the kitchen like a batch of happy, excited children.

"Awesome announcement!" Lani called out, even though it was only the three of them in the kitchen that evening.

Alva clasped her hands. "How exciting!"

Dre actually looked up at that. Of course, Baxter was back in the room.

Riley dried her hands on the towel tucked over the apron strings wrapped around her waist, and turned to face them. "What's up?"

"Great news, and Riley, we're hoping it's good news for you, too."

Riley's eyebrows climbed. "Me? Why?"

"Well, you know I'm finishing up the second cookbook, and a third was proposed, but we've never moved forward on it. With the latest season of *Hot Cakes* in the can, I've finally wrapped up the second book."

"That's wonderful," Riley said, "Great job!"

"That's not the news," Baxter said, "though thank you. It's a great relief because just today, my agent received an offer to officially contract for a third book."

Lani linked her arm through her husband's. "*We've* been offered the contract," she amended.

"I was getting to that part, luv." Baxter leaned down and bussed her on the top of the head, then beamed at the group. "This time around, they'd like me to collaborate with my brilliant wife, and put together a book that charts our culinary odyssey from working our first kitchen together in New York, through putting Gateau on the map, to coming to Georgia and starting a whole new chapter in our lives." He looked down at Lani, who beamed right back up at him.

Riley's heart stuttered . . . and her thoughts went straight to Quinn. And the way he'd looked at her. And the way she felt when she looked at him. Nowhere did Jeremy, or any part of her past life, enter into the equation. She wanted what Lani and Baxter had. There was no hopscotching over the scary parts to get to that, and no guarantee if she started the journey, she'd reach that desired destination. Riley had been convinced, standing on that beach, feeling overwhelmed by Quinn and all that he was so certain of, that she needed more time by herself. Needed to be more sure of herself.

As she watched Lani and Baxter, she wondered just how badly she was letting her fears of repeating the past ruin her chances of ever having love again in her future.

"Congratulations," Dre said, which, for her, was the equivalent of giving them a standing O.

Riley jerked her thoughts away from that path and focused on the good news, the celebration at hand. *Yes, tuck it away, ignore it, and it will just go away.*

Alva's eyes twinkled and she raised her clasped hands until they were propped under her chin. "Now then, that's just wonderful news, isn't it? And well deserved. Your love story does deserve to be told."

"We'll only be exploring the culinary part, but —"

"Nonsense," Alva said, "your culinary journey is your love affair. It's your passion for food and each other that has made you who you are."

There were more googly eyes shared between husband and wife, followed by a surprisingly hot, hard kiss on the mouth.

"Still in public," Charlotte reminded them, always the arbiter of decorum.

"My, my," Alva added, though she didn't look particularly disturbed by the display. Possibly quite the opposite.

Riley's thoughts precariously teetered once again, which prompted her to say, "Let me add my congratulations to the pile. I think it's great! And very well-deserved. If you don't mind my asking, though, what does it have to do with me?"

Lani pushed at Baxter's chest, then pushed harder when he leaned down and kissed her again. "All right, all right," he said, both of them laughing. He looked at Riley, that spark still flashing in his eyes, and she felt a surprisingly sharp jab in the center of her chest.

"So, here's the deal," Lani was saying, but Baxter pulled her into a face-planting hug, muffling her voice against his chest as he grinned at Riley over her head.

"We've seen your amazing work in *Foodie*," he told her. "In fact, Lani looked it up right after you arrived. We discussed talking with you about this on the last cookbook, but you were new here, and had just left Chicago behind. We . . . didn't want to intrude. But we had trouble getting the photos for the second cookbook; we struggled a great deal with the team we ended up working with."

Lani, laughing and pushing at her husband, managed to squeak free just enough to blurt out, "So we pitched your previous work to Baxter's editor — who I guess is our editor now," she amended quite gaily. "We wanted a green light before even talking to you." She grabbed Baxter's hand when he laughingly tried to subvert her again. "We want you to be the food stylist for the cookbook!" she said in a rush, then looked smugly up at Baxter, before lifting on tiptoes and kissing his pouting bottom lip.

Baxter retaliated by pinching her backside, which prompted a wolf whistle from Dre and an eyeroll from Charlotte.

"I believe there should be a new rule, effectively immediately," Charlotte said. "No hanky-panky in the kitchen unless we all have equal opportunity hanky with our own personal panky."

"Says the only other person in the room who happens to have a panky," Dre grumbled.

"What's a panky?" Alva wanted to know.

It was all a buzz in Riley's ears, because she was still trying to digest what Lani had blurted out. Style food again. For a cookbook that was a surefire bestseller even before it was written.

"Would you be willing to consider it?" Baxter asked.

"Obviously you'll have a lot of questions, but . . . would you?" Lani lifted up on her toes, clasping her hands together under her chin, much like Alva had earlier, but looking far more winsome. "At least consider it?"

"Wow," Riley said on a nervous laugh, skating along the edge of hysterical laughter. *Were they kidding? Consider it?* "When would we start?"

"Is that a yes?" Lani squealed.

"We'd get a production meeting set up, then figure out the filming dates," Baxter said, far more reasonable, but looking nonetheless equally thrilled. "As soon as we can swing it. A month at the most."

"Don't you have to plan it all out, test the

recipes, and all of that?"

"Yes, of course," he said. "It will take some time to complete the whole project, but we need to put together a sampler, something for marketing purposes for the publisher, as soon as possible. They have some other events they want to be able to promote up front, so there will be a lot of work to do, straight off."

"We know you have other commitments," Lani added. "But, being as it's now almost October — and winter is a slow time for you, typically, right? — we were hoping —"

"I only have one winter under my belt here, but yes, it was slow last season. Given how spotty things have been already coming into this fall, I think it's a safe bet this season will be the same. I'm sure I can work around my staging jobs." Riley's brain was spinning, but she couldn't catch her breath enough to really let it all sink in.

"Actually, we'd want to have you on board full-time, for the duration," Baxter said. "Naturally, you'll be given prominent credit."

Lani elbowed him. "Don't overwhelm her." To Riley, she said, "We'll talk this all over, professionally. Hopefully tomorrow or as soon as you can make time for us. But right now, I say this is cause for a double celebration!"

The timer for Riley's cupcakes went off exactly at that moment, and everyone jumped. Their laughter filled the room.

A bottle of champagne was produced from somewhere in Lani's office, and Dre retrieved paper coffee cups from the front of the shop. "Franco is not going to be happy he missed this," she said, coming back into the kitchen.

"I'll talk to him tomorrow. He's helping Carlo and me with the fall charity ball." Charlotte smiled her little demure-but-devilish smile as she poured the champagne. "Besides, I don't think he will be too upset that he's not here."

"Is he entertaining his new young man again?" Alva inquired.

Charlotte's hand wobbled the champagne bottle, and Dre ducked her head to keep from being seen with a totally uncool smile, so it was left to Riley to respond. "Yes, Miss Alva, I believe he mentioned something about a dinner." She shot the other two quelling glares, then smiled back at Alva. "I gave him one of my recipes for pan-seared duck."

Alva smiled approvingly. "He's being a thoughtful host. Setting a good table. Good boy. I do hope they practice safe sex." She

341

took the coffee cup from Charlotte just then, which was a good thing. Otherwise it might have ended up straight in her lap.

Riley thanked Char as she took the next cup and hid her smile behind the rim. Alva was such an odd amalgamation. None of them ever knew quite what to expect from her. Just when they thought she couldn't shock them, she'd say something like that.

"To Baxter and Lani," Charlotte said, lifting her glass.

They all sipped, then Lani lifted her glass again. "And to Riley, who is going to make our cookbook look like a million bucks!"

Everyone sipped again and the room devolved into excited chatter as a dozen questions were aimed at Baxter and Lani. Riley took the moment to turn and get her cupcakes out of their pans to finish cooling on the racks. She worked by rote, her mind reeling in so many different directions, no single thought sustained itself for more than a few seconds.

She didn't have a single tool of her trade, she'd have to talk to Baxter about meeting with the photographer; she wondered how he'd feel if she suggested they talk to Chuck and Greg. It was vital that the relationship between stylist and photographer be simpatico if they wanted shots worthy of a glossy coffee-table book, no matter the finished scale of the book itself. Richer was always better.

So lost in her thoughts was she that she jumped slightly when Baxter touched her elbow. "I know this has to seem like an avalanche of information, but Lan and I are so pleased you're considering it. Please know that, when we get the chance to discuss all the logistics, if it's not something you want to commit yourself to doing, we'll understand." He smiled. "Pout, throw a tantrum or two —"

Riley laughed. "I do have a lot of questions," she said, being honest. "I know you've done two of these now, so it's a process you're familiar with, but I have my own style and process, too. We'll really need to go over every detail before any of us should commit to doing this together. Friends and business, you know what they say —"

"You can trust your friends." He looked over at his wife. "I married my best one."

Riley's smile softened, even as that tweak pinched her heart again. "That you did," she managed. "I don't have any bookings tomorrow, and my appointment with the new bed and bath vendor canceled, so if you'll be staying on the island — or did you need me to go to Savannah?"

"No, this isn't part of my television production. We can handle this from my office here on Sugarberry. I don't have to be back on set until the first of next week to begin editing, so if we can manage it before then, that would be great. Actually, I'm getting the creative director I used with the first book, along with some of the production team, to come this way over the next few days."

"Okay, well, good. I should be able to sit down whenever you want me. Why are you bringing the entire crew here? Are you going to want to do the book shoot here?" Riley thought, given the theme, maybe he planned to use Lani's bakery kitchen, or perhaps their home.

Lani slid underneath Baxter's arm and tucked herself next to him. "Did you tell her yet?"

"Was just about to."

"Tell me what?" Riley asked.

"I had one of those brochures from when you styled the bungalow," Lani said. "I showed it to Baxter a month or so ago, because I thought about maybe leasing it for that amazing kitchen space."

"I've been thinking of perhaps filming some of the next season here on Sugarberry instead of in Savannah," Baxter said. "But I can't take over Leilani's kitchen, and our home isn't suitable for filming purposes."

"So, on his way back here tonight, Baxter thought about how the bungalow with that amazing kitchen would be perfect as a backdrop for the preliminary stuff we need to shoot," Lani interrupted excitedly. "It's upscale, modern, but reflects island life, our life. It would be great neutral territory, not disrupting either of our regular day-to-day work spaces. If it all works, who knows, maybe we'll do the whole book there."

Lani's words turned into a buzzing inside Riley's head that only got louder when Baxter ended with, "I've already had a brief chat with Quinn about setting up a meet, just to see if the logistics work. I don't know how long he's leased the place, but he's probably not going to be staying around for a long time, so if it works as well as we think it will, we'll just arrange another short-term lease after he moves out."

"That brochure was a double bonus, because Baxter's publisher loved what you did styling the place. That and your work at *Foodie,* and she was completely sold on bringing you on board." Lani took Riley's arm and squeezed. "Isn't it exciting? It's all falling into place, like it's meant to be."

Riley nodded, suddenly feeling a bit light-headed. In the span of one evening, she'd gone from firmly deciding not to pursue things with Quinn, to having to play poker in his home, to feeling jabs of doubt about her choice, and now . . . working around him. For who knew how long. "Yeah," she managed weakly. "Meant to be."

CHAPTER 15

Quinn couldn't type the words fast enough. When he was writing introspection, or action elements, he had to sit and work through the right thoughts or staging dynamics. But when it came to the dialogue and byplay between Joe and Hannah, it flew fast and furious. It was a challenge to write as fast as the words filled his brain.

His hands were cramping, his back and shoulders tight; he had no idea when he'd eaten last. The music he'd put on earlier had stopped some time ago, but none of that registered.

"Bam!" he grunted, hitting the final period on the keyboard. Flinging himself back in his chair, he whistled out a long, slow breath, feeling as if he'd just completed a marathon — which he had, of sorts. A mental marathon. It felt good to stop worrying about recording every word as it came into his head before it vanished, to give himself a mental break from thinking. Only then did the growling stomach, aching shoulders, and echoing silence filter back in.

He looked around and noticed the sun was already past zenith, casting long shadows across the back patio. He liked the cooler nights and lower humidity now that autumn was finally beginning to make itself known. He was probably the only one who didn't mind the days growing shorter. He wrote better in the winter, for some reason. Something to do with hibernation and cave mentality, he was sure. But it was easier to focus.

He pushed himself out of his chair, then leaned forward and snapped his laptop shut. No more tonight. But he smiled. It was a good feeling to know that he was tempted, that he had more to say. Already ideas were waltzing around in his mind, snippets of conversation, thoughts his characters needed to have. He even started to look for a pad and pen to make additional notes, but forced himself to turn and walk into the kitchen.

"It'll all be there tomorrow," he told himself, then grinned. For once, he knew it would be. Right now, though, he wanted food. A glass of wine. Maybe sit on the deck to eat, pipe some music from the house, read a chapter or two of something written by somebody other than him. "Get a life," he added to the list.

As he wandered into the kitchen his thoughts traveled straight to Riley. With her silence the past two weeks, she had made her choice clear. He really needed to stop those thoughts from getting on that train anymore. Mercifully, his new fictional friends were taking care of that for large portions of the day, but when writing time was over, his thoughts did wander.

He stared past the open door into the fridge, and thought about heading into town for dinner at Laura Jo's. He'd been doing more of that and less of breakfast lately, as he'd pretty much hit the ground running, writing almost as soon as he opened his eyes in the morning. By the time he came up for air, it was lunch. More often than not, he spent that time hitting the beach for a good mind-clearing run.

And, if he were being honest with himself, a slim hope that a certain behemoth of a dog would accost him again. And bring his lovely owner along for the adventure. So far, no such luck.

He closed the fridge door. He didn't feel like cooking. "Diner it is." Grabbing his wallet and keys from the foyer table, he pulled the door open just as Riley was lifting her curled fist to knock on it.

Startled, she stepped back, then belatedly lowered her fist.

"Sorry," he said, almost too stunned to speak. "I didn't know you were there."

"Of course, how could you have?" she said, trying for dry humor. The dark splotches of pink in her cheeks, and along the sides of her neck, gave away the true state of her nerves. He didn't think he'd ever seen her that red.

"What can I do for you?" He leaned casually on the doorframe, pretending his heart wasn't racing a thousand miles per second. Or that he wasn't ridiculously happy to see her. All of which made him foolish and pathetic. *Shut it down, Brannigan. What part of thanks, but no thanks, didn't you get?*

Riley's brows knitted together as she noticed the keys and wallet in his hand. "I'm sorry, were you heading out? Did they change the meeting time? Isn't it supposed to be at seven?"

"What meeting?"

She frowned fully. "About the setups for the first shoot? For the cookbook? You and Baxter did agree to shoot some preliminaries here tonight when you spoke a few weeks

350

back? Maybe I got the date wrong." Another splash of color joined to the rest.

Quinn frowned along with her, then the lightbulb went on. Baxter. Cookbook. "Oh. Right. Is it Friday already?"

She smiled, a bit as one would when looking at a crazy person. "All day."

"Good thing I didn't leave for the diner then." He stepped back and motioned her inside, feeling discombobulated and anything but smooth and in control. "That would have been rude. Come on in. Let me get you something to drink."

Riley waited until he stepped out of the doorway before she moved into the foyer. "I'm fine, that's okay. I'll just . . . I can wait in the kitchen until they get here." She turned back as he closed the door. "In fact, if you want to head out to eat, I can let everyone in and show them what's what. You won't need to stay." Her voice trailed off a bit as she added, "You know, if you'd rather not."

Just like that, it was awkward. He wasn't sure which thing he hated more, the awkwardness or the fact that Riley hadn't once met his direct gaze.

"I gather *you'd* rather me not."

She sighed and looked more defeated than he could recall ever seeing her. In fact, he'd never seen her defeated. "I should have called you. Come by. Something." Riley finally looked at him. "I didn't know what to say. I don't think straight when I'm with you, and I was —"

"Afraid I'd talk you into something again."

"You didn't talk me into anything. I made my own choices. I was just trying to do what I thought would be better for us both, down the line. I really . . ." She shrugged. The helpless look that accompanied it was worse than the defeated one. "You were right. I can want what I want, but that doesn't mean I'm ready to handle what I'll get."

"That's fair, and the only reason I haven't turned up on your doorstep with Brutus bribes and a list of reasons why I think you should give us a chance."

She gave a flicker of a smile at that, and a few small pieces of his heart shifted back into place. He was sad, and sure, he was hurt. Maybe even a little angry, not at her, but at the gods, or fate, or whoever thought putting her in his path had been a good idea in the first place. But none of that was her fault. She'd been trying to tell him all along that she wasn't ready.

"I appreciate that. I'm not sure I deserved the consideration." That tiny hint of smile resurfaced when she added, "Just make sure

Brutus never finds out what I just turned down."

Quinn made the lock and key motion over his mouth, as she had that day on the beach.

Her expression softened then. For just a moment, real warmth crept into her eyes, mixed in with what looked like regret, or maybe he was just seeing what he wanted to see.

"What are you doing for the cookbook?" he asked, searching for the right tone, the right balance. The longer she stood there, the harder it was starting to be. He wanted to do the right thing by her, especially when the last person she'd let in had done so wrong. He still knew none of the specifics, nor had he tried to find out. The aftermath was all he needed to see, to know.

"You mean, why am I here? Oh." That seemed to set her back. "I'm sorry. I thought you knew. Wow, that just makes this even more awkward," she murmured. "I didn't mean to make it a surprise. Thought it was all — anyway, I'm styling the food. For the prelims, and if that goes how we hope it will, for the whole book."

He smiled. It was something of a relief to have an honest and sincerely happy moment between them. "That's great. I mean, I'm assuming it is. You said you loved your work."

"I did. And yes, this is a dream come true. Totally out of the blue and, well, pretty exciting."

He was happy for her. But he wasn't happy about how she was trying to downplay it, as if being happy in his presence was somehow rubbing it in his face. "Riley, it's okay to be happy, to be excited. I'm truly excited for you. I'm sorry, about the us part, okay? But that's all I'm sorry for."

She didn't speak right away; then she took in a steadying breath, and let it out slowly. "Okay. Thank you. That's . . . good."

And still so damn awkward he wanted to scream.

"How is the book coming?" she asked, always the trouper, trying to make things okay for everybody else.

"Flying. Editor's happy, publisher's happy, I'm happy, the characters are happy."

Her lips curved, and she finally looked comfortable and not so tense and jumpy. "That's great. Really." She pointed to herself. "Reader is happy."

His responding grin came fast and naturally, and so did the clutch in his chest. God, he wanted her back. He missed her so much, even though he'd never really had her. In his arms, his space, his bed . . . his life.

He let that yearning show through on his face.

And she shifted her gaze away again. "So, do you want to go —"

"Riley, listen —"

They stopped, both faltered.

He motioned to her to go first.

"I was just asking if you wanted to go eat. If this works, the book, I mean, I'll — uh, I can make up a schedule. Of when I'll be here. Just so you know."

"You don't need to do that. And I wish you didn't feel you have to tiptoe around or act like you're at a funeral. I'm not fragile and I'm not dead."

"I know, I know. I'm not good at hurting people I care about," she said. "And I know I hurt you. Maybe not a deathblow or anything, it was just a kiss, but still . . . it's not something I ever meant to do."

"I know that," he said quietly. "You did exactly what you were supposed to do. You were honest with me. And yourself. No one can ask for more than that."

She didn't say anything, as her gaze wandered the foyer, then fell back to her hands, which clutched the small tote she was carrying in front of her in a white-knuckled grip. She remained silent for a long moment, as if trying to decide whether or not to say what was on her mind.

"Is there something else?" he asked. "No point in censoring your thoughts now."

She looked up at that. "Part of me wants to tell you all the things I've been thinking about the past few weeks, so maybe you'll understand how much I didn't want either of us to be hurt."

"And the other part?"

There was a hint of . . . desperation, almost, in her eyes. But, she squeezed them shut, and dipped her chin. For the first time since she'd entered the house, he had to curl his fingers into his palm to keep from reaching for her.

He opened his mouth to tell her he would go to the diner for the duration, but her head shot up, and her eyes were open again. Huge and . . . scared.

He stepped forward without hesitation. He took her arm, but stopped short of pulling her close. "What is it?" He was actually alarmed. "Is everything okay? Did something else happen?"

"Yes." Her voice was shaky . . . as was she. He could feel the tremors in her arm. "Something did happen."

"Riley, what —"

"God, I feel like a fruitcake or something. I thought I could come here, and do this. Okay, no I didn't. I had no idea how I was going to work here, be here, around you. Just because I decided I couldn't handle it doesn't mean the want goes away. And now . . . you're going to think I'm . . . well, whatever you think I am, I'm sure I'll deserve it."

"What are you talking about?"

"The thing that happened was me trying to figure out how I'm ever going to bridge my past to get to my future. I watch Baxter and Lani, and Char and Carlo. Heck, Alva's even been seeing Sam Shearin on the sly, though she thinks we don't know about it. Franco has a new beau. It's all around me. I can't escape it, can't stop thinking about it . . . can't stop wishing I had it." She lifted her free hand. "I know, I know. I could have it. It's staring me right in the face. All I have to do is grab for it."

She lifted her gaze to his and his heart squeezed until it about broke in two when he saw those twin pools go glassy with tears. Her lip was quivering. "I want it so badly." The words choked out on a hoarse whisper. "I do, Quinn. I do. And I haven't, for even one second, stopped wanting it." She was almost pleading with him. "But I'm so scared. I know it's dumb, and I should be strong, but I'm just not. I'm not, and the fear is real and it's big. It's swallowing me up. I'm so ready to be happy . . . but I don't know if I can go through being hurt again. I want to make that grab, but then I think about last time, and how hard I've worked just to get to where I am now. And I don't know how to get to what comes next."

He felt her shoulders jerk and her body shake, and he tugged her hard and fast against his chest, folding her into his arms, wrapping her up tight. "It's okay." He pulled the tote she'd been carrying from her hands and blindly shoved it on the foyer table behind him, not caring about whatever it was he'd just shoved off the table to the floor, then pulled her more tightly against him. "I'm so sorry you were hurt." It was the God's honest truth, and the only part of the truth he could afford to let himself think about, or he'd get angry all over again and want to go asshole hunting. "I hate it. I wish like hell I could give you a guarantee that nothing will ever hurt you again —"

She sniffled. "I know, I know. No one can."

He tipped back just enough to nudge her chin until he could look into her eyes. His heart teetered and squeezed, as big fat tears rolled down her cheeks. "But I can make you a promise. No matter what role we play in each other's lives I will always be honest with you. Even if it hurts. You'll always know where I stand, what I feel. And if you don't, ask me. You can trust me, Riley. Today, tomorrow, and every day after that. I can't promise I'll never hurt you, because it happens. It happened on the beach to me, and I know you didn't want to hurt me. But you were being honest, and that's what I need to be able to count on. I won't play you, I won't lie to you, I won't disrespect you. You have my word on that. Those are the guarantees I can make."

She nodded, tears still gathered at the corners of her eyes, her body still shuddering a bit in his arms. "Thank you," she whispered.

That single sentiment sounded so damn . . . grateful, he felt the hot sting in his own eyes. She deserved so much more than to feel freaking grateful because someone was going to treat her the way she should automatically be treated right from the get-go. What the hell kind of number had that guy done on her?

Quinn tucked her close again, his heart pounding; then relief flooded through him when she tentatively slid her arms around his waist. When he instinctively tightened his own hold, she did the same, as if she were holding on for dear life.

And maybe she was. Because he sure as hell considered her life dear to him.

Slowly, the trembling ebbed, as did her sniffles. He stroked her hair, soothed a hand up and down her spine, and just . . . held on.

"I wish I had the answers," he said quietly, gently. "I don't. I've never been where you are. I don't know how you reach out a second time. Or a third, or a fourth. I was half scared to death trying to figure out how to do it for the first time."

Against his shirt, he heard her say, "How did you get yourself to do it?"

"Same as you did. I was honest about all of it." He smiled briefly against her soft curls. "Then I just up and kissed the girl." His smile faded. "And, turns out, I made her cry."

Riley pulled her head back at that, and lifted damp cheeks and wet eyes to his. "No, you didn't. It wasn't you who made me cry."

"Point is . . . I might. Someday. Won't mean to, but I'll hate having added to any tears that came before. Maybe you've cried enough. But for all the fear, and the being scared, and the chance of feeling the way I do right now, which is hurt, angry at the

360

fates, at your ex, and missing you more than I thought it was possible to miss a person . . . I know I'd do it all over again."

"Why?"

"Because I made you laugh, too. And you made me feel like the cleverest guy in the room, every time you did. Because of the way you looked at me, whether it was the dry smile, the avid listener, the curious monkey, or even the eye roll of I-can't-believe-he-just-said-that. Because of that single, amazing first kiss." He smiled. "And the second one. And the hope I felt, getting a gift like that, like anything is possible after all." He looked down at her upturned face, and smoothed the hair clinging to her damp cheeks. "Maybe that's it right there. I'd do it all again, because you gave me hope I could someday have it all. I've never once felt that, but I've always wanted to."

Riley stared into his eyes almost helplessly, then finally lowered her head and pressed her cheek hard against his chest. He could feel her shake her head.

"What?" he asked.

"I just . . . wish I was worthy of all that."

He tilted her head back again, and for the first time, he felt a sliver of irritation with her. "You don't get to judge that. I do. And saying you're not worthy of my affection, or interest, or any other damn thing I want to feel about you, is a pretty big slap at me, don't you think?"

She looked shocked by his retort, and immediately remorseful. "That — that's not what I meant."

"But it is what you said. You may not value youself, but that doesn't mean I don't. Or can't. Maybe you can't see it because you are convinced it's not there. But I can see it. And so do all your friends. How many people are going to have to value you before you stop judging yourself by the one selfish bastard who didn't?"

Her eyes widened at that, but rather than look hurt, or stung, or even insulted, she looked . . . thoughtful.

"Is that what I'm doing?" she asked, the words a hushed whisper.

"Only you can say. But . . . it sure seems that way."

"Well, it's not what I meant." Her voice grew steadily stronger. She looked like she was getting a little mad, too.

He didn't mind that at all. That was the Riley he knew, that was the Riley he'd thought he'd be getting to know better. And he was so damn thankful to see that Riley finally step up to the damn plate.

"I know I have value. I know I'm good at

what I do. And I know I'm a good friend. I know I'm good to my dog. And I know I have value to all of those people, and to myself. The only thing I don't know — the only thing — is whether I'm a good partner. I thought I was." She looked at him, holding his gaze evenly, steadily. "And I was wrong. So, that's the place where I don't feel like I know anything, where I question what you see in me, where I question if I have what you think I have."

"I believe you do," he said. "I wish you did, too."

She looked disgusted, whether it was at him for provoking her, or herself for realizing how far down the rabbit hole she'd let herself sink, he didn't know. But when she looked at him, there was a fire there, one he couldn't ever recall seeing.

But one he responded to, with every fiber of his being.

"Well," she said, "I guess you're right. There is only one way to find out."

"How is that?"

"Lay it all on the line. Then just kiss the boy."

And so she did.

CHAPTER 16

Quinn went still for approximately two earth-shattering seconds. Then he gripped the back of her head and kissed her back.

He groaned against her mouth, and Riley gripped his head, slanted her mouth on his . . . and jumped right off the cliff.

Quinn grinned against her open mouth. "Dead cat."

"What?"

"Dead cat." He kissed and nipped along her bottom lip, her jaw, making her tip her head back in thrilling wanton abandon, of which he took immediate and full advantage. "We should have known all along." He punctuated the words with kisses, his hands very — very — busy. "We're both too curious, by nature . . . not to find out."

"Find out what?"

He turned and neatly backed her up against the wall. "This." He dove straight back in, kissing her like a man not set on claiming, or languidly exploring, but going for every bit of gusto the two of them could muster.

She wanted to laugh, she wanted to howl at the moon, but most of all, she wanted him. "I'm still terrified," she told him, gasping when he flicked the tip of his tongue over a sensitive spot on the side of her neck, moaning when he nipped the same spot, her body jerking in response to the sweetness in him . . . and even more so to the savory. Or maybe that was the unsavory, she thought, riding a giddy high as his hands slid up her waist, his thumbs pressed against the center of her torso, his palms splayed wide, coming to stop just below the weight of her breasts.

"Join the club," he readily agreed. "Better to not be alone in the dark, though, right?" He nudged the shoulder of her camp shirt open, and continued his seductive tyranny along her collarbone.

"Right." The single word ended up a long, satisfied groan when he finally slid his thumbs up just a little higher, then dragged them across her painfully hard nipples.

She moaned in the back of her throat, and opened for him as he slid his tongue past her lips. The moan continued, long, low, almost a growl, as he rolled one nipple gently between his fingers. "I want these bared. I want to feel them, lick them, taste them."

She shuddered — hard — against him, and he pushed up against her, making them groan when the rigid length of him pressed into all the softness of her.

He hiked her up on the wall, and she slid her knees up the outside of his thighs, to his hips, pressing tight. She whimpered when his fingers left her swollen nipples so he could slide his hand between the wall and the small of her back. That whimper turned to a grunt of raw heat when he arched her back and slid himself more fully between her thighs.

He made that growling noise again, and her hips bucked against him of their own volition. But he was too tall, and she couldn't grip him tightly enough with her thighs to gain any real leverage to shift herself higher, to get herself where she most needed to be.

God, there was such a glorious freedom to be found in simply giving herself permission to stop thinking and only feel. Thinking had gotten her into panicked trouble, whereas feeling was getting her into rhapsodic amounts of pleasure. It wasn't hard to do the math.

Now that she'd opened the floodgates, the hunger, the need, was voracious. She wanted to submerge herself in it, wallow, revel, swamp, drown. From everything he was doing and the sounds he was making, he was quite willing to let her pull him under with her.

"I can't — reach —" She bucked against him.

He broke away from her mouth long enough to say, "Hold on to me." The command was rough, but coated with all that warm honey, his accent having strengthened from the moment he'd pulled her into his arms.

She couldn't let herself think about that. She couldn't let herself think about anything. The only way she was going to scale that giant wall she'd spent two years so cautiously and thoroughly erecting was to go sailing over it on the wings of lust, and want, and need. And trust, not just him . . . but herself. She'd either crash and burn all over again . . . or hit the ground running.

She wrapped her legs around him without hesitation and thought, *I guess you're going to find out!*

He lifted her from the wall and kept her wrapped around his big, hard body. As it had before, the way he swept her up so ef-

367

fortlessly thrilled her straight down to her toes. She wrapped her arms around his neck and pulled his mouth back to hers.

He grunted in surprise, but when she started to pull back, he halted their progress long enough to turn his head, and take her mouth in a hot, hard kiss. "Remember where we left off," he said, then tucked her against him and started for the stairs.

His foot had just hit the first riser when a knock came at the front door.

They froze, wobbling badly as Quinn turned them back around, Riley still wrapped around him.

The knock came again. "Yoo-hoo. It's just me!"

Riley and Quinn looked a bit wildly at each other. "Alva?" Riley hissed. "Oh crap!" How had they forgotten all about the meeting? Well, she knew exactly how. "Put me down," she told him, flustered to the extreme as she struggled to straighten her clothes and make a half-assed effort with her hair, which had to be totally wild. "Baxter and the crew should have been here ages ago."

"I didn't know Alva was coming," Quinn said, straightening his own clothes, raking a hand through his hair, looking a bit wild and undone himself for a change.

"I'm sure I look like I've been ravaged —"

"And liked it," he said with a grin.

She swatted at him, but her grin matched his.

"Why don't you duck into the guest bathroom off the hall and I'll find out what Our Lady of Untimely Interruptions wants?"

"Not untimely," she corrected him. "Baxter and company should have already been here. If she hadn't come by when she did, they could have walked in and found us —"

"Right." Quinn's eyes flashed all over again, and Riley had to fight the urge to fling herself at him and to hell with the rest.

"I'm going to need more than whatever is in the guest bathroom, but I'll work with what I've got."

Quinn wiggled his eyebrows as he slid a hot gaze over her. "Then you'll be more than fine."

The doorbell rang this time. "Hello? Anyone home?" Alva pressed the buzzer again.

Riley silently went through an entire string of swearwords. "Stall her, for at least a minute or two. And keep a lookout for the production trucks. Big white vans, three of them."

"I think I can manage that." He snagged

her arm as she went to dash off, spinning her neatly around right back up against him. He planted a sizzling hot, very short, but incredibly intent kiss on her mouth.

When he lifted his head, she dazedly asked, "What was that for?"

"We're not done with this . . . conversation. No ducking back behind barriers and stuff."

She surprised him, and herself, by smiling right back at him. "Like that's going to keep you out anyway. I don't know why I bothered trying."

His smile curved slowly into a deep, incredibly sexy grin. "That's what I was trying to tell you. Just a couple of dead cats."

She swatted him again, then tugged him down by his shirt-front for a fast, hard kiss of her own. Then she did something completely out of character for her, but hell . . . fair was fair. He'd put his hands all over her, hadn't he? Before she lost her nerve, she impulsively ran a hand down his chest . . . resting it on his belt buckle as her thumb caressed just below. His body twitched, and he jerked her against him. She slid her tongue in his mouth, and pushed it and her hips against him at the same time, before releasing him and stepping back.

"Get the door, smart guy," she said, panting as hard as he was, enjoying immensely the somewhat stunned, glazed look in his eyes. She knew the feeling. "And give me two minutes."

She ducked out, but heard him say quite clearly, "Oh, I'm pretty sure you're going to get all the time from me that you need."

"What in the hell did you just do, Riley Brown?" she murmured on a breathless laugh as she swung into the bathroom and closed the door behind her. "What in the *hell* did you just go and do?" But she was grinning like a loon when she said it.

CHAPTER 17

Quinn knocked on the side of the boat before stepping on board. "Honey, I'm home!" he called out, hoping the greeting would make her smile. Truth be told, he was nervous, though he couldn't have said exactly why.

He hadn't seen or talked to Riley since the rather ragtag assemblage had finally converged on the bungalow two nights ago. It turned out Alva had come by to talk about the poker tournament. The production trucks had been pulling into his drive when he'd opened the door to her.

Quinn was pretty damn sure that without Alva ever laying eyes on Riley, her eagle sharp senses had picked up on enough little signals to know she'd interrupted something more than a production meeting. Fortunately Baxter, Lani, and a gaggle of production crew types had rolled in as he was still chatting with Alva on his front porch.

He'd made alternate plans with Alva, which they'd completed yesterday afternoon, over lunch at Laura Jo's. While Baxter and crew had swarmed his kitchen, he'd opted to take his laptop out on the deck and pretended to do just about anything but pay attention to what was going on inside his house. He'd had no clue how well he and Riley were concealing anything from the equally sharp intellects of Baxter and Lani, so decided leaving the field of play was the better part of valor, along with the best shot of preserving Riley's privacy.

Baxter had come out at the end to set up another shoot date and confirm his plans to move forward.

Quinn knew from their preliminary talks that Baxter intended to lease the place after Quinn moved out. Had his life stayed on the planned course, it would have been by the year's end. He wasn't so sure about that anymore.

It was, in part, why he was standing on the dock next to Riley's houseboat early on Monday morning. The sun had barely crept up to cast thin, pink streamers of light over the line of sails moored on the far pier.

"Quinn?" Pushing a mass of blond curls from her still sleepy face, looking lush and warm and soft and delectable wearing an ever-so-alluring pair of pink and green flannel boxers and an old, faded Bulls T-shirt, she poked her head through the rear glass doors, blinking a few times in the spare dregs of morning light. "What are you doing here?"

He wanted to wrap her up in his arms and slowly wake her rumpled, sleepy self with a long, deep, slow kiss. He wanted to feel her come alive and alert, until she smiled up at him, that full-dimpled, rich-chocolate-brown-eyed smile. And he wanted to drag her straight back to her stateroom like a caveman and tear the clothes from her warm, delectable, voluptuous body — with his teeth — and sink every last hard inch of himself into the welcoming and ready hot, wet core of her.

He shifted his stance, and angled the slim black leather satchel he carried so it was in front of him. He hadn't known what to expect from her with this surprise visit, but he supposed he should have known better what to expect of himself. He lifted the cardboard tray balanced in his other hand. "I come bearing Laura Jo's coffee and egg sandwiches. I think she snuck two apple Danishes in there, too." He tried for an endearing, please-don't-shoot-the-delivery-boy grin, knowing Riley would see right through it, which somehow made it even more fun to try. "She took pity when I explained about my plans. I didn't know if you were a morning person or not, but she seemed to think maybe something sweet might be in order."

"I am a morning person," she grumbled. "But this isn't morning. This is just night-time thinking about becoming morning. Eventually. What time is it, anyway? Why didn't you call first?"

"I don't have your number." And he hadn't wanted to risk her turning him down.

"Sure you do. It's on all the paperwork from the leased furniture and stuff."

"I sent all that to David, since he's handling it, and it didn't occur to me until after the fact that I'd shipped off your contact information with it." He smiled briefly. "At the time, I didn't think I'd be needing it. If something went wrong with anything at the house, I'd have had David contact you anyway. Just to spare you any awkwardness."

"Unlike now, you mean."

He shrugged and tried for abashed. "I didn't know where else to go."

"Because, what, the bungalow washed out to sea last night?"

"No, because Baxter's crew showed up before the crack of dawn this morning to start with the lighting setup and staging. I can't work with all the noise. I figured you'd be at the bungalow to do whatever is on the schedule to be done today, so I'd talk you into swapping spots for the day. Or however long you'll be over there."

"Really."

He nodded. "Truly." He lifted the coffee offering again. "I did come bearing gifts."

She didn't look at the tray of coffee and food. She was still staring rather grumpily at him. Say what she wanted, she was *not* a morning person. It should have been a clear warning to him regarding just how far off the cliff he'd already dived when he found that fact rather endearing.

"So, is that why I haven't heard from you about continuing the . . . conversation? Because you lost my number?"

"We started that . . . conversation, a little more than forty-eight hours ago," he reminded her. "We've both been rather busy during that time, with all this accelerated cookbook sampler stuff going on."

"So?"

He grinned at that. He couldn't help it.

"What's funny?"

"Not a thing." Deciding to take matters into his own hands, he slid his satchel to the deck, and set the tray down on one of the fish wells. Then he stepped over to her and simply pulled her through the door and right into his arms.

"What makes you think you can just climb on my boat and have your way with my person?" she asked, blinking up at him, making absolutely no effort whatsoever to extract herself from his hold.

"This." He bent down and kissed her.

She didn't respond, for at least the span of three seconds. Then there was a little . . . whimpering sound, and he felt her body soften against his. She gave a soft little moan in the back of her throat, then gave up entirely and slid her hands behind his neck, and molded his mouth more firmly to hers.

He'd only intended that slow, sweet, warm, good morning kiss he'd imagined earlier, but it was quickly moving along toward the caveman scenario by the time he managed to break free and lift his head. She was smiling up at him just as he'd hoped, only there was a bit of smugness there. Probably because his heart was beating like a wild man, and he looked and sounded a bit the part, as well.

"Well," she said. "When you put it that way."

He grinned at that. "You weren't changing your mind, were you?"

"I might have been." She was a terrible liar. "Of course, you wouldn't know, since you didn't bother to call, come by, send smoke signals. A tasteful carrier pigeon would have been welcome."

"I know. But if you recall, you all were at that first shoot until three or four in the morning. I didn't see or hear from you Saturday."

"I was unconscious Saturday. I haven't done that kind of work in a couple years."

"I did come by here that afternoon —"

"You did? Oh. I drove into Savannah. I had a ton of things to replace, put my tool kit back together, all the tricks of my trade. Char and Carlo asked me out to dinner. I wanted to call you, tell you to come meet us . . . but I didn't have your number, either. And I hadn't heard anything. Where were you yesterday? I came by the bungalow."

"You did?" He grinned. "You know, we might want to avail ourselves of some modern technology."

"I was thinking the same thing."

"Good. I had to drive to Atlanta to do some press stuff for the book that's out now. I didn't get back until late last night."

"You were in Atlanta yesterday?"

He nodded. "Being away was torture — which should appease your need to punish

378

me if you feel the need to do so."

"I'm not disagreeing with that part, but next time, punish yourself some other way, will ya? Depriving you, deprives me."

"Well," he said, echoing her earlier statement. "When you put it that way."

And the caveman scenario won.

She squealed when he scooped her over his shoulder. "You can't haul me off my feet and —"

"Can too. And I prefer the more romantic *sweep,* if you don't mind."

"Well, I don't sweep easily, either." She giggled when he slid his hands up her waist and adjusted her so they could make it down the narrow passageway to her stateroom.

Sliding her down his body, he ducked and cleared his head through the opening to the stateroom.

"I have no idea how you managed that," she said on a breathless laugh. "I can hardly make it down that hall without elbow bumps and bruises to show for it, and probably would even if this thing didn't bob and sway."

He smoothly whirled her into his arms and around in a tight circle, without either of them clearing a thing off any surface. "That's why you need me around. I'll keep you safe from all the bobbing and swaying."

She looped her arms around his neck and let him whirl her again. "Is that right?" She squealed again when he scooped her up against him so her feet left the floor.

"In fact, it's possible we can find a way to make the bobbing and swaying work to our benefit." He wiggled his eyebrows and made her laugh again. Then he slid his hands up and under the edge of her flannel boxers, cupping the soft, delectably full curves of her buttocks, turning the laughter into gasps.

"What time are you due at the bungalow?" he said, nuzzling her neck.

He felt her fingertips dig into his back as he continued nuzzling, which tugged the thin cotton across her plump, hard nipples.

"Eight," she breathed.

"Good." He stepped up so he could lower them to the bed. "It's possible you might still get there on time."

The boat rocked just as he was lifting her onto the bed, which landed her closer to the middle. She laughed again, and covered the top of her head to keep it from bumping the headboard. Quinn tugged off his polo shirt and levered himself up . . . and over her.

"You have way too many clothes on," he

said, bracing himself above her.

"The same could be said about you," she replied, sinking back into the tousled linens of the unmade bed she'd just crawled from.

He grinned. "We could probably fix that."

"Probably." She started to reach for the hem of her tee, but he stopped her.

"That's no fun."

"No?"

He nudged her hands away and levered himself so he could sprawl on the bed next to her. The bed itself was wide, though a bit short for his long legs. "Well, more fun for me, if I get to do it — which may mean more fun for you."

She lifted her hands away and let them rest over her head. "Really? Huh," she said, trying for insouciance, but the gleam in her dark eyes betrayed her anticipation. "Who knew?"

"I could explain —"

"You are very good with words."

"— but as writers, we're taught to show, rather than tell."

"Is that so?" She lifted one hand to toy with his hair, just above where it brushed his ear. "This would be another one of those things about your work that fascinates me." She ruffled his hair. "It's grown. Since you've been here."

"I haven't found a barber. Or looked, really."

"Don't." She smiled when he lifted his eyebrows. "Not on my account, anyway. It makes you look —"

"Heathenish?"

"I was going to say a little rough around the edges. Less like that book jacket guy." She teased his hair with her fingertips. "You're always so effortlessly groomed. This makes you seem, I don't know . . . more like us mere mortals."

"Good to know. Being godlike can be such a burden." He leaned down and placed his lips over one plump nipple, making her gasp and her hips buck up.

"I can only imagine," she managed, her hands falling limply next to her head when he shifted his attention to her other nipple. "Oh . . . God," she gasped, when he used his fingers to gently rub and massage one nipple, while suckling the other hard through the thin cotton of her shirt.

"Yes?" he said, lifting his head and giving her his best celestial leer.

She snorted out a laugh, then almost choked on a sharp indrawn breath, her hips bucking again as he went back to teasing and tormenting first one tight tip, then the other.

She fisted her hands in the loose linens as he nuzzled the hem of her shirt up, exposing the creamy white skin of her tummy. "You have the softest skin."

"With freckles galore," she said. "Everywhere. If you squint in the right light, they look just like a tan."

"I like them just the way they are," he said, kissing one, then another. "In fact, I think I'll make it my mission to catalog each and every one." Quinn lifted his head to look at her. "After all, I'm very good at research and keeping track of lots of tiny details."

She lifted her head to look at him, whereupon he dropped his mouth to one freckle, then another and another, all while keeping his gaze intermittently focused on hers.

"Hmm," he said. "I've a quandary."

"That's a good word," she said, moving restlessly beneath him. "Quandary," she repeated, drawing it out, rolling her hips in a sinuous motion as she did so. "Who knew vocabulary could be so hot?"

That got a chuckle out of him.

"What is your quandary, sir?" She rolled her hips again.

"Well, it seems I've gotten to all the freckles in my immediate research area. I'm torn now between exploring northward" —

he nuzzled her shirt up another few inches, until the plump undersides of her breasts were exposed — "or taking a more leisurely southern route."

She let out a long, satisfied groan when he nudged the wide elastic band of her boxers down below her bellybutton, then further down, until they clung to the faint crests of her hipbones. "I hear the south is lovely this time of year," she croaked out as he kissed and teased his way lower . . . then higher, then back lower again.

"There's another skill that writing and researching has helped me to hone."

"Hone," she repeated, drawing the word out and making it sound remarkably earthy.

He was already rigidly hard almost to the point of pain, but that got another surge and twitch out of him, making him swallow his own groan. She had absolutely no idea how utterly carnal she was. Goddess in her own right.

"Go on," she urged.

It took him a moment to recall the thread . . . he was sidetracked by how decadent it was, seeing her sprawled half beneath him, a hint of those voluptuous breasts exposed, threatening to spill out of that thin, worn cotton. And that wide flat band of flannel-covered elastic, caressing the softly rounded swell of her stomach, exposing the creamy freckled sweetness to his hands and mouth. Teasing him, so close to revealing the truth of her blond hair, downy and waiting for his tongue to toy, part, and plunder.

She was all but vibrating beneath him, a coiled spring, as he continued to linger around her navel, dipping his tongue in, then drawing it out, then darting it in again, until her hips moved in unison and her soft moans became urging growls.

"Multitasking," he murmured against the sweet, freshly exposed skin below that elastic band, which he pulled down farther . . . and farther still, taking advantage of the way her hips pumped up hard in shock when his fingers slid under her tee and closed over her swollen nipple. He gently rolled and caressed it while tugging her flannel shorts down with his free hand, so she could kick them loose.

"Move up," he urged her, shifting them so they lay diagonally across the wide bed. He kicked off his worn docksiders and shucked his shorts down and off, as she wrestled off her tee. "You're glorious, Riley," he said, easing his body between her legs. He had to keep his long legs bent slightly, but he could prop his toes against the stateroom wall, which gave him leverage. "Scoot back, just a — yes, right there." He leaned down and kissed the sweet, tender skin of her inner thigh. "Hold on," he said, then slid his tongue deep into her.

Her surprise shout of pleasure ended on a long, shuddering groan, as he began to toy and tease, stroke, and caress. He stopped long enough to slide two fingers into his mouth, then returned to his slow, languorous exploration. He slid his hand back up her body, reaching her nipples with his slick fingers, toying, flicking, and rolling them with a bit less gentleness as her hips started to buck in earnest.

"Quinn," she panted.

"Right here," he murmured against her slick, sweet flesh.

She shuddered hard as she went over, her body jerking beneath his questing and plunging tongue, as he pushed her longer, higher, harder.

"Can't, can't," she panted.

"Can," he said gruffly, focusing on the throbbing nerve center with the gentlest of swipes with the very tip of his tongue . . . while sliding a finger, slowly, deeply, inside her.

She cried out loudly, and thrashed beneath him.

Then she was grabbing his hair, leaning up to claw at his shoulders, her body still bucking and quaking with the aftershocks of her release. "Here," she commanded, pulling him up and over her body. "Now."

"Now?" he asked, poised over her.

Her eyes were so dark, the pupils had all but swallowed the sweet dark chocolate of her eyes. "Now," she growled almost angrily.

He grinned, even as he throbbed almost in pain he was so hard. "I like a woman who knows what she wants. Let me grab —"

"No," she said, which made him lift a brow. "I'm — I'm safe. Pill. We don't need, I mean . . . unless you want —"

"I only want one thing." He gripped her hips and dragged them up and off the bed so he could drive himself between them, sheathing all of himself inside every last sweet, hot, wet inch of her in one smooth, steady plunge.

She cried out, bucked hard against him again, and he realized she was climaxing. Again. Thinking of her he thrust again, and again, and she almost sobbed as she cried out, her nails digging into his shoulders, then his buttocks, as she urged — no, demanded — that he keep on. Faster. Deeper. Harder.

Her command was absolutely his wish.

He'd have gone longer, for as long as she wanted him to, but her tight muscles throbbing around him ripped him to release before he even knew it was going to happen. He'd been on the brink since he'd slid his tongue inside her. Or, more honestly, since she'd stuck her head out the sliding glass door, all sleepy and flushed in those ridiculous flannel shorts.

Panting heavily and trying to find his breath, he moved to roll away, so he could take his weight from her, only to have her hook her ankles around the backs of his calves and pull his head down to hers.

"I'm heavy," he said, his voice sounding like that of a drugged man.

"Stay," was all she said. Then she pulled his head down the rest of the way and kissed him.

They'd coupled more like wild beasts than lovers. There hadn't been anything intimate about it. He knew that because the kiss . . . her kiss . . . the one she was tenderly giving him, so sweetly exploring, and soft, as if she'd never kissed him before, as if they hadn't just mated like wild jackals — was truly intimate. Not the way she'd responded to his slightest touch, not her multiple orgasms which had, in fact, made him truly feel somewhat godlike. No. It was this genuine and pure kiss, freely and fully given, all vulnerabilities laid bare.

He knew enough about her, understood enough about what scared her, to know that this was the true gift of herself. It was that, more than anything that had come before, that completely undid him.

He slid from her then, and eased his weight off her, pulling her with him when she would have ended the kiss to protest the shift in position. He kept her with him, tucked her against him, and continued to glory in the most amazing gift he'd ever received.

As he pulled her closer, sheltered her with his body, as if protecting her was and would always be his natural, default directive, he knew he'd do everything in his power to always be worthy of that one, single kiss.

CHAPTER 18

"What time is it?" Riley murmured, coming awake slowly, realizing as she became aware of being wrapped up against Quinn's big, hard body, that they must have dozed off — while still kissing, if she recalled it properly. She smiled against the warmth of his skin as it all filtered back.

She rolled her head just enough to see the bolted wall clock. Just after seven. Good, she had a little more time before embracing the real world.

"Is someone else on the boat?" Quinn's deep voice was even sexier when rough with sleep and a little honest fatigue. "I hear footsteps."

"That's just Brutus."

Quinn's eyes cracked open. "Brutus is on-board? How did I miss that?"

She laughed. "Where did you think he was? Out in the backyard, treading water?" She started to roll over and sit up, but a very strong arm hooked her right back up against an equally strong body. Since that was exactly where she wanted to be, she let him. "He sleeps up on the front of the boat, and nothing wakes him until the sun comes up."

"What if it's raining?"

"He goes under the awnings."

"Never in here?"

Riley grinned. "Let's just say he goes wherever he's most comfortable. That storm we had last week? I found him wedged between the barbeque and the life preserver bins. I try to get him to stay in here, but I think he just likes being outside. If it's really cold, he stretches out in the main cabin in front of the little space heater. Mostly I don't mind him not being underfoot."

"I can imagine." Quinn grinned and rolled his head so he could press a kiss against her hair. "I liked you being under me." He toyed with the long tangle of curls that spread across his chest, sending delicious little tingling sensations skittering all over her skin. She really thought this was perhaps the best use of an early morning she'd ever had.

"Yeah," she sighed. "That I didn't mind so much."

There was another thud from somewhere

on board.

"He's jumping down from the front of the deck to the side rails."

"Sounds like he's really gotten accustomed to boat living." Quinn drew his fingertips through her curls, slowly untangling them. "I guess you both have. How long did that take? Do you take it out much? I've never been on one of these — how does it maneuver in open water with the waves and all?"

She laughed. "Curious monkey and silly wabbit. I have no idea how to even turn the thing on, much less steer it anywhere. You don't honestly think Chuck and Greg would want me to take their big expensive toy out for a spin, do you? I mean, they have been around me for more than five minutes. It's a testament to their inexplicable affection for me that they agreed to let me even step onboard."

"How did you get it up here from Jekyll then?"

"The same way any self-respecting klutz would. I paid Chuck's uncle to do it."

Quinn chuckled at that. "Well, given my extensive, if youthful, life aboard ships of various sizes and modes, what do you think the chances are your very dear friends would let me take us out for a spin?"

She lifted her head to look at him. "I'm sure they'd be delighted to, but . . ."

"But what? Do you get seasick?"

"No, I don't think so. I didn't on the boat ride here, anyway."

"Is that the only time you've ever been on a boat?"

"Yes, why?"

He grinned. "It's funny to think someone who's never been in or around boats, lives on one."

"I know. I feel the same. And yet, here I am. I have to admit, I have come to really like it."

"So, why don't we take her out for a spin?"

"Because I finagled a space on the docks here by promising I wouldn't stay long. No one has said anything, but I'm afraid if I take it out they won't let me back."

"Don't you have a contract or something?"

She shook her head. "Just month to month. I dump an envelope in the slot at Biggers' and they leave me to my own devices."

He surprised her by sliding her body over and more fully on top of his much bigger body, making her feel lithe, and petite and anything other than how she'd always felt before. "Well, maybe I could put David on that for you. He's very good at making things happen."

"Why?" she asked. "I mean, thank you. I would feel better if I had something in writing."

"You're welcome. It's purely selfish. I'd like a sunset cruise around the sound with you. That's where my grandfather and I sailed in the evenings after work. I'd like to share something of that with you."

She softened, and her heart teetered dangerously. This was the intimacy she wanted, the kind of opening up and sharing. "That sounds very lovely. If David can work his magic, I accept the invitation."

"Good." He looked inordinately pleased.

Riley braced herself, mentally anyway, for the fears to kick in. Making Quinn happy — she wanted to do that, and much more — but the fact that she could implied she mattered to him. That should scare her.

It did . . . but it didn't make her want to hide. She considered it forward progress made, and left it at that. "Fair warning, though. I don't know if I'll make any better a first mate than I do a captain."

He slid his hands down and cupped her bottom, then lightly pinched the soft flesh. "You're doing really well on the mating scale so far."

"Ha, ha," she said, but felt the warmth of

pleasure at his comment fill her cheeks. She leaned down and kissed him. "So are you, Captain." She moved to roll her weight off him, but he wrapped his arms around her and kept her there.

"Few more minutes. You don't have to go yet, do you?"

She shook her head. And probably would have stayed, even if she knew she'd be late. Just a few more minutes sounded like heaven.

"I have one other request."

She slid her hands down his sides and pinched the side of his butt. "Getting awful cheeky," she said, enjoying the surprised snort of laughter that got from him. "What is the request?"

"Will you mind if I stay here to work while you're at the bungalow? Tell me honestly, because I can find another place —"

"No. I kind of like the idea of you being here. Uh, could I maybe ask a favor in return? Would you mind if I left Brutus with you? Say no if you'd rather not. I know you need to concentrate. But he's really no trouble. Just walk him down to the end of the pier to the grassy area every once in a while. He'll let you know."

As if on cue, there was a jarring thud overhead, then a big, panting dog face appeared in the tiny window in the wall above their heads.

"Would that constitute letting me know? And how the hell did he get up on the fly deck?"

"There's a ramp. Sort of."

"A sort of ramp. I probably don't want to know."

"I think he likes the windier breeze up there. Or maybe he just likes playing king of the world." Riley grinned. "But right now I need to get the king out for his royal stroll. It'll just take a minute. And I . . . need to shower, before I go. I'd ask you to share, but it's tiny."

"Asking was nice." He tugged her down for one last fast, hard, and very hot kiss before letting her crawl off him and off the bed to search for her shorts and T-shirt.

Riley's thoughts flashed back to that hot and hard kiss Baxter had dropped on Lani the night they'd announced the cookbook deal. The one that had got her wondering all over again, and really questioning what she wanted in her life — who she wanted in it — and how she was going to get to where she could have it. She smiled privately to herself as she quickly pulled on her clothes. Maybe what she had with Quinn wasn't the love affair of the century, like the Dunnes' was, but, for what it was right now . . . it would do. It would certainly do.

"A shame," Quinn said.

Riley looked over her shoulder to find him sprawled back, sheet half over his naked body, arms propped behind his head. She was surprised she didn't outright drool, but it didn't keep the *you lucky dog* thought from skimming through her mind. "What is?" she asked him, wondering what he thought when he looked at her. He certainly didn't seem put off.

"Putting clothes on that body. When we take our sunset cruise, can we have naked sailing time?"

Her responding grin was swift and honest. He made her feel good about herself, and just . . . good in general. Even swifter than the grin was the infusion of warmth his sincerity gave her . . . not to mention the healthy boost it gave her ego. Maybe she shouldn't need that, but after everything she'd been through, and all the self-examination that had followed, she was too human to deny it felt pretty damn good.

"Only if you have five billion level sun block."

"I'll take that as a yes then."

She shot him a dry smile. "Of course you will."

Brutus scratched at the window.

"I'm coming, I'm coming. Keep your collar on."

"When you come back down, why don't you grab the stuff from the diner. We can nuke it, have a little reheated breakfast, and —"

"Uh-oh."

"Uh-oh what?"

"I forgot about that. About the food. Someone distracted me."

Quinn grinned, quite broadly and somewhat smugly. "And?"

"And I'm pretty sure I won't have to feed Brutus this morning."

It was entertaining how quickly Quinn's smug grin turned into a droop of disappointment. "Oh."

"Right. But I can put something together for you."

"Do you have eggs, some bacon? I can fix us something quick while you walk the dog. I've cooked onboard before."

"Which is dandy, because I have not. Hence no eggs, no bacon."

"You're in a cupcake baking club."

"We keep the spoilables in the shop kitchen so we don't have to haul everything back and forth. Char, Dre, and Franco come over the causeway from Savannah, sometimes straight from a job or school, so it helps to keep all refrigerated stuff on-site. I just bring the dry ingredients, or replace what I use of Lani's."

"Makes sense. But I wasn't referring to the lack of eggs. You're a food stylist. You have culinary training of some kind to do that, right?"

"I'm a trained chef, yes, though I didn't work in the field as one. My slant was always the photography aspect, though I ended up in design and styling." She grinned and shrugged. "I love food, trying new things. Not so much preparing all the intricate and involved dishes myself, but I have great respect for those who do, as well as for the final result of the food itself. When I figured out I could combine my love of photography with my love of international cuisine, and make a living at it, it seemed like a no-brainer to me."

"So you don't cook," he repeated. "At all?"

"I said I don't cook onboard." She gestured to herself. "Clearly I'm not wasting away here, so I manage. I either nuke stuff — you'd be amazed how much cooking you can actually do in a convection microwave — or I beg, pout, and say pretty, pretty please, and Carlo sends in with Char on club nights whatever dish he's experimenting on."

She held up her arm so he could see the Bullwinkle Band-Aid on the back of her tricep. "Rope burn from tying down the deck stuff before that storm — when the water was still flat as glass and there was no wind." She turned sideways and lifted the hem of her shorts to show a faint, almost healed bruise. "Banging against the dining room table, off-loading bags of groceries. The boat barely even rocked. No way am I turning on anything with the potential to catch fire."

"I suppose that makes sense." He sat up, stretched, and the sheet slid farther . . . and farther, down his lap. "Would you mind if I gave it a go?"

"Knock yourself out — not literally of course — but like I said, there's nothing in the pantry to be cooked. Nuked, yes, Grilled, fried, or scrambled, not so much."

He slid from the bed, making her entire body wobble with want, and walked to her buck naked, simply too good to be true. He framed her face, bent down, and kissed her soundly on the mouth. "That's why they make markets. I'll go pick up some stuff and make us dinner. You'll be back by then, right?"

All she could do was nod, and whimper a little. How could she ache all over again?

She should be a walking collection of sore muscles in need of great recuperation time. But had he even nodded toward the bed, she might have been the one to drag him there. Or to the floor. Or the nearest wall.

A huge, thundering *woof* made them jump.

"Right. Sorry, Brutus," she called out, then looked back at Quinn, whimpered again, turned and fled. It was that or attack him.

That she heard him chuckling all the way as she dashed though the main cabin and out the back sliding door didn't help matters any. She really needed a better poker face.

She checked that thought and changed her mind as she clipped the lead on the dancing dog. Did it matter if Quinn could read her every thought if he seemed to be of like mind?

Brutus leaped from the boat to the pier. Riley tried her best to keep him from dislocating her shoulder on his mad dash to the grass, but her thoughts were still back on the boat. And with Quinn. She definitely hadn't seen this morning happening . . . not like it had, anyway. But she was thankful and relieved. If he'd called and asked to see her on some kind of official date, she'd have been a nervous wreck. She'd have overthought her choice of clothes, overthought how she should act, overthought how the whole transition from date to possible sex might go, not to mention the getting naked part — speaking for herself anyway — followed by spending far too much time worrying about every single aspect of that dynamic.

Instead, he'd just shown up, been funny, charming, sexy, and somehow made her feel the same, despite being in dorky sleep clothes with massive bed head. He had literally swept her off her feet and taken her to bed, where they'd had the most amazing sex she'd ever experienced.

It had been thrilling and fierce. He made her feel like a femme fatale siren goddess. For that alone, she'd be forever in his debt.

Brutus bumped his head against her leg and she got a bag, cleaned up after him, then started back to the boat after depositing it in the big trash can.

What she and Quinn had done hadn't been anything like lovemaking, not really. It had been hot, but not necessarily intimate. Of course, for a first time . . . She paused as Brutus sniffed some particularly intriguing fishy smells, and her thoughts drifted to after, when he'd pulled her close to him, and then after that, when they'd kissed.

She sighed deeply. Her body felt all warm and achy — in a good way — just thinking about that kiss. Hands down, that had been the most intimate act they'd shared. It had gone on and on, and she'd felt truly connected to the part of him that mattered.

He knew his way around a woman's body — like a violinist intent on making a Stradivarius weep. But he'd been the first one to admit that his relationships never got past that part.

She'd loved the snuggling, the banter, after they'd woken up together, and how he'd wanted to keep her there with him. He'd made her feel alive and desirable in her own skin, not just comfortable, but sexy and naturally at ease. He was a hedonist, making her aware of every single cell in her body at all times, and making her feel good about it.

She remembered how he'd laid himself bare to her, standing in his foyer, when she'd cracked under the pressure of her own fears. She knew he could open up and be more than a very skilled lover. A whole lot more. Would those two parts of him eventually blend? Could he open himself up fully and make love to her?

And, more important, would he want to?

She shook her head, and smiled dryly at

her own thoughts. "He makes you feel like Cleopatra and Sophia Loren all wrapped into one exotic package and you're already worrying about what happens next?" She let Brutus lead her back to the boat, thinking about the irony that Jeremy had loved her for her mind, her offbeat humor, and her skills with the work they shared. He'd made her feel strong, respected, valued . . . but he'd never made her feel comfortable in her own skin. In fact, she'd always suspected that while he claimed to love her body, the lushness of it had always been a little too much for his true personal taste. He was taller than she was by a few inches, but slender. In fact, they weighed close to the same. She'd never sprawled herself across his body as she had Quinn's. As years went by, they learned to satisfy each other's needs and their sex life remained a healthy enough one. Was it any surprise she'd assumed he'd come to love her body as he'd come to love her? Just like she'd come to love his skinny, long bird legs and the complete lack of hair on his chest?

Wasn't that what a couple did?

She thought again about how Quinn had brought every part of her body to a feverish pitch, kept her there, vibrating on the edge, then effortlessly teased her up and over, again and again, to a series of the strongest climaxes she'd ever had. Or known she was capable of having. She was not a screamer. She smiled privately. *I am now.* That had certainly not been in the repertoire with Jeremy. Their lovemaking had been ardent at times, but much more . . . staid. Jeremy wasn't particularly earthy.

Riley let Brutus hop onboard, then followed him along the walkway and on deck. Something smelled amazing. She'd thought it had been coming from one of the other boats, but almost all of them were battened down for the winter.

"Quinn?" She climbed down the companionway and found him in the galley.

Tousled hair, rumpled khaki slacks, no shirt, towel tucked sideways in the waistband of his pants like a short apron. He looked up, spatula in one hand, and grinned. Her heart fluttered, flipped, then did a lovely little freefall — which made no sense. He always looked hot. And had shot her that sexy grin more than once.

Of course, this time he was half naked in her own kitchen, but still. She thought her heart had higher standards than that. Or at least more integrity than to be swayed by a hunky chef. *Who plays your body like a violin,* her little voice reminded her. Needlessly.

"Come taste this," he said, lifting up the spoon.

Rather than duck past the galley for her shower, and the very wise distance and time it would give her to sort through her jumbled thoughts, she walked right over to him. "What did you even find to make?"

He carefully tipped the spoon to her lips. "Rice, cheese, and mushrooms. Some flour from your baking supply stash, milk, and a few of your spices to make a sauce. Here, try."

She took a nibble, then felt her eyebrows climb halfway up her forehead as the rich, creamy, incredible flavors burst all over her tongue. She closed her eyes and groaned as she finished off the nibble. "Where did you learn to do that?"

He shrugged. "Necessity. I hate eating out all the time. And you forget, I was chief biscuit cutter in Grams' kitchen."

"Right, right. Never underestimate the culinary powers of Grandma."

"Did you learn to cook from yours?"

"What? No. I never knew my grand-parents. Two of them were alive when I was born, but infirm. We were stationed over-seas." She shrugged. "They were both gone by the time we returned stateside."

"Military brat then?" he asked.

She nodded. "My dad was killed by a land mine when I was little. I don't remember him."

"I'm sorry, Riley."

"It's okay. I lived on base, so I wasn't the only kid who went through it. Maybe because of that it was — well, it wasn't normal, of course — but it was part of the culture of that life. You got yourself through it, as those around you did."

"And your mom?"

"Also military." When he looked surprised, she said, "That made it hard — she was gone a lot. I got shuffled around a lot. But I kind of liked the freedom I had . . . and the security of knowing I lived on a military base. It was an interesting combination."

"And now? Your mom? Still serving?"

Riley shook her head. "She passed when I was in college. Complications from pneumonia."

Quinn's expression was tender and sad. "I'm sorry for that. I know what it's like."

"Thank you. It's okay now. I was thankful — very — that I'd grown up as independent as I had. Helped me move forward and be okay."

"It explains a lot about you," he said.

It was her turn to look surprised. "As in?"

"All good," he said, echoing her words

from the beach that day, when she'd been describing how she saw him. "You have this innate strength and you've definitely tackled life, even when it hands you rough stuff. You hung in, you pushed through. Maybe there is something about losing parents young that makes us wary of allowing ourselves to want something, or to let someone else contribute to our feelings of security. We know, quite literally, how fleeting life can be."

She thought about that, and nodded. "You probably have a point. I think, in my case, though I avidly pursued my career, I was too eager for the sense of security that came with someone suddenly being there for me. Maybe because my parents largely hadn't been, even when they were alive? I don't know. I do know that I sucked it all in, draped it all over myself, and paraded it around. I loved everything about being half of two, rather than only one."

"I can see that. Reacting that way. It helps me understand how you went the other direction after it was over. I'm glad you told me."

"Good," she said. "I don't want it to be awkward."

"If you mean your past relationship, I don't want it to be either. For the record, I don't need to know about it. That's your business. I understand the general dynamics enough to understand why this leap was hard for you to take. I don't need or want you to mine your own pain just to help me understand you better."

"I — thank you." Riley ducked her head for a moment, surprised not only by his words, but by this welling of . . . she didn't know how to label the emotions he was making her feel. Except to know that instead of scaring her, they made her feel good. As if she was on solid ground. And that was . . . a lot. "You promised me you'd always be square with me. I promise you the same thing. So, if you want details, I'll give them to you. But I feel . . . sturdier, with you. Than I thought I would. I very much like being in the present, especially this one right now, with you."

"Then the present is where we'll stay. Though I do have one last dead cat question."

She didn't exactly brace herself, because that teasing gleam had come back into his eyes. She realized not only how well she'd come to read him . . . but that she'd also come to trust that what she found there was real. "And what would that be?"

"Where did you learn to cook? Or what

made you want to learn?"

"Oh, that's easy." She laughed. "Military base food. I never had family cooking, even when staying with other families. It was always my luck to get stuck where meals were prepared much as ours were — leftovers and quickly thrown together potlucks. I remember watching TV and seeing families on those shows always gathered around a big table, enjoying all that food together. I wanted to be an honorary Walton." She laughed, and a bit of pink warmed her cheeks.

He grinned. "Well, if it makes you feel any better, I'll call you Riley Sue."

"Thanks, Quinn Bob."

He laughed outright at that. "If you're going to grab a shower, you might want to do it now. I'll put a plate together for you."

"Okay." she said, grinning, too. "Thanks." But she didn't make a mad dash to the shower. She stood right where she was for a few moments longer. As soon as she moved, he took her arm in a gentle hold and turned her back to face him.

"Everything okay?"

"Amazing." There was nothing about the last hour and a half that had been anything short of that. And she had a lot more than hot sex to base that judgment on.

"But?"

She dropped her chin, which he lifted right back up. "You always do that," she said.

"What, not letting you hide? Or wanting to know what's bugging you?"

"No, reading my mind so you know there's something bugging me in the first place."

"More of my godlike skills." He offered her a crooked grin. When she didn't smile back, his faded. "Come here."

"I should really —"

"Come here, is what you should really do." He gently cupped her head and tilted her face up to his. "Did I do something wrong?"

Another part of her simply melted. "No. You're everything that's right."

"Too much still?" His gaze searched hers and she realized that maybe he needed reassurance as much as she did.

That it mattered to him, that she mattered, did reassure her . . . even as it made her nervous. "I —" she began, then faltered, not sure how to put her thoughts into words.

She was falling in love with him.

"We probably should have waited," he said, "given everything else. We should have spent more time getting to know each other with our clothes on first."

That got a spontaneous laugh from her. "You might be godlike in many ways, but neither of us is superhuman. Given what happened this morning — and in your foyer, and on the beach — just how long would we have been able to hold out?"

"Well" — a teasing light came into his beautiful blue eyes — "when you put it that way. We were simply victims of the primordial order of things. There was nothing else to be done but surrender to the inevitable."

"Something like that," she said with a wry smile. "Maybe that's the way the whole thing is going to be with us. Explosive and primordial and completely incapable of going at any other speed than full tilt." She paused, and dipped her chin.

After a moment he very gently tilted it back up again until their eyes met.

"So, yes. It's still too much," she said softly. "But I'd rather have too much, too fast, than nothing at all."

"I don't know if this helps, but it feels that way to me, too.

It's all a new roller-coaster ride for me. So, hell yes, it's too much right from the starting gun. But you're right. I'd rather hurry and play catch-up than ditch the ride altogether."

Her lips curved.

"What is that smile all about?" he asked.

"What a pair we are, Quinn Brannigan."

He leaned down and kissed the tip of her nose. "Finally," he teased. "That's what I've been trying to tell you all along." Gathering her in his arms, he kissed her the way a man did when maybe, just maybe, he was falling, too.

CHAPTER 19

"It's coming along really well, Dad." Quinn stretched his feet out on the deck in front of him as he leaned back in his chair for leverage, and launched the huge stick toward the pergola. Brutus dutifully watched it hurtle and fall into a large palmetto, then hauled his butt up and trotted over to retrieve it. Quinn shook his head and smiled, then shifted the phone to his other ear. "It's a departure from what I've been doing, so I'm excited and a bit nervous to see how it will be received."

"Sounds good," his father said, which was the same response he'd have given if Quinn had told him he'd decided to paint his body blue and jump out of a plane. "I've got a meeting. Good to catch up."

"Yes, Dad, you, too. Love you," he said as his father signed off. His father wasn't comfortable with expressing emotions, or receiving them. He was a policy wonk on

Capitol Hill, which suited his sober, serious nature and allowed him to avoid pretty much all emotional ties. If his dad didn't regularly play racquetball and golf, most often with a small group of guys who dated all the way back to his far more social frat days, Quinn would worry about him more. But, all in all, he seemed content with the status quo. Quinn knew his father loved him, and he figured his dad could put up with hearing it expressed occasionally from his son.

He looked over his shoulder into the breakfast nook off the kitchen. Still a busy beehive of activity going on in there. Baxter and Lani were baking up a storm, along with a handful of assistants; then there was the art director, the photographer, Riley, and who knew who else. They were finishing up principal photography for a glossy booklet that would be stuffed in bags and handed out at huge, regional cooking shows around the country.

Quinn laid his phone on the side table next to his closed laptop. He'd been on the boat earlier, but had decided to come back here. It was a gorgeous day, above average temperature, but no humidity, so he figured he'd camp out in the pergola and enjoy the perks of making his living on a mobile device. He heard a squeal, then something crashed, but he didn't turn around. He smiled to himself and leaned down to pick up the slobber-covered log Brutus has deposited. "Ten-to-one your mom just busted something expensive," he told the dog, who offered a baleful stare in return. "I know. That's what I said." Laughing, Quinn launched the log across the back yard again, and watched as Brutus made his slow and steady trek toward it.

Quinn had come to have a great appreciation for the way Brutus observed life. He was all for balance and not sweating the small stuff, which the mammoth dog seemed to have down to a science. "It doesn't hurt that you get regular meals and lots of love from a beautiful woman. I'd take that life."

Quinn's cell phone chirped and he picked it up.

That wasn't my fault.

He grinned, but before he could text Riley back, another one came through.

This time.

Brutus returned and dropped the log, then sat and let his tongue loll to the side as he stared at Quinn. The tongue lolling meant he'd had enough of the game. Quinn reached in his pocket and pulled out one of the superdog-size Milk-Bones he'd stashed away there, tossed it into the gaping maw that was Brutus's mouth, then watched with bemused pleasure as the dog sank into a boneless heap and munched on his treat, as if it were nothing more than his due. He picked up his phone again, smiled . . . and typed out a message.

What are you wearing?

A moment later: You're such a guy. And then: Thank God.

Come out and play with me.

I can't. I'm drizzling glycerin all over the top of this nice, plump red cherry so it looks all sticky and sweet.

You play dirty.

And sticky, she wrote back, which made him bark a laugh out loud. It even startled the dog.

Fine, fine. Me and Brutus will just sit out here in the garden and eat worms.

Nothing came back after that, which meant she was busy making pastry look naturally sumptuous by using a blowtorch, or motor oil, or spray deodorant. Who knew what? As she'd explained it to him, under the unrelenting heat of the lights, hot foods still cooled, cool foods grew warm, frozen foods melted, greens wilted, and moist foods went dry.

It wasn't enough to keep fresh duplicates on hand to swap out. Staging one individual dish could take hours all by itself, so swapping wouldn't work. Good stylists learned all kinds of tricks to sustain and extend the original look of the food by using a few less than natural — or even edible — items to create the necessary illusions.

She'd caught him looking through her Supergirl Tool Belt the other day after climbing out of the shower, and — after copious curious monkey comments — had given him quite the education on how stylists made the food in those magazines and print ads look so luscious. She almost put him off chocolate sauce for life.

He tossed the phone back on the table, and stretched his legs out again. He'd told himself he'd come back to the bungalow to work, and let Brutus have a bit of a romp, but he knew he'd come back so he could be closer to Riley. He missed her — which was kind of crazy, since they'd shared their mind-blowing, life-altering morning together only two days ago. At least, that was how he'd viewed that morning in the grand scheme of things.

They'd spent zero time alone together since. Not all her fault. Or his. She'd gotten hung up that day through the evening and into the wee hours planning the initial shoot with Baxter, Lani, and the art director. The following morning she went back to Savannah, frantically searching for specialty gadgets she needed for the first shoot and ordering the rest of the equipment she'd need.

He'd likely passed her on her way back to Sugarberry, as he'd had to go into Savannah to meet with a producer and screenwriter who'd been dogging him for rights to his current release. David had tried to keep them at bay, but when they'd offered to bring the meeting to him, Quinn had finally agreed to have a dinner meeting and be done with it. That dinner meeting had gone to the wee hours. In the end, though, it had been worth it for all parties involved.

He'd come back to the bungalow after the meeting instead of going to the houseboat, thinking he would just show up with breakfast at the boat in the morning and see if he could start their day in the same spectacular fashion he had two days before.

He'd zonked out and slept straight through his alarm. By the time he'd gotten himself together and out the door, the vans were already pulling in for the day's shoot. Riley showed up right behind them, leaving little time for any private conversation.

She'd told him the boat was his as long as he wanted, that they'd definitely be running long that day, and apologized for being so rushed. Someone had called her name and off she'd dashed. He hadn't even given her a kiss good morning. Or gotten one.

The desire for her kiss had hovered over and around the edges of his mind the entire morning as he tried to write. He'd managed to pull a few decent pages out of his distracted brain, then had spent another hour digging into some research about horses for the book, but had finally given up and decided maybe he'd get his concentration back if she were at least within viewing distance.

"So much for that, big guy. Right? At least we have modern technology on our side now."

Brutus responded by heaving his weight to his side and stretching his legs out more fully as the late afternoon sun warmed his half-exposed underbelly.

Quinn smiled to himself as he admitted that he'd developed a whole new appreciation for the connective powers of text messaging. He might not have spent any alone time with Riley in two days, but since she'd hopped off the houseboat that morning with his cell number in her back pocket, they hadn't been apart-apart for more than a few hours at a time. They hadn't used their phones for actual talking yet. With her being on set or him being in that meeting almost the whole time, they hadn't been able to.

Tapping out secret little messages to each other tickled some other place inside him that he was coming not only to appreciate, but to enjoy as its own, separate way of having fun with her. There was a kind of passing-notes-in-class, breaking-the-rules vibe to it that felt a little naughty and rebellious.

"I promise this tastes better than worms."

Startled, he looked up to find Riley standing over him with the most amazing, piled-high version of a napoleon he'd ever seen.

She had her hair pulled up in a messy knot on her head. Glasses he didn't know she wore were shoved up into the tangle of curls. Her face was flushed, he supposed from the heat of the kitchen and the lights. She was wearing what he'd come to think of as her standard uniform — loose khakis, long tee, with an open camp shirt thrown over it. The new addition of her Supergirl Tool Belt was slung low around her hips, but he wasn't really paying attention to that. Or the amazing napoleon, for that matter.

The way the breeze caught and lifted the front panels of her camp shirt away from her body, revealing just how perfectly the long tee hugged her amazingly beautiful breasts, made his body stir. He'd had those breasts under his thumb, under his tongue, between his lips . . .

He groaned under his breath and reached out to pluck off the cherry from the top of the dessert, then dragged it through the thick and foamy frosting. It wasn't going to come close to the taste of her bare breasts, but it would make a decent second choice. He paused with the treat halfway to his open and waiting mouth and lifted a single brow in question.

She raised her hand, palm out. "I swear, no glycerin has been used in the making of this dessert."

He plopped the cherry in his mouth, then closed his lips over it and groaned. Still not naked nipples, but . . . "My God," he said, his mouth still full. "That's amazing."

She set the plate down on his side table, along with silverware tucked inside a rolled linen. "Don't talk with your mouth full."

"Okay." Still savoring the last of the frosting, he elicited a squeal from her when he tugged her down across his lap. "You can keep me from talking for a few minutes."

"My tools," she cried out, as various things jangled and clanked.

"Will be fine. I have a big lap." He pulled her in for a long and languorous exploration. The kiss was heady and sweet and better than any napoleon could hope to be.

When he finally lifted his head, her eyes were dazed and sparkly, and he suspected his might look the same.

She smacked her lips. "You taste yummy and creamy."

He grinned. "Bring a few pieces of that back to the boat and I'll make you taste yummy, too."

Her eyes went dark and he was pulling her back down for another round, when he spied the rather large bandage on her elbow. He lifted her arm up in front of them. "What happened?

"It's nothing, just a scrape, and before you mock me —"

"I would never mock." He leaned down and pressed a kiss next to the bandage. "I understand my role here is to kiss the boo-boos, confirm that it really wasn't your fault" — he reached down beside him and fished blindly in his leather computer bag, then brandished a small box in front of her — "and provide copious quantities of cartoon character Band-Aids."

The way her expression instantly softened, as if he'd given her flowers, or diamonds, for that matter, made him glad he'd given in to the impulse. He'd hoped she'd be amused rather than offended.

"You're such a guy, though."

"A nice guy," he amended, handing her the box.

"Spiderman?" She offered him a wry grin. "Was your manhood threatened by getting Hello Kitty or Powderpuff Girls?" She tucked the pack in her toolbelt, but he didn't miss the sweet smile she privately allowed herself as she did.

"It was all they had. Well, it was that or plain brown, and on your lovely skin, a plain brown wrapper simply wouldn't do."

She laughed. "Well, I appreciate your attention to aesthetics and I take it all back."

He slid his palm along the back of her neck, nudging her closer again.

"The whole crew is still in there. I have to get back," she cautioned.

"You know, I didn't get the chance to kiss you good morning earlier."

"That's true. I don't guess you did. But we just kissed two seconds ago. Doesn't that count?"

He shook his head. "You have to call it first. Official make-up-kiss rule." His smile stayed in place, but he caught her gaze and held it intently. "I missed getting to do that." He reached up and traced a finger along her lower lip, following the motion with his eyes, then lifting his gaze back to hers. "I missed you." He felt a fine tremor shiver through her, and his body responded with equal enthusiasm.

"Boy" — her voice was a little shaky, though she was striving for casual and light — "give a guy a nooner before breakfast and he gets all needy on you."

"Spectacular as that was" — he traced her upper lip, delighting in the way her body instantly responded — "I've missed you every day since I met you." That was the simple truth of it. She hadn't left his thoughts since the day she'd first entered them. He leaned in and replaced his fingertip with his lips, taking her mouth softly, sweetly, working hard to get a grip on the more ferocious needs that ignited the instant he tasted her again. "And I missed kissing you," he said against her lips, "before I ever tasted you."

She sighed, and he felt her body relax and soften on his. He continued the slow, steady exploration, urging her to open to him, languidly sliding his tongue into her mouth. Both moaned as he coaxed her tongue into his mouth, then pulled it in more deeply.

He kept his hand cupped on the back of her neck as she lifted her mouth from his, keeping her close, in the intimacy of the moment they'd created. "Good morning."

She smiled at him, and it wasn't just the obvious parts of his body that responded to the affection and light that entered her eyes. He also felt a tightening in his chest and throat. And he couldn't stop the thought that he could easily stand to see that look in those eyes every single day for the rest of his life.

"Good morning," she responded. "I missed that, too. I'm sorry I didn't know about the rules sooner."

"Well, I would have told you that morning on the houseboat, but you went and distracted me with your wicked, wanton ways."

She laughed. "Right, because baggy shorts, a basketball jersey, and crazy bed head just shout *take me!* to a man."

"You don't need to shout," he said, pulling her mouth back to his.

"Why is it you always say the absolute perfect thing?" she asked, on a sigh against his lips.

"You forget, you're playing with a professional," he told her, making them laugh even as their mouths stayed fused together.

He shifted his kisses to the side of her jaw, then along the side of her neck. "You could be wearing a cardboard box with holes cut out for arms, and I'd still want to rip it off you."

She gave a mock shudder. "Ew. So would I." Then she surprised him by turning her head and catching his mouth with hers for a fast, hard kiss. "But I like your reasons much better." She lifted her mouth and leaned back.

"Not to intrude on the poolside canoodling here, but do you think maybe you could let her come back inside to work sometime soon?"

Startled by the close proximity of the new voice in the conversation, they jumped, but it was the poleaxed look on Riley's face that got Quinn's attention. He'd completely forgotten no one had seen them together yet. "Uh-oh," he whispered, though he was sure Lani could hear him. "Looks like Mommy and Daddy know you have a boyfriend." When Riley merely narrowed her eyes at him — though there was a distinct threat of a smile hovering around the corners of her mouth — he silently mouthed *sorry*.

Quinn glanced up at Lani, but kept his arm locked around Riley's waist. "Did you know that four out of five people on a survey I'm sure has been taken somewhere say workers who spend at least fifteen minutes a day canoodling perform at a much higher standard than those who don't?"

Lani's lips twitched. "I hadn't heard that. I'd have to do some independent research analysis on that, and get back to you."

Quinn looked at Riley. "I like her."

"Yeah," Riley said. "She makes it hard not to."

"In the meantime," Lani said, "could we have her return to her slave labor job?"

Quinn consulted his watch. "I believe we need at least three more minutes. You know, for optimal performance."

Lani gave him a dry smile. "We'll risk her being slightly subpar."

"You both realize I'm sitting right here."

"Oh, I'm very aware of where you're sitting," Quinn said, making Lani bark out a laugh. It had the unfortunate affect of startling Brutus from his doggie dreams.

Belying his more usual speed-of-sludge style, he heaved himself up, blinking and swinging his head around, as if looking for the source of the noise. He also heaved the top-heavy deck chair over, sending both of its occupants directly into the pool.

428

Quinn reached instinctively for Riley, and pushed her to the surface first, following her a second or two later.

Lani was standing poolside, hands on her hips, with a very innocent-looking Brutus sitting ever-so-politely beside her. "You know, some people will do anything to get their extra three minutes." She grinned. "Of course, if it cools off some of the steam rising off that deck chair when I came out, then maybe it's for the best. Kitchen's hot enough."

Quinn guided Riley to the edge so she could hold on while scraping a mass of wet blond curls from her face. "I lost my scrunchie."

"I hate it when that happens." Quinn smiled when she stuck her tongue out at him. "Careful where you aim that thing," he warned, then helped her pull her heavy, wet hair away from her face.

"I'm pretty sure no one has seen me so consecutively at my worst, ever. This is now officially a record."

"You look like a mermaid with bed head." He leaned in and kissed her smiling mouth.

"Oh my God," Lani said. "You're soaking wet and still there's steam. I'm surprised there's not fog over the water. Not that anyone is listening to me."

"I am," Riley said. "Just let me find my way out of this pool with a tiny shred of dignity, if that's possible. This tool belt weighs a ton wet and it's possible I may have a serious wardrobe malfunction with my pants as I try to exit the pool area."

Quinn scooted behind her. "I believe I can be of some assistance with that."

"Oh, brother." There was laughter in Lani's voice. "I'm going back inside before I see things I don't need to be seeing. Still in public!" she called out in a dead-on impression of Charlotte as she headed back to the house.

"Says the woman who is the cause of all Charlotte's constant admonitions," Riley shouted back.

Lani turned at the French doors and sketched a bow. "I may be the reigning queen of Kingdom Gettaroom, but I believe you may be in the running to topple my crown." She waved her hand in a swirly motion in front of her forehead as she bowed. "Sim-salah-bim. Now please get your most excellent, wet royal fanny inside as soon as you can. The semifreddo is melting . . . melting." Wavering the last word, she cut loose with a fairly excellent Wicked Witch of the West cackle as she ducked inside.

"Her skill set is even broader than one

would imagine," Quinn stated, staring at the closed patio door.

"You have no idea. Whatever you do, don't get her started on boy bands of the nineties."

"You don't like boy bands? Huh. I'll make a note of that. No impromptu Backstreet Boys medleys under the moonlight during our naked time dinner cruise."

Quinn had guided them to the set of wide stone steps leading out of the small pool, but Riley turned back. "The fact that you're even aware of who the Backstreet Boys are is disconcerting and oddly hot."

Quinn leaned down and put his mouth close to her ear and sang the first two lines of the chorus from "I Want it That Way."

Riley clamped a hand over her mouth, whether to stifle peals of laughter or utter shock, he couldn't be certain. Her eyebrows probably would have climbed just as high either way. She flung her arms around his shoulders, bussed his cheek with a loud kiss, and whispered in his ear, "If you ever sing that to me while we're in bed, I will either die in sure-to-be mood-killing laughter . . . or you'll be able to have me any way you want me. I can't decide."

"I'm thinking it might be worth the risk just to find out."

She caught his gaze, and they snorted. Quinn put his hand over his heart as if he were about to break out into song again, which sent Riley into snickering peals of laughter. They were full-out laughing as they dragged their wet, soggy selves from the pool. Water ran from her tool belt like its own miniature waterfall.

She looked down and pouted. "It took me a full day of hunting to find all my special Supergirl stuff."

Quinn looked down at the soggy nylon pockets. "If you give me a list, I'll be happy to help out. I've got some time tomorrow." Frowning, he reached in and pulled out a package that read ICE POWDER. He looked at her and lifted his eyebrows.

She wiggled hers in response and snatched it back. "If you're really nice to me, I'll show you a few of its many uses. Only some of which are for photographic purposes."

Grinning, he impulsively hooked his hand on the front of her tool belt, tugged her against him, and dropped a hard, fast kiss on her mouth.

"What was that for?" Riley asked, looking a bit dazed.

"My life is so much better with you in it."

She chuckled. "Yes, well, it's not every man who dares to live in Calamityville."

He framed her face. "Actually, I meant that." He dropped a softer, sweeter kiss on her lips. "Before you say anything, or get nervous, I just mean you make me happy, that's all." Worried he'd pushed a little too much, he said, "Let's get inside. I'm sure I have something you can pull on. At least you'll be dry. I know you have work to do."

Inside was only a notch or two below utter and complete chaos. He brought down an old sweatshirt and sweatpants for her to change into, but that was the last he saw of her until the chefs and crew packed up shop on the far side of midnight.

By half past twelve, he'd gone upstairs after texting her to come find him to say good night before she left.

He woke up when he heard the vans backing out of the drive. Thinking Riley would show up at his door shortly, he debated the relative merits of talking her into staying with him, if for no other reason than it was the more expedient route to getting some sleep after what he knew had been a very, very long day for her.

He heard another vehicle engine start up, and managed to look out his bedroom window in time to see her pull out, with Brutus enthroned in the passenger side of the Jeep.

He glanced at the clock, and saw it was just after two in the morning. He supposed he couldn't fault her for not coming up and disturbing him. She'd likely assumed he'd gone to sleep. He checked his phone. No text from her, either. He'd never thought of himself as a pouter, but he pushed out his bottom lip a bit right then.

He didn't like his chances of getting right back to sleep, so he went downstairs to grab a bottle of water. He was more than a little stunned to see that what had looked like the aftermath of a nuclear bomb the last time he'd popped his head in had been restored to his nice, clean kitchen. There were still cables, lighting, and cameras everywhere, but the immediate cooking area was spotless.

"Well done," he murmured, in what he thought wasn't a bad Baxter Dunne imitation. He'd come to know the famous chef fairly well in the brief time he'd been loaning out his kitchen to him. Baxter was a likable guy, as tall as Quinn, with an effortless kind of affable charm, but there was also an intense edge about him. Quinn supposed it was the latter that had made him the rock star chef he was.

Quinn had enjoyed the few chats they'd had, and had been surprised to find they had a lot more in common than he initially thought. Not just the books, and dealing with various aspects of celebrity — though Baxter dealt with way more than Quinn did — but also making adjustments to life on Sugarberry after city dwelling for a long time. Not to mention their involvement with two of the island's more prominent citizens. In Baxter's case, he'd married her and was now a full-time resident himself.

Quinn wondered how inappropriate it would be to ask Baxter if he had any advice where Riley was concerned. He didn't regret the comment he'd made to Riley by the pool, about his life being better with her in it. He wished he knew how to convey those happy feelings without making her nervous. He was probably overthinking it, just as she had said they both had a tendency to do. Of course, he probably wouldn't be having wee-hour musings at all if she'd left him some kind of good night message.

"Oh yes, old chap, you're in veddy, veddy deep, indeed." He popped open the door to the fridge, and spied the bone-in roast he'd optimistically moved from the freezer that morning to thaw. The stray thought that he'd better save the bone for Brutus had him shaking his head. "Deep end, deep," he murmured. Unlike Riley . . . the nerves he felt about where their relationship might be heading bred more excitement and anticipation than any sort of dread or concern. Standing in front of the open fridge door in the wee hours of the morning, he knew he was in for the duration.

It wasn't some revelatory epiphany. It was thinking about that spontaneous kiss by the pool, and what had motivated him to do it. His life *was* better with her in it. He was happy. Deep-down happy in a place he didn't even know existed. She made him happy.

It was that simple.

He had to hope and trust that Riley would give herself a chance to get to that same place.

That's when he found the note.

Grinning so broadly he thought he'd pull a facial muscle, he plucked the small, handwritten note off the top of the carton of eggs, which was stacked on top of the pound of bacon he'd bought at the market the day before. He straightened as he scanned what she'd written.

I didn't want to wake you. I was thinking maybe a round of pirate and wench at sunrise? I'll bring the pirate ship. Your job is to bring our hearty apres-pillaging repast. Oh, and I call dibs on the good night kiss we missed. And where to deliver it. It could have something to do with my tongue being forced to walk a certain . . . plank. Hope you dreamed good stuff, matey. Har har.

— Riley

"I don't have to dream it," he murmured, his heart tripping right over the edge into that fast slide straight into love. He closed the refrigerator door and shuffled back upstairs to bed, note still in hand. He propped it on his nightstand where he'd see it first thing when he opened his eyes, and buried his stupid-grin smiling face into his pillow. "I'm living the good stuff."

CHAPTER 20

Riley woke up to the heavenly smell of bacon, decided she was clearly still dreaming, and rolled back over so she could enjoy it a little longer, delaying the harsh reality of the cold, dry breakfast cereal that actually awaited her. But, snuggling in more deeply, she still smelled bacon. Then she abruptly sat up. *The note!* Bacon, eggs . . . and a pirate.

She grinned. "Har har, indeed." She hadn't known if Quinn would see the note, much less in time to do anything about what it said. She looked down at the baseball jersey and pajama pants she'd dragged on when she'd come home in the middle of the night to a chilly stateroom. "Not exactly wenching clothes."

Of course, bacon was already on the griddle, so perhaps there would be no time for pillaging. They were apparently going straight to the hearty après pillage repast

438

portion of her proposed morning's activities. She pushed her hair out of her face and checked the clock. Seven. Fortunately call time had been moved back to eleven that morning, as Lani had no one to cover Cakes by the Cup. She had to open the shop until Alva was done with her weekly set and starch (as Lani privately called it) at Cynthia's. Of course, Quinn probably didn't know that.

Hmm. A slow smile spread across her face as she wondered what Quinn's schedule looked like that morning. And just what kind of wenching attire she could throw together in hopes of enticing him into a bit of raid and pillage.

She slid her feet out of the covers and over the side of the bed, felt the cold air, and pulled them right back in, deciding wardrobe planning would be better undertaken while staying warm and tucked in.

She stilled when she thought she heard something coming from the galley that sounded like . . . She grinned. Quinn was singing. Not loudly, but still. She strained to make out the tune, then covered her face with a pillow so she could laugh out loud when she heard him bust out the refrain to New Kids on the Block's "The Right Stuff."

She flopped back with the pillow still on

her face, but found herself wiggling her hips in the tangle of sheets as the song flooded her mind. "Oh, oh, oh," she sang along. Flinging the pillow aside, she took a full slide into the second refrain, singing a heartfelt, "All that I needed was you!"

"Ahoy, matey," came a deep voice from the door.

She slammed the pillow back on her face, immediately starting to snicker, which led to full-out laughter.

A second later the pillow was gently peeled back from her face, sending her into a fresh peal of laughter when she spied Captain Jack Quinn looming over her, complete with handmade black patch strapped over one eye and red bandana wrapped around his head.

"If it's dancin' in the sheets ye wanted" — he gave it his best Jack Sparrow — "I believe I can be of some assistance." He tossed the pillow aside. "But first, let me usher my worthy sidekick to his observation post off the portside bow."

He straightened and glanced to the side, drawing her gaze downward . . . where it landed on Brutus, who was also sporting an eyepatch. A bandana bowtie was attached to his collar.

"They were out of parrots at ye olde pirate

shoppe," Captain Quinn offered by way of explanation when she lifted her gaze to his in openmouthed disbelief.

"I can't believe he let you do that."

Brutus looked up at Quinn, and his tongue lolled to one side.

"Okay. Yes, I can." Riley flopped back on the bed, the laughter making her breathless. "First pirates who sing sea chanteys complete with a solid bassline and synchronized dance moves, and now this. I've no restraint left." She flung one arm wide and the other dramatically over her eyes. "Have your wicked, wanton way with me, Captain Quinn. I know I've stirred your manly ardor with my wicked, wanton attire."

She cracked one eye open and spied Quinn sliding off Brutus's patch and nudging him out the stateroom door, which he promptly closed behind him. A moment later, they heard a thud, indicating Brutus had parked himself in his standard boneless heap just outside the door.

Quinn turned back to Riley. "No one can save you now, my pretty." She felt his weight on the side of the bed a moment later. "And if it's restraints ye be wantin' . . ."

She lifted her arm slightly to look at him. "Wait —"

He just grinned, and reached for his patch.

She grinned. "Leave it on."

"Aye aye, Cap'n," he said, and rolled on top of her.

He pushed her hands over her head, pinning them down as another breathless laugh escaped her. But that laughter quickly faded as he ran his hands down her arms, and straight over her breasts. She moaned and arched up hard against him as his fingers closed over her nipples.

"Oh, aye. A wench ye are indeed." He slid down and shoved her shirt up . . . and suddenly things shifted from light and funny to lusty and hot. He suckled one nipple and tore her shorts off as she yanked the white linen shirt he'd worn, thankfully open to the waist, from the waistband of his pants. In seconds she was naked and he was pulling on the buckle of his belt and dropping his pants on the floor.

She drove greedy hands into his hair and dragged his mouth to hers as he fell on top of her, parting her legs with the weight of his body. They growled as she shoved her tongue in his mouth just as he yanked her thighs up high on his hips and drove into her.

It was hot and wild. His mouth never left hers and he plundered it in the same rhythm and thrust as he plundered her. She didn't even try to keep from shouting as she came . . . and neither did he.

He collapsed on top of her while still throbbing inside her. She shuddered in the throes of rippling aftershocks. They were breathing so hard, neither could speak. He finally rolled off, tugging her hard against him, her body half splayed across his torso and legs as they dragged air into greedy lungs.

With her cheek pressed against the damp, hot skin of his chest, she felt his hands slide into her hair, stroking, toying. He tucked her foot around his ankle, and slid his other arm over the small of her back. Little things, instinctive things, they were the things that made her know he was always aware of her. Always. And he wanted her to know it.

She slid her hand up his chest, and cupped her palm to the side of his face. That was all, just pressed it there. With a little tilt of her head, she pressed a kiss over his heart. Because she wanted him to know it, too.

As their pounding hearts slowed along with their rapid intake of breath, he let the fingers that were teasing the ends of her hair wander slowly, lightly, across the tops of her shoulders, then traced a path along the length of her spine.

She moved the hand cupping his cheek so

her fingers could slide into his thick hair, toy with it, tracing her fingertips around the shell of his ear.

And slowly her body began to stir all over again as she felt his begin to do the same.

Silently, wordlessly, he eased her to her back. Pushing her hair from her cheeks, he caught her gaze. The patch was gone, and his eyes were like blue crystals, dark and flashing, belying the exquisite gentleness of his touch and the protective way he sheltered her body with his own.

He cupped her face, and she felt the finest of tremors shaking his fingers. He tipped her mouth up to his, keeping his gaze locked on hers as he lowered his lips. The intensity was something she'd never seen in him before. When he kissed her it was as if her body, her mind . . . her heart — everything she was, or had ever wanted to be — opened to him. He'd laid her utterly bare, but in doing so, had bared himself to her as well.

As he took the kiss deeper, she gave herself over to him. In what was the most intimate act she'd ever experienced, it was the most vulnerable, honest, and elemental way she knew how.

He finally moved on top of her, and took her slowly, almost reverently. His rhythm was steady, powerful, claiming . . . just as it was nurturing, compelling, protective. He took her up, higher, sweeter. The only sounds were her gasps, as he took her right to the brink, and kept her there, winding slowly, ever tightening, until she thought she'd splinter into a thousand pieces if he didn't give her release — which was exactly when he jerked her gently over the edge. Pleasure cascaded through her like a waterfall, gently flowing until it went thundering over the edge and into the abyss.

He kissed her again, framing her face as he pushed deeper, and harder, and she could feel his heartbeat, thundering like her own, pressed against her.

"Riley." He said just the one word, the only word he'd spoken. She locked her gaze on his as he pushed one last time, hard, deep, and claimed her mouth as his body bucked, shuddered, and shook.

And that, she thought as she wrapped herself around him, holding the weight of him on top of her and him inside her, was how you made love.

They drifted, slept, and when she finally opened her eyes fully again, it was to discover at some point he'd pulled the covers over them. Quinn was on his back with her curled against him, her head on his chest, her leg entwined between his. His arm around the small of her back held her to him, and his other hand was tangled in the lengths of her hair as it draped across his chest.

His steady, even breathing didn't change as she slowly came awake, and she knew he was still deep in sleep. Staying where she was, which was right where she wanted to be, she let her thoughts wander where they would.

She closed her eyes and listened to the beat of his heart. *Well, you don't have to wonder if he's capable of being vulnerable with you.* She had no idea where that thought had come from. Maybe the intensity of their first time had left them with nothing to protect their more vulnerable selves.

She didn't know what she was feeling. But she knew she was herself with him, utterly and fully, all the time, in every moment they shared. And that apparently wasn't going to change.

She realized her ability to be so relaxed with him, so herself, was because she'd never had to strategize, or worry, or plan. She might wish she'd not been a klutz here or a dork there, but it went far deeper than that. At first that had been scary, had made her feel exposed, like her guard was con-

446

stantly down. Thinking about it, she realized it wasn't because she was stripped bare of her defenses . . . it was because she had no need of them.

If she could purely be her true self there was nothing to defend, no inner part to protect. That begged the question . . . protect against what? What had she been so afraid of? Jeremy hadn't been harsh or critical. She had wondered what his true thoughts or feelings were at times, but he'd never overtly made her feel defensive.

She thought more about that. Though it might seem odd or wrong to be thinking back over personal times, intimate times, spent with one man, while lying in bed in the arms of another, it wasn't. She was so comfortable, relaxed, at peace, she could finally peel back some of those painful layers and put aside the hurt brought on by betrayal. She could finally look at what her life had been then in a more rational, objective, maybe even impersonal, way.

It was true that Jeremy had been somewhat picky about certain things — particular, he called it. She had known there had been a certain amount of passive-aggressive manipulation on his part, to get what he wanted from her. But it had been so benign. She was, by nature, a pleaser, and she'd loved him, and he'd loved her, so she'd never thought of it as anything other than what someone does when they're in a relationship.

With the luxury of dispassionate hindsight, she played back moments, and comments, reactions, interactions. Patterns of behavior began to emerge. Not just his, but hers as well. She'd never really asserted her opinions or her wants with him. She'd been so happy to be part of that pair her focus had been on making it a happy, joyful world to exist in. If she'd been asked then, she'd have said she had everything she wanted. If he was happy, so was she. Certainly, he had habits that annoyed her, routines that didn't mesh with hers, opinions she didn't share, but those were all things she knew were just part of their yin and yang. It was normal. What wasn't necessarily normal, and what she saw now, was while Jeremy wasn't the type to directly point out her flaws or shortcomings as he saw them, he found a way to make it known to her that maybe it would be better — for her — if she changed this, or did that.

Even that was part and parcel of a relationship. She didn't have to make any of those adjustments, though she always had. Making him happy had brought her joy. But, she realized, she'd never let him know about those same sorts of little things that bugged her. Not because she'd been afraid of making him angry. He was the most even-tempered person she knew. She had loved that about him, in fact. It had made her feel safe and secure knowing he'd never fly off the handle. No, that wasn't it at all.

She realized she hadn't pushed any of those opinions, or wants or needs at him, because she'd suspected he wouldn't have been moved to do for her what she so happily and willingly did for him. It wouldn't have mattered to him. Making her happy in that way was not something that motivated him, especially if it meant doing something he didn't want to do.

She'd been so busy making both of them happy, and maintaining the status quo, it had never occurred to her he wasn't really having to do much of anything. She'd felt needed by him, vital to his happiness. She supposed she had been, but not in the way she'd thought, or the way she should have been.

It wasn't until the images and memories finally began to coalesce into an accurate picture of what their lives had really been that she understood the real, painful truth: he'd never loved her. Of course, it might have been the only way he knew how to be a partner, how to love. What did that say? What she saw so clearly was that he hadn't loved her the way she'd assumed he had, or in the way she'd counted on him to. Much less the way she'd loved him.

What she'd thought of as their inseparableness had been Jeremy's neediness. He'd relied on her for everything. It had made her feel wanted. Strong. Equal. Loved. But when had he ever been there for her? Those times when he appeared to anticipate her needs, brought home dinner — or got her a spa day — she saw that he was really serving his own needs.

That led her to a more personal, painful truth. She'd spent most of the time after their breakup wondering what had been lacking in her, where had she gone wrong, what hadn't she done right, or what did she need to improve about herself. The only person she'd been letting down and disappointing, whose love she hadn't been living up to . . . was her own.

What she'd needed to do to improve herself was, essentially, grow a pair. Value herself. Acknowledge she had needs that were at least as important as his. Stand up for herself. *Be* herself.

Somehow, somewhere along the way since

coming to Sugarberry, she'd become that woman. The woman she should have been, and should have lived up to, all along.

That woman wouldn't have put up with Jeremy's "particularness," at least not without asserting some "particularities" of her own. That woman would have seen through the affection and recognized it as clinginess. In fact, had she been then the woman she was right now, she'd never have fallen in love with Jeremy Wainwright in the first place.

Riley's eyes blinked wide open. *Wow.* When, exactly, had she stopped loving Jeremy? And how?

Had it come from finally making choices purely for her self? Had it come from making new friends, real friends? From gaining confidence in who she was, merely by getting up every day and being that person without having to make adjustments for any other person? On the heels of that realization was another revelation. While Jeremy definitely made it known what he expected from her, she realized she'd made a lot of personal adjustments in anticipation of what he'd want. That was entirely on her. Oftentimes, he'd never even asked. She'd made sure he didn't have to — which meant keeping expectations that, in essence, she'd created herself.

Not that Jeremy wasn't a complete and utter bastarde! for what he'd done to her, but if she'd been remotely the person she was now, she'd have seen through his bullshit so early on, he'd never have had a chance to pull that selfish stunt on her. She'd have dumped his self-centered ass long before.

She laughed silently at herself, wondering why on earth if felt so good to realize what a ridiculous, blind, needy, clinging dork she'd truly, truly been. Finally . . . she got it. She really got it. She knew exactly who she was. And therefore . . . who she'd never, ever be again.

That brought her to Quinn.

She shifted, propped her chin on his chest, and watched him sleep. Had he been part of the transformation? She knew the answer to that. And it was a relief. No. She'd already become who she needed to be, a better woman, a better friend. She'd done that for herself, no one else.

She thought about Quinn's words that day on the beach, about her valuing herself, trusting herself, and finally she understood what he'd been trying to tell her. She'd been that better woman. She just hadn't tried her new confidence out yet. He'd given her the chance to see herself for who she was now . . . and to put that newfound knowledge to work.

Just as her friendships with Lani and Char had helped her to see her value as a friend, Quinn had allowed her to realize her true value as a partner. He had been that final piece falling into place, showing her what a real partner was in return. It was what she'd seen with Lani and Baxter, Char and Carlo. Quinn was someone who would be there for her, see her for who she really was . . . and support that person. Maybe even love that person. He'd encouraged her, pushed her to believe in what he knew to be true, to believe she was the woman he was falling for. And trust that woman could handle falling right back.

And she had. Oh yes. Yes, indeed she had.

CHAPTER 21

Quinn had been awake for some time before he let Riley know about it. He lay there, almost hearing the singing of the wheels as they spun around, furiously, inside her head.

He wished like hell he knew where those spinning wheels were taking her. He couldn't see her face, so he had no easy gauge.

He hadn't forgotten a single, heart-searing moment of what they'd done together in that bed this morning, and he knew she hadn't either. It had been wild and raw, driving him so far past anything he'd experienced in the way of pure, unadulterated pleasure. They'd given themselves over to it with utter abandon and intensity, and had been amply and exhaustively rewarded.

He knew there was trust in that, to let go and to reach like they had. It wasn't just about heart-slamming, body-pounding sex. What they'd done was possible only because they'd given themselves to each other, trusting the other to match them shout for shout, thrust for thrust.

And then there was that second time . . . He squeezed his eyes more tightly shut against the sudden hot sting he felt as tears welled.

He loved her. Hard. Complete. Epic. It was his grandparents' love story. It was the reason Joe and Hannah's love story was thumping out of him. And it was going to be his own love story. . . . if he hadn't just scared the living bejesus out of her while he'd let everything bottled up inside him come pouring out in one steady flowing, never-ending stream of gushing emotion.

For the very first time, he understood the depths of the soul-chilling fear that had kept Riley from reaching for love again. It would hurt more than a little if she left him now, if she decided, nope, this wasn't going to be it for her.

She was it for him. If she walked away, she'd be ripping out everything that was good inside him, and taking it right along with her.

How did anyone go on after something like that? How did anyone even think such a risk was anything other than the most insane act they could ever willingly embark upon? Who in their having-ever-loved mind would put themselves in that place, knowing firsthand the risks they were taking?

Riley had, his little voice snuck in and whispered.

She had at that. She'd taken the initial leap. She might not land where he wanted her to, but the respect he had for how innately strong she truly was had grown to stratospheric heights as he'd lain in bed. He doubted he would ever be able to do the same.

It also gave him a new understanding of his father's choices. Riley might not understand what she'd done in moving forward, but Quinn understood it. His father had chosen the opposite of Riley. He'd chosen to completely close himself off from feeling anything for anyone. He'd turned inward, focusing on things meaningful to him, like his work, that he could walk away from at the end of the day.

Riley hadn't done that. She thought she'd closed herself off from risking her heart. But look what she'd done. She'd taken her dog and run away to hide, yes. But she'd made a home for herself here. Made friends, good friends. Made a place for herself in the community, cared for people, as they'd come to care about her. Started, in essence, the family that her fiancé's choices had robbed her of having. To take it one step further, she'd taken on a job that allowed her to turn house after house into home after home, to pour all of what she wanted into everything she did. He wondered if she realized that instead of closing any part of herself off, she'd put herself out there.

He hoped he'd have done the same. He thought about his life. He kept people at arm's length. Friends were casual, or more associates and peers than real buddies. He'd tried to reach out to his father; it wasn't that he didn't want family. The bottom line was, the people who presently had the deepest entrée to his personal life were on his payroll, for God's sake. Not that they hadn't developed an honest respect and affection for one another . . . but was that the best he could do when it came to building a family?

And there was Riley.

Maybe he'd just needed someone to show him the way. How to bridge the gap between himself and his father . . . to his grandparents.

Thank God for her all over again. He'd been correct, believing that when it was the right thing, it became more all on its own. Important and special, there was no other way for it to be. It was the most mysterious thing, and the simplest thing in the world to see — when he'd finally seen it.

What in the hell could he do so she'd love him back?

He felt her subtly shift her weight, and felt her gaze, even with his eyes still closed, steadily on his face. He debated on how to handle this morning. What he wanted to do was open his eyes and tell her he loved her, straight out. He realized that he was dying to tell her, to share it with her . . . as he did every other thing that happened as his days bumped along. She'd so swiftly become his friend and his lover, his companion and his cohort. How could he keep something so important from her?

He cracked one eye open, and her brown eyes were shining right into his. A smile immediately curved those beautiful, lush lips. Everything inside him relaxed.

Calm down, Brannigan. He had time. Thank God. No need to rush things and blow it. She was happy and smiling. That was enough. For now. He'd tell her when she was ready. He could wait for that. He'd waited his whole life, after all.

He opened his other eye and let himself enjoy the simple and exquisite pleasure of drinking his fill of her, understanding he was already half-buzzed on love.

"Morning, Cap'n," she said, all double dimples, and looking like the cat with the proverbial canary.

His grin was slower, but curved just as deeply. He lazily wrapped one of her blond curls around his finger and tugged her gently closer. "So" — the word came out as a gravelly drawl — "I can't wait to play doctor and naughty nurse."

She snorted a little giggle, which made him chuckle. "Can we take turns with the roles?"

He lifted his eyebrows, but pretended to give it some thought. "Okay. But candy stripes really aren't my color."

There was a scratching sound at the stateroom door.

Riley lifted a warning finger. "No stethoscope for Brutus. He'll just eat it."

Quinn laughed huskily. "So noted." He glanced at the clock. "Uh-oh. Somebody is really late for work." He lightly slapped her butt. "Naughty pirate wench."

"I didn't get the chance to tell you earlier, as you were too busy ravaging my lusty and voluptuous pirate booty. I don't have to be there until eleven."

"That might be the second best news I've had so far today. What say we go avail ourselves of that hearty repast?"

"That sounds heavenly. I'll take your pirate matey out there in the hall for his walk if you'll do the reheating."

"Deal."

She started to shift so she could sit up, but stopped and leaned down, kissing him, not on the mouth . . . but on his chest. Right over his heart. She looked up, and there was a spectacular shine in her eyes. "What was the first best news you've had today?"

All of his carefully laid plans went right up in smoke.

"That I love you."

She froze.

He closed his eyes. *Seriously, Brannigan?* The single most important thing, the *only* thing he had to get right, and —

"Good," she whispered.

He froze.

"Quinn."

He opened his eyes.

She was smiling, dimples winking, brown eyes dancing, freckled cheeks blooming pink. Her hair was a wild halo around her head. She had a Bullwinkle bandage on her elbow, and her massive dog was heavily snort-breathing under the bedroom door. "I didn't want you to have your eyes closed the first time I told you I loved you."

Suddenly it was the Fourth of July inside

his head, his heart, and he was pretty sure all over the universe as he knew it. He rolled her to her back, framed her face with his hands.

"You do." Making it more statement than question, he needed to make sure he hadn't gone to some parallel dimension in his head after blurting out his own admission. "You're sure?"

She placed her hand over his heart. "I, Riley Brown, love you, Quinn Brannigan, with my whole messed-up, beat-up, but resilient-as-all-hell heart."

"How?"

She spluttered a laugh. "*How?* What do you mean, how? Hopefully really, really well."

He tried to get his galloping heart and his even more unruly thundering thoughts under control. "It wasn't that long ago that you couldn't even —"

She touched his lips with her finger. "You helped me figure it out, to see who I'd already become. You pushed me, you believed in me, you badgered me . . . and this morning you loved me. At least that's what it felt like to me."

"It was. I am so head over heels in love with you."

Sudden tears sparkled on her lashes, but

the light in her eyes was a joyous one. "That's what I knew I wanted to get to. I watched you sleep this morning, and I thought over everything, and I have clarity now. I see what it was with Jeremy. What I was. And what I wasn't. I know who I've become, Quinn. A woman who wants to love and be loved, and who finally understands how. Then I looked at you . . . and realized I'm already there."

"Would you have told me? Had I not —"

"I don't know." He appreciated that truth. Because it helped him to believe the rest.

She smiled again. "Were you planning on telling me?"

"I wanted to. I wanted to shout it. But I wanted you to have time and space. I wanted you to be more sure. Of me. Of you."

"What happened?"

"You kissed my heart, and then you smiled at me with your heart in your eyes. When you asked me what the best news was, there was nothing to say but the God's honest truth. I couldn't *not* say it."

Her eyes grew extra shiny and the self-deprecating laughter that followed was sweet music. "I'm pretty sure that's what I would have done, too. But I'm glad you said it first."

"Sure, sure," he teased, "piggyback on." Just like that, everything slid back into place, that rhythm, that space they'd carved out just for the two of them, that only they understood, where only they existed.

"Look at it this way," she said. "You got to hear it like I did, all curled up in our bed, happy and satiated after an amazing morning of hot sex and wonderful lovemaking. Left up to me, you know I'd have probably blurted it out at the most inappropriate time, in God only knows what place, or in front of who knows who." She lifted her head, and kissed his mouth. Gentle, sweet, pure. "I'm glad we got to have it right here on our little pirate ship, just between the two of us."

A bellowing, door-rattling *woof* reverberated around the stateroom.

"Three of us," she amended, and they laughed.

"Can I tell you the third best news?"

"You don't have to be the one to take him for a walk?" Riley guessed.

Quinn rolled to his back and slid her on top of him. "You said our bed."

"Well, it is our bed. Wait, you don't think we're going to share it with —" She nodded to the door.

He barked out a laugh. "Uh, no. He can

463

sleep on the floor if he wants though." He nestled her more snugly on top of him. "I just liked that instead of yours and mine . . . there's an ours now."

"Yeah," she said, and leaned down. "Yours," she breathed, as she kissed him long and slow, bringing all those banked embers back to life. "Mine," she panted, sliding his hand down until it covered her breast, where he rubbed, rolled, tweaked.

He lifted her hips even as she started to do so herself, sliding her body down over his, until they were fully, completely joined.

"And ours," they said together.

Outside the door, Brutus rested his mighty head on his paws as he made himself more comfortable. He'd wait. It was okay. After all, he had a family to look after now.

With that in mind, he rolled slowly over to his side, letting out a long, sleepy sigh as he relaxed his back against the door. Yep. It was a job he planned to take very, very seriously. As laughter pealed on the other side of the door, and someone burst into song, he closed his eyes . . . and let his tongue loll happily to the side.

EPILOGUE

Riley glanced at the clock in Quinn's kitchen, and sidled over to the crystal cupcake display. Half past one in the morning. The poker tournament had finally wound down and was officially over. Thank God.

"Lost twenty bucks," Quinn said as he came in through the door from the deck.

"How'd that happen?" Riley eyed one of Lani's few remaining dark chocolate and raspberry cupcakes, but decided it was just too late to give in to temptation.

Quinn bent down and pressed a kiss to the side of her neck. "There was a pool going as to whether the police would be summoned before or after midnight. Person picking the closest time in a fifteen-minute interval wins."

"The police weren't here, were they? What did I miss?"

"Nothing," he said, turning her into his

arms. "That's why I lost the twenty."

"Ah," she said, smiling. "Sucker."

"Apparently." He leaned down and trailed his tongue along her jaw, to her ear. "And yet, you never seem to complain . . ."

As tired as she was, he stirred her body to life. She should be used to that by now. Or dead. She had no idea where their stamina was coming from. She figured it was a good thing they both had jobs to do or they might never wear clothes. Turned out naked sunset cruise time was pretty fun.

"How did that last part of the scene you were working on go?" she asked. "Did you get all the right info for the dressage stuff, for the horse show?"

"I did. Then they ended up not going."

"Why?"

He grinned. "Never could get them out of that damn hayloft."

"Ungrateful characters. After you did all that research."

He shrugged. "That's okay. It didn't suck to be me today, either way."

"Well, when you put it like that." Riley leaned up and kissed him. "Although I'm beginning to see a trend with this sucking thing and you, today."

"Day's not over either." Quinn plucked a cupcake from the display and dangled it in front of her. "Pirate's ship or knight's castle?"

"I'm so tired, I don't know if it's going to matter. So don't go dangling your . . . cupcakes at me."

"Still in public," Char sang as she swooped into the kitchen with another bag of trash.

Riley looked past Quinn's shoulder. "You said get a room, you didn't specify which one."

Quinn turned her around and pulled her back against him, looping his arms around her waist as he rested his weight on the breakfast nook table. Only Riley understood the real reason for his snuggled pose. It was presently pressed against her backside.

She wiggled, just slightly, and his arms tightened like steel bands. He leaned down and pressed a kiss near her ear. "Careful what you wriggle for," he whispered.

"Do you need a hand with that," Riley asked Char, then wriggled, just a tiny bit, once more.

"No, this is the last round."

"Outstanding menu," Quinn said to Charlotte, who was scooping up the last few disposable plates and cups and adding them to her trash bag. "The savory and the sweet. Please give my regards to Carlo. I'll pass the word to my agent and publisher. They often have to entertain at things like regional book-fairs, writers' conferences, that sort of thing, and are always looking for the best and most interesting."

Charlotte smiled. "Thank you. That's very kind." To Riley, she said, "Okay, we'll keep him." Adding the full trash bag to the ones already lined up along the wall, Char snatched up another empty tray and bustled to the door, at which point she glanced over her shoulder.

But Riley beat her to it. "It's only still in public because the public isn't leaving."

Quinn chuckled as Charlotte sailed out.

"She's just grumpy because her panky isn't here," Riley told him.

Char's catering service had been double booked at the eleventh hour. By stepping in and taking over a birthday celebration bash for one of the mayor's closest aides when his caterer backed out at the last minute, Char and Carlo were likely to get many other bookings, not to mention being owed a favor by the mayor. It meant Charlotte had run Alva's event, while Carlo had done the birthday party.

"What's a panky?" Quinn asked.

"Long story," Riley said, just as Dre hustled in with another loaded tray. Because of the double booking, she'd stepped in to help serve.

"She was dealing off the bottom," Dre was saying. "Hey, Riley. Hey, Quinn." Dre turned back to Franco as he came in behind her. "I saw her with my own eyes."

"No one said a word to her," Franco responded, and Dre leveled a look of disbelief at him. "Okay, fine," he went on, "but if Alva was dealing from the bottom, why wasn't Beryl getting better hands? Suzette took half the pot tonight."

"I said I saw her deal from the bottom. I didn't say she was any good at it. And, if you noticed, Beryl won the trip to Baxter's taping *and* one of Quinn's books."

"This is true."

Charlotte came in again. "This is the last of it." To Quinn, she said, "Are you certain you don't mind me coming back tomorrow to get all my stuff? Carlo is stuck in Savannah. The party is going way over, and I won't get our van back until —"

"It's fine, really," Quinn assured her. "Is there anything I can do to help?"

"No. I'll have some helpers with me tomorrow. We need to come get all the equipment for another event the day after tomorrow."

"It's an anti-versary party," Franco added.

"For a group of divorcees. Should be interesting."

"Interesting is certainly one word," Charlotte said. "Can you still drive me back tonight?"

"Of course, ma petite." He looked at Dre. "You ready?"

"As ever." Dre took off her Sweet and Savory server's jacket.

"You are godsends, both of you," Char said. She turned back to Riley and Quinn. "We leave you in privacy."

"You did good," Riley told her. "All I heard were raves."

"Except for old Mrs. Lauderberg," Dre added. "But considering she was sampling all the garnishes and not any of the actual food, I don't think that counts. She kept complaining how bitter everything was. I tried to tell her parsley snips weren't part of the serving menu, but she smacked my hand when I tried to take her plate." Dre examined the back of her left hand. "Turns out she wears a lot of rings. Heavy ones."

"Tough audience," Quinn offered.

"You said it."

Saying their good nights, they all headed to the door.

"We'll see ourselves out," Franco said.

Char was the last one out, then turned

470

back. "Oh, I almost forgot. When you see Lani tomorrow night — tell her I'm sorry I won't be there. I have to get all this transition and prep done, but let her know I think I have the perfect person for her to talk to."

Riley frowned. "About?"

"The mail-order business she's thinking about starting, as an adjunct to the cupcakery. Requests for mail orders keep flooding in every time the *Hot Cakes* road trip show is repeated. With Baxter being a constant draw to the area, and their joint cookbook coming out sometime next year, she thought it would be a good idea to get the mail-order division up and running. I'm surprised she hasn't said anything about it, with all the time you've spent working on the cookbook."

"She mentioned it. I just didn't realize she was going to move on it so fast."

"Well, only if they can find someone she can trust who can handle it, and hit the ground running. Anyway" — Charlotte fished in the pocket of her chef's jacket — "I'll just put her card here. Her name is Kit Bellamy."

"I'll make sure Lani gets it. I know she was bummed she couldn't be here." At one time, Riley had hoped she'd get sick so she could miss the tournament, but Lani actually had.

Char smiled. "Between you and me, I don't think she was that bummed."

Riley's eyes widened. "Are you saying she played hookey?"

"Maybe. Baxter got back from New York a day early. But you didn't hear it from me. Okay, I'm really leaving now." She looked at Quinn, then back at Riley. "Nice panky, I will give you that. Have a good night."

"What is it with this panky business?" Quinn said, barely waiting for the front door to close before he turned and neatly pinned Riley between him and the breakfast nook table behind her.

"No hanky-panky in the kitchen on club night unless everyone's hanky has a panky. Or something like that."

"Ah. That clears it right up."

"It made perfect sense at the time."

"So . . . I'm your official panky, am I?"

"That you are."

"Well, it's awfully convenient that we're in a kitchen. And you're the only hanky here."

"Hmm. You make a good point."

He pressed against her, and she grinned. "More than one, it would seem."

He lofted the cupcake again, then peeled the paper liner off with his teeth. "Did I mention that I'm plagued by this fantasy

I've had? It involves you, a cupcake, some amazing chocolate frosting . . . and me getting the chance to lick it off."

"Funny, sounds like I've heard that story before."

"All but the licking it off part."

She pretended to think about that. "No . . . that was definitely part of the story." A slow smile spread across her face. "At least that's how I remember it playing out. And I remembered it . . . a lot."

"Funny, so did I."

"Huh. What should we do about that?" she asked.

"I think we should compare stories. See how they . . . stack up."

"Hmm. I think you're the one who told me that writers should always show . . . not tell."

"It really is the best way." Quinn popped open the buttons down the front of her blouse one at a time with his free hand.

Riley looked down. "You're very good at that."

"I'm very motivated at the moment. I'm really good when I'm motivated." He pushed her back onto the table, her blouse sliding down her arms as she braced herself. He flipped open the front catch of her bra on the first try.

473

"I've noticed that." Her breathing started to hitch a little as he spread her legs with his thighs . . . and dragged his finger through the thick, dark chocolate ganache frosting.

"Now, in your version of the story did I paint the frosting on?" He drew his frosting covered finger down the center of her torso. "Or did I decorate the cupcake with a little . . ." He pressed the top of the cake onto her nipple, making her gasp.

"I — can't remember. Maybe . . . refresh my memory?"

Quinn pushed her all the way back on the table and leaned down over her, so he could retrace his actions . . . with his tongue.

"Still not sure," she managed, and earned a wicked chuckle as he lifted her hips off the table and slid pants and panties off.

"What time are you meeting Chuck to look at final brochure prints tomorrow?" he asked, as he reached for his pants buckle.

"Eight."

He grinned. "You might make that." Then he dipped her other nipple in frosting. "Or not."

She smiled up at him, then reached up and yanked him down on top of her. "I'll just blame it on the cupcakes."

In *Sweet Stuff,* Lani has Quinn and the rest of the Cupcake Club crew taste-test her newest creation, the Reverse Caramel Apple Cupcake. Just like a caramel apple, but with the caramel coating on the inside as filling. Now, this was a fictional cake — I just made it up — but it got me to thinking . . . hmmm . . . that *would* be yummy! So, as part of my ongoing research into all things cupcake, I set about figuring out how to make my own.

Naturally, the first step was to call my mom and find out if we had any great apple cake recipes in the family, and sure enough, we did! She sent me her Johnny Applesauce Cake recipe, which I adapted from loaf pans to cupcakes. Next, I had to figure out the caramel filling. I'm envisioning getting caramels and melting them, or using ice cream topping heated up — something like that. Color me surprised when I found out that you can make your own caramel. From scratch. I mean, of course *someone* had to make the first caramel at some point, but I thought it was kind of like Oreo cookies, i.e., you can't make them yourself. Wrong! You can. And I did! (And lived to tell!)

Of course, as soon as I saw words like "candy thermometer" and "360 degrees Farenheit," I immediately put my local hunky EMT on speed dial. Partly because, if you've read my cupcake research blog at www.cakesbythecupblog.com, you know that I've learned a local hunky EMT can come in really (really) handy at those times when you're trying not to blow things up or burn things down. And partly because, if you have a hunky EMT in your life for any reason, why not keep him on speed dial?

So, below is my "every baker" version of Lani's Reverse Caramel Cupcake. You don't even have to be a big-time fancy pastry chef to make them. Enjoy!

Reverse Caramel Apple Cupcakes

Johnny Applesauce Cake
1/2 cup butter (1 stick, cut into pieces)
1 3/4 cups sweetened applesauce (1-pound can or jar)
2 cups flour (not self-rising)
1 cup sugar
1 teaspoon salt
1 teaspoon soda
1 teaspoon cinnamon
1 teaspoon nutmeg
1/4 teaspoon ground cloves
1 cup raisins or chopped nuts (*optional*)

1. Preheat oven to 350 degrees F. Line

20–24 muffin tins with paper liners.

2. In a small sauce pan, melt cut-up pieces of butter over medium heat.

3. In a large mixing bowl, combine all dry ingredients except raisins and nuts.

4. If you're making the cake, add in raisins or nuts and stir thoroughly. (For the purposes of caramel-filled cupcakes, I left out the raisins and nuts.)

5. Add in the applesauce and melted butter, and stir until well blended.

6. Spoon the batter into the paper cups until each is two-thirds full.

7. Bake 20–22 minutes until test toothpick comes out clean, or until a cupcake springs back when lightly touched in center.

8. Let cool in pan for 5 minutes, then transfer to wire rack to cool completely.

9. Use a paring knife or apple corer to remove the centers of each cake. (Reserve the cored pieces.)

Salted Caramel Filling

2 1/2 cups sugar
2/3 cup water
1 tablespoon light corn syrup
3/4 cup heavy whipping cream
2 1/2 teaspoons sea salt

1. Heat sugar with the water and corn syrup

in a heavy saucepan over high heat, stirring occasionally, until syrup is clear; clip a candy thermometer to the side of the pan and stop stirring.

2. Cook until syrup comes to a boil.
3. Boil until mixture is caramelized and just reaches 360 degrees F. (You can swirl the caramel in the pan as it boils to keep it from sticking to the sides, but be very careful as this mixture is very hot.)
4. Remove from heat and slowly pour in cream, stirring with a wooden spoon (plastic can melt at this temperature) until smooth.
5. Stir in sea salt.
5. Fill cupcakes immediately. If caramel begins to harden, heat again until soft.
6. Use a spoon to fill each cupcake with the caramel filling. The caramel will seep into the cake, so add a bit more to fill.
7. Plug the top of the cupcake with a piece of the cored filling before frosting.

Vanilla Buttercream Frosting
1 package powdered sugar (approximately 4 cups)
1/2 cup butter (1 stick), softened
3 tablespoons milk
2 teaspoons vanilla

1. Beat sugar and butter together, then add milk and vanilla with an electric mixer at low speed until well blended and smooth.
2. If the frosting is too thick, add more milk, one teaspoon at a time, until the frosting is smooth enough to frost the cupcakes.

Makes about 2 1/2 cups frosting for 20–24 cupcakes.

As part of my research for the Cupcake Club Romance series, I've been learning all about baking cupcakes. Beginning back in January 2011, I started sharing my adventures in baking with everyone via my author blog at www.donnakauffman.com/blog, as well as my designated research site, www.cakesbythecupblog.com (named after Lani's bakery, of course!) It's become a fun cupcake recipe destination for both readers and cupcake bakers alike. So, last summer, my wonderful publisher Kensington decided to amp up the cupcake excitement by launching the Original Cupcake Recipe contest. The prize? One very lucky reader would see his or her recipe published in an upcoming Cupcake Club Romance book. The contest was on!

Word spread quickly, and recipes started coming in from all over the world. Then

Amazon.com heard about the contest, and asked if they could be part of the cupcake fun and judge the final round. Of course, we said yes! It was very challenging narrowing the field down to the final three, but we did, then sent off samples of the finalist cupcakes to Seattle for Amazon's final decision. They were so torn between Chocolate Meringue, Sweet Peach Tea, and the Fluffy Elvis that they asked to have the recipes sent their way for an in-house bake-off! In the end, it was close . . . but see the winning recipe below, submitted by Stephanie Gamverona, all the way from South Korea. (And if you're curious about the other two finalists, see the blogs mentioned above for those recipes.) We were thrilled with Amazon's choice. Stephanie's Sweet Peach Tea cupcake recipe truly embodied everything we thought was perfect for Sweet Stuff and the Cupcake Club Romance series, from the wonderful Georgia locale of the books to the complexity of the flavor profiles in the cake itself. This recipe is truly worthy of a cupcake that would be featured at Lani's Cakes by the Cup bakery. Enjoy! (I certainly did.)

Sweet Peach Tea Cupcakes

Sweet Tea Butter
1 cup unsalted butter
32 grams (about 1/3 cup) whole-leaf or loose-leaf black[*] tea

1. In a small saucepan, melt butter on medium-high heat until just melted.
2. Add tea leaves.
3. Continue heating mixture for about 5 minutes on low heat. Make sure mixture does not reach simmering point.
4. Remove from heat and allow to stand for another 5 minutes.
5. Pour mixture through fine sieve, pressing hard on tea leaves to squeeze out as much butter as possible.
6. Let tea-infused butter cool to room temperature and refrigerate until solid.
7. Use for Tea Cupcakes recipe below.

Tea Cupcakes
1 1/2 cups sugar
Zest of 1 medium-size lemon
2/3 cup Sweet Tea Butter
3 eggs
1/2 teaspoon ground ginger[**]
1 1/2 cups all-purpose flour

1/2 cup milk
1 cup finely chopped overripe peaches***

1. Preheat oven to 350 degrees Fahrenheit.
2. Line muffin tins with paper or foil baking cups, and spray lightly with cooking spray.
3. In a small mixing bowl, mix sugar and lemon zest. Allow to sit for at least 30 minutes.
4. In a large mixing bowl, stir Sweet Tea Butter with lemon sugar until mixture is smooth.
5. Beat in eggs, one at a time.
6. Beat in ginger.
7. Beat in flour, one cup at a time, alternating with tablespoons of milk.
8. Gently fold in peaches.
9. Fill prepared cupcake liners two-thirds full.
10. Bake 18–23 minutes.
11. Frost with Peach Whipped Cream Frosting when completely cooled.

* Earl Grey may be substituted.

** Cinnamon may be substituted.

*** Canned lightly sweetened peaches, drained, may be substituted, but of course they don't taste as good as the real thing.

Peach Whipped Cream Frosting

1 cup heavy whipping cream
1/2 teaspoon pure vanilla extract
1 tablespoon sugar
1/2 cup lightly sweetened peach puree *or* peach preserves

1. In a large mixing bowl, place whipping cream, vanilla extract, and sugar, and stir with wire whisk to combine.
2. Cover bowl, and chill in refrigerator for at least 30 minutes.
3. When chilled, beat the mixture until soft peaks form.
4. Add sweetened peach puree a little at a time, beating just until stiff peaks form when whisk is raised.
5. Taste, and fold in more puree, if required.
6. Frost Tea Cupcakes once cupcakes are completely cooled.

Makes approximately 18 cupcakes.